HERMAN MELVILLE

A Biography

Herman Melville

A Biography

by Leon Howard

UNIVERSITY OF CALIFORNIA PRESS
Berkeley / *Los Angeles* / *London*

UNIVERSITY OF CALIFORNIA PRESS
Berkeley and Los Angeles
California

UNIVERSITY OF CALIFORNIA PRESS, LTD.
London, England

Copyright 1951, by
THE REGENTS OF THE UNIVERSITY OF CALIFORNIA

ISBN: 0-520-00575-9

Illustrations by Robert Else
Designed by Adrian Wilson
Printed in the United States of America

4 5 6 7 8 9

To

Jay Leyda & Harry Hayford

who
browbeat me into doing this

Preface

THIS BIOGRAPHY *grew out of a casual meeting with Jay Leyda during the winter of 1944–1945 when he was just beginning to follow the train of curiosity which has since led to the completion of his monumental Melville Log. At the time I had a small store of information about Melville which seemed more valuable than it has since proved to be, Mr. Leyda possessed a hardheaded inquisitiveness which was rare even among scholars, and the two of us had enough in common to keep in touch with each other while his project matured. His plan, as it developed, became one of gathering all the available facts of Melville's life, some examples of the literary use he had made of them, and various documents relating to his background and of putting them together in such juxtaposition as to give an impression of the man as he existed in reality rather than in the minds or imaginations of later readers. As a sort of cinematic experiment in biography, it was new and exciting—and particularly interesting in its application to a subject about whom so much misinformation was in print.*

But, as a new experiment in biography, the plan could not take full advantage of some of the more conventional techniques of drawing inferences from the materials and dealing in causal relationships; and, as a result, Mr. Leyda proposed a coöperative venture in which I should undertake a formal narrative biography while he pursued his original plan, each of us checking on the other, sharing such information as we could gather, and troubling one another with the problems that arose out of our different procedures. The outcome, I am afraid, was that I supplied most of the questions and he most of the answers; but the two projects remained complementary rather than competitive, and each of us has remained in constant touch with the other's progress. The Log, consequently, provides both the source material and the documentation for this biography: even when I used more complete documents than could be printed in the Log, I have tried to make my own text circumstantially allusive to it in a way which would enable an interested student of Melville to locate my basic sources of information. Both the Log and the biography, I should add, have been from the beginning greatly indebted to the generosity of such scholars as Harrison Hayford, Merrell Davis, William Gilman, and Wilson Heflin, whose careful and clearheaded investigations of Melville's life and works have added more precise knowledge to the subject than has yet appeared in print.

The major aim of my own researches has been to place the basic facts of Melville's life in their proper physical, historical, intellectual, and literary contexts and to draw from them the inferences necessary for a coherent and human narrative. My only departure from conventional biography, perhaps, has been in the amount of attention paid to the writing of Melville's books as a series of important events in his life. There is, of course, a certain amount of logic in assuming that a biography of an author should contain as much as can be conveniently said of his authorship; but a greater justification for this procedure, in my own mind, at least, is that Melville has suffered more than most American prose writers from the current tendency to dehumanize the humanities and that the human element in his books most genuinely needs restoration. An account of the actual motives affecting Melville's composition and of the methods by which he put his books together may distress some of his admirers, but, in the long run, it may be well to recognize the fact that memorable literature is something which has risen above the frailties of its human origin rather than descended from some perfect inspiration. To those critics who insist that a work of literature makes its most admirable appearance as an independent object of aesthetic experience, I can only suggest that the arts which we call the humanities are, as a matter of fact, unavoidably human. Of them, literature is the most comprehensive and illuminating in its humanity; and, for my part, the knowledge of human beings, in all their complex relationships, which can be gained from literary study is one of the greatest incentives to its pursuit. I cannot, in short, share the apparently widespread feeling that a rereadable book is so delicate a plant that it needs to be removed from its natural environment before it can attract the imagination.

Nor can I share another widespread assumption: that literature draws most of its peculiar nourishment from the substrata of the author's mind, below the level of his conscious motives and desires. No book can survive for long, of course, if its roots are entirely near the surface. But the sort of critical botanizing that confines itself to speculations about the taproot and admiration of the foliage is not to my taste, and in dealing with Melville's books I have concerned myself primarily with the observable evidence of their growth. There is guesswork aplenty involved in that, for a biographer's relationship to his subject, at best, can be no closer than that of father and son or husband and wife; and the attempt at a reason-

ably well-informed and intelligent interpretation of words and behavior seems to me the most secure foundation on which such a relationship can rest.

However all this might be, the following pages were written with no other intent than to understand the author of Moby Dick and other books as a human being living in nineteenth-century America. He did not turn out to be quite the sort of man whom I expected to emerge at the conclusion, but I made no attempt to adjust his appearance either to my own expectations or to those of his other readers. So far as I know, I have made no statements of fact or probability which are not reasoned conclusions based upon the best available evidence; and the only real freedom I allowed myself was that of making inferences without attempting to reproduce the arguments leading from the evidence to the conclusions. For example, the statement that the Acushnet hid out for a day after Melville and Toby escaped in the harbor of Nuku Hiva was based upon the fact that her position, as given in the "Abstract Log," was behind a neighboring island on one day and back in the harbor on the next. Thus the conclusion stated was drawn from a check of the position upon a contemporary chart and from a knowledge of the habits of whalers which was gained from reading numerous journals and logbooks, but it was not something which could be readily documented by reference to a single source of information—although specific testimony to that effect turned up later. Similarly, to cite another example, statements concerning Melville's financial situation during the late 'fifties were based upon all the information available from the records of his borrowings, his dealings with his publishers, his recorded real-estate purchases, and his declarations of real and personal property in the Pittsfield tax offices. They may be wrong, and they certainly go contrary to tradition, but they are the only ones which make calculated sense in explanation of the existing records. On the whole, it seemed to me better to draw such inferences freely and have the wrong ones eventually corrected than to be so judicious as to be noncommittal.

The most difficult sources from which to get trustworthy information concerning Melville's life were his autobiographical books. In no case have I accepted his own personal narratives without some sort of circumstantial evidence to give them support and without making every reasonable effort to discount material he may have derived from other books. A study of the sources of Typee and Omoo and an examination of contemporary maps of the Marquesas and of Eimeo enabled me to exercise discrimination in the use of his first two autobiographical works, and this discrimination, of course, was assisted by that of other scholars and sharpened by that of a colleague, John T. Stark, who had mapped the island *of Eimeo, and his friend, James Norman Hall, who was not only thoroughly familiar with Eimeo, but had made an effort to follow Melville's footsteps in the Marquesas. Maps and histories of Liverpool influenced my use of Redburn, and the researches of Charles R. Anderson were particularly valuable in connection with* White Jacket. *It should be evident from the text, I believe, that my consistent approach to Melville's books was to consider them as significant indications of what was in his mind at the time he wrote and to assume that their substance was derived partly from a memory of his own experiences, partly from reading, and partly from an invention which combined his real and vicarious or imaginative experiences in an effort to tell as good a tale as he could make sound plausible.*

In some respects, the incidental images in Melville's books were more useful and trustworthy sources of biographical information than the narratives themselves. Almost nothing can be documented concerning his early trip to Illinois, for example, except the date of his departure and the approximate date of his return. Yet a collection of the western images found in the entire body of his prose and verse formed a regular pattern of observations going westward through the Great Lakes and down the Mississippi to the mouth of the Ohio for his return. The journal of a traveler who went westward within a day or two of Melville's trip also provided a check on some of the unusual images by showing that a great storm did occur on Lake Erie on the first of July, 1840, that Indians actually camped "on the beach" of Mackinac Island during the Fourth of July celebration, and that the flowers were in full bloom on the Illinois prairies at the time Melville presumably crossed them. The only inexplicable western image in his books, in fact, appeared to be his reference to a Minnesota Indian village in White Jacket; *but a surviving manuscript fragment, once intended for* The Confidence Man, *revealed that he had paid a visit to the Falls of St. Anthony, and the tourist literature of the period showed that the village was one of two regularly visited by steamers carrying tourists from Galena to the Falls. But normally there was substantial documentary evidence for all the events recorded, and there are few long periods in Melville's life which remain a mystery or even offer an excuse for farfetched inferences.*

Whatever sound value may be found in this account of Melville's life, however, is largely the result of the generous assistance I have received from others. My colleague at Northwestern University and one of the finest scholars I know, Harrison G. Hayford, rivaled Jay Leyda in providing me with information and with the benefit of his sound and discriminating judgment; and two other colleagues, Elmo P. Hohman and Edward B. Hungerford, were generous in allowing me to profit by their knowledge of whaling as an industry and of ships and naval history. Merrell Davis, of the University of Washington, turned over to me the extraordinary collection of information he had gathered in connection with his study of the genesis of Mardi. William Gilman, of the University of Rochester, and Wilson Heflin, of the United States Naval Academy, shared their new discoveries concerning Melville's early life and sea-going years; and Howard Vincent, of the Illinois Institute of Technology, allowed me to use the books, charts, photostats, and microfilm he had collected for his study of Moby Dick and his edition of Melville's Poems. Mrs. Eleanor M. Metcalf, with her usual kindness, admitted me to the large group of Melville scholars who have gained both stimulation and knowledge from her library and from her conversation. In addition, Messrs. Leyda, Hayford, and Vincent have read the entire manuscript, and Messrs. Davis and Gilman, Mr. and Mrs. Philip Durham, Mr. Merton M. Sealts, and my wife are among the dozen or more people who have read it in part. To all of them, as to the many writers on Melville from whose printed books and articles I have received assistance, I am deeply indebted.

Although I have leaned heavily upon the industry and generosity of other people, I have also made productive use of various libraries and am especially grateful for the friendly coöperation supplied by the staffs of the public libraries of Nantucket, New Bedford, Boston, and New York; the Library of Congress and the National Archives; the Newberry Library and the Henry E. Huntington Library and Art Gallery; and the libraries of Harvard University, Northwestern University, the University of Chicago, and the University of California, Los Angeles. Without the tolerance, over a period of years, of Mr. William A. Jackson and Miss Caroline Jakeman, of the Houghton Library, I should never have been able to get along very far with this job; and without the financial assistance of the Research Committee of the Northwestern University Graduate School I should not have completed it within any reasonable length of time. Finally, as this goes through the press, I should like to add an expression of indebtedness and gratitude to Mr. Glenn Gosling for his unusually alert and sympathetic editorial talents, to the many members of the University of California Press who took such interest in the book's progress, and to Mrs. Elsie Leach, who struggled with the Index.

L. H.

Los Angeles, July, 1950

Contents

1 The Open Road   1

2 At Sea   19

3 The Pacific: Outward Bound   41

4 The Pacific: Recoil   61

5 Settling Down   89

6 The World of the Mind   112

7 Second Growth   150

8 Misdirections   180

9 Magazine Writer   207

10 The Quest for Confidence   226

11 Critic and Commentator   254

12 The Customhouse   283

13 Recollection and Renown   319

Index   343

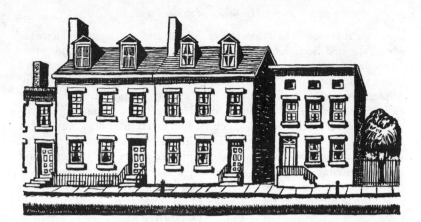

I

The Open Road

I

LATE IN APRIL, in the depression year of 1839, the widowed Maria Gansevoort Melville returned from Albany, New York, to the small town of Lansingburgh with a hundred dollars she had obtained from her two brothers as an advance upon the estate of her mother. By the twenty-third of May the money was all gone, and she was desperately rendering her accounts to her closest brother, Peter Gansevoort, with a further appeal for a remittance that week. Forty-eight dollars had been required for the payment of bills and small loans, thirty-one and a quarter for rent on her home, and twenty dollars and seventy-five cents for the expenses of running her household. It had not been enough to keep her family in the state of respectability upon which she was determined. She had again been under the painful necessity of borrowing from her cousin, Mrs. Peebles, and was still in debt to the shoemaker. Something definite would have to be resolved upon for her support, she wrote, until her sons were able to "do" for her and relieve her mind "from an insupportable weight of uncertainty."

Maria could hardly have found seventy-five cents a day adequate, by any standards, for the subsistence of herself and the eight children for whom she had been responsible since the death of her husband Allan seven years before. The four girls—Helen, Augusta, Catherine, and Frances, ranging in age from twenty-one to eleven—were economically helpless, as were all well-bred young ladies at that time. And of the four sons on whom she rested her hopes, the oldest and most promising, Gansevoort, was still in the bed to which he had taken after an injury to his ankle nearly a year earlier. He had failed in business in the spring of 1837, and now, although he was gaining in the power of self-control and would sometimes walk with the aid of a cane, he was, at the age of twenty-three, a nervous invalid. The third boy, Allan, at sixteen, was an unwilling apprentice in the law office of his uncle Peter in Albany. The youngest, Thomas, was only nine. The pressure to be out and stirring fell entirely upon Maria's second son, who was still only nineteen, and of his activity she assured her brother: "Herman has gone out for a few days on foot to see what he can find to do."

Herman Melville was probably the one son on whom Maria was least willing to base any great hopes. Born in New York City during America's first great postwar depression, just before the hot midnight of August 1, 1819, he had grown up in an atmosphere of constant strain, to which he had reacted with a sensitivity which branded him as a backward child. His father, Allan, was ready enough to find superior qualities in any of his children, and before Herman was eighteen hours old wrote proudly to his relatives of his "chopping boy" with "good lungs" and a "kindly" habit of feeding. But by the time Herman reached the age of self-consciousness he knew that his severe father looked with greatest favor upon his first-born. Gansevoort, at the age of four, had received a "ticket of Merit" on his first day at school and had been engaged in a triumphant progress from that time until he was struck down by the panic of 1837. Herman's own progress at school during his sixth year was such that he impressed his mother as a lad who "does not appear so fond of his Book as to injure his Health"; and when he was allowed, just after his seventh birthday, to visit his grandmother Gansevoort and uncle Peter in Albany, he was accompanied by a paternal letter explaining that he was "very backward in speech and somewhat slow in comprehension" though "both solid and profound" within the limits of his understanding. Yet even the heavily whimsical Allan—who was rarely heard to laugh aloud, yet gave the name Augusta to the third of his children born in the eighth month of the year—found him "of a docile and amiable disposition" and felt that if he could be kept from "green Fruit and unseasonable exposure to the Sun and heat" he would be a satisfactory guest. He required an apology only because he could not measure up to the higher standards set by his older brother, who was then being sent to Boston for a visit with his Melville grandparents.

The summer was an important one in the lives of both boys. Herman found a loyal friend and supporter in his uncle Peter Gansevoort while his brother was attracting the favorable attention of Lemuel Shaw, Allan's boyhood friend who was to become the chief justice of Massachusetts, and they were both to need older friends and patrons. Their father had survived the depression of 1819 and professed to have learned the lesson of contentment with little; but he had moved to a more expensive house before his importing business fully recovered from the scarcity of hard money and within a couple of years was to move into another, at almost twice the rent, on Broadway. In the meantime he was speculating in an effort to support his ambitions and borrowing heavily from his father, Major Thomas Melville, in Boston, while also striving for security by making a "confidential" connection with a prosperous commission merchant. The result was an entanglement of affairs which placed the head of the household under an increasing strain, although his family and friends were aware only of the fact that he had given up all outside interests and was devoting himself entirely to business. Later, his sons were to find themselves caught in the tangle and in serious need of outside help.

There were other stresses within the family during the period of Herman's childhood. By the time his mother had borne her fifth child and third son, Allan, in 1823, her health was such that she remained above stairs for longer than her customary ten days, and within a year she had begun to suffer from "unpleasant fainting fits," which her brother believed could only be cured by "rest and exercise." The five-year-old Herman watched them with an attentiveness which seems to have made a lasting impression upon him; and perhaps one reason why he and Gansevoort were so regularly sent away to spend the summer with their grandparents was the tension produced by the impact of pent-up boyish energy upon overstrung nerves. For the senior Allan Melville was determined that his children should be kept off the "streets," and Maria's nerves remained on edge for as long as the family remained in New York. Shortly after Herman's eleventh birthday, his father wrote that her spirits were occasionally "more than ever depressed" and that he feared a permanent injury to her health unless she soon obtained some "relief from mental excitement" through a favorable change in the family's "condition and prospects." "She is very desirous of removing to Albany," he added, where she would feel "at home and if possible happy, which she never has been, and never can be here."

The tension was often lessened by long summer visits to relatives in

Albany and Boston, but there were other times when it was increased by the misfortunes of kinfolk outside the immediate family circle. Thomas Melville, Jr., Allan's older and only living brother, who had moved from Paris to a farm in Pittsfield, Massachusetts, had allowed the family name to be dragged through the courts at about the time of Herman's birth and after two years of legalities had been jailed for debt—to Allan's pained disgust, and to his indignation when he learned that the situation jeopardized his father's position as an officer of the Port of Boston. Allan made an agitated trip to Washington in behalf of his parent (whose position was actually saved by the intercession of Daniel Webster), and relations between the two brothers were cool for some years thereafter. When Herman was nine and Andrew Jackson was in power, Major Melville actually was despoiled of his office for the benefit of the new Democrats; and the aged veteran of the Boston Tea Party, bowed by his sons' financial difficulties as well as by his seventy-eight years, was made free to totter about the streets of Boston in his old-fashioned knee breeches and cocked hat until a young spriggins named Oliver Wendell Holmes put him into a poem as "The Last Leaf" on a forsaken bough. His sons denounced the spoils system in indignant rhetoric, as was their nature, but it did no more good than the martyred patience with which Allan faced his other family trials—the periodical absences of his family during the fever season, the unseasonable visit of Maria to Albany during her sister-in-law's prolonged illness, the lameness of Helen which was later to be cured by an operation, the months of invalidism suffered by his sister Priscilla during a visit, his own illness and Herman's ill-health at the same time, and the attacks of influenza, whooping cough, measles, and scarlet fever which affected all his children as their number increased biennially until it reached a total of eight in 1830. Most of these troubles were a part of normal life, but they were sufficient to keep a worried father and a nervous mother from relaxing long enough to create the wholesome atmosphere in which a growing child could feel secure and completely at ease.

Yet most of the tension within the Melville household existed below the surface. Outwardly, the family gave every appearance of the prosperous respectability which was its birthright. Each of the moves the Melvilles made in New York was into a larger and more comfortable house in a better neighborhood—from No. 6 Pearl Street, where Herman was born; to 55 Courtlandt a year later; to Bleecker Street, where they had a basement playroom and a garden and a view of the "elegant white Marble Houses in Bond Street"; and to Broadway, where Maria always wanted to live. They regularly kept a cook and a nurse and a "waiter" until they acquired an inexpensive governess for the girls and convinced themselves that they were more "comfortable" without a manservant. The children were all promptly baptized into the Dutch Reformed Church and sent to dancing school as soon as they were able to trip, and Allan paid tuition for his boys to attend the New York Male High School, where they were taught subjects and arts not included in the common school curriculum of reading, writing, and arithmetic. If Allan did not keep a private carriage of his own, his family used one when they traveled, even though it might mean crowding seven passengers into one vehicle for a five-day trip from Boston to Albany. When Maria made her summer visits to her mother, she generally made them with her entire entourage of cook, nurse, governess, and children; and at least one captain of the overnight steamer was so impressed that when he docked at an unexpectedly early hour he went personally to their home near the Courtlandt Street landing and rang the bell to get Mr. Melville out of bed and inform him that his family was preparing to disembark. No one could take the Melvilles for merely ordinary people.

In such an environment Herman grew up more normally, it would seem, than either of his closest brothers. As a youngster of five he became an unendurable tease to the eldest without attempting, at home, to rival him in scholarship or in the ostentation which made Gansevoort such an unremitting reciter of "pieces." Yet the "sedate but not less interesting" Herman, who was considered "less buoyant in mind" than his older brother and perhaps less "bewitching" and "intelligent" than the younger Allan, occasionally astonished his family by showing signs of unexpected progress and talents: "You will be as much surprised as myself to know," his father wrote Peter Gansevoort in February, 1828, "that Herman proved the best speaker in the introductory department" of the High School, where Gansevoort, he reported as a matter of course, "still ranks among the A^s N° 1 in the senior class." The achievement, however, may not have been as unexpected to uncle Peter as it was to Allan, for the boy had preserved the good impression he had first made in Albany and had also become and remained a "decided favorite" with his Melville grandparents in Boston. In Bristol, too, he "delighted" his father's older sister Mary, with whom he spent the summer of 1828, two years after the return of her husband, Captain John De Wolf, from a prolonged voyage to Russia. But Allan continued to display an incapacity for enthusiasm about his second son, and as late as 1830, after speaking highly of Gansevoort's distinction and of Helen Maria's natural talents, he wrote: "Herman I think is making more progress than formerly, and without being a bright Scholar, he maintains a respectable standing, and would proceed further, if he could be induced to study more —being a most amiable and innocent child, I cannot find it in my heart to coerce him, especially as he seems to have chosen Commerce as a favorite pursuit, whose practical activity can well dispense with much book knowledge."

The commercial pursuits which Herman seemed to favor, however, required more talents than his father possessed. At the time he wrote, Allan Melville was failing in business, and his affairs were rapidly approaching a climax. Two years before, he had begun to find it necessary to call upon friends and relatives for assistance as each quarter day approached, and by midsummer of 1828, judging from the dates of his appeals, his term of credit had been reduced to forty-five days instead of the customary ninety. He borrowed so much from his father that in February of the following year Major Melville, at Allan's suggestion, added a clause to his will making the loans a debt against his estate—a debt which was increased by thirty-five hundred dollars in 1830 until it amounted to considerably more than Allan's share of the property. Yet despite such assistance he so completely exhausted his resources by the end of the third quarter of the year that he shut up shop, packed his furniture, and moved to Albany, leaving behind an unpaid obligation for a quarter's rent on his home on Broadway and other bills which made him liable to prosecution and jeopardized the new start he hoped to make in his native town. He settled his family in a house at 338 North Market Street, but was obliged to depend for their support upon occasional loans from his brother-in-law Peter while he desperately called upon his father for the five hundred dollars necessary for temporary relief.

In the meantime his two oldest sons were put in the Albany Academy, enrolling on October 15, 1830, only four days after Herman and his father arrived from New York. There Herman did so well in the work he was taking in preparation for a commercial course that at the end of the school year he received the first prize in his class for excellence in the "department" of "ciphering books." But Allan was too hard pressed to show, or perhaps even feel, any surprise at the achievement of his "sedate" son in outshining the more brilliant Gansevoort on a public occasion. He had been trying to conceal his inability to make a new start among his numerous connections in Albany, but in April had been obliged to confess his situation to his father, and on August 11, a week after the end of school, he set out for Boston to see his parent, accompanied by Maria, Gansevoort, Herman, and Augusta and traveling by stage instead of private carriage. At Pittsfield he had a tender reunion with Thomas, to whom he had become a brother in misfortune as well as in blood, and left Augusta for a visit with her cousins before proceeding to Hadley, where he dropped off Herman with other relatives, and to his ultimate destination. Whatever assistance he received as a result of the trip was not enough to put him back on his feet, for after returning and reëstab-lishing his boys in the Academy on September 1 he was forced to turn again to Peter Gansevoort for a loan of two thousand dollars in October, apparently for the purpose of setting himself up in a business of his own. At the end of November he left for New York, traveling as a deck pas-senger on the steamer, and started homeward in the same economical fashion on the seventh of December. The river was frozen, however, at Poughkeepsie; and he was obliged to proceed in an open wagon to Rhine-beck and, through a second day of exposure, to Hudson. A covered sleigh took him to Greenbush, but he had to cross the river on foot at nightfall on December 10 with the thermometer at two degrees below zero. Sheer determination brought him home exhausted.

Nearing fifty and unaccustomed to such hardship, he should have gone to bed until he recovered from the exposure. Instead, he drove himself to his business with a diligence that brought about a high state of excite-ment and sleeplessness. It was not until the end of the first week in Janu-ary, 1832, that his friends could persuade him to remain at home; and by that time his excitement had become so completely uncontrolled that on the ninth he "occasionally manifested an alienation of mind" and on the tenth, in the words of Peter Gansevoort to Thomas Melville, Jr., presented "the melancholy spectacle of a deranged man." Thomas im-mediately hurried to Albany and after four days of exhausting watchful-ness wrote Lemuel Shaw, with his own temperamental and Gallicized excitability: "Hope is no longer permitted of his recovery, in the opinion of the attending Physicians and indeed,—oh, how hard for a brother to say! —*I ought not* to hope it. —for, in all human probability—he would live, *a Maniac!*" The situation endured, however, for nearly two weeks; and although Allan occasionally recovered his senses enough to call for members of the family, he remained generally in a state of excited delirium until his death, at half past eleven o'clock, on the night of January 28. Three days later he was buried and his wife and children were left to take stock of their resources and begin a new and more realistic phase of their existence.

II

The flutterings of family conferences after Allan's funeral led to a deci-sion that both of his older sons should be withdrawn from the Albany Academy on the first of March and set to work. Herman, not yet thirteen, was to put his commercial course to profitable use by becoming a clerk in the local New York State Bank, which included among its directors Peter Gansevoort and a relative by marriage of his uncle Herman. His brother Gansevoort, then three months past sixteen, would undertake to operate the business which his father had worked so industriously at establishing before his death. The new firm consisted of a fur and cap retail store and manufacturing plant, situated at 364 South Market Street, in which Allan had invested some six thousand dollars in cash and for which he had obtained credit for merchandise amounting to an even greater sum while on his trip to New York. Putting so young a boy in charge of a business establishment was a recognized gamble. But the entire family had always placed an extraordinarily high estimate on Gansevoort's abilities, free legal and financial advice was always available from Uncle Peter, and the worst immediate loss from the gamble could be no greater than that from a forced sale of the stock already acquired. Accordingly, on March 28, 1832, Maria signed a certificate of accountability for all debts contracted by her eldest son and made a businessman of him while Herman was given the responsibility of improving his handwriting until it came up to clerical standards.

Gansevoort was mightily pleased with his position, especially after he made a trip to New York in May and discovered that "all the furriers in town" knew him as "the young man who lately began the cap manufacture in Albany." But Maria had a meager perception of her sons' responsibilities; and when the cholera broke out in Albany in the middle of July she fled with her entire brood to Pittsfield, where Thomas' farm was immediately overrun by the children. A firm letter from Peter Gansevoort persuaded her to send Herman back to his job in the bank, but she kept Gansevoort with her in Pittsfield while his business, apparently, was left in the hands of employees or perhaps even closed. In any case, it showed few signs of prospering during the year that followed. The death of Major Melville, on September 16, revealed the true state of Allan's indebtedness during his lifetime and made it necessary for Maria to confess her inability to pay her husband's notes and, later, to subject her children to a friendly suit from the executors of the estate. Although all of Allan's sisters (with the exception of Mary, whose husband, Captain De Wolf, was one of the executors) joined in the effort to protect Allan's heirs from the due processes of the law, Maria felt that her children had been the victims of an "utter" and "inexplicable" desertion by their Melville grandparents and aunts. Relations between Albany and Boston began to show signs of strain, and Judge Lemuel Shaw, who was the only executor outside the family circle, was placed in the position of a mediator with an increasing feeling of responsibility toward the children of his old friend.

On the other hand, the relationship between Allan's family and the Thomas Melvilles grew closer as Maria found Pittsfield a convenient place for the customary summer vacations of herself and children. Herman was there during his week of freedom from the bank in August, 1833, and perhaps again for a while during the following summer. Thomas' nine rustic and uneducated children were not precisely the companions Maria would have chosen for her own, but the two families were thrown together by circumstances and by Thomas' genuine though poverty-stricken hospitality. Maria's mother had died in 1830, and her brother Peter had recently taken a young bride and was beginning to think of a family of his own. The oldest brother, Herman, for whom Maria had named her son, had a wife who refused to welcome her sister-in-law's children to the family estate in the village which bore the Gansevoort name. After the Melvilles moved in Albany from the home in which Allan had first placed them and into a new residence at No. 3 Clinton Square, the old house in Pittsfield became more and more like a single spot of stability in a world of changes. The road lined with elms, the larch-shaded porch looking across the meadows to South Mountain, and the great old-fashioned fireplace in the kitchen came to be, in Herman's mind at least, symbols of a tranquillity which was as singularly uncharacteristic of Thomas Melville's existence as it was of his own.

For misfortune continued to beset the two families. In the spring of 1834, the section of Gansevoort's establishment used for the preparation of skins was destroyed by fire with an immediate loss (above insurance) of between fifteen hundred and two thousand dollars and a lingering further loss from the "derangement" of the business. But Gansevoort (who was really working seriously at his job) went ahead with the expansion he had planned before the fire, and in March, 1836, advertised in the Albany *Argus* for twenty "trimmers" to be employed immediately in the new factory. In the meantime, Thomas had been in jail twice again for debt, first in the summer of 1835 and then in October of the same year, at which time he was debating whether to gain his release by taking a debtor's oath or by going into "close confinement" and thus forcing his creditor to choose between the charity of paying his board and that of letting him out. After escaping by one means or another he ran into further troubles through the death of animal stock by sickness and accident during a severe winter; and, when an early freeze caught him the following November with his turnip crop still in the ground, he was ready to give up and go west to Illinois in the spring for a new start on the prairies at the age of sixty-one.

In the midst of these troubles Herman was growing up and quietly exhibiting unexpected signs of strength and ambition. It was probably during 1835, rather than 1836 as he later remembered it, that he went to Pittsfield to help his cousin Robert with the farm work and watched with fascination the gray but unbowed figure of his uncle, during the latter's period of freedom, leaning upon his hayrake and taking a pinch of snuff with the "aspect of a courtier of Louis XVI, reduced as a refugee, to humble employment, in a region far from the gilded Versailles." The Melvilles, with their background of life in France, had cut fine figures a generation before; and if the Gansevoorts were the more solid citizens among Herman's relatives, there was a suggestion of something more adventurous and a faded hint of greater distinction among his father's kin. Whatever his practical shortcomings may have been, Thomas Melville was able to stir a boy's imagination and make him aware of a world greater than the commercial environment to which Allan committed both himself and his second son.

Herman was already reaching for something beyond a clerkship. On January 29, 1835, he had followed his brother Gansevoort into the Albany Young Men's Association for Mutual Improvement, gaining access to a large and varied library at a cost of two dollars a year; and by the spring of 1835 he had transferred from his job in the bank to that of clerk in the fur and cap store, probably in order to secure irregular hours that would permit his attendance at the Albany Classical School. There he was later remembered by his professor as an undistinguished mathematician and an enthusiastic writer of themes; and there he acquired, before the autumn of 1837, the education which qualified him to become a schoolteacher.

While Herman was retailing caps and improving his mind, Gansevoort was getting into the difficulties that eventually helped put him to bed and forced Herman to take the road. The financial situation of the country as a whole was beginning to tighten during the last half of 1836, and the family business was being operated with so little free capital that it could not meet its obligations without prompt collections from its wholesale customers. A delay in receiving remittances meant that Gansevoort had to risk an overdraft at the bank if he were to make his own remittances in time to preserve his credit. In order to avoid constant appeals for Peter Gansevoort to intercede with the cashier of the New York State Bank, Maria, on October 22, 1836, mortgaged part of her property in real estate to the New York Life Insurance and Trust Company. This maneuver, however, was not adequate. The financial panic of 1837 struck the country in the spring and caught Gansevoort in the trap that his father had blessed himself for avoiding eighteen years before. As a result of optimistic salesmanship which outran collections, he failed, on April 15, for the amount of the mortgage and for an additional four thousand dollars which his uncle Peter obtained in order to preserve the family honor. His mother, on April 28, was forced to sign a bond for fifty thousand dollars to the president and directors of the New York State Bank.

At the moment, Gansevoort was not greatly stricken. He bravely left home to seek his fortune in New York. Allan, the third son, who had reached the age of fourteen, was taken out of school and put to work in Peter Gansevoort's law office as a clerk and an apprentice. Herman found a school to teach near Pittsfield, where his uncle Thomas had made a pessimistic report on educational conditions shortly before leaving for Galena, Illinois, with his son John in early June. The school was a typical, one-room, elementary affair in the rural Sykes District five miles out from the village in the direction of Washington Mountain. In it Herman found about thirty scholars "of all ages, sizes, ranks, characters, and education," some of them as old as himself but still incapable of doing a sum in simple arithmetic. Five of his students were included among the twelve children of the rugged "Yankee character" with whom he was boarding in December, 1837, on the top of a "savage and lonely" mountain a mile and a half away from the schoolhouse. Later tradition has maintained that he was obliged to assert his mastery over half-wild charges by force—as he probably did, for in a report to his uncle Peter at the end of December he declared that he faced precisely the obstacles and difficulties portrayed in John O. Taylor's realistic book on the "District School," which his uncle had given him for guidance. Disillusioned though he was by the American "system of common school education," as he found it in practice, he nevertheless managed to stick to his job for another six weeks before returning to Albany.

By this time Maria had acquired more worries than a less self-centered woman could have endured. Her creditors had made her very "unhappy" by calling for a settlement during the preceding November, and she was threatened with the loss of her home and property at a time when her brother Peter was almost at the end of his resources and her older brother Herman was unprepared to render any considerable assistance. The Pittsfield Melvilles were preparing to leave the farm during the summer of 1838 in order to join Thomas and John in Galena. Peter had abandoned the family home, and Herman Gansevoort's wife still lacked any enthusiasm for the Melvilles. Maria had no place of refuge if she should be sold out. Under these circumstances, young Allan was also becoming a problem. Though less high-strung than Gansevoort, he seems to have been more nearly spoiled than Herman had been and was proving less able to get along with his uncle.

Even Herman was being difficult. Before taking over his district school, he had been an active and aggressive member of the Philologos Society—

a debating adjunct to the Young Men's Association—which had evidently languished during his absence from Albany. Upon his return, he revived the organization, obtained a room in Stanwix Hall for its meetings, and at a rump session had himself elected president. His indignant opposition publicly denied the constitutionality of the reorganization in the columns of the Albany *Microscope* for February 17, 1838; and for nearly two months the injured "Ex-President," a young man named Van Loon, and his energetic successor quarreled bitterly in public. Writing under the signature of "Philologian," Herman denounced his former friend as a "silly and brainless *loon*" who stood "in the *van*" of that "class of individuals, who are of so narrow-minded and jealous a disposition that deserving merit when developed in others, fills their bosom with hatred and malice." The "Ex-President," in turn, referred to "Hermanus Melvillian" as a "moral Ethiopian" and a *"Ciceronian baboon."* The exchanges probably marked the first appearances in print for either of the young men, and they were obviously as excited by their own rhetoric as they were by each other. A fellow member of the Society who called himself "Americus" tried to make peace between them in the *Microscope* for April 7, and the controversy died out too soon to indicate whether Herman got a job and remained in Albany for the next six months or went back to his school in the spring.

On the first of May, the Melvilles were forced into a drastic move. They abandoned their home and friends in Albany and reëstablished themselves in the village of Lansingburgh where they could obtain a house pleasantly situated on the banks of the Hudson for a hundred and twenty-five dollars a year and where, in all other respects, their living expenses would be smaller. Allan was left to board in Albany, in resentful sight of a lumber yard, with an eccentric old-maid cousin; and Maria, the four girls, and the eight-year-old Thomas began to adjust themselves to new surroundings in which the bedridden Gansevoort soon became an additional problem. Maria found the adjustment to new surroundings and undisguisable poverty hard to make. She was habitually careful of appearances but not of the appearances she was now forced to consider. Soon after she was settled, when the June sun began to pour into the house, she offered her landlord a half year's rent in advance if he would put up blinds immediately; and Peter, who was aware that she had not paid for her last barrel of flour, was forced to write her a blunt letter: "I send by Mr. Holme one hundred dollars as requested by your letter of Saturday last— You might rather have done without the blinds, than give your landlord or your neighbors the false unfounded idea that you have means to pay rent in advance— I do not object to the thing itself, so much as to the effect upon your comfort and peace of mind, which such an impression may produce." Her creditors were becoming impatient and she should be made aware of her "true situation," he explained, for "if the creditors hear that you are living handsomely at Lansingburgh, and particularly that you pay rent in advance, they will be inclined to annoy you by a sale of your furniture."

Maria was apparently able to learn the art of calculation and did without her blinds, for on August 2 she wrote her brother again, complaining that the quarter day just passed had found her "unprepared." In October, she complained once more that Peter's absence from Albany had forced her to go in debt for the winter's supply of coal. But she was not consciously begging for charity. Her brother was an executor of her mother's estate and the manager of her own affairs, which had not yet been settled, and her ignorance of business kept her from recognizing the fact that her liabilities far exceeded her resources and that Peter was also hard pressed for ready money. When Herman decided to prepare himself for a profession with a future, there seems to have been no family objection to the loss of his income or to the added expense of keeping him at home. Accordingly, early in November, he made arrangements to attend the Lansingburgh Academy and on the twelfth of that month paid his tuition fee of five dollars and a quarter for the first term of a course in engineering and surveying.

In the midst of the continued severe depression throughout the country the one promising sign of activity visible to upstate New Yorkers was the bustle along the Erie Canal, which had been granted funds to expand and improve its facilities. Herman may have been advised to look in that direction by his farsighted uncle Peter, and it is not impossible that he undertook his special course in the Lansingburgh Academy with his eye on the construction work anticipated in the spring. In any case, on the evening of April 3, 1839, his uncle introduced him to William C. Bouck, one of the five canal commissioners, who gave him enough encouragement to send him scurrying for a certificate of his education and a letter from the principal of the academy to the chief engineer of the canal. Peter Gansevoort enclosed them both in a formal letter he wrote to Bouck the next day. His nephew was "a young man of talent and good education," he declared, who had "endeavored to prepare himself for the business of surveying and engineering" and was anxious to make that business "his profession." "He however submits his application, without any pretension and solicits any situation, however humble it may be, but he indeed would prefer a subordinate station, as he wishes to advance only by his own merit." Any "kind interference in his behalf," his uncle added, "will be considered a personal favor."

While waiting for a notice of his appointment—which was never to arrive—Herman occupied himself with what were evidently his first attempts at literary composition. On April 20 the *Democratic Press and Lansingburgh Advertiser* appeared with a notice to correspondents that the communication of "L.A.V." had been received and that "an interview with the writer is requested." At the interview Herman learned that Gansevoort was not the only promising literary member of the family, for his epistolary essay was accepted for publication in the May 4 issue of the newspaper and he was probably encouraged to become a regular contributor of the sort of "lively" prose that early nineteenth-century editors so often inveigled from their readers. He adopted a heading, "Fragments from a Writing Desk," suitable for a regular column, and produced a more ambitious humorous narrative for the issue of May 18, numbering the two contributions "1" and "2" as though they were the beginning of a series. But he could not afford the leisure required for a continuation of such amateur experiments with literature. It was at about the time of the appearance of his second "Fragment" that his mother's money ran out and she was forced to borrow from Mrs. Peebles. His practical prospects of getting a job with the Erie Canal were fading, and economic circumstances kept him from the impractical enjoyment of a local literary success. However spirited the "Ciceronian baboon" may have become during the maturing months of teaching away from home and purposeful study in Lansingburgh, it was with no lightheartedness that he took the road, on foot, to see what he could find to do.

III

Amateurish and precious though they were, Melville's "Fragments from a Writing Desk" have preserved the clear stamp of an individuality hitherto only faintly revealed by records smudged with family prejudices and emotions. At this time he was approaching manhood, and his stocky figure was within an inch of its mature height of five feet, nine and one-half inches. The fair complexion visible above his homemade clothes was yet untanned by salt winds and tropic suns, and his thick brown hair covered a fine head marred by incongruous features. In contrast to his oversized ears, his small blue eyes appeared slightly piggish; and the long upper lip separating his rounded chin from his straight nose made the latter seem smaller than it really was. He was neither a handsome nor a distinguished-looking young man, and his more elegant older brother sometimes audibly wondered, as older brothers will, whether he could be said to look like a Christian. There was nothing about his appearance to make him self-conscious either through pride or shame. If the "Fragments" show that he was capable of describing his "pretty corpus" as "the envy of the beaux, the idol of the women and the admiration of the tailor," they also reveal a high spirit to whom the joke was not bitter. He could fancy himself as having overcome a "hang-dog modesty" and acquired an extraordinarily effective way with the ladies without indicating that he took his blemishes or his embellishments very seriously. The "Fragments" were from the "Writing Desk" of a youth who had abundant energy and more animation of mind than he seems to have allowed himself to display within the family circle.

He was also surprisingly literary for a boy whose early interests were supposed to have been entirely commercial and whose most recent studies had been devoted to engineering. Much of his erudition was mere pose, indicating that he had made affected use of such volumes as Lindley Murray's *English Reader* and *The London Carcanet, Containing Select Passages from the Most Distinguished Writers,* which he had received as his Albany Academy prize eight years before. But he referred knowingly to Byron, and his quotations from *Hamlet* were not from "select" passages which normally would be included in collections of Shakespeare's "beauties." Although it is quite evident that he was not above reading with unsophisticated interest the romantic and sentimental fiction introduced into the house by Gansevoort and his sisters, his impulse was to parody rather than imitate it when he took his own pen in hand. For the second of his "Fragments," in particular, was a narrative hoax which created a conventional atmosphere of romantic mystery around a silent though inviting beauty and then discomfited the reader's expectations by revealing that she was deaf and dumb. It was crude humor, but the tensions in the Melville home restrained any subtle play of the comic spirit; and the appearance of any kind of humor in such an environment, especially from the son of Allan and Maria, was almost unbelievable. Later when he went "Over the hills and far away" he left in the hands of a young lady his copy of *The London Carcanet* inscribed with John Gay's words for that appropriate air in *The Beggar's Opera* and left in the village a gossipy tradition that he had run away from a girl in "trouble." Whether or not there was any connection between the gossip and his humorous representation of himself as a wandering Macheath panted after by a village Polly, he was more than once, in the future, to be placed in the infuriating position of having his jokes taken seriously as evidences of an eccentric mind or improper behavior.

The financial troubles of the Melville family, however, continued to be serious enough. When Herman returned, on May 24, 1839, from his unsuccessful job-hunting trip, he found both Gansevoort and Allan in a restless mood—the older brother prepared to leave his bed and go to New York, and the younger ready to quarrel with their uncle Peter and go with him. Herman remained behind. He may have had hopes of a position as a schoolteacher for the following year but had no prospects of any occupation before fall. Restless and well prepared with an excuse for taking any kind of temporary work that offered itself, he evidently asked Gansevoort to arrange for his employment, if possible, on a sailing ship which would make a summer's round-trip voyage across the Atlantic.

It was not at all unnatural that Melville's thoughts should have turned to the sea as a means of escape from the financial problems which seemed so inescapable on the depression-ridden land. Although both his grandparents had been soldiers in the Revolution, seafaring was in his family background as a means of achieving success through unaided effort. His uncle by marriage, Captain John De Wolf, in whose home he had spent a summer vacation in his boyhood, had achieved a modest fame as a sea captain and had established himself as a merchant as a result of his voyaging. More important, three older cousins of his own generation had gone to sea under circumstances similar to his own. After his uncle Leonard Gansevoort had died in 1821, leaving eight children, Melville's cousin Guert had entered the United States Navy and as a young midshipman had impressed the Allan Melvilles in New York during Herman's boyhood. Later the younger Leonard, only three years Herman's senior, had followed his older brother to sea and had, in fact, only a year and a half before made exactly the same voyage on a packet ship to England which Herman was now contemplating. There was no reason for him to suppose that a seafaring life was a particularly easy one, for his cousin Thomas, the oldest of the Pittsfield Melville boys, had recently distressed his family by disappearing from view—presumably on a miserable whaling vessel —after being forced to resign from the Navy by repeated failures to take his midshipman's examination. But, on the other hand, there was no reason at all why an active young man should not give the sea a trial, especially since the experiment involved a change in scenery and a small amount of highly desirable income during an otherwise unoccupied summer.

Gansevoort was prompt about making arrangements. On Friday, May 31, he wrote to his family that he had obtained a place for Herman in the crew of a merchant ship which was due to sail immediately. Maria already had her son's clothes ready, and "preparation" for the voyage "forthwith commenced" with the packing of everything that she considered useful and instructions for Gansevoort to "secure for him everything within the range of his means that will make him comfortable." "Herman is happy," she observed sympathetically, "but I think at heart he is rather agitated." There is no doubt but that his mind was agitated by doubts and his heart by mixed feelings as he separated himself, for the first time, completely from his family; but he caught the Sunday boat for New York City, joined his brothers at the home of Alexander W. Bradford, and signed the ship's articles the next morning. The ship proved to be the fast-sailing *St. Lawrence* with a cargo of cotton for Liverpool in charge of Captain Oliver P. Brown. It was a medium-sized vessel of 356 tons burthen, with room for cabin and steerage passengers, and carried a crew of sixteen including the mates. Although the cargo was not complete at the time Melville signed on, the ship was advertised to sail on Tuesday, and he had excellent prospects of getting back before the opening of his school.

The *St. Lawrence* was actually a day late in sailing and Melville probably spent the entire intervening period with his brothers at the home of Gansevoort's friend Bradford, whose father had been the pastor of the Dutch Reformed Church into which the first of the Melville children had been baptized in Albany. He was also probably indebted to Bradford rather than to Gansevoort for the practical arrangements for his voyage— as he was to be again in the future—for the handsome and successful young lawyer had the knowledge and acquaintances necessary for the prompt action taken in Herman's behalf. In any case, Melville was not the forlorn boy he was later to describe in his story *Redburn*. His estimates of his equipment and plans for additional purchases were most likely made with good advice given more abundantly than was necessary. In the company of an older brother trying to act *in loco parentis,* a younger brother who would have liked to be going somewhere himself, and a well-informed older friend whose wife took a motherly interest in the whole affair, he could hardly have allowed himself to appear less happy than he had seemed when he got the news of the arrangements at home.

Whatever his appearance may have been when the *St. Lawrence* cast her moorings and swung out into East River to await a tug through the Narrows, Melville probably had a feeling of complacency, if not of happiness, more deep-seated than the agitation he tried to conceal. His father had been a great traveler in his youth, estimating his mileage as almost equal to the distance around the earth by land and twice as much again by sea. Had his financial circumstances and growing family permitted him to make the last voyage he planned across the Atlantic, the elder Allan would have been able to boast of spending two years of his life, all told, upon salt water. His three sons who were together in New York were all aware of their father's vanity over his carefully recorded achievement, and they could hardly have avoided an awareness of the fact that at last one of them was following, however humbly, in his wandering footsteps. Each had probably dreamed in secret of undertaking such an adventure, and the one actually doing so was neither Gansevoort, his father's pride, nor Allan, his namesake, but the sedate and docile Herman. Beneath whatever superficial air he exhibited and his ill-concealed trepidation, the nineteen-year-old boy was buoyed up by a feeling of satisfaction as he grasped his capstan bar to perform the first of his duties as a sailor. Gansevoort might go back to his sickbed, and Allan might hurry back to Albany "at once" as his mother had ordered four days before. When he saw them again he would be a man who had gone over the horizon and could talk of strange places that his father had seen before him but which his brothers might never see. The devious ways of another mind can only be followed by guesswork, but there seems to have been an impulse toward security as well as toward escape involved in Melville's first voyage. His desire to escape the atmosphere of anxiety and the nagging sense of responsibilities he could not meet, both of which he felt at home, was possibly no greater than his more secret desire to return home with the security of a manhood that had proved itself in action and found some sort of place in a pattern of experience which was a part of his family heritage.

The way that lay ahead as his ship passed through the Narrows and moved into the great Atlantic was an open road. Hitherto his course had been hedged in by necessity and his goal determined by circumstances. Now he was, for the moment, a free man. His failure to find employment two weeks before when he had gone out on foot had released him from immediate obligations to his family, and his departure relieved his mother of a fraction of the financial burden which he was planning to share in the fall. He had temporarily shed the responsibilities that he could not meet and was facing only such difficulties as could be overcome by willingness of mind and strength of body. He had grasped a chance to prove his manhood to himself and his independence to his family. He may also have had a quiet notion of acquiring some fragments of experience which would be useful to a young man with a writing desk. How seriously he may have thought of following the sea as a profession is uncertain. But whatever his purpose may have been—whether it was to find himself, to find material for his immature literary ambitions, or merely to find a way to become self-supporting—he was for the moment healthy and free with the world before him. His essays could remain on his desk unwritten. His school could stand untaught. The money so badly needed at home could remain unearned. Although he was never to escape the pressure of duties and obligations, his actions were never again to be determined by a family council: the long path before him was to lead wherever he chose.

2

At Sea

I

AFTER the *St. Lawrence* cast loose from the tugboat which had escorted her through the Narrows, transferred the pilot to the little schooner which awaited farther out, and began to roll in the swell of the Atlantic, Melville found himself in a new world. It was a world in which the captain of the ship was lord and master of every soul aboard, and the members of the crew, at least, were immediately informed of the fundamental law under which they would live until the end of the voyage. Gathered before the sacred quarter-deck in the after part of the ship, they learned that their primary duty was unquestioning and quick obedience to the absolute authority invested in the master and exercised by him through his two mates. All distinctions of breeding and education were left ashore. The captain became unapproachable under normal circumstances except by the chief mate, both mates became "mister" when they were being approached and "sir" when their orders were being acknowledged, and the men were left free to arrange themselves in an unofficial hierarchy determined by agility and force of character. The most active of the sailors would take the positions of honor at the yardarms in reefing sails, and the one with the dominant personality might take charge of the distribution of food in the forecastle; but all of them were, as a class, inferior to the second mate, no matter how intimately he might work with them or how incompetent he might prove to be.

The social adjustment from the position of being master of a village school to that of being an inexperienced member of a thoroughly subjugated group was a hard one for Melville to make; yet he had to make it while experiencing all the difficulties of learning a new language by which he was directed to all sorts of new activities. Before leaving port—if his own later fiction can be trusted with reference to such incidental details of actual experiences—he had been given the customary greenhorn's instructions to "slush down the main-top mast" and had been told, rudely enough, that it meant taking a bucket of grease aloft in the rigging and greasing the mast as he worked his way down. At sea, however, strange orders often came without explanations. He had to learn by watching his companions and without appearing to hold back that an order to "lay aloft" required him to scamper like a monkey up a rope ladder and out on a rope stretched below the yard or crosspiece which sustained one of the vessel's heavy sails. Hanging on his dizzy perch, the height of a six-story building above the deck, and rolling at intervals out over the water, he had to learn further that to "reef" the sail he was obliged to let go his hold, lean over the yard, claw at the canvas until he could grasp a "reef point" or short length of rope attached to the sail, and haul away with all his might while trusting his own weight and that of the sail mostly to his footrope. After the process was repeated until all the spare sail was taken in and the last "point" knotted, the men would race down the rope shrouds which extended from the masthead to the sides of the ship. It was exciting duty, especially in bad weather when it had to be performed most quickly and efficiently; and a greenhorn was lucky if he was first sent aloft at sea, as Melville was, to loose a sail, although he might risk the danger of suddenly being pulled higher than he intended to go by his companions on deck who hauled up the yard as soon as the sail was free.

For more routine duties on board, the sailors were divided into "watches" under the command of the two mates. Excluding the cook and the steward, whose normal responsibilities were the galley and the captain's cabin, there were six men for each watch on the *St. Lawrence;* and the term of their duties was measured in "bells" struck at half-hour intervals. Because eight bells was the full measure of a watch, the members of the crew had alternately eight and only four hours in their bunks at night, although those who had the longer period on deck had a chance to sleep for two or three hours after breakfast or to nap during the two-hour "dog watch" which immediately preceded their first call at eight o'clock in the evening. All hands were on deck from noon until four in the afternoon, and all were kept busy during every minute of their exposure to daylight. The early morning watch greeted the rising sun by scrubbing down the decks, taking in or letting out whatever sails had to be adjusted, and filling the scuttle butt from which the men received their daily allowance of fresh water and around which they had an excuse to gather and exchange the gossip usually repressed by their officers when they were at work. After a breakfast of cornmeal mush, salt beef, and hard sea biscuit, washed down by coffee of a sort never tasted before by a young man like Melville, the forenoon watch began its unceasing job of keeping the ship in repair.

However carefully the ship had been rigged in port, the first few days at sea always revealed the necessity of making adjustments in the hundreds of ropes which held its sailing mechanism together and made it workable. If the "standing" or permanent rigging—such as the stays or shrouds which supported the masts, or the horizontal ratlines which made the shrouds also rope ladders—became slack, it was necessary to remove the tarred cord seizings which held the ropes together, bouse the lines taut with the help of a block and tackle, and refasten and cover them with tar. The halyards, sheets, and other pieces of running rigging used to hoist or control the sails had to be examined regularly for signs of wear, and all weak sections had to be replaced by careful splicing which interwove the strands with such skill that they could move freely through the blocks or around the belaying pins used in handling them. Most of the materials used in these repairs were manufactured on board by the sailors themselves, whose otherwise idle moments were devoted to unraveling old cable and cordage called "junk," tying the bits together into "rope-yarn," and spinning it into "marline" for seizing and other uses. There was always rust to be chipped off the anchor and chains, a proper deck was not only regularly scrubbed but at intervals holystoned, and the effects of hot sun and salt water called for frequent applications of paint. Other miscellaneous jobs took up all the spare time of one sailor who doubled as ship's carpenter and another who called himself a sailmaker, and occasional demands were made upon the skill of a blacksmith. Melville soon learned that before he could become an able-bodied seaman worth sixteen dollars a month he would not only have to acquire the agility of a cat, the digestion and constitution of a goat, and the thick skin and strong back of a mule, but he would have to supplement these qualities with the habitual industry of a good housekeeper and the assorted skills of a Jack-of-all-trades.

A variety of skills was necessary to keep a ship in operation, and a fourteen-hour day was equally necessary to keep the sailors out of trouble. The only space in which they could spend their leisure time was the forecastle crowded with bunks and sea chests and occupied twenty hours a day by members of the off watch who were trying to sleep. Subjected to the direct buffetings of the sea and located beneath the latrines at the "head" of the ship, it was at best a place made noisy with the reverberations of pounding waves and tramping feet; and, at its worst, it could be a noisome hole which could turn the stomach of a green hand before he got half way down the hatch. For it was completely unventilated except for such air as might circulate through the single narrow opening which connected it with the deck and which had to be kept closed in wet weather or in heavy seas, and it was rarely free from the mixed odors of tobacco juice, stale food, oilskin garments, and unwashed bodies wet with salt water and heavy with fatigue. To a young man brought up in a home where housekeeping was a solemn ritual, the change in living conditions came with almost as great a shock as did the change from a position of social importance to that of a cursed and despised menial who did not understand the nautical language of the orders he was required to obey.

Yet Melville was young and active and free, for the first time in his life, from any unexpressed expectations concerning his behavior. Despite the fact that he was later to represent his first voyage as a miserable experience, there is no real evidence that he suffered or, in fact, did anything other than thrive in his new environment. The chance to prove himself by his own merits in particular circumstances rather than by comparison of his general qualities with those of a brilliant older brother and an idealized father was inevitably a relief to him and also a compensation for the new difficulties he had to overcome. There were other compensations, too. Outside the forecastle, the salt air of the Atlantic was fresh and invigorating, and salt beef and sea biscuit made healthy fare for a still-growing boy with a sharp appetite. If custom required that he spend most of his waking hours in the fore part of the ship, he spent them in the section which enabled him to become acquainted with the ocean in its most fascinating aspects: in the night watches he could hang over the fiery bow as it splashed its way through the phosphorescent ocean and in the daytime he could marvel over the great schools of porpoises that raced ahead of the vessel and lunged above the water to breathe. In the late afternoon of a clear day an imaginative boy might keep secret from his companions the fancy that his ship was trying to escape the past by sailing away from the sunset, yet he was always conscious of going over the horizon; and the shortness of the theoretical half hour between seven and eight bells at noon was a constant reminder that he was really moving over the rounded surface of the globe. One's impulse on shipboard was generally to look ahead; but if the declining moon invited a homesick glance backward, the ship's rigging appeared as a moving screen between the present and the troubles left behind. Before the *St. Lawrence* was four or five days out and into the Gulf Stream Melville should have realized the peace of mind which comes from being out of sight of land and unable to do anything about the events of yesterday and the responsibilities of tomorrow.

How many of the events later recorded in *Redburn* actually occurred on the outward voyage of the *St. Lawrence* is of course uncertain, but it would have been only natural that the quiet and well-bred Melville should have found himself at first "a sort of Ishmael in the ship" and that he should have acquired the enmity of such a sailor as one of his ship-mates, Robert Jackson, later proved to be. On the other hand, as he began to prove his seamanship in the cold fog and bad weather off the banks of Newfoundland, he would normally have been accepted by his fellows and even his good English would have been forgiven. There is no reason to doubt, especially in the light of his later actions, that before the voyage was over he really "took great delight in furling the top-gallant sails and royals in a hard blow": "There was a wild delirium about it"; he wrote, "a fine rushing of the blood about the heart; and a glad thrilling, and throbbing of the whole system, to find yourself tossed up at every pitch into the clouds of a stormy sky, and hovering like a judgment angel between heaven and earth; both hands free, with one foot in the rigging, and one somewhere behind you in the air. The sail would fill out like a balloon, with a report like a small cannon, and then collapse and sink away into a handful. And the feeling of mastering the rebellious canvas, and tying it down like a slave to the spar, and binding it over and over with the *gasket,* had a touch of pride and power in it, such as young King Richard must have felt, when he trampled down the insurgents of Wat Tyler." To a young man who had spent his entire life measuring his strength against intangibles there was an emotional fulfillment in the physical mastery of unruly canvas, in learning to slide down the bare stays instead of crawling down the shrouds, and in becoming familiar with the many arts and the complicated terminology of seamanship. By the time they sighted the coast of Ireland, after nearly four weeks at sea, he could do these things; and if he was still too inexperienced to steer a passenger ship or pass as a genuine "sailor-man," he was enough of a seaman to recognize the symptoms of an approaching calm in the rattling of the quadruple rows of reef points along the topsails and to tie his points with a secure square knot in the midst of a blow.

Melville's first glimpses of foreign lands were disappointing. Ireland was hardly more than a cloudlike effect on the northern horizon, and the purple mountains of Wales were too far away for him to observe the hedgerows of the little farms which made them different from the familiar Catskills. Even after rounding Holyhead, picking up a pilot at the mouth of the Mersey, and working up the river to within sight of the city of Liverpool, he saw nothing which seemed really new. The forest of masts on the river front with the buildings of the city in the background and the spire of St. Nicholas towering above them all made the new scene not unlike New York; and it was not until the crew of the *St. Lawrence* had begun to haul and pull their ship into the basin and from there, at high tide on the afternoon of July 2, into the great Prince's Dock that Melville had what he called a "realizing sense" of the difference between Liverpool and his native city. For the massive docks of Liverpool, enclosing ninety acres of water and packed with shipping, were the wonder of the maritime world. Prince's Dock, one of the two largest of the fourteen, itself was nearly twelve acres in extent and was usually filled with ships from America tied up in close contact with occasional native vessels from India or China. The quays to which ships were tied were surrounded by high stone walls penetrated by gates leading to the warehouses and the city beyond. Guarded by customs inspectors at each gate, every dock was a kind of free port in which visiting sailors worked for a few hours a day while eating, sleeping, and amusing themselves in the town.

Although Liverpool was becoming noted for the magnificence of its public buildings, the sights of the city which most impressed sensitive Americans were the slums. Five years before Melville's arrival, an estimated twenty thousand of its inhabitants were living in dark cellars, almost as crowded as the forecastle of a ship, and at least twice as many more occupied dwellings above ground which were almost as dark and damp and equally as filthy. Since that time the population had been increased by thousands of emigrants from Ireland, drifting migrants from Wales, and refugees from the industrial cities of the English midlands, and this large influx was responsible for the growth of the port. In the year of Melville's visit, imports of cotton and wool had fallen off severely; and there was probably more unemployment than usual in the districts from which Liverpool drew some of the more poverty-stricken elements of its population. From the squalid dens these people called their homes they swarmed into the smoky fog of daylight and provided a visitor to the water front with a never-to-be-forgotten sight: groups of haggard and hopeless men, young women nursing babies at dirty bosoms, women of all ages with bare splay feet and burdens on their heads, and children who appeared never to have known the touch of soap and water. With a public house for each one hundred and fifty inhabitants, there seemed to be a gin mill every few steps in the poorer sections of the town; and there was no attempt at supervising the dingy alleys and bystreets. In them could be found someone who would cater to every vice and weakness of every sailor from the fifteen hundred vessels which used the port each year.

As Melville and his companion left Prince's Dock at noon and at four o'clock each afternoon, they made their way first up Queen Street and then turned right through a bystreet called Lancelot's Hey to Chapel Street and their boardinghouse in the neighborhood of the old church of St. Nicholas. Lancelot's Hey had been the scene of a great fire five years before which destroyed eight dwellings and fourteen warehouses, and it was in one of the surviving ruins of this catastrophe that Melville seems to have witnessed a sight which gave him his most vivid single impression of Liverpool. "Once, passing through this place," he was later to write in *Redburn,* "I heard a feeble wail, which seemed to come out of the earth. It was but a strip of crooked side-walk where I stood; the dingy wall was on every side, converting the mid-day into twilight; and not a soul was in sight. I started, and could almost have run, when I heard that dismal sound. It seemed the low, hopeless, endless wail of some one forever lost. At last I advanced to an opening which communicated downward with deep tiers of cellars beneath a crumbling old warehouse; and there, some fifteen feet below the walk, crouching in nameless squalor, with her head bowed over, was the figure of what had been a woman. Her blue arms folded to her livid bosom two shrunken things like children, that leaned toward her, one on each side. At first, I knew not whether they were alive or dead. They made no sign; they did not move or stir; but from the vault came that soul-sickening wail." For two days he tried in vain to secure them assistance—from three different policemen in the main thoroughfares, from the ragged scavengers who knew the mother by name, from the watchman in the warehouse across the way, and from his own landlady and cook. Bringing them water in his tarpaulin hat, he discovered that the woman was clutching a meager third child, a baby who had been dead for hours when he first saw the group. On the morning of the third day, the odor of death was unmistakable, and at noon a heap of quicklime was glistening in their place. Merry England could, at least, bury its dead.

Although Melville did not know it, the situation which made so deep an impression upon him was the result not of "modern civilization" but

of the feudal organization from which the town of Liverpool was only
then beginning to escape. For generations before the Municipal Reform
Act of 1835 the city government had been divided among discordant
authorities which had proved inadequate to deal with the problems of
rapid growth, and the recent establishment, at the time of Melville's
arrival, of a centralized and more efficient administration had not yet
brought about many changes affecting the general welfare. The appointment of a public health officer who might have dealt with Melville's
problem, for example, was still nine years in the future. The impressionable young sailor, however, would not have been interested in historical
explanations of a situation which rubbed raw the nerves of his hitherto
sheltered humanity. Having fled from what he considered poverty and a
cold world at home, he was profoundly shocked by the discovery of in-
digence and inhumanity of a sort which he had never imagined. At
the moment, perhaps, the impression made upon him was only one of
shock. But three years later, when he found himself spending another
period of weeks in another foreign land, he was to compare the advantages of civilized and savage life in such a way that one suspects his
disillusioning experiences in Liverpool as having formed an important
frame of reference for his observations in the South Seas.

Because of the awkwardness of unloading ships onto the unprotected
quays in a rainy climate and transporting goods by drays to the warehouses, a transatlantic vessel normally had to stay in port for as long as a
month; and the difficulty of getting an adequate cargo for the depression-
stricken United States kept the *St. Lawrence* there for almost six weeks.
The crew slept and boarded ashore but reported to the ship morning and
afternoon for makeshift work and as a guarantee that they were not
running loose through the countryside. They were free on Sundays,
however, and after four o'clock on the long summer afternoons; and
Melville had plenty of time to see the formal sights of the town and the
surrounding country, although he wrote his mother that he would give
them all "to see a corner of home." Soon after his arrival he evidently
picked up a thirty-one-year-old "Stranger's Guide" to the town, *The
Picture of Liverpool;* and, sentimentally assuming that his father might
have used the same book, he tried to follow its directions from sight to
sight. Not knowing that Riddough's Hotel had been actually torn down
before the date of his father's visit, he took its location as his starting
point and pursued a series of imaginary dotted lines to the major points
of interest, noting particularly that the old fort had been replaced by a
tavern and that the famous Old Dock had been filled to provide a site
for the magnificent new customhouse. As a young man who liked to read,
he probably looked longingly at the newsroom at the Exchange and at

the Liverpool Lyceum, but his story in *Redburn* of being literally kicked out of the latter place almost certainly belongs with such whimsical fantasies as his circumstantial account of his father's notes in the old guide-book.

Most of the visual observations he later incorporated in his book were, of course, based upon actual experience; and his schedule of duties allowed him adequate time for excursions into rural England. But if he ever made a trip to London over the fast new railroad and engaged in any gaudy adventures there, his absence from Liverpool is not noted in the collection of papers which contain Captain Brown's oath to the effect that on August 6 five of his crew—including Robert Jackson and the Greenlander Peter Brown—had deserted. Jackson and Brown, however, returned to duty before the date of sailing, and the three missing men were replaced by new recruits who gave the names Henry Gill, Anton Ton, and Thomas Moore. The probability is that Melville spent his last five days in England just as he had spent the preceding five weeks and that he had no blot on his good record as a sailor on the morning of August 13, when he helped work the *St. Lawrence* out of the Dock, through the basin, and into the Mersey.

On its homeward voyage the *St. Lawrence* carried two passengers, Messrs. L. A. Kettle of England and Andrew Coats of Scotland, in the cabin and thirty-two in the steerage. The trip was an unusually long one, lasting until September 30, but it was made without any of the gruesome dramatics that Melville was afterwards to introduce into his account of it. If the emigrants suffered from an unexpected length of time upon the ocean, they did not suffer from unusual crowding as others may have done in other ships from which Melville may have picked up elements of his horror story. Captains were held to a strict accounting for the members of the crew, and Captain Brown was able to discharge his with their proper certificates. He had no missing man to account for with a strange tale of something like spontaneous combustion. Jackson, at the age of thirty-one, may have been "the foul lees and dregs of a man" that Melville described; but he was last seen walking off the ship rather than falling into the sea from a blood-spattered yardarm. Melville's own greatest worry upon his return voyage was whether he would reach home in time for the opening of the school he expected to teach. His trip had matured him and released him permanently from the apron strings to which he had been tied, but it had not freed him entirely from the financial responsibilities to his family which he would once again try to accept.

When Melville reached home he found that his mother's financial position, instead of improving during his absence, had grown worse. On October 4 one of her creditors sent word that "he had been played with long enough" and could no longer put off the sale of her furniture. Allan, to whom she immediately forwarded the news, had been working in a law office in Albany at a pittance of five dollars a month and could be of no help; but he communicated at once with his uncle Peter Gansevoort, who was in financial difficulties himself and sufficiently distressed to write Judge Lemuel Shaw, in Boston, of Maria's situation in the evident but unexpressed hope that the Melvilles' old friend would renew his interest in the family. It was most probably on this evening or the next morning that Herman reached Lansingburgh. He had learned that his expected job as a schoolteacher had materialized and that he was to begin work promptly at the near-by Greenbush Academy, but, since he could hardly conduct classes in his red baize sailor's shirt, he needed his first quarter's salary for clothes and board and had little or nothing in the way of cash to show for his summer adventure. He was sure that he could provide his mother with between a hundred and fifty and two hundred dollars a year once he got established in his position, but at the moment he could do no more to meet the emergency than could Allan or the unemployed and still-languishing Gansevoort.

Herman had sailed back into exactly the same sort of family crisis that he had sailed out of in June. His mother felt strongly that her two brothers should contribute a fixed sum for her support, and sent Herman to Albany with a letter to that effect apparently on the afternoon of his first week-end visit from Greenbush. As usual, her brother Peter patiently explained both his and her situation: "My inability to contribute a fixed sum for your support has arisen from the same cause of which you have been reduced—I am at this moment apprised of the note, which was discounted for you after Gansevoort's failure, and which I am unable to pay, without great sacrifice—and the large debt due by you to the State Bank, the payment of which I was obliged to guaranty, remains unpaid —under the circumstances, is it reasonable that I should be heavier laden with debt and responsibility—when our brother Herman has not incurred any responsibility for you." He had been hoping daily to hear from their older brother, although he realized that Herman, too, was financially embarrassed, since "money has not for many years been more scarce than it is at present." Nevertheless, he advanced her fifty dollars, with which young Herman returned at once, and somehow the crisis was passed without the loss of the furniture.

In all other respects, Herman's new year began pleasantly enough. As a submaster at Greenbush he had less responsibility than had been forced upon him in the Sykes District School, and he was living among friends and developing an intimacy with a young man named Eli James Murdock Fly, to whose sister Harriet he paid attentions and in whose home he often visited. On one occasion at least he seems to have returned to his "writing desk," publishing in the *Democratic Press and Lansingburgh Advertiser* for November 16, 1839, a sketch called "The Death Graft" under the nautical name of "Harry the Reefer." A youthful combination of sentiment and Gothic horror, it contained a raw exhibition of the sort of fancies he was to introduce so skillfully, many years later, into *Benito Cereno;* but it was less personally revealing than the earlier "Fragments" had been. When he came home again for Gansevoort's twenty-fourth birthday on December 6, however, his mother wrote Allan that she felt "cheered" by his prospects and his interest in his occupation; and Herman himself indicated, in a humorous postscript to his mother's letter, a buoyant disposition which could not be repressed by a protracted and very bad cold. He visited home regularly during the autumn and early winter, and Maria looked forward to having all her children, and also Herman's friend Fly, with her for the Christmas holidays.

Yet despite the preservation of her furniture and the relief from her worries concerning her second son, Maria was growing increasingly bitter about her own situation. On December 14 she wrote once again to Peter, complaining of being left by her two brothers to "struggle with absolute want" which was only momentarily relieved by reluctant remittances in response to begging letters. People who were in the "habit" of wearing shoes, she observed, could hardly postpone buying them "until the times become easy," and not even a "good manager" like herself could keep a family of five children on less than fifty dollars a month. She and her four daughters could not give up their maid of all work, to whom she paid ten shillings a week, but she did threaten to break up the family and disperse its members—although, she added: "I know Brother Herman has no desire of domesticating either of us—you can best answer for yourself. Elsewhere—I have no claim." Peter was being equally hard pressed at the same time by his widowed sister-in-law in the interest of her youngest son, Stanwix Gansevoort; and he passed Maria's case over to Brother Herman, who wrote, through Peter, that he could provide a hundred dollars on the first of the year. Peter, conscious that his own embarrassment was principally caused by his sister's circumstances and hurt by her charges of coldness and indifference, tided her over the holidays with a check for twenty. The family gathering for Christmas could hardly have been a lighthearted one.

Nor did the new year promise to be very prosperous. Herman went back to Greenbush in such a state of numb withdrawal from the complexities of existence that he was reluctant to call at the post office for mail. From New York Gansevoort shrewdly diagnosed Herman's mental state in a letter to Allan on the twenty-first of January: "I know no other reason for his remissness but laziness—not general laziness by any means —but that laziness which consists in an unwillingness to exert oneself in doing at a particular time, that which ought to be done—or—to illustrate—that disinclination to perform the special duty of the hour which so constantly beset one of the most industrious men of the age—Sir Walter Scott." As the winter wore on into a disappointing spring, his withdrawal changed from a sensitive reaction to an apologetic unhappiness because of his inability to carry out the promises he had made during the first quarter of his school year. On April 3, 1840, Gansevoort again wrote Allan that he had heard nothing from Herman, although Helen had informed him that their brother had "not yet received any money for his services during the past winter"—"very singular conduct," he remarked, "on the part of the Trustees of the institution" who were distressing all the Melvilles by allowing Herman to accumulate an indebtedness for board for which the family felt responsible.

By the middle of May, however, some financial arrangements had been made by the trustees, and Herman was evidently able to settle part of his board bill and walk home on the fifteenth with three meager dollars for his mother. Although further sums were due him, he expected his school to be discontinued at the end of the following week for lack of funds and had no hope of being able to help pay his family's quarterly rent bill which was already past due. Maria was a hundred and fifty dollars in debt—the exact amount of her son's minimum promise during the fall—and had written three times to her brother Herman without receiving an acknowledgment "in act or deed." Turning again to the long-suffering Peter in an effort to obtain fifty dollars if he could "do no more," she wrote: "I feel unusually depressed and troubled, and cannot throw it off. I feel as if my poverty and consequent dependence, have robbed me of the affection of my dear brothers, at a time when true love and Friendship is alone to be tested, *in adversity*. . . . If you cannot possibly send me fifty, in mercy my dear Brother send me the amount of the rent." She sent the letter to Allan by Herman with instructions that her younger son should hand it to his uncle and "await his reading of it." Peter made a note on the document, "Gave answer to her son Allan who delivered this letter," but left no indication that he had been able to render assistance.

At this time Herman was more at sea emotionally than he had been when he left home a year before. He knew that the poverty of which his mother complained so bitterly was genuine only with reference to her proud standards of decent living, yet he was approaching the age of twenty-one and knew that he must do something to relieve the overwrought condition of the Melville household. The prospects of local employment were no better than they had been the preceding spring, and as soon as he had received notice that his school would close he thought of going west where his uncle Thomas Melville was located and where his cousin Robert was expecting to go during the summer. Allan had obtained a better job in Albany, but he was hardly doing more than making his own living; and Gansevoort was no better off in New York, where he was worrying about his health and trying to study law. The least Herman could do, for a second time, was to get out from under foot and hope for the best in the future. When his school closed there was evidently some sort of financial settlement which provided him with funds for an economical trip west, and he may have taught for a couple of extra weeks in the town of Brunswick in order to have additional money to pay his debts. His friend Fly was eager to go west, too, and they began to plan the trip. On June 5, apparently on the eve of his departure, Herman made out a receipt to the trustees of the School District No. 7 of the Town of Brunswick for the sum of six dollars "in full of all demands to this date." If he left it with his mother or brother to be used when the money was available for collection and for the payment of his board bill in Greenbush, the action was his final boyhood gesture of misguided optimism: the unendorsed receipt is still among the Melville family papers.

II

The disillusioned schoolteacher and sensitive second son who set his face westward promptly disappeared from his family's view more completely than he had when he took a well-known ship to cross the Atlantic. The great basin of the Erie Canal, into which he and Fly seem to have dropped from sight, was not unlike the docks of Liverpool, although the boats were smaller and the chaos greater. The young men who turned their backs to the brown tiers of houses from which Albany overlooked the Hudson had before them all the bustle of a growing country whose rapid expansion could not be halted by hard times. They stood at one of the major links in the chain of commerce and immigration which connected Europe with the prairies of Illinois. From their right came the steamboats from New York City towing barges of freight to be transferred to canalboats, which in turn would be towed in strings through the locks to the north, across the long aqueduct, and turned loose to be pulled westward by animal power. Boats by the hundreds were tied to the wharf, which ran for nearly a mile along the embankment separating the basin from the river, and the whole scene was noisily alive with people moving and checking cargoes, bargaining over passages westward, dodging about with an air of urgent business, or lounging on the decks and shouting the latest gossip to their neighbors. It was not a new sight to either Melville or his friend, but it was more exciting than it had been when they had no expectation of becoming a part of it; and an ex-sailor could observe with new interest the women and horses that gave an unusual character to the Albany basin as a nautical scene.

For every boat which arrived or departed had to disembark or take on board the animals by which it was normally moved, and usually the boat had a woman cook to do the captain's washing, help him steer, and otherwise comfort him on the long slow haul to Utica, Rome, and eventually Buffalo. Melville, who was later to describe himself as having been "a vagabond" along the canal, and his friend probably managed to talk themselves from stage to stage of their journey aboard different freighters instead of taking passage on a regular passenger boat, walking along the towpaths when necessity required and getting a ride whenever the occasion permitted.

Such a trip would have made demands on most of the experience and toughness Melville had acquired during his voyage across the Atlantic and his six weeks in the Liverpool slums the summer before. Winding its way for three hundred and sixty-three miles between the Hudson River and Lake Erie, climbing mountains by means of locks, and crossing swift streams as a great aqueduct, the canal was a placid stream forty feet broad and four feet deep, with smooth towpaths on either side for the plodding mules which drew the freighters or the trotting horses of the faster packet boats. From a distant hilltop it seemed invested with romance as the spectator looked down upon the creeping eighty-foot boats and listened to the mellow echoes of the horns with which the boatmen announced their approach to a lock, bend, or another vessel. But within its clearly defined limits the canal possessed an unromantic life of its own which provided a rowdy contrast to the quiet countryside through which it passed. The teen-aged, tobacco-chewing, gin-drinking teamsters were the despair of the occasional missionaries who realized that there were worse heathen at home than there were abroad; and those who toughened into maturity and grew tired of being boatmen, without a boat and a "cook" of their own, generally had to conceal their past if they wanted to be accepted in any other environment—even in that of a whaling vessel. There were good canallers, of course, just as there were good sailors; but since it was always possible to desert ship by a single leap ashore canalmen were under little more restraint than sailors were in port, and their normal lives were undisciplined by either necessity or convention. Furthermore, the mooring basins in every large town were the resorts of thieves and harpies, and notorious gangs of robbers roamed the banks, especially in the region of the great Montezuma swamps between Syracuse and Rochester. Unattached travelers who did not stay on the regular passenger boats could rarely feel entirely secure either in their property or in their lives.

Melville must have had some genuine experience with the dangers of the canal, for he was later to express his hearty thanks for a "good turn" done him by an anonymous canaller who had "as stiff an arm to back a poor stranger in a strait, as to plunder a wealthy one." He also had other experiences that were not recorded. At Rome, a lock of the canal touched the site of old Fort Stanwix, where his maternal grandfather, Colonel Peter Gansevoort, had defeated the British and Indian troops of Colonel Barry St. Leger during the Revolutionary War and thereby prevented them from reënforcing General Burgoyne before the Battle of Saratoga. While his boat was passing through the lock Melville had time to stand where his heroic ancestor had earned a formal vote of thanks from the Continental Congress, and he might have recalled the sound of the British drum which had been captured during the engagement and later presented by the then General Gansevoort to the Albany artillery company. At other points along the canal the young vagabond found less historical provocations to thought. The state was spending more than three and a quarter million dollars during the depression year of 1840 upon the project of building new locks and aqueducts and enlarging the canal to seventy feet in width and seven in depth, and every sign of activity must have reminded Melville of his own fruitless effort to become an engineer on a job which was to last for over two decades. For miles after leaving behind the new improvements and the remains of Fort Stanwix, he could have meditated the differences between a young wanderer hoarding the thin resources of his pocketbook and a young engineer who might have been developing in peace a section of the country his grandfather had saved in war.

As they approached the western end of the canal, the two travelers may have gone out of their way to visit Niagara Falls, perhaps investing ninety-four cents each in the novelty of a railroad passage from Lockport or a similar amount for the trip from Niagara to Buffalo behind an engine which carried a man on the cowcatcher to look out for and hammer down the loose strips of iron that covered its wooden rails. The thriving town of Buffalo surprised Melville with its macadamized streets and the variety of people who walked them—Indians in deerskin trousers, platoons of soldiers, backwoodsmen, German emigrants, wild-looking Irishmen, dainty lady tourists, squaws with papooses on their backs, an occasional British officer in a red coat or an English farmer in gaiters, Frenchmen, and Canadians from across the river. If he climbed to the elevated residential

area above the town he could look backward across a landscape of un-
broken primeval forest or down upon the busy wharves to which several
large sailing ships and some forty steamboats and canalboats were tied
on the last day of June. For ten dollars one of the steamers would take a
passenger on the week's trip to Chicago, and Melville and Fly evidently
embarked without delay, for they were to reach Illinois before the flowers
stopped blooming on the prairies in early July.

To the young man who had crossed the Atlantic the summer before,
the voyage through the lakes offered almost as many novelties as it did to
his companion who had never been to sea. On Lake Erie, vessels normally
followed the shore line and made several stops before reaching Cleveland
—where Melville was again surprised by the neatness of paved streets
—and then turned out of sight of land on the direct route to Detroit. The
dark green lake water was often choppy and crested with foam, and if
Melville crossed it on the night of the first of July he had adequate reason
to write later of the lakes' "Borean and dismasting blasts as direful as any
that lash the salted wave," for Lake Erie was swept that night by a storm
which made experienced travelers from Europe, and even horses, seasick. By morning, however, the passengers on a steamer could appreciate
the steadiness of their ungainly wood burner, for it had kept its course
during the tempest and reached the archipelago off Point Pelee, where
a major naval engagement of the War of 1812 had been fought and where
the islands appeared as romantic in the morning sunshine as anything
Melville was later to see in the South Seas. The historic city of Detroit
was disappointing in comparison with the active canal terminals, Cleveland and Buffalo, but it was rich in associations and was already in the
process of changing from a center of the fur trade to a railway center and
an important landing port for immigrants. From Detroit the travelers'
way took them across the glassy Lake St. Clair and up the St. Clair River,
where the clean sailing vessels often had to beg motive power from the
sooty steamers and on which the steamers themselves could be chased
and overtaken by the birch canoes put out by the wild Indians from their
peltry wigwams along the shore.

With Lake Huron the genuine wilderness began. As the traveler
looked over its dark water he could see only what Melville was later to call
"ancient and unentered forests" marred only rarely by the shacks of summer wood choppers who provided the lake vessels with their fuel. The
frequent military establishments of the Americans and British had been
left behind, and every voyager who approached Mackinac Island from
the east was impressed by the loneliness and the grandeur of the American
fort which crowned its heights. Some three hundred feet below the bat-
teries and white buildings of the fort were scattered the houses of the

town and the wigwams of the Indians on the beach. There the visitor could observe at close hand the proud Ojibways, the ugly Menominees, or the dark and shaggy Winnebagos from the west; or he could wander through the town examining the rude houses built by the French more than a century and a half before or the more impressive modern church, mission house, and home of the Indian agent, Mr. Schoolcraft, whose researches were to provide the legendary material which Professor Longfellow was eventually to find more interesting than the European literature he was then teaching at Harvard. Leaving the island, they skirted the ruins of old Fort Mackinac, which had been destroyed by Pontiac, passed through the straits, and turned southward along the eastern shore of Lake Michigan past uninhabited miles of forests, cliffs, and sand dunes before crossing over to the new town of Milwaukee, for which many new settlers were bound.

Chicago, in the summer of 1840, was by far the most thriving of the western towns. In seven years it had grown from a fort and three frame dwellings into a city of between six and seven thousand inhabitants with hotels and warehouses to accommodate the great flow of travelers and goods that passed through it. Leading westward, the Illinois and Michigan Canal—larger than the old Erie—was nearing completion, and soon it would be possible to go by boat to Peru and from there down the Illinois River through Peoria to the Mississippi at Grafton. But the upper Mississippi was reached by stage or horseback over a route which led through Elgin, Rockford, and Freeport to Galena. Although the triweekly stage was cutting prices on its western trip that summer, Melville and his companion probably used the cheaper mode of transportation by horseback and were free to leave the road and "wade" through the tall grass, which came as high as the horses' saddles and made a permanent impression upon the mind of the future author of *Moby Dick*. After some thirty miles of flat country just west of Chicago the prairies took on the rolling appearance which so regularly reminded visitors of the ocean, and in late June and early July they were covered with flowers—acres of purple, or yellow and red and blue, rainbow mixtures, and fields knee-deep in the striped tiger lilies that Melville was later to remember most vividly. Occasionally the landscape was broken by small islands of trees, but for most of the three-day journey its only variety was to be found in its color; and lonely riders had ample time to meditate upon the herds of buffaloes which had once roamed the land and fought off the slinking wolves whose descendants still howled around the camps of wayfarers. The rugged country around Galena marked the end of a journey which was both novel and memorable.

In Galena, Melville found that his uncle Thomas had achieved a fairly prominent but hardly a prosperous position in the community. He was the official notary public for Jo Daviess County and a commissioner for taking acknowledgment of deeds and depositions for the states of Massachusetts and Maine, and at the most probable time of his nephew's arrival he was away from home serving as a member of the convention of delegates who were trying to settle the northern boundary of Illinois in a meeting at Rockford. He had also been secretary of the Galena chamber of commerce for two years and had recently been made treasurer as well, but such small town offices and honors were of the sort that commonly distinguish the citizen whose breeding is better than his business sense. In a town of less than two thousand inhabitants, Thomas Melville was still recalling the boulevards of Paris while trying to support his family by commissions earned by dealing in real estate, paying taxes, and collecting debts for people who lacked the experience or the time for managing their incidental business. It was a new country, full of strangers, of course; and there were outside interests to be represented in the affairs of the flourishing lead mines across the river at Dubuque or in the lead manufactory in Galena. But Thomas Melville was not prospering, and he could do no more for a young nephew than he was able to do for his own sons, one of whom was eventually to become a clerk on a steamboat while another went into the lead mines.

Herman Melville had, in fact, picked the worst possible year in which to go west, for the financial depression which blighted his earlier prospects at home had moved ahead of him across the country. He may have learned from the most recent immigrants' guide that schoolteachers were in great demand in all the western towns, but when he reached Galena he discovered that actually one of its two schools had been closed and that the building was being advertised for rent as suitable for the residence of a bachelor or a small family. Other residential property was standing vacant with no prospect of occupancy as the summer drew toward a close, services of craftsmen were being offered at lowered prices, and Thomas Clark, the proprietor of the Galena hotel, had announced a twenty per cent reduction of all charges "in consideration of the hard times." Melville was to stay with his uncle long enough to see the silks of the prairie corn turn brown in the autumn and to receive the impressions later incorporated in his poem, "Trophies of Peace," but there was little for him to do. The only activity reflected in his novels was that of a conventional tourist's trip to the Falls of St. Anthony, where he observed the magnificent forests from which the limpid headwaters of the Mississippi flowed. Sixteen years later he started to use a description of the scene for the opening chapter of *The Confidence Man* but rejected it, and the only recollection of the excursion to be preserved in his published writings was a fanciful reference in *White Jacket* to the Sioux Indians who inhabited the village of Kaposia and whose miserable condition was regularly noted by travelers in Minnesota.

At the beginning of autumn there was nothing for Melville and his companion to do but turn homeward with the hope of finding some sort of employment in New York. They took a river steamer from Galena to Cairo, passing in sight of the old Mormon settlement at Nauvoo and stopping off at St. Louis long enough to visit the Indian mounds across the river in Illinois; and from this region, and from his casual notice of the Jewish settlers who first came to Chicago in the summer of 1840, Melville garnered impressions which were to last more than three decades and become a part of his philosophical poem *Clarel*. Below St. Louis his boat passed by the low, vine-covered banks which kept the river from overflowing into the famously rich "American bottom" of Illinois—banks which Melville observed were as "flat as tow-paths" and to which the picturesque shot towers on the cliffs of Herculaneum and the limestone bluffs above Ste. Genevieve on the Missouri side made a dramatic contrast. Above Cape Girardeau the cliffs bore such names as the "Devil's Oven" and "Devil's Anvil" and below it the river twisted and turned until it came to the swampy and squalid, mosquito-infested flats which to the south-borne traveler signified Cairo. All of this scenery and the river boat from which it was observed was later to appear, although not always in its proper order, in the first half of *The Confidence Man;* for in that book Melville allowed his voyagers to observe the scenery only so far as he himself had gone down the river, and the only geographical allusion in the latter part of the narrative is to the junction of the Muskingum with the Ohio, up which the author himself had turned in these days of his youth.

The last stages of Melville's trip homeward are not clearly recorded in his later writings; but he probably left the Ohio, after a week or ten days and nine hundred miles upon the river, at Wheeling, Virginia, and took the broad "national road" across the Alleghenies, acquiring en route his lasting impressions of the Virginia mountaineers. The uniform regularity of the houses in Philadelphia provided him with a figure of speech for one of his later novels, and by the middle of November he reached New York, where his brother Gansevoort was persistently enjoying ill-health and studying law. "Herman is still here," the latter wrote on the twenty-sixth of that month, reporting that both of the returned travelers were on the lookout for jobs while living at a cheap rate of two dollars and a half a week—exclusive of dinner, which they took "with good appetites" at Gansevoort's expense at "Sweeney's." There they could get a plate of meat for six cents and vegetables for three. "They are both in good health and tolerable spirits," he commented; "Herman has had his hair sheared and whiskers shaved and looks more like a Christian than usual."

Although willing to make some concessions to convention while job hunting, Herman was reluctant to return home. Since his school had not paid the small amount of salary due him for the year before, he still owed seven dollars for board and had no interest in whether or not the school had reopened. His mother's financial position was as bad as usual, and if it had not become worse it had at least become more clearly apparent to the whole family, for, under the direction of her brother Peter, she had consolidated her debts in October and had signed a note for nineteen thousand dollars to the New York State Bank. Peter Gansevoort's home in Albany had been saddened by the recent death of his infant son, Herman, and Robert Melville had at last decided that as bad as conditions might be in Galena they were no worse than those in Pittsfield and had really given up the farm and gone west to join his father. There was no direction in which Herman could turn without the prospect of becoming a burden. Neither his own nor Gansevoort's resources could support him in idleness, and his sensitive older brother probably warned him against any expectations from his Boston relatives. When Fly finally succeeded in getting a position as a copyist and Melville realized that his own youthful failure to perfect his handwriting disqualified him from the one means of employment available in hard times, his position became psychologically, if not actually, desperate.

Both he and Gansevoort thought of the sea. The older brother believed that a winter voyage to the West Indies would restore his health and enable him to pursue his legal studies with greater efficiency upon his return, and he had reason to believe that Judge Lemuel Shaw, whose protégé he had become, would be sympathetic to such a therapeutic adventure. Herman, able-bodied, experienced, and determined not to be a nuisance to anybody, was quite capable of taking a ship for anywhere he chose without assistance. It was inevitable, perhaps, that his mind should have turned to the Pacific; for even in the innermost regions of the American continent he had not been far from a consciousness of the South Seas. All the time he had been in Galena his uncle and aunt had been worrying about the fate of their oldest son Thomas, who had returned from one whaling voyage and disappeared upon another; and Herman, having heard romantic accounts of his cousin's earlier experiences on the other side of the world, may have speculated more than once upon the attractions of faraway places to a relative whose family would not believe that he was "utterly depraved." The entire Melville family had probably read with unusual interest the story, published in the *North Western Gazette and Galena Advertiser* for July 17, of the long captivity of Seaman Joseph

Forbes who had been caught by the natives of Timor in 1822 and only recently released by the captain of a British vessel. It was not a pleasant story, but it was almost as exciting in some of its implications as the fiction of James Fenimore Cooper's *The Red Rover* which Herman was also reading "far inland" that summer. In New York, one of the most recent books of general interest was *Two Years Before the Mast*, by Richard Henry Dana, Jr., and as Melville read it with "strange, congenial feelings" between vain applications for jobs he may have been struck by the South Sea experiences of Dana's young English acquaintance whose adventurous footsteps he himself was soon to follow after his own more respectable fashion. The Atlantic Ocean had provided him with a means of escape from the temporary problem of unemployment eighteen months before. Now that the problem had begun to seem permanent, the Pacific might, by its very breadth and distance from home, serve the same purpose just as effectively for a longer period of time.

Whatever Melville's motives were in undertaking a whaling voyage to the South Pacific, he did not "get away from it all" in the manner of lonesome desperation which he was later to attribute to Ishmael in *Moby Dick*. As he had done on his first trip, he made his preparations in advance of his actual joining a vessel, in consultation with Gansevoort and perhaps with the advice of his brother's friend Alexander Bradford. At any rate his family received a note from Gansevoort on Sunday, December 20, saying that on Friday "Herman's destination would be decided"; and his mother wrote Allan that he would hear the particulars when the family saw him—presumably on that Friday when the Melvilles were all expecting to get together again for Christmas. If Herman actually got home for the holiday, the family reunion must have been more talkative if no more happy than the one of the year before. All the news of the Galena Melvilles and all the adventures of Herman's western trip would require hours of telling, and the girls were probably not averse to speculating upon the relative charms of the sights they expected their brothers to see in the West Indies and the Cannibal Isles. But amidst the vivacious gossip and speculation they could not have avoided an uneasy awareness that this might be the last time they would all be together. Their cousin Guert Gansevoort was later to "blame" Herman seriously for going to sea, and they knew in advance that a voyage on a whaler would be shocking to their relatives and friends—especially since the mystery of their cousin Thomas was a familiar reminder of how readily a man could be lost to his family even though he might survive the dangers commonly associated with whaling.

Neither the gaiety nor the uneasiness of the occasion could have lasted long, however, for Gansevoort probably went to Boston to make financial arrangements with Judge Shaw for his cruise on the ship *Teazer*,

which was to sail from New York for the Caribbean and the Gulf of
Mexico about the middle of January, and Herman signed an affidavit of
American citizenship in New Bedford on December 26 and then crossed
the river to Fairhaven, where he was to get a berth on the new and still
unregistered whaling ship *Acushnet*. Two of its owners were Bradfords,
and whether they were relatives of the Melvilles' Albany and New York
friends or members of the Vineyard Quaker family of the same name there
was evidently some connection between the ship and the circles in which
the Melvilles moved in New York. On Thursday, December 31, the
young adventurer—now twenty-one and full grown, with a complexion
tanned by prairie suns—signed the articles as an ordinary seaman whose
"residence" was Fairhaven and received the sum of eighty-four dollars
as an advance against his prospective earnings. About nine-tenths of this
would normally have been applied to the purchase of a standard "outfit" of shoddy clothing and blankets, straw-filled mattress and pillow,
sheath knife and razor, and the various incidentals that went into the
sea chest every man was required to buy; but there was enough left over
for him to start the new year with a little money in his purse and with no
serious demands upon it in the visible future.

For three days Melville may have renewed his acquaintance with a
sailors' boardinghouse while the *Acushnet* lay at the wharf and took on the
supplies necessary for the voyage, literally cramming itself with the large
oaken casks that rolled toward every whaler in a steady stream in the
days preceding its departure. Some were knocked down and stored away
in crevices to be put together by the ship's cooper at the end of the trip.
Others were empty and ready to receive the first oil. But many were filled
with fresh water, salt beef and pork, biscuit dried to worm-resistant hard-
ness, spare sails and cordage, trade goods for distant ports, or articles of
clothing and miscellaneous items for the "slop chest" from which the
members of the crew would draw their personal necessities for undetermined months to come. Since the crew did not ordinarily go aboard until
shortly before sailing, Melville had plenty of time to explore both Fairhaven and New Bedford. In the latter place he visited the Whaleman's
Chapel, which he was later to identify with Father Edward T. Taylor's
more famous Seaman's Bethel in Boston, and may even have attended a
religious service there, under the Reverend Enoch Mudge, either on December 27 or January 3, before the *Acushnet* cast her moorings and got
under way for Buzzard's Bay, Cape Horn, and the far Pacific. As Melville looked at the bleak New England coast he was leaving on that winter
afternoon, he must have experienced a feeling of escape without any
accompanying sense of relief: the pride that started him on his long
voyage was cold, and it would be nearly four years before he returned.

3
The Pacific: Outward Bound

FEW YOUNG MEN ever boarded a whaler under circumstances more auspicious. If Melville's decision had been "forced by the united influences of Captain Marryat and hard times," as he later hinted, he already knew enough about the sea to discount the romance of Captain Marryat's novels, and the "hard times" he had seen on shore had been sufficiently real to make him appreciate the economic security of the years that lay before him. If not a protégé of the owners, he was at least a person of some interest to the major shareholders in the ship, with whom the captain himself was in partnership; and he had every reason to expect as friendly treatment as the master of a vessel could give a common sailor. He also had reason to be sure of his ability to deserve such treatment, for although his limited experience classified him as an ordinary rather than an able seaman he knew that he could trust his sea legs and his grip on a rope and was sure that he would compare favorably with the green hands in the usual whaler's crew. Any passing doubts that he may have had concerning his seamanship would have been normally quelled by a merchantman's traditional scorn for the overmanned, unkempt floating factories at which the smaller crews of trimmer vessels regularly jeered.

The *Acushnet* itself was as good a whaler as anyone might pick—brand-new and of standard design, with two decks, three masts, and a square stern. She measured a hundred and four feet, eight and a quarter inches in length; twenty-seven feet, ten inches in width; thirteen feet, eleven inches in depth; and slightly over three hundred and fifty-eight tons in burthen. She represented an investment of over thirty thousand dollars on the part of the owners, plus perhaps two-thirds as much again for stores and equipment, but if she returned fully loaded to her capacity of twenty-eight hundred barrels of sperm and whale oil (as very few did) her cargo would more than equal the value of the entire investment. Of this an ordinary sailor's "lay" or share in the net proceeds might be as much as two hundred dollars if he had not drawn too heavily on the "slop chest" for clothing and tobacco during his three to five years of absence. In the meantime he would have had board and lodging and freedom from responsibility, and that was more than Melville had got out of teaching school. Instead of occupying a comfortable bed, of course, he would be obliged to sleep in a narrow, straw-filled bunk, wedged with seventeen others in double tiers along the sides of the squat parabola of an unventilated forecastle hardly twenty-five by twenty-five feet in size at the bow of the ship; and instead of sitting down to the generous table of a farmer, he would squat over a tin plate of boiled salt beef or pork with hardtack on weekdays and a "duff" of hard-boiled dough sweetened with molasses on Sundays. But he was young and, at the moment, had a better appetite for adventure than for comfort and good food. He could face his ship cheerfully enough.

The members of the crew were also somewhat above the average quality to be found in whaling vessels at that time. According to the best modern authority on labor conditions in the whaling industry, the *Acushnet* "carried a relatively mature crew" in that six of its members had reached the age of thirty and only four were under twenty. It included a number of ne'er-do-wells recruited by shipping agents (two of whom deserted before the voyage began), and its roster recorded the presence of the usual mixture of free Negroes, Portuguese, and strays from the north of Europe; but a majority of those listed had good New England names, and Melville was agreeably surprised to find that many of their holders had possessed "early advantages" in education and background. The provision of the new ship with a library and the fact that the crew was fully recruited without the necessity of stopping at the Cape Verde Islands for additional Portuguese both indicate that Melville was better off for companions than he would have been in any "average" vessel at a time when even the shoddiest and most inexperienced sailors were extremely hard to obtain for sperm whaling.

The early part of the voyage certainly bore out any good expectations that Melville may have held. Although the Atlantic rarely held a Pacific whaler for long, captains were generally anxious for enough hunting to break in green hands, find the proper combinations of men for the boats, and work the whole crew into a sound state of discipline before they made the dangerous and often heartbreaking circuit of Cape Horn. A school of porpoises, speared from the martingale stays, might provide an excuse for uncovering the tryworks—two great pots of a couple of hundred gallons capacity each, set amidships in a framework of brick which contained a shallow furnace chamber and a space beneath to be filled with water for the protection of the wooden deck. In these the fat blubber, spliced and peeled off the bodies of any variety of seagoing mammals, was reduced to oil very much as the country boys on board were accustomed to rendering lard, except that the fire was fed with crackling, thus intensifying the smell and covering the entire ship with greasy black smoke. A school of larger blackfish provided an excuse for lowering the boats and breaking new men to their oars with considerable sport and a minimum of danger, for a good harpooner might attach his boat to several of these animals at once and let the men bet on their strength as they pulled at cross purposes. Oil from the porpoise and blackfish was not very good, but it sold at the price of whale oil if properly distributed among the casks and thus allowed a captain with a Yankee conscience to train his men while preserving a meticulous regard for the interest of his owners.

Despite the custom of placing a lookout at the masthead soon after leaving port, sperm whalers had little expectation of finding their primary game north of the Tropic of Cancer. But as soon as they were well into the central latitudes every man on a ship became alert to the long cry of "blo-o-o-o-w" which would signal the first test of his courage and of any training he had received on the way down. For the great sperm whale, which might be half as long and a third as wide as the ship, or even larger, was caught and killed from a five-hundred-pound whaleboat which was crowded with an officer, four oarsmen, a harpooner or "boatsteerer," and a half ton of gear, including the three-foot tub containing some four hundred yards of thumb-size Manila line to which the harpoon was attached. It required both courage and discipline for a crew to row within arm's length of the unpredictable monster and even greater courage and discipline for them to obey orders and handle their oars after the dangerous line had begun to whiz down the middle of the boat, while the mate who handled the killing lance and the harpooner who handled the steering oar changed places after the strike, and when they never knew but that the whale's mighty flukes were rising twenty feet or more above their bowed backs. Once attached, they had to stay with their prey until the mate found its heart with an eight-foot lance, although the boat might be pulled over the horizon in the "Nantucket sleigh ride" of a straightaway run, almost swamped by a deep sounding, or tossed like a chip in the rolling waters of a dying "flurry." When they reached the Pacific they would count themselves extraordinarily lucky whenever they could start a new chase while still oily with blubber and black from a sleepless night at the try-pots. They needed all the training and hardening they could get before they reached there.

The crew of the *Acushnet* were lucky in getting their training early. By the time they reached Rio de Janeiro on March 13, after two months and ten days at sea, they had enough oil aboard to send one hundred and fifty barrels north by the brig *Tweed* and could count themselves experienced hands. They had learned the slippery art of making fast a whale to the side of the ship, balancing upon the swaying cutting platform beyond the carcass and above the gathering sharks, and peeling off great slabs of blubber eighteen inches wide that were raised high in the rigging before being cut off and lowered into the blubber room for slicing into the large "horse-pieces" later minced into the "bible-leaves" required for the pots. They were familiar with the Brobdingnagian butchery involved in cutting off the whale's monstrous head and either hoisting it aboard the stern or securing it so that the pure liquid oil could be bailed out of its hollow "case." They knew the sort of exhaustion that seems to suck the very marrow out of men's bones. They had felt the sliminess of the black grime that made them look like feverish devils working around the fierce flames of the tryworks. They had felt the sweet spermaceti that had to be squeezed into fluid before being tried out and stored away in the great six-barrel casks. They were, in short, tried and proved men, ready for a spell of relaxation on shore.

Instead, they learned that a sailor's life on the ocean wave was not a mere figure of speech. The *Acushnet* remained in the Rio harbor for only one full day, too short a time for shore liberty, and if Melville was allowed to set foot on dry land the privilege was an insignificant reward for rowing a boat in line of duty. On the fifteenth, with discipline unrelaxed, they left "the bay of all beauties" and Sugar Loaf Mountain behind and turned toward Cape Horn. With only one recorded chase en route they made rapid progress southward and exactly one month after leaving Rio sighted Staten Land looming through the mist two leagues directly ahead. Swinging around, they ran for the Cape; and although they came into a heavy squall the next day they beat out the westerly gale that usually followed and on April 17 saw the island of Diego Ramírez to their right and slightly behind them. Sailing almost directly west for safety, they caught another squall on the eighteenth; but when the gale broke early in the following day they were in a position to fight it and even gain a few miles in its very teeth. Thick weather and the fear of another blow kept them facing their prospective danger for three days more before they were able to swing their bowsprit to the starboard and beat their way north toward sunshine and security. On May 7 they passed between Más Afuera and Robinson Crusoe's island and two days later were chasing sperm whales west of Valparaiso. They had experienced just enough Cape Horn weather to give them a yarn but not enough to have given them any real trouble.

Melville was also acquiring other experiences that gave him material for yarns. One of the stories told and debated periodically in the forecastle was that of the whaler *Essex* which had been stove and sunk within ten minutes by a sperm whale in 1819. Owen Chase, the first mate of the vessel, had published an account of the event insisting that the attack was deliberate, furious, and apparently made in revenge for the harpooning of three other whales in the shoal to which the attacker belonged. The story was one which invited argument from beginning to end and would naturally have called to mind all the wild legends that had grown up in the whale fishery about other aggressive monsters including the white-humped Mocha Dick. The fame of this peculiar whale had been spread abroad, shortly before Melville made his first voyage, in an article for the *Knickerbocker Magazine* which had since been reprinted in several cheap collections of tales for sailors. The curious and apparently fascinated young man (who seems to have been on good conversational terms with his officers) learned that the second mate, an Englishman named John Hall, had twice sailed under Owen Chase but could tell him no more about the man and the incident than he already knew—although Hall "always spoke of Chase with much interest and sincere regard." The story stayed in Melville's mind, and, when he later discovered Chase's son aboard a vessel the *Acushnet* spoke beneath an equatorial sky, he eagerly questioned the boy about his father and was allowed to read the son's own copy of the published *Narrative*. Some time afterward the *Acushnet* spoke another ship in the same neighborhood, and its captain, whom Melville evidently took to be Owen Chase in person, came aboard for a visit. Although a foremast hand had no opportunity to talk with him, Melville studied the visitor with careful attention and romantic admiration, finding verification of his *Narrative* in his face and deciding that he was "the most prepossessing-looking whale-hunter" he had ever seen. This interest, as much as any physical event of the voyage, was to bear fruit later.

In the meantime, the *Acushnet* was continuing northward with occasional lowerings for whales, passing inside St. Felix Isle on May 17 and bearing toward the coast of Peru. The ship approached the coast on

June 9 and followed past the Pacific headquarters of the American Navy at Callao to the harbor of Santa, where Captain Pease dropped anchor for a ten-day stop on June 23. One member of the crew, David Smith, who afterwards committed suicide in Mobile, had had enough and deserted two days before the ship got under way again. But Melville was in no way discontented. He wrote his brother Gansevoort that he was in perfect health and not dissatisfied with his lot, and that he was afforded constant gratification by his good fortune in "being one of a crew so much superior in morale and early advantages to the ordinary run of whaling crews." On this occasion he undoubtedly had an opportunity to make some observations of the South American civilization which apparently interested him greatly, and he probably had a cheerful sense of seeing the world when his ship left port, on July 2, for a cruise outside the Galápagos and just below the equator, where sperm whales were supposed to be plentiful at all seasons of the year.

Although reports brought home by other vessels are confusing because of the oil sent home from Rio, the *Acushnet* apparently had at least two hundred barrels on board when it left Santa; and between the time its crew sighted their first game on July 25 and the time they spoke the *William Wirt* two months later they added two hundred and fifty more, all collected while swinging back and forth in the neighborhood of 4° S. and 105° W. On October 1, during a rugged squally day, they made the sort of killing that captain, crew, and owners dream of: a round hundred barrels, as they figured it after days and nights at the tryworks. Their casks had been nearly a quarter filled, and half of their total cargo had been collected on the voyage out and half after little more than two months on the real hunting grounds. When they were seen by the *Joseph Maxwell* of their home port, Fairhaven, on October 11, they were probably lighthearted with the expectation of a short and prosperous voyage; for many whalemen believed that the best season along the line came in the winter, which still lay before them. Their extraordinary day of good luck, however, was almost their last. Before the end of the month Captain Pease had turned in disgust back toward the Galápagos Islands. On the thirtieth Albemarle Island was sighted to the southeast, and the *Acushnet* cruised in its neighborhood for several days in company with a number of other ships, including the *Rousseau* of Nantucket, from which Melville was to recall getting another wild tale of its having had its bottom pierced by a swordfish—although it was the *William Penn* which was actually laid up by such an accident, to the great wonder of the whaling fleet, a year and a half later. All sorts of curious stories, however, seemed to collect around this desolate group of scoriaceous lumps on the bright surface of the Pacific; and it had been reported that whales could be herded like cattle in Albemarle's twin bays. But for twenty days the

Acushnet saw nothing either to herd or to chase. Finally Captain Pease decided to return to the coast of South America in order to recruit or resupply his ship for a longer cruise farther out along the line.

Before leaving the Galápagos, he came to anchor for six days at Chatham's Isle—possibly for the purpose of capturing some of the giant tortoises for which the islands were named and which, without being fed, could provide a ship with fresh meat for months. There Melville made his most prolonged and intimate acquaintance with the arid, volcanic, and reptile-infested surface of a land which quickly disenchanted any common sailors whose expectations might have been raised by hearing their navigation officers refer to the islands as the "Encantadas" because of the way their unpredictable currents upset calculations and made the islands seem to jump around in the empty ocean. After getting under way on November 25, the *Acushnet* made fairly good progress eastward, and although they sighted sperm whales in pleasant weather off the Gulf of Guayaquil on the thirtieth they apparently had poor luck in the chase, for they came to rest in the harbor of Tumbez, the port of Payta, on the second of December.

There, during the thirteen days they lay outside the breakers, Melville and his companions had a chance to see their first coconut trees rising above the grass huts of the plantations; and they may have gazed in wonder at the famous "oyster tree"—a willow which, at low tide, displayed bivalves clinging to its branches—or visited the still-remembered grave of the seaman Collins, who had been shot to death by an angry mate. But he could hardly have left in as good a state of mind as he had displayed in Santa nearly six months before. He had learned about the burning sun above the mast at noon as he had learned about the albatross off Cape Horn, and he found it considerably less exciting—especially after he had come to realize how long it could burn upon an empty ocean. And Captain Pease aimed to recapture his luck by the exercise of grim determination beneath that same copper sky. He tried his Christmas fortunes without success on the On-Shore Ground and then swung northward, passing Cape Blanco on December 27 and Point St. Elena the next day before beginning a zigzag run below the equator which carried him past Hood's Island and Charles Isle in the southern Galápagos without a stop on January 6 and headed him through an open sea that extended a quarter of the way around the globe.

At first there were indications of a change in luck, but the Off-Shore Ground was crowded that season and the whales had taken alarm at the number of their hunters. The master of another vessel, John B. Coleman of the *Charles and Henry,* after covering the same section of the Pacific sent his Nantucket owners an unstopped flow of querulous indignation

from the Society Islands in November, 1842, to the general effect that
"whales have been very wild that I have seen and seems almost impossible to get nigh them though I can assure you that I have not got the best
whalemen in the world, my boat steerers have missed two hundred and
fifty bbls." Captain Pease probably had the same experience and the
same feelings, for although he added one hundred and fifty barrels to
his cargo between early January and early May he could hardly have
made a killing from more than two or three of the nine pods of whales
he sighted during that period. On the hazy day of June 6 his crew saw
the bloody spout of a dying whale for the last time during a disappointing cruise that had covered half their equatorial stretch of open sea. After
trying out and coopering down the fifty barrels of new oil they missed
another capture in the same neighborhood and continued westward, speaking the *Herald* of New Bedford on June 16 and making a report of their
cargo. The *Herald* was full and homeward bound. The *Acushnet* had
lost its chance to make a record voyage and, at the rate it was filling its
casks, had no prospect of returning home for several years to come. Captain Pease, who had already been at sea as long as the threat of scurvy
permitted, decided to drop down to the uncivilized Marquesas for recruiting; and on June 17 he turned his vessel southward, ending a tedious
season of plain bad luck.

II

Such luck was unusually bad for a crew whose master was a part owner
who had invested his savings in one last voyage with the expectation of
retiring on its profits. Furthermore, Captain Pease was possibly already
showing signs of the ill-health which was to lay him up ashore twice before the year was out and make him so quarrelsome that his first and third
mates left the ship at the first civilized port. The tyrannical disposition
revealed by his disappointment and irritability was even less endurable
to the touchy and somewhat thin-skinned Herman Melville, who had
no eye for extenuating circumstances and who, for years afterward, was
to explain that his subsequent actions were impelled by the captain's
brutal cruelty. The parting with the *Herald,* however, had probably increased his own sensitivity. Furthermore, the "superior" qualities of the
crew were becoming less evident as the strain upon their tempers increased
and one of them began to show symptoms of the disease which released
him from service two months later with the familiar, revealing notation
"went ashore half dead" as his last record. When the *Acushnet* dropped
anchor in Taio Hae or Anna Maria Bay, Nuku Hiva, on June 23, 1842,

Melville was in no state of mind to write home again about his "gratification" with the morale aboard his vessel.

Yet the sight that met his sea-weary eyes was one that might well have
inspired a special letter home had he been the first of his family to see
it. The high rocky islets between which his ship had passed guarded the
entrance of a horseshoe bay nine miles in circumference and surrounded
by mountainous ridges towering nearly half a mile above the level of the
sea. Immediately before him was a curving beach of surf-beaten sand
which formed the mouth of a shady valley, split by the dark channels of
mountain streams and rising gently inland until it divided itself into deep
canyons. These came to an end against sheer cliffs, over which vines
climbed toward the green crests and the gray and basalt heights above. On
a clear day the scene had a breath-taking quality of natural design, and, in
Melville's case, its effect may have been heightened by anticipation. He
could have known something of the South Seas from the accounts of the
naturalist Langsdorff, who had visited Nuku Hiva and had written up
his experiences in the same book which told of his later travels in a ship
commanded by Melville's uncle, John De Wolf. Or he may have heard
indirectly of the Marquesas by way of his cousin, Thomas Wilson Melville, whose family he had just been visiting in Illinois, who was even
then somewhere at sea in a whaler, and whose name Herman was to use
in his imminent adventures. The original "Tommo" Melville had spent
two weeks at Nuku Hiva nearly thirteen years before as a midshipman
aboard the U.S.S. *Vincennes,* on a trip which also had been described in
a book Herman Melville might have read before he left home; and if
the younger cousin knew little in particular about the older one's visit to
the neighboring valley of Typee, he undoubtedly was aware that there
were supposed to be cannibals in those hills before him and eyed with a
curiously ambiguous thrill the bamboo huts of natives who were reported
to be embarrassingly uninhibited in public and dangerously so in the
privacy of their more secluded valleys.

For however much the sailors may have discussed the cannibal propensities of the islanders, they approached anchorage with feelings of enthusiastic amiability toward the natives who "absolutely" supposed, in the
words of the commanding officer of the *Vincennes,* "that all our objects
in visiting them are secondary to the enjoyment of female favours." The
squally weather in which the *Acushnet* dropped anchor, as recorded in
the ship's log, of course precluded the immediate appearance of "a shoal
of 'whinhenies' " or young women swimming out in obedience to their
absolute suppositions—just as it precluded the greeting from a solitary
canoe, gliding over the unrippled surface of the bay, which one of Melville's shipmates later described to the respectable citizens of Sandusky,

Ohio. Melville's account of the ship's reception was of his expectations rather than of the reality, but he probably saw enough during the days that followed to become impressed with the spontaneous friendliness and hospitality of the Marquesans and be convinced that he might expect other and more conventional favors if he should desert the *Acushnet* and escape into one of the valleys that was not directly under the white man's eye.

He made his plans carefully. He realized that whatever charms an American had for the natives were less than those of a bolt of calico or a musket that the captain might offer as a reward for his capture and return, and he knew that he would have to postpone his effort until he could profit by his captain's readiness and eagerness to put to sea. For two weeks, while the ship lay at anchor, he was able to collect information about the island and apparently learn a few words of the native language. His best chance, obviously, was to escape over the uninhabited ridges and into one of the valleys that led away from Anna Maria Bay. To his left, as he faced inland and meditated the country, the land beyond the mountains sloped down to the bay of Tai Oa (or Tior, as he was to spell it in his later book) some five miles away as a bird might fly. The "queen" of Nuku Hiva herself had recently set a royal precedent for fugitives by escaping to the valley of Tior and there defying her royal husband. She had been brought back home by the new French masters of the island only two weeks before the *Acushnet*'s arrival, and although Melville could not have witnessed the subjugation of the valley, as he later claimed, he could hardly have avoided learning that its inhabitants were currently inhospitable to refugees. To his right, at a somewhat shorter distance and in the direction pointed by the customary landing beach, the other side of the mountains descended toward Comptroller Bay, which the French had not yet invaded. By the logic of geography and the loopholes of French imperialism, that was the necessary direction of his flight; and he began to calculate his chances accordingly, examining the countryside for unobtrusive routes away from the beach and the ship for signs of its departure.

Before he had finished his calculations he became aware that the mind of one of his watchmates, a somewhat smaller lad who called himself Toby, was turning in the same direction, and the two completed their plans together. They had learned that the nearest of the three valleys leading into Comptroller Bay was inhabited by a tribe of Hapaas, or Happars, who were of good repute among the natives of Taio Hae and that the central valley was the abode of the Taipis or Typees, who were dreaded by the local natives and the Happars alike as traditional enemies and notorious cannibals. The greatest of their risks, as they figured them, was the danger of getting into the wrong valley. What they did not realize was the seriousness of this risk, for their carefully discreet inquiries could not have revealed that the Happar Valley was little more than a relatively shallow extension of two beaches, whereas that of the Typees extended deep into the mountains and was the one in which a cross-country traveler would most likely find himself.

As soon as it became evident that the ship was nearly ready to sail and the next trip ashore for their watch would probably be their last, the two adventurers made their preparations by securing as much tobacco as possible and concealing it beneath their clothes with their ditty bags, shaving kits, a little food, and a few yards of cloth. As Melville was later to describe their actual escape, they went ashore with their watch in the morning, slipped away from their companions during a heavy tropical shower, made their circuitous and difficult way to a ridge they had selected in advance, and, after being sighted from below, scurried along its crest toward the mountains into which the natives were unwilling to go. Three hours before sunset, on July 9, they had scaled the basalt cliff of the highest mountain and stood, Melville said with some exaggeration, three thousand rugged feet above the *Acushnet* and the French vessels in the harbor. Beyond them, instead of the beautiful valley they expected, they saw only a broken country, in which they were to be completely lost by nightfall. Although Melville's published narrative does not suggest it, the two boys, who had innocently expected to find coconuts and fruit in the uninhabited mountains, must have been frightened; for, instead of turning east toward the Happar Valley, they apparently plunged almost directly across country. Melville himself was suffering from chills and fever and from a mysterious infection of his leg which was to bother him for the next three months. On the afternoon of the second day, however, they caught sight of an inhabited valley and began to debate the wisdom of an immediate descent to its attractive floor.

The Irish optimism of Toby persuaded him that the valley offered plenty to eat. The Dutch caution of Melville made him dwell upon the chances of being eaten. Eventually they compromised by deciding to cross a high ridge that lay to the southeast, in the hope of finding a smaller uninhabited valley in which they might discover the comfort Toby wanted without the risk that bothered Melville. Had they been able to carry out their new plan they might have reached the Happars—perhaps on the very day that the *Acushnet* (which, after spending an extra day in the harbor, hid out behind a neighboring island for twenty-four hours in order to give the fugitives a sense of security) returned to Nuku Hiva for news of her missing men. But the agony of working his way down and up the sides of the seemingly innumerable gorges that lay between them and the ridge was too much for Melville's endurance. After another miserable night and a small pill of sweat-soaked, tobacco-flavored bread for breakfast he had little disposition to worry over the danger of being eaten at some time in the indefinite future. He yielded his leadership to the high-spirited Toby, who proposed following the course of the stream by which they sat into the valley they had seen the day before.

Such procedure might have been good woodcraft in the Berkshires or in the Genesee Valley, but in the torrentially eroded volcanic mountains of Nuku Hiva it was an invitation to worse trouble than the two unfortunate travelers had yet experienced. For three more days they worked their tortuous way down the stream, over rocks, around waterfalls, along the most difficult route they could have selected and one which they could not retrace. The emotions he experienced during the ordeal made a lasting impression upon Melville, and his astonishment at their eventual success made his account of it in *Typee* one of the finest "yarns" in all his books—the sort of story, in which reality is suspended in wonder, that made so many of his later friends remark on his genius for dramatic narration. But he could have felt little more than a dull discouragement, too weary to become despair, when on the evening of July 13 he stood at the head of the last waterfall and looked again down into the valley he had first seen from almost directly above more than four days before. After another soaking night filled with delirium and dire anticipations they made their perilous way down their final hundred yards and, with Toby feeling almost as subdued as Melville, stood at last upon the ground which they soon found to be inhabited by the notorious Typees.

For three weeks and five days the valley was to be Melville's place of uneasy refuge. There he was to make the observations of native life and customs which enabled him, three or four years later, to collect the accounts of other visitors to the Marquesas and work them into a circumstantial narrative of personal experience that gave him his literary start and the profitable notoriety of being known as a "man who had lived among cannibals." How cannibalistic the Typees actually were is still a matter of debate among anthropologists; and it is altogether improbable that any of them ever eyed him hungrily even after he had been settled in one of their spacious bamboo huts, fed, rested, bathed and generally restored to decency in appearance. Melville certainly kept a careful eye upon the diet of his hosts, however, for of all their customs that he wrote of later the ones he described most precisely without the help of other authorities were those dealing with the preparation of food. By his lameness and by the insistence of the natives, his movements were restricted to the upper part of the valley; but he had the good fortune to be kept in the chief village of the tribe, where the range of his observations was extensive.

He was interested in the natives' method of making their "tapa" cloth by patiently beating out the bleached inner bark of a mulberry tree with scored wooden mallets, and he found a somewhat horrible fascination in the fine art of tattooing. The social customs of the savages were equally interesting, although he was less sure of what he thought of them. He was impressed by the good humor, the tolerance, and the easygoing dispositions of his new friends and enthusiastic about their complete freedom from the strain of getting and spending which had been the root of all his own troubles. But he never quite grasped the complexities of a social system in which a hereditary ruler had little authority over his subjects, which permitted young girls complete sexual freedom yet kept them out of canoes, and which tolerated all manner of disrespect to the gods while enforcing all sorts of minor prohibitions with the utmost rigidity. Nor does he seem to have understood the peculiar marriage customs that he observed until he read of them, at a later and perhaps for a second time, in the works of other visitors.

There can be little doubt, however, despite the suspicion cast upon them by many of his contemporaries and some later readers, that his observations were genuine and that he looked around him with an alert if not a comprehending eye. Some of the early native stonework, still identifiable, he described or located in a manner that could not have been derived from secondary sources; and he undoubtedly attended some sort of harvest or memorial festival which he later described, with some secondhand additions, as a "feast of the calabashes." His account of his discovery of the remnants of some other feast, which verified his worst suspicions concerning the secret habits of his good-natured associates, is less credible. For when he wrote up his experiences for public consumption he could hardly have afforded to give the impression that his real fears were really unfounded or have allowed his readers to close the book without being relieved of the suspense in which the hints of cannibalism had held them throughout the entire narrative. The only thing one can say positively of his life with the Typees is that he dwelt among them not unpleasantly but not at all happily until he had a chance to escape.

The circumstances surrounding his escape are not entirely clear despite his dramatic account of the event and despite Toby's unexpected appearance—as a respectable sign painter, Richard Tobias Greene, of Buffalo, New York—with a further explanation of some of the events leading up to it. When it became evident, after a week of care, incantation, and primitive medical attention, that Melville's infected leg was not getting better, the sympathetic natives were apparently willing to let Toby go to Anna Maria Bay, actually only a few hours away by trail, for medical assistance. And when Toby had been injured and turned back by the unfriendly Happars, whose territory he was obliged to skirt, the Typees actually encouraged him to try again in the company of "Irish Jimmy" Fitch, a tabooed beachcomber who appeared several days later and exercised his powers of persuasion upon them. According to Toby's own later testimony, the beachcomber's good offices were no more than a successful bit of trickery designed to get him signed aboard another whaler and force him to sail away without making any attempt to rescue his companion. Nevertheless, by the time still another whaler put into the bay, some two weeks later, Melville's unwilling presence among the Typees had become well known; and its captain was sufficiently hard up for men to go to some trouble and expense to rescue him.

The rescue was certainly by boat, for an examination of a chart based upon the French survey of Comptroller Bay in 1844 shows that Melville could hardly have written the concluding chapter of *Typee* without a firsthand knowledge of the territory to which he alludes. But the same chart provokes doubts concerning the melodramatic quality Melville introduced into his account of his departure: unless a band of barefooted savages dashed furiously over a mile of coral along a coast so rocky that for generations it had kept them separated from the neighboring Happars, they did not swim out from the headland to intercept their escaping prisoner and so give Melville the chance to make the Byronic gesture of thrusting his boat hook into the throat of the ferocious one-eyed chieftain. For all we can know, the captive may have been told to go in peace. We do know that on August 9, 1842, he was signed on the small Australian whaling barque, *Lucy Ann,* Henry Ventom master, as an able seaman and for a one hundred and twentieth share of the profits from the succeeding voyage.

III

Whatever the conditions that caused Melville to desert the *Acushnet,* he soon found that those on the *Lucy Ann* were worse. Australian whalers were generally notorious for their lack of discipline, and the *Lucy Ann,* with its crowded quarters, incompetent captain, and drunken mate, was a particularly bad specimen of the Sydney blubber barque. A short time before, the second mate, the carpenter, and seven members of the crew had deserted at Resolution Bay; and two sailors had been delivered under arms to the local naval commandant for arrest in the French frigate *La Reine Blanche,* transhipment in irons to Valparaiso, and trial for mutiny. The rest of the crew was almost as disaffected, for some weeks later Henry Smith had Melville write from the *Lucy Ann* to George Lefevre, who was still imprisoned on the French warship:

You know we all agreed to hang out on your account when we came aboard from the Corvette, but it so happened that those who talked loudest were the first who returned to their duty. I was the last one that went forward, and would not have turned to at all, but that I found it was of no use,—so after being in double irons for some time I thought it best to go forward and do my duty as usual.

He and "young Smith," he added suggestively, often talked of their former companion in the night watches. He might also have added that at Nuku Hiva he had attempted, in company with John B. Troy and William Matthews, to desert the ship and had been ignominiously returned. All three were subject to severe punishment for their action, and Troy, the steward who had been in charge of the medicine chest, was held liable to the criminal charge of embezzling the value of the medical supplies he had taken with him and concealed on shore for the natives to find and return. The crew that Melville joined was not only inadequate but divided between suspicion and uneasy foreboding.

To this unhappy lot had already been added two other dubious individuals in the persons of Nicholas Utley and Charles Watts, who had been picked up at Nuku Hiva the day before Melville was rescued on August 9. But additional men were needed, and Captain Henry Ventom continued to search the Marquesas for other beachcombers and deserters who might provide sufficient man power to work his boats. At Dominica he found a boat steerer, John Garritson, and two additional seamen: William Bunnell, who was probably the avowed beachcomber from New England whom Melville later remembered as "Salem"; and the Portuguese Amado Sylva, a known deserter in whom the American authorities were interested. These were enough to enable Captain Ventom to testify later that he left the Marquesas on August 20 with a full complement of men but not of officers. The only officer on board besides the captain was James German, the first mate, who had been with the ship since the signing of the crew in Sydney on January 25 and who was, by the testimony or implication of all accounts, a vigorous and seemingly able man though given to drunkenness even at sea. The petty officers, on whom a considerable amount of responsibility inevitably devolved, consisted of the three harpooners—a reckless Maori named Benbow Byrne, a Portuguese called Immanuel Senora, and the new man Garritson—plus a makeshift carpenter, Joseph Jackson, and a disaffected cooper, Andrew Blackburn, who seems to have been the most mutinous talker and the least dependable man on the ship. Five of the sixteen seamen, according to the captain's testimony, were observably "ailing and ill of the venereal."

In such a crew Melville was one of the minority who were rated as able

seamen, and it is not improbable that his kindly recollections of his recent cannibal associates began as soon as the *Lucy Ann* turned westward
away from the Marquesas. Other whaling crews no better than this had
been brought into a state of discipline by the driving power of hard-
bitten captains, but the master of the *Lucy Ann* was not of their tough
breed. Within a week he began to suffer from an abscess in the perineum
and by September 4 was unable to walk and confined to his cabin. The
crew, who probably mistook the nature of his ailment, thought he was
dying; and their normal uneasiness was increased by the mystery which
the chief officer began to make of his daily observations of position. They
could not know that German was more worried than they and with unexpected discretion had changed course for Tahiti on his own responsibility. After four days of confinement, however, the captain himself
recognized the necessity for getting medical assistance and gave orders to
sail for Papeete, which they reached on September 20, laying outside the
harbor where they could be in reach of help without giving the sailors
an opportunity to escape the ship.

The events that followed, like those of the brief voyage itself, were
later to be remembered inaccurately and distorted with fiction by the
yarn spinner who wrote *Omoo*. Nor are they entirely clear from the official
records, which are sometimes inconsistent or obscure in details—especially
in dates during the first days in which the testimony follows the Tahitian
calendar. Yet the main facts of the narrative are unimpeachable: The
first mate went ashore and in the afternoon returned with the local medical
officer, Dr. Francis Johnstone, who diagnosed the captain's ailment, verified his fears concerning the seriousness of his condition, and insisted
upon his removal to the town. On the next day (September 22, according to the local system of reckoning introduced by missionaries who had
reached Tahiti from the west) the chief officer lowered the captain in a
boat, took him ashore, and returned with the Acting British Consul
Charles B. Wilson and Dr. Johnstone. While Wilson mustered the men
aft in order to hear complaints and sound them out concerning the future,
Johnstone gave a medical examination to the five ailing sailors and to
Herman Melville, who had limped hopefully into line with them. Henry
Smith and Nicholas Utley were pronounced too ill for further service and
ordered ashore before the vessel left on its cruise. The others, William
Matthews, John B. Troy, James Smith, and Melville, were certified capable of duty after a week or two of "care" and were therefore not released
from their articles. In their interview with Wilson, four of the men picked
up with Melville in the Marquesas apparently expressed their unwillingness to sail under German; but the acting consul ignored them and
reported to Ventom that there was no objection to a short cruise under the

temporary command of the first officer provided the ship was supplied with two mates and with two sailors to replace those left behind. This Wilson undertook to do on the following day; but, despite his assurances to the captain, he could hardly have been easy in his mind about the situation. He employed a boat to take the new men out instead of letting German trust the crew with the ship in his absence or with a boat to come ashore.

In the meantime, the sailors were trying the mettle of their prospective commander. The six men who had been on the sick list, standing on their rights as certified invalids and convalescents, refused to join their customary watches; and Charles Watts, Garritson, and Sylva (of the four who had originally protested against serving under German) refused duty. They were joined by three members of the original Sydney crew, Henry Burke, James Watts, and David Fraser, leaving only ten men to divide watches and handle the ship. There was no clear-cut mutiny, however, for by the following evening James Watts at least was back on duty and assigned to the watch of Benbow Byrne, the Maori harpooner who was second to the mate in authority. The best indication of the situation on board is perhaps to be found in the implications of German's own testimony concerning his part in the affair which followed. Having instructed Byrne to spread the jib, the mate retired to his cabin and made no appearance on deck during the ruckus which began when the Maori ordered Watts to carry out instructions, received certain anatomical suggestions in response, and attempted to enforce his authority with his fists. Watts boldly invaded the sacred precincts of the cabin to report the incident to German, who accepted the sailor's version of the escapade and "then told said Benbow that he had no business to strike said Watts." The men could have had little reason for trusting either the mate's sense of responsibility for the ship or his ability to maintain discipline among his subordinates, and even Wilson privately noted on the records: "Mr. German not fit to take charge for continually drunkenness."

On the following morning, German reacted to the crisis which had developed precisely as he had reacted to the captain's illness: disregarding his standing orders, he turned the vessel toward the safety of port and dropped anchor in Papeete harbor. Wilson came aboard and again interviewed the crew. When the showdown occurred William Bunnell, who was accused by German of being one of the ringleaders in the affair, played a role which Melville later adopted for himself in the fiction of *Omoo* and cast his lot with the mutineers. The real Herman Melville, with a medical certificate which protected him from the formal charge of mutiny, stepped out of such bad company. Captain Ventom filed a formal complaint against the ten men, including the other convalescents, who remained defiant; and Wilson arranged for an armed boat from *La Reine Blanche,* which was in the harbor with the *Lucy Ann*'s earlier mutineers still aboard, to take them into custody.

The imprisonment on board the French vessel, as more experienced wrongdoers than Melville may have suspected, was a bluff; for Captain Ventom could hardly have afforded to send the British authorities in Valparaiso two sets of mutineers along with reports of desertions that, all together, accounted for more than four-fifths of his original crew. In any case, the second group remained in irons for only two nights before being transferred to the British open-air calaboose on the evening preceding *La Reine Blanche*'s departure on September 26 (or, according to the proper calendar followed by the ship's log, September 25). When the bluff failed to work, Wilson called the men before him for another interview; and Melville, having seen the threat of naval shackles disappear beyond the horizon, joined them in their continued refusal to go back to work on the *Lucy Ann.* He was sent with them when they were returned to the calaboose—a thatched roof above rude wooden stocks into which the native jailer trained his prisoners to thrust a leg at night or at the approach of a European in the daytime. Otherwise they were free to roam about at will and were quite prepared to wear out the patience of the acting consul and the ailing captain.

Wilson was already tired of his unexpected responsibility, and Ventom was worried about the loss involved in keeping his vessel idle while the whaling season approached and an unoccupied crew had to be fed both afloat and ashore. Those on shore were again called up on October 5 for a final attempt at getting rid of them: Formal depositions were taken from the captain, mate, harpooner, the loyal members of the crew, Dr. Johnstone, and the acting consul; and, when the legal ceremony made no visible impression, Wilson gave up in disgust. He sent the men back to the calaboose to await the arrival of some British warship in the indefinite future, made a vain attempt to place the whole matter in the hands of the higher authority represented by the French provisional council for Tahiti, and gave permission for the enlistment of a new crew for the *Lucy Ann.*

Whether Melville was ordered back to the stocks with his companions is uncertain. His name appears on the official list of those to be left on shore as "revolters" but upon none of the four lists of those who were formally recommitted to prison on October 5. His behavior throughout the affair was such that he could hardly have been considered a dangerous character, and he may have appeared rather obviously out of place in a crew of which he was one of the two or three literate members—at the most—who did not show signs of tropical wear and tear. Wilson, who seems to have had a better private understanding than he could officially display, may have treated him with an unobtrusive discrimination which the young man did not appreciate. Actually it made little difference in his situation. The calaboose was his headquarters and a more agreeable home than the beach; and Dr. Johnstone gave Melville's address as the "stocks" when he charged the ship for two "embrocations" of laudanum, turpentine, and soap liniment, on October 16 and 19—although the week or two of care he had originally prescribed were well over and Melville himself referred to the first visit as an occasion on which he was absent and remembered the second by the pulling of the doctor's leg rather than the rubbing of his own.

Either as a prisoner or as a free man, Melville spent the time before and a few days after the sailing of the *Lucy Ann* on October 16 in a way that was both pleasant and educational. His situation gave him his first opportunity for a leisurely observation of the progress of civilization in the South Seas, and he made the most of it. Within sight of the calaboose ran the famous Broom Road, paved by the good intentions of missionaries who tried to enforce blue laws in Beulah Land with the assistance of native "kannakippers," or religious police, assigned to uncover peccadillos which received punishment measured out in yards of spread gravel. Over its shaded route, between the mountains and the sea, passed the traffic of the island: carefully European missionaries and their families, in broadcloth coats and silk or gingham, with an ocasional party on horseback; sailors in loose frocks, stained with tar and patched at the elbows; native women in awkward straw bonnets, white cotton petticoats, and loose Mother Hubbards; and brown men, with and without pantaloons, sweating in buttoned-up pea jackets or cool in foreign hats and native breechcloths. The westward course of empire was on triumphant parade and Melville did not like it.

Although respectable Europeans, with the exception of a genial Irish priest Father Murphy, avoided his company, he got on excellent terms with the natives and learned from them about their English spiritual and French political masters. They might be ninety per cent "mickonaree," as they termed their allegiance to Christian civilization; but the one Commandment to which they could not subscribe was the one that might have protected them from the worst scourge of their new era, and no observer could avoid noticing how they strained other Commandments which had been unconsciously observed in the heathen valley of Typee. Well-brought-up young man that he was, Melville conscientiously attended church on Sunday, but the pidgin English translation of one sermon he heard did not impress him with the depth or the spiritual effectiveness of the missionaries' appeal. Nor did he find much utilitarianism in the civilization of Tahiti. If he had looked for the greatest happiness of the greatest number he would have cast his eyes back upon the unspoiled inhabitants of the Marquesas rather than upon the declining, poverty-stricken, unoccupied population around him. His immediate opinion of the French is less evident, for he was even closer upon their imperialistic heels in Tahiti than he had been in the Marquesas, and the antagonism he was to express in his books was largely supported by information he obtained later. Yet there can be little doubt that he was affected by the main topic of conversation during his stay there and shared the natives' resentment at the loss of their formal independence so sympathetically that, by the time he left, he was ready to believe the French had done as much damage in six weeks as the English had in six decades.

During his stay at Papeete, Melville seems to have become increasingly intimate with John B. Troy, the former steward of the *Lucy Ann* who was consistently signalized by the ship's officers as an embezzler as well as a mutineer. By Melville's own account, against the background of official records, Troy was a well-educated and experienced young reprobate (though some years older than Melville) with a quick wit and a reckless disposition, a familiarity with drugs which enabled him to get laudanum from Dr. Johnstone while the other sailors were cheerfully drinking paregoric, and a missionary's zeal in spreading the worst evil of the civilization Melville denounced. He was certainly the most entertaining companion among the crew, however; and Melville, whose shy loneliness caused him to form unusually strong attachments, seems to have been sincerely convinced that he was a ship's surgeon who had been demoted after an admirable outburst of temper, a man of the world whose eccentricities should be viewed charitably, and a gallant whose pursuit of the opposite sex, like his avoidance of work, was an amusing evidence of lightheartedness. A tall, thin, colorless blond, whose appearance justified his nickname, the "Long Ghost," was a remarkable sight to the natives and had a way with them which Melville envied. Originally drawn together on shipboard by a common interest in books, the two friends became foraging companions and sufficiently close confidants on land to put their heads together and plan an escape to the neighboring island of Mooréa or, as it was then more commonly called, Eimeo, from which they might expect to ship without the hindrance of a bad reputation.

4

The Pacific: Recoil

I

IF MELVILLE was still on Tahiti, as he seems to have been, when Dr. Johnstone made his last recorded visit to the stocks on Wednesday, October 19, he made his escape immediately afterward. According to his own story, he and the Long Ghost stole down to the beach at the appropriate hour of midnight, slipped into a boat concealed in the shadow of a grove, quietly rowed out beyond the reef, and set sail for Eimeo ten miles away. The rescuers who operated the boat were two planters, a tall backwoodsman from Maine named Zeke and a little cockney known as Shorty, who cultivated potatoes in the valley of Maatea (which Melville spelled, with his customary soundless *r*'s, Martair), at the southern foot of the highest peak on the island. By morning they had angled past the eastern coast, made their way through the Mooréan reef, and beached their boat in safety, with the whole island between them and the nearest whaling port and with two or possibly three ridges separating them from their hosts' closest European neighbors.

Whether the two refugees had actually engaged themselves to work on the plantation is doubtful, for the real course of events hardly permitted them enough time in the fields to convince Zeke and Shorty that they had got a poor bargain in hired men. If they made their escape on Wednesday night, Melville's later account, in *Omoo,* of the succeeding five days is circumstantially probable. After spending Thursday resting and recuperating from their overnight adventure, they divided Friday between digging potatoes and hunting wild cattle in the hills and spent Saturday in a planned shooting expedition for both wild cattle and wild pigs. On Sunday, October 23, Melville characteristically persuaded Shorty to take him to the mission church at Afareaitu or Arfrehitoo while Zeke and Long Ghost remained at home to prepare the hunting feast, and they all spent the next morning loading Zeke's boat with potatoes to be sold in Papeete. But they could not have lingered long after Zeke's return at dawn the next day, and if they made their visit to the lake and village of Temae or Tamai (which Melville completely mislocated in the map he had especially drawn for *Omoo*) they made it with considerable dispatch. Winding along native paths, "through wood and ravine, and over hill and precipice," they could have passed through the rugged interior of the island in the course of the leisurely day Melville described. But they would have had to return the next day without waiting to be scared out of the village by the approach of missionaries and without having had time to arrange the Marquesan dance Melville later reported having seen there.

For, whatever their adventures during their first week on Eimeo might have been, they were evidently back at their headquarters in Martair near the end of that time, arranging with Zeke for something like a sailor's "certificate of discharge" which would protect them from arrest as they made their way around the western beach to the royal village of Papetoi, where a solitary whaler was reported at anchor in the harbor. The fifteen-mile circuit of the beach should have been an easy dawn-to-sundown tramp for even a pair of poorly shod sailors, but Melville and Troy were curious about their surroundings, accustomed to receiving native hospitality, and in no particular hurry. They may have spent as much as two full days on their way, arriving in Papetoi in time to find a native host and establish themselves in his household before Melville again attended the local mission church on October 30. The coquina church was the most impressive building on the island and could contain almost the entire population of the eighty grass huts that formed the most attractive village Melville had seen since he left the valley of Typee. The natives appeared almost entirely unspoiled by the European influences which so distressed the visitor to Papeete; for the permanent foreign residents of the village consisted only of the two missionary families, and the rarely frequented anchorage inside Tareu Pass accommodated no more than one whaler at a time. Such a harmless and useful stranger as the English carpenter Willie, whom Melville ran across, might be allowed to settle down;

and a disgraced naval officer, whose "trial" Melville professed to have witnessed, might be tolerated so long as he behaved himself. But runaway sailors were either hunted down if their ship lay in the bay or driven back among the ridges, like those from the *John Adams* which was then at Papeete, as soon as they made too free with the village. The Bells, who operated the sugar plantation across the bay, had few visitors of their own sort upon whom they could exercise their hospitality; and the charming Mrs. Bell, according to later gossip, had already taken to drink at the time Melville was fascinated by a single glimpse of her, and was even then riding toward an early grave.

The setting of the village was as attractive as its unspoiled character. Spread out through a shady grove, it was divided by a stream which ran into a narrow bay deep set upon the right among mountains a half mile high and expanding at the left toward the anchorage and the surrounding reef. Directly across lay the green plain on which the Bells had their sugar plantation at the foot of the ridge separating Papetoi from Cook Bay, the only other harbor of the island. If a pair of wandering sailors followed the road that cut across the stream they would reach, at its northern end, the "palace" of Queen Pomaree—a group of large native houses, surrounded by a bamboo picket, which projected from the grove onto a coral pier built into the bay. There Melville and the Long Ghost humorously professed to seek "preferment" and actually succeeded in satisfying their curiosity concerning the mixture of barbaric and Victorian splendor of the royal household before they were put in their place by being "waved" off the premises. It seems evident that Melville spent several days wandering about the neighborhood of the village, but the most attractive sight he saw anywhere was the whaler anchored in the bay trying to supply itself with provisions. When two of its crew ran away he investigated the ship, and he later approached the captain and apparently persuaded him that he was a respectable character and an able and responsible sailor. By Thursday, November 3, according to the Tahitian calendar (or Wednesday, the second, on the ship's proper log), the captain was looking upon him—but not upon his companion—with favor, and he was in a fair way to escape the island without having had to stay there long enough to deserve an application of the epithet "beachcomber."

The captain whom Melville approached in anticipation of his third whaling voyage was the same John B. Coleman, of the *Charles and Henry,* who had been so querulous about the conditions on the Off-Shore Ground which had got Captain Pease's dander up and caused Melville to desert the *Acushnet.* If his two runaway seamen were not captured and returned, he was reluctantly prepared to ship some of the men from the *John Adams* in their stead, although he would have preferred to fill out his ordinary crew with natives. But he had also discharged a boat steerer, according to his letter of November 2 to his owners, and was "going to ship another tomorrow." For this job his only likely prospect seems to have been the future author of *Moby Dick,* who was later to vouch for that book to an English publisher on the somewhat exaggerated authority of "the author's own personal experience, of two years and more, as a harpooner." But whatever his position may have been, Melville became a member of the crew; and the vessel sailed shortly afterward, for it was reported at Tahiti on November 7, although it did not drop anchor in the Papeete harbor, where Coleman might have heard reports that would have made his new man appear worse than a runaway from the *John Adams.*

Melville had no inclination to stay in the neighborhood any longer than was necessary. He must have known that his captain had been disappointed in his efforts to obtain potatoes and other "recruits" on Eimeo, yet he seems to have made no attempt to put Coleman in contact with Zeke and Shorty; and the ship probably finished recruiting at the unfrequented islands of Rurutu and Ravavai to the south of Tahiti. In his letter to his owners, Charles and Henry Coffin of Nantucket, Coleman had signified his intention to disregard their instructions and go to the coast of Japan. But the northern season did not begin until spring, and in the meantime he leisurely made the southern Pacific voyage Melville later described in *Mardi*—southward and then east to Más Afuera, toward which the *Charles and Henry* was sailing when it was sighted, on January 27, 1843, a few days' journey from the South American coast. During a cruise of nearly three months the ship had not taken a single barrel of oil, and by this time the captain, who was young and nervous about his responsibilities, had definitely made up his mind to take matters into his own hands. Instead of making the customary trip up the coast and around the Galápagos Islands to the Off-Shore Ground, he turned directly northeast and sailed for the Sandwich Islands and Japan as rapidly as the trade winds would carry him. By February 9 he was in the equatorial zone with fifty barrels of new oil and enough hope for a change in luck to cruise the neighborhood of the line for nearly three more months. The result was a mere hundred barrels in addition, and very little experience for Herman Melville as a possible harpooner. On April 26 the *Charles and Henry* dropped anchor in the roads at Lahaina, on the island of Maui, and on the next day Coleman officially declared five hundred barrels of sperm oil as the return of his twenty-eight months of sea and announced his intention of clearing for Japan.

Unlucky though it may have been, the voyage had not been unpleasant for Melville. The *Charles and Henry* was twenty tons smaller than the *Acushnet* and crowded with a crew to man four whaleboats instead of the *Acushnet*'s three. But he was to remember the captain and the sixteen other Americans and ten foreigners (most of whom were probably natives) who were shipmates agreeably enough in later years, and his third whaling experience is reflected slightly but pleasantly in his books. He may have had a better position on board than he had ever had before and better quarters amidships than he was accustomed to in the forecastle. He certainly parted from the *Charles and Henry* under circumstances better than those that marked his separation from the *Acushnet* and the *Lucy Ann*. For he had evidently signed aboard for the single cruise and was given an honorable discharge without controversy. If he had not been forced to draw too heavily on the ship's "slop chest" for clothing and tobacco, he might have stepped ashore with as much as twenty dollars as his share of the profits of the voyage—more money than he had seen since leaving home nearly two and a half years before. In any case, the American vice-commercial agent, John Stetson, who certified his discharge at Lahaina on May 2, 1843, also certified that neither Melville nor his shipmate Joseph Whiting was "on his hands" as a case for relief. He was free, for a while, to do as he pleased.

Lahaina was a favorite stopping place for whaling captains, if not for their crews, because it was so difficult for sailors to get in trouble there. The famed "blue laws" that levied a six-dollar fine against a vessel allowing a cooking fire on Sunday had also abolished prostitution by the "whinhenies" who had once swarmed over incoming ships, forbidden the sale of alcoholic liquors, and even restrained the natural propensities of the islanders in their own homes. For two decades or more sailors fresh from the United States and expecting to see savages had been disappointed by the many stone and adobe houses to be found among the matted-grass cottages of the poorer natives and by the well-kept plantations and groves of coconut and breadfruit which surrounded the town. The stone church could hold a congregation of eighteen hundred—more than half the population—and the seamen's chapel was built to accommodate two hundred worshipers from the thirty or more whalers that on some occasions lay anchored outside the ledge which protected the beach from the full force of the sea. Visitors from New England might not find all the proprieties of home, for one of them had become "quite sure," after some experience with the native girls' curiosity about his person, that "they went much farther than our American girls would, in public, at least"; but Lahaina was more nearly a missionaries' town than any other settlement in the Pacific.

By this time Melville was too experienced to be bothered by the curiosity of the natives and had been sufficiently long at sea to have developed an active curiosity about the sights of civilization and the news of the world. The most conspicuous sign of civilization at Lahaina, visible from the deck of a ship at sea, was the large white building of the Lahainalulu Seminary on the mountainside between two and three miles behind the town. There missionary teachers tried to give native boys who, according to the admission requirements, possessed "some character" or were "as little polluted as possible," the semblance of an education in the liberal arts while encouraging them to a certain amount of industry. Tramping up the dusty road between the student-built stone walls that offered decayed evidence of New England's moral empire, Melville visited the educational institution and overlooked its unkempt state in his astonishment at the sight of "a tabular exhibition of a Hawaiian verb, conjugated through all its moods and tenses" and covering "the side of a considerable apartment." He also visited the still-unfinished royal summer palace which had once been occupied by Queen Kaahumanu but was then being neglected by King Kamehameha III, in preference for the more private native apartments behind it. There were few other sights to see. The clouds of fine red dust that hung above the roads made long walking trips unpleasant, and the mountains, more than twice as high as those he had seen in the Marquesas, closed Lahaina in from the east. He probably spent many hours watching the natives at their favorite sport with surfboards and discussing political events.

Later Melville was to recall having seen the famous Dr. Gerrit P. Judd "making up his diplomacy from fat natives lolling in the shade" at Lahaina, but, as was so often the case, his "memory" was a collection of impressions fancifully grouped around an emotional attitude. The political events that required Dr. Judd's diplomacy were occurring in Honolulu, and they demanded a shrewd calculation of local interests and of foreign imperialism. Less than three months before Melville's arrival in the islands, Lord George Paulet, of the British navy, had arrived in the Honolulu harbor with various demands on the native government and on February 25 had accepted a temporary cession of the islands to Great Britain. Since that time the government had been in the hands of a commission consisting of Paulet, two officers from his warship, and Dr. Judd as a representative of the king; but on May 8, six days after Melville's discharge from the *Charles and Henry,* Judd had resigned from the governing body in protest, among other reasons, against Paulet's relaxation of the blue laws. American and British residents of the islands found the state of affairs provocative of almost infinite discussion. Common sailors and representatives of commercial interests were generally antagonistic to the severe controls exercised by the missionaries and were delighted to see the government freed from their influence. Yet American nationals were traditionally distrustful of Great Britain and not at all enthusiastic about finding themselves under the British flag. On the other hand, the Union Jack was a guarantee that they would be protected from French imperialism, which was active in the Pacific and considerably worse than that of England. At Lahaina, where one employed seaman had observed that wandering sailors were considered "poor and miserable" creatures, the sympathies of most of Melville's associates would normally have been with the new government which formally recognized the recreational desires of their fellows in Honolulu; and in the discussions along the water front Melville himself, fresh from his experiences with the French in the Marquesas and Tahiti, would probably have undertaken to influence opinion in favor of any power that would save the islands from France. He would neither have understood nor cared about the fact that Dr. Judd was taking the course best designed to keep American influence predominant, and his emotional attitude toward the ex-missionary adviser to the king would inevitably have been one that caused him to remember the doctor's diplomatic practices in a derogatory way.

On May 18, when the schooner *Star* was scheduled to take the relief cases and other discharged seamen to Honolulu, Melville had his chance to reach the commercial metropolis of the islands, where he could find opportunities for employment which did not exist at Lahaina. Even though he had been living in a community where students at the seminary were boarded for a year at an expense of seven and a half dollars and where there were few inducements to extravagance, the small returns from his cruise on the *Charles and Henry* would not have maintained him long in idleness. A casual acquaintance later recalled having known him in Honolulu "at a time when he was setting up pins in a ball alley"; and the missionaries, who were proud of having converted King Kamehameha from the vulgarity of bowling to the respectability of billiards, damned the author of *Typee* and *Omoo* as a former hanger-on at the alleys. But if Melville acquired his later expertness with a bowling ball during his stay in Honolulu, he did not support himself for long in places of recreation which then possessed the social connotations afterwards acquired by the village pool hall. He promptly made the acquaintance of a respectable resident who was planning to open a general merchandise store on July 1 and on June 1 signed a formal contract with him, engaging to serve as a clerk and bookkeeper at a salary of one hundred and fifty dollars a year, payable quarterly, and free board, lodging, and laundry service.

In Honolulu Melville found much that reminded him of social conditions at Papeete. There was the same contrast between the handsome dwellings of the prosperous foreigners and the wretched abodes of the natives, whose bright-colored garments were picturesque but did not conceal their diseased misery. The slightly more than four hundred

American residents made up less than five per cent of the population, but they, with the British merchants and a few Europeans of other nationalities, made Honolulu a "town of strangers"; and, according to Melville's observation, the members of the native government allied with the strangers were more indolent and corrupt than their subjects. The difference between the upper and lower classes was dramatized, more than it had been at Papeete, by the stories Melville heard of the autocratic cruelty of the late darling of the missionaries, Queen Kaahumanu, and by his own sight of the "Kanaka cab-horses" who trotted through the dusty streets drawing the four-wheeled carts in which sat the wives of the men who had been sent out from Boston to save their souls. Not until he visited Honolulu, he wrote later, did he become aware of the fact that the natives "had been civilized into draft horses, and evangelized into beasts of burden." The impressions he had begun to form in the Marquesas and Tahiti were crystallized in the Hawaiian Islands.

The process of crystallization, however, was not entirely spontaneous. The merchant with whom Melville formed a connection was a young Englishman, three years Melville's senior, named Isaac Montgomery, who had come out to the islands from Cumberland in 1838. At that time the question of Roman Catholicism was vigorously alive as one of the periodic symbols of dissent between the missionaries and their local enemies, and Montgomery apparently fell into the camp of Stephen Reynolds and several other older merchants whose antagonism toward the American Board of Commissioners for Foreign Missions and its influences had led them to have the children baptized into the Catholic Church some ten years before. Montgomery had acquired the capital for his business adventure by acting as a bill collector and an auctioneer, so fascinating the king with his fluency, according to Melville, that His Majesty had tried to make him a member of the royal household, where his spiel might vie with the music of the royal violinist whose leg had been bitten off by a whale. There is also not much doubt but that he was the Englishman whose "confidence" Melville enjoyed and "who was much employed by his lordship" Paulet during the period of English government. In short, he seems to have been an active, articulate, and vigorous opponent of the American missionaries and all their works, an enthusiastic partisan of Lord George Paulet, and the sort of person who appeared to know everything about everybody and could generally support his opinions with arresting illustrations and anecdotal evidence. Over a young man with Melville's hunger for intellectual companionship such a benefactor and friend could have exerted an extraordinary influence.

Other influences were also at work in the crystallization of Melville's attitude toward the missionaries and other evidences of formal civilization in the Pacific. An unemployed common sailor, who had no claim on consular relief, possessed fewer rights and less respectability than a Kanaka cab horse; and on one occasion during his stay in Honolulu, on June 6 when the *Acushnet* was in harbor, Melville found it wise to lie low although he had no way of knowing that Captain Pease had just sworn to his desertion before John Stetson in Lahaina and had probably been informed that his man could be found in the metropolis. To know that identification and a complaint could place him among the "white slaves" in the fort was a humiliation in itself, and the knowledge aroused no sympathetic feelings toward the respectable society that was so indifferent to the appeals of the unfortunate wretches who had been placed there. Although Melville was later to write that he had "no development at all" until he reached the age of twenty-five, his residence in Honolulu, where he passed his twenty-fourth birthday, was an important formative period in his life. In it he acquired one of the major attitudes around which his intellectual development took place.

The *Acushnet,* which was still short on luck, spent only one night in the harbor before putting out to sea, and Melville settled down in security. The carpentry work on Montgomery's store was not finished on schedule, possibly because Montgomery himself was busy auctioning off the books of the Sandwich Island Institute and sugar from the estate of F. J. Greenway; but on July 13 it had its grand opening, and Melville measured off enough calico cloth at two bits a yard to convince his employer that the retail counter was more profitable than the auctioneer's platform as a place for disposing of "old goods." In the meantime he was a witness to the mounting pressure against Paulet's government. On July 7 the U.S.S. *Constellation* arrived in the harbor under the command of Captain Lawrence Kearny who issued a protest against the cession of the islands to the British and threatened to hold the commissioners personally responsible for any damage to American interests. Rumors began to circulate that Kearny was planning to advise his fellow countrymen to ignore the Paulet government, and although these seem to have had no foundation there was a general weakening of authority. On July 21 Levi Chamberlain wrote to the Reverend Rufus Anderson that "affairs at the islands are in an unsettled state": "The floodgates of licentiousness have been opened by the removal of law, and our streets exhibit scenes of intemperance and debauchery exceeded only by the darkest times of heathenism in the islands." In the midst of the restlessness the king issued his own public protest against the British regime, and on July 26 Admiral Richard Thomas arrived on the British frigate *Dublin* with an authority superior to Paulet's. He immediately conferred with the king and announced his intention of restoring the islands to the native government. The formal ceremony of restoration took place on the morning of July 31 with twenty-one gun salutes from the British warships, an acknowledgment in kind from the Hawaiian fort, and miscellaneous firing from all the whaling and merchant ships in the harbor that could make a noise. Three days later, after announcements had been sent to neighboring islands, some three thousand people gathered above the city at Nuana to celebrate the restoration with a feast of fish and fowl, pork and poi, washed down with cold water. The missionary regime had returned.

Most of the Americans in Honolulu were as relieved by the lowering of the Union Jack as the natives were delighted by the raising of their own flag, but such extreme antimissionary merchants as Stephen Reynolds were not. Among the extremists were probably Isaac Montgomery and certainly Herman Melville. The latter was to undertake a vigorous defense of Paulet in an appendix to *Typee,* basing it upon an antimissionary attitude so strong that he seems genuinely to have "remembered" the breakdown of law and order of which Levi Chamberlain complained ten days before the restoration as being characteristic of the ten days following that event—although, as a matter of fact, the natives were probably out of control during both periods. It was the strength of this attitude that led him to refer to the missionary-controlled king as an "imbecile," to Dr. Judd as "a sanctimonious apothecary-adventurer," and to the Calvinistic representatives of the American Board of Commissioners for Foreign Missions as "a junto of ignorant and designing Methodist elders." The young man who for so long had allowed himself to be pushed around by circumstances was beginning to form strong opinions, right or wrong, which would not enable him to be happy in Honolulu.

Yet Melville seems to have intended to remain in the Sandwich Islands for the term of his contract and to have written home of his intentions, because replies to his letters were being advertised in a local newspaper more than a year later. His mind reached home before his letters did, however, and began to dwell on familiar surroundings as it had done in Liverpool. When the American frigate *United States* dropped anchor in the roadstead after sunset on the day of the king's feast, he must have speculated, feeling as he did about the restoration, upon the vessel as a possible means of getting back to a civilization in which he might find a more secure place. In the days that followed he became acquainted with the sailors and learned from them that a man could enlist in the Navy for either the conventional term of three years or for the cruise, whichever was shorter, and that the *United States* would end its cruise in Boston. "Conditions" made it easy enough for him to rationalize his reluctance to continue measuring calico in Honolulu, a new experience at sea was tempting, and the eventual prospect of home was appealing. Two days before the ship was due to sail, Melville yielded for the last time to the curious combination of impulsiveness and security seeking which had led to all of his adventures: on August 17, 1843, he enlisted as an ordinary seaman in the United States Navy, homeward bound.

II

At the time when Melville joined the Navy he was not only anxious to get home but was inclined to be impatiently critical of American authority in the South Seas. The impulse which sent him adventuring had worn itself out in Tahiti, and in Honolulu his mind had begun to recoil upon his experiences in a way which made him shrink back from the kind of civilization he saw being imposed upon the natives. He had observed in them little of the natural depravity which the missionaries advertised and had noticed that the civilization represented by the missionaries was doing more harm to their bodies than good to their souls. He had become particularly sensitive to the sort of civilized brutality which, according to his observations, had the effect of brutalizing people who were not at all bad at heart.

On the *United States,* he had hardly finished balancing on one leg, assuring the assistant surgeon that he had never suffered from such a typical sailor's disease as the "gout," and learning to sling and unsling a hammock in the twenty-two inches of swinging space allowed him on the berth deck before he was compelled to attend an exhibition of greater brutality than he had yet witnessed. A sailor had been found guilty of striking a sentry on duty and another had been caught smuggling liquor, and after inspection at nine o'clock in the morning all hands were called to "witness punishment." A wooden grating sometimes used to cover a hatchway was placed on deck in the shelter of the starboard bulwarks, and the first culprit, stripped to the waist, was tied by his ankles to the grating and by his wrists to the hammock nettings above. The boatswain opened a green baize bag and produced the official weapon of punishment, the cat-o'-nine-tails, consisting of nine knotted leather thongs attached to a heavy wooden handle, and at a signal from the captain a boatswain's mate "laid on" a dozen vigorous strokes, raising a hundred and eight blood welts over the victim's back. The procedure was repeated, with a fresh cat and a fresh mate, for the second culprit and then gone through again for two little apprentices who had been found guilty of fighting and using abusive language and were whipped with the lighter "kittens." The experiences were Melville's formal introduction to naval life, and although he was to witness the flogging of a total of one hundred and sixty-three seamen and apprentices on board the *United States* before he finished his cruise he was never to become hardened to the sight. A flogging conducted with all the formality of institutionalized civilization became his symbol of all the indignity that man could heap on man, and that symbol was to dance before his eyes during his entire term of naval service and remain vividly in his memory for many years thereafter.

But Melville hardly had time at the moment for brooding upon symbols or upon anything else. At the time he enlisted, the *United States* had only a little more than two days to remain in port, and a new recruit had to learn new duties, become acquainted with a new ship, and generally appear busy at all hours of the day when the vessel was bustling with preparations for departure and the captain was entertaining last-minute guests from on shore. Most of Melville's duties were to be learned at sea, but his assignments were made at once: in addition to a number indicating the spaces in which he would hang and store his hammock, he was given numbers identifying his sailor's responsibility for handling sail, his battle station at a gun on the quarter-deck, and his mess. All of these required a preliminary knowledge of his way about a ship which, although only seventy-five per cent larger in its over-all measurements, was five times the tonnage of the *Acushnet* and carried almost twenty times as many men. The *United States* was indescribably crowded with sailors employed in all the familiar duties of seamanship on the main spar deck or exercising various kinds of craftsmanship on the gun deck below. The part of the spar deck abaft the mainmast, of course, was the captain's sacred quarter-deck, and the port side of the gun deck was reserved for the officers; so that each sailor had fewer square feet for himself than he could claim for a pauper's grave, and sometimes he could occupy these only by virtue of his ability to squeeze himself into corners and avoid the eye of an officer or the feet of a companion on duty. The low space between the gun deck and berth deck was forbidden entirely to the men during the hours of daylight, and few of them ever had occasion to visit the storerooms of the orlop deck below the water line. Even the crowded *Charles and Henry* seemed spacious in retrospect.

The problem of staying out of trouble under such crowded conditions, Melville discovered, was an insoluble one for many of the men; and after three of the bandsmen were flogged for drunkenness on the nineteenth, it was a relief to know that on the next morning the crew would be gathered around the capstan to weigh anchor rather than around the mainmast to witness punishment. A fine breeze took them out to sea, and they stood to the south and westward in the direction of the Marquesas.

The routine established for the men at sea kept them out of mischief.

At a boatswain's pipe and the early morning cry of "all hammocks up" the men tumbled out of their swinging beds, put on such clothes as they had not been sleeping in, rolled up their bedding and stowed it in the hammock nettings above the spar deck bulwarks, and began to swab down the decks. By breakfast time the ship was clean, and the pieces of canvas spread for each particular mess were for the protection of the deck rather than the food placed upon them. The cooking was done in three great copper cauldrons behind the mainmast on the gun deck; in these were boiled, after their daily cleaning, the morning coffee, quantities of salt beef or pork, water for the evening tea, and such special dishes as the individual mess cook could prepare out of his stores and cook by boiling in a numbered canvas bag. Service was from a carrying bucket or "kid" into tinware kept with individual allowances of sugar, molasses, tea, cheese, flour, and any supplies the men might buy for themselves in a "mess chest" on the berth deck. Members of each mess took turns serving as cook and steward, and when a meal was over the men who were not cleaning up were free until the morning inspection at nine o'clock.

For six of the twelve hours that Melville was on duty he was free from the crowd. His assignment to the maintop meant that he spent two hours out of every watch on a platform more than seventy feet above the deck, surrounded by straining canvas and creaking ropes and out of sight from any officer who might put him to work at makeshift tasks. There he could stretch at ease and gossip with the companions of his quarter watch while shaded from the tropic sun by the sails above. His own particular duty required him to scamper up a second set of shrouds leading from his platform to a smaller one above and then up a jacob's-ladder to the main-royal yard nearly two hundred feet above the deck and there handle the topmost piece of canvas on the ship. From that high perch the *United States* looked smaller than any vessel in which he had ever sailed, and when the roll of the ship sent him far out above the water he was in a world of his own out of which he could be called only by a strong voice through a megaphone. Melville sometimes indulged his desire to escape the crowd by remaining on the main-royal yard when he was off duty, and it was while he was aloft, perhaps, that he most often turned over his experiences in his mind and began to see them from the point of view he eventually displayed in his books. But most of his time he spent on the secure platform just above the mainsail and in better communication distance from the deck.

His enforced intimacy with his companions of the maintop gave Melville a close acquaintance with the only man in the Pacific whom he was later to remember with unreserved admiration. John J. Chase was an Englishman by birth who had served in the British navy before joining that of the United States and becoming a boatswain's mate on the U.S.S. *St. Louis.* The most unusual episode in his career had been his desertion from that vessel in the harbor of Callao on November 18, 1840, in order to take service in the Peruvian navy during the war with Bolivia. During the period that Melville had been on the *Acushnet* Chase had been wearing the gold braid of Lima and walking a quarter-deck; but in the latter part of May, 1842, when the American fleet was in the Callao harbor and after the strife-torn Peruvian government had made peace with Bolivia, Chase returned to American service with a particular request from the Peruvian admiral that he might be pardoned for his desertion. Commodore Thomas ap Catesby Jones had acceded to the request but had transferred Chase to the *United States.* On that ship he had been enrolled as an ordinary seaman and after six weeks promoted to the position of captain of the maintop. At the time of Melville's enlistment he had been in his new position for more than a year and had impressed his superiors as a splendid seaman, a man of intelligence, and a born leader. One of the midshipmen on board later testified that "his topmates adored him, although he kept them up to the mark," and Melville certainly shared the admiration in which he was generally held. To him Jack Chase was a finer gentleman and a better scholar than anyone he had actually known to claim these titles. He had a kinder heart than usually went with the soft palms of the conventional gentleman; and he was a master of languages who could recite long passages from Camoëns' sailors' epic, *The Lusiad,* in the original Portuguese, and talk in English of Rob Roy and Don Juan, Macbeth and Ulysses, and Bulwer's Pelham. Chase, according to Melville's later account, took the new recruit into his own mess, acted as his protector, and taught him to respect good seamanship and the honor of a position in the maintop. He also probably contributed a great deal to Melville's growing interest in literature, for in the free and easy companionship of six hours a day for fourteen months the two had time to dwell reflectively upon almost everything either had read.

Strangely enough, Melville found himself in literary company for the first time in his life while serving as a common sailor in the United States Navy. Among his other associates was a young poet from the afterguard of seamen who were responsible for the mainsail and with whom the maintop men sometimes had to work in concert. He was a fellow New Yorker from Auburn of about Melville's own age named Ephraim Curtiss Hine. Hine was touched by homesickness and given to sentimental verse, but he had enough humor to make a good story of Commodore Jones's "conquest" of California the year before as an occasion when seventeen members of the Monterey garrison fled during the night after receiving the American ultimatum, leaving only eight men and a bulldog to surrender with dignity on the following morning. The two young men had much in common, although Melville was amused by the other's attempts to pursue the muse and preserve her offerings despite the obstacles put in his way by the crowded conditions on shipboard. Later, after *The Haunted Barque and Other Poems* had been printed in the conventional fashion, Melville was to tell a fantastic story of a different sort of publication given the manuscript—that is, of its being fired from the mouth of a cannon in which the author had concealed it. Another literary member of the afterguard was a tall spare man of mystery who had little to do with his companions, kept a saturnine silence about his past, and went under the assumed name of Edward Norton. Attracted by his dignity and reserve, and suspecting literary interests from his consorting with the poet, Melville managed to engage him in conversation during a quiet night watch when most of the maintop men were dozing on their platform and the afterguard on the carronade slides. "That night," he wrote later, "we scoured all the prairies of reading; dived into the bosoms of authors, and tore out their hearts." "And that night," he added, a young maintop man "learned more than he has ever done in any single night since." The two became intimate enough to be sight-seeing companions during later shore liberties, but Norton's reserve was such that it was not until sixteen years later, when he had settled down under his real name Oliver Russ, taken a wife, and named his son after the young man who had scraped his acquaintance in the night, that Melville became aware of the value the "man-of-war hermit" placed upon his companionship.

There were a number of other men on board who were interested in writing—Melville knew of at least three who were keeping journals of the cruise—and Jack Chase apparently stimulated so great an enthusiasm for poetry in the foretop that one of his men strained his memory for a dozen lines from Felicia Hemans which he put on paper and inscribed to "J.J.C. by his sincere Friend G.W.W." The plagiarist was possibly the happy-go-lucky ex-peddler and ex-pedagogue from Maine, Griffith Williams, the "laughing philosopher" who had enlisted with Melville at Honolulu. Williams' middle initial is unrecorded, but he was, in any case, Melville's fourth and only other close friend on board the *United States*—a man "full of mirth and good humor" whose original stories of country frolics and sweethearts provided balance for the rhetorical enthusiasm of Jack Chase, the sentiment of Hine, and the earnest penetration of Norton.

The companionship of men whose minds could escape their immediate surroundings and take refuge in literature was of unusual value to Melville at this particular time. Ordinary sailor talk had long ago lost the charm of novelty, and the activity of his mind which had become evident in Honolulu made him eager for intellectual discussion of any sort. Furthermore, he found life in the Navy neither exciting nor pleasant. The routine begun before breakfast in order to keep the men occupied was maintained all day, and although the men off duty during the forenoon watch were not put to specific tasks they were not allowed to retire to their hammocks and sleep, after the custom established on merchant and whaling vessels. With each watch on duty for eight hours every other night, this meant that each morning half the men on board the ship had spent less than four hours in their hammocks and that many of them roamed the decks half-consciously or learned to lounge against a gun and doze standing up. If the morning happened to be that of a scrubbing day, when all hands were called before dawn to scrub their hammocks and clothes and holystone the soapy decks, the entire crew was wet and sleepy and too tired to be revived by the two ounces of whisky doled out to each man before he broke his sixteen-hour fast with his morning meal. The men on duty during the forenoon had all the miscellaneous tasks of merchant seamen plus the job of providing the "glittering bright-work" and "neatly flemished rigging" which, according to naval tradition, should always accompany "snow white decks." An insistence that all ropes should be kept in neat, flat, free-running coils seemed reasonable enough to a man who was familiar with a whale line; but the amount of work required to keep the brightwork glittering was almost intolerable, even to a foretop sailor who spent half his watch high above the deck. For the *United States* not only showed far more metal than a merchant vessel but she mounted thirty "long guns" on the gun deck and two more in addition to the twenty carronades on the spar deck, and the highest standards of efficiency required that the guns themselves and their twenty-four- and thirty-two-pound shot should be kept free from rust. The scouring dust was one of the most hated substances aboard a man-of-war.

Unlike merchantmen, naval vessels kept "watch-and-watch," leaving the members of the crew who had been on duty during the forenoon free to follow their own devices after their midday meal. Thus in the afternoon half the "people" either were busy at such personal tasks as overhauling their clothes and practicing the amateur craftsmanship which whaling men called "scrimshaw" or were trying to kill time by reading, talking, playing checkers, or engaging in crafty gambling with lookouts posted against discovery by roving officers or the master-at-arms and his corporals. At all hours of the day cooper, carpenter, tinker, cobbler, and tailor could be seen at work on the starboard side of the gun deck, where the school for midshipmen was also held in the mornings. There too the ship's barbers practiced their art on shaving days, Wednesday and

Saturday, rolling with the ship as they trimmed hair and scraped off surplus whiskers for the men perched upon upturned kegs balanced upon shot boxes. At eight bells or four o'clock in the afternoon, however, all such miscellaneous activities were brought to an end with the cry "Clear up the deck!" Sweepers brought out their brooms, the drums rolled for the day's second "tot" of grog, supper was piped and quickly eaten, and the evening dogwatches began.

The short dogwatches which were begun with supper, separated by the evening inspection at six o'clock, and brought to a close with the order "Stand by your hammocks" before eight, provided the period of greatest relaxation throughout the ship. The men were well fed after their third meal in eight hours, warmed by their tot of grog, and stimulated by the change introduced into the normal four-hour rhythm of their lives. It was a time for promenading, for arguing, for storytelling, and for singing. During this time the order of watches was reversed: men who had been sleepy all day could look forward to six or seven hours in their hammocks, while those who were fresh from a good sleep the night before would take over the long duty to come. Unless some kind of punishment had to be measured out and witnessed at the six o'clock inspection, it was the one time of day when the ship was free from grumbling.

Gradually, during the months that followed his enlistment, Melville was to grow so much accustomed to this routine that it became an unconscious round of activity which he could not in later years relive in his memory without external assistance. Its interruptions, however, were unforgettable. The first came when they had been at sea for less than a week and the crew received a call to general quarters for battle training. Since the ship normally went into action with the main royal furled, Melville had no duty in the rigging and was stationed instead at one of the carronades on the starboard side of the quarter-deck, where he was readily available for service aloft if long-range maneuvering required it, or for handling the ramrod and sponge in the short-range action for which his gun was designed. It was a position of honor which he appreciated more than he liked, for rumors of possible war were afloat on the Pacific and there were sailors aboard the *United States* who had seen action and liked to entertain their younger companions with stories of blood in the scuppers and butchery in the hospital. The quarter-deck, these warriors never failed to point out, was the most dangerous part of the ship because it was exposed not only to the canisters of chain and miscellaneous old iron fired at the rigging but also to the raking of small arms directed at the commanding officers. Such stories appear to have encouraged Melville to meditate upon the foolishness and futility of war, but his real objection to battle practice was less to the chance of blood than to the certainty of sweat. For his heavy carronade was fastened to the bulwarks by great ropes to prevent its being knocked across the deck by its recoil, and after every shot the ropes had to be loosened and Melville was required to help roll it back before he sponged out the barrel and rammed home the charges of powder and ball. Rolling it into place again and jumping out of the way before it fired all added up to entirely too much hot-weather activity for someone who had learned that the best way to endure the tropics was to lounge quietly in the shade—especially when his only relief from a straining back was that of dancing around with a pike or cutlass in an active pretense at repelling boarders. Such antics were hardly to the taste of a young man so recently habituated to the charms of easy savage life and so skeptical of the boasts of mechanized civilization.

But worst of all was the feeling of extra compulsion which accompanied every exercise at arms. Melville had lived long enough on ship-board and had been exposed to enough danger to accept the necessity of disciplined seamanship and a certain amount of busywork, and although he may have believed that the Navy was overdoing a good thing he could adapt himself to a new situation, as he had done so often in the past, and stay out of trouble. Military discipline, however, made new and more arbitrary, less comprehensible, demands upon his rebellious disposition; and it made them without regard to the rights of human beings about which he had become sensitive in Honolulu. He became fully conscious of war's harsh disregard for humanity for the first time on September 3, when the crew of the *United States* was mustered around the capstan to hear a reading of the articles of war. Then he learned that the officers of his ship had a power over him which was more severe than the power to flog and that it could be exercised for shortcomings less tangible than drunkenness, fighting, and failure to obey orders. As the voice of the captain's clerk, pitched to the ears of five hundred men, beat in upon his consciousness, the young ex-deserter, ex-mutineer, and anti-imperialist discovered a liturgical ruthlessness in the refrain "shall suffer death." As the ceremony was repeated, according to naval regulations, on the first Sunday of each succeeding month, the liturgy became a part of his main-top meditations until he was aware of all its implications as another illustration of the essential barbarism of civilized society and its institutions.

Another memorable interruption came four weeks later when one of the seamen, Conly Dougherty, died of a heart disease and Melville witnessed his first recorded burial at sea. After the body had been weighted with shot, wrapped and sewed in canvas, and carried to the starboard gangway, all hands were called for the burial service, which was read by the chaplain while the corpse was tilted and allowed to slide into the water. Melville was to see the same ceremony four more times before he got home, and he was never to forget the contrast between the solemnity of the occasion and the irreverence of some of its witnesses, whose rudeness was tempered only by the variety of their superstitions. For some sailors advocated the old custom of taking a "last stitch" through the nose of the corpse to prevent its rising from the sea, while others insisted that the spirit invariably did rise and hover about the ship in the form of a bird or a light.

The most remarkable of the deaths aboard the *United States,* however, occurred on one of the hammock-scrubbing days in early October, when David Black, the ship's cooper, climbed out on the projecting "cat's head" to which the anchor was attached, in order to wash his hammock by towing it in the sea. Hoping apparently to avoid the labor of scrubbing by forcing water through the canvas, he tied lanyards to the four corners, got literally a death grip upon them, and threw overboard what any ordinary seaman could have told him was a sea anchor. He went over with it, and, although the ship was immediately hove to and the barge and a cutter were launched for a five-hour search in the heavy seas, neither he nor the life buoys cut loose from the stern were ever seen again. The accident was especially remarkable to the superstitious sailors, who normally believed that every extraordinary event was foreshadowed by some sign, because the cooper had been told shortly before that his life buoys leaked and had replied that "If a man cannot save himself with these, he ought to drown." The incident gave Melville new food for meditation and perhaps caused him to think enough about superstitions and the foreshadowings of tragedy to use them as major literary devices for the purpose of unifying a later romance of the Pacific.

III

Except for these interruptions of the daily routine, the voyage of the *United States* was a leisurely and monotonous one over a part of the ocean which Melville had sailed before. The ship took time to cruise about for an entire day in September taking soundings and keeping a lookout in a vain effort to verify the existence of a shoal marked on its chart, but after the death of the cooper it made good speed toward the Marquesas and on the afternoon of the following day hove to off the entrance to Nuku Hiva harbor and hoisted a signal for the pilot, who brought the frigate through the Sentinels and to anchor in Anna Maria Bay. The fifteen months which had elapsed since Melville fled up the familiar ridge and over the mountains had brought changes. The French, represented still by *La Reine Blanche* and a couple of smaller vessels, had forcefully established themselves and were building a fort and preparing to settle a colony of convicts whose tents were pitched near the construction work. The king was happy in a French military uniform, rich with gilt and topped off by a three-cornered hat with waving ostrich plumes. But his young queen, who was then only fifteen years old, was still incalculable in her behavior. Although the sedate chronicle of a visit from the royal pair merely says that she was "tattooed on all visible parts," Melville later recorded that in her enthusiastic inclination to compare decorations with an old sailor she left practically no parts invisible. That was the nearest he came, however, to a renewal of his acquaintance with the unspoiled children of nature, because the *United States* remained anchored only thirty-three hours before being towed out of the harbor by the boats of the French squadron and setting sail for Tahiti.

Reaching Tahiti on October 12 after a voyage of five days, Melville again found himself among familiar surroundings although he had less opportunity than he had found at Nuku Hiva for renewing former acquaintances even if he had cared to do so. For the *United States* dropped anchor for its week's stay in the bay of Matavai rather than in the harbor of Papeete some eight or nine miles to the west, and it was possible to supply the ship with fresh water from a spring running into the bay while the sailors' mess was replenished with fresh pork, vegetables, and fruit from the native boats which swarmed about them. But the stop was primarily for the purpose of making an informal investigation of conditions and recent events in the Society Islands, and Melville would have had no trouble in getting a summary account of the relations between the French and the natives during the past year. Some such information may, in fact, have reached the ears of a curious sailor from Queen Pomaree's royal consort, who paid the Americans a visit on their last afternoon in port, spoke good English, and doubtless was thoroughly pumped for news before he was allowed to depart with a salute of thirteen guns. On the morning of the nineteenth they weighed anchor and set sail for Valparaiso. Their business in the middle Pacific was finished, and they were starting in the general direction of home.

As his ship skirted Eimeo, Melville was able to get a good farewell view of the village of Papetoi and the bay from which he had sailed on the *Charles and Henry* and of the western beach along which he and the Long Ghost had tramped almost precisely twelve months before. That afternoon they were becalmed a few miles off the southern reef of the island, and through the remarkably clear atmosphere Melville may have been able to observe once again, from his position on the royal yard, the dark shadows of the valley of Martair. But there was no going ashore. The fresh evening breeze filled their sails, and they set their course south and eastward to catch the same winds that had taken Melville once before toward the coast of South America.

The thirty-day passage which followed was the most agreeable made by the *United States* since leaving home, except for the accident that occurred on October 28 and provided Melville with material for a later tale. On that day James Craddock fell from a mizzen yard and suffered fractures of the arm and leg, and as a consequence became a victim of the ship's surgeon. After passing the familiar island of Más Afuera in the late afternoon, the captain ran close in to Juan Fernández on the morning of October 19; and all the men had a near view of the picturesque island which the literary sailors knew as the refuge of Alexander Selkirk and the inspiration of Defoe's *Robinson Crusoe* and Cowper's poem beginning "I am monarch of all I survey." They saw tall mountains rising three thousand feet above the sea with slopes covered with bright meadows and dark myrtles and among them an abrupt wall of bare rock resembling a monstrous blacksmith's anvil several hundred yards in height. Two days later they reached Valparaiso, exchanged salutes with the U.S. frigate *Constellation* and two British and two French warships which lay in the harbor, and dropped anchor for a stay of thirteen days.

The grogshops and señoritas so readily found on and between the two hills known as the "Main and Fore Top" were considered too dangerous to the wealth and health of the Navy for American sailors to be allowed the run of the port, but there were various occasions for going ashore and four men deserted and three times as many more were flogged for misbehavior before the *United States* left for Callao. It was customary to permit one member of each mess to purchase fresh supplies when a ship lay at anchor, and Melville would have needed only one such visit to the local market in order to see all the sights of the town. Most of its thirty thousand inhabitants lived in low adobe houses or thatched huts plastered with mud, overlooked by the more conventional homes of the American and English merchants upon the hillside above the city. The customhouse, two churches, a small theatre, and an open-air *chingano* for dancing were the main public buildings; and the most striking recollections usually carried away by visitors were of the four-foot-thick adobe walls designed to resist earthquakes, the animated haystacks formed by peasants bringing grass to market on horseback, and the musical cry of the night watch sounding out over the quiet harbor. The men probably looked forward to putting out to sea again for the ten-day run which was to take them up the coast to the headquarters of the American fleet in Peru.

Although Callao was a town of only about three thousand inhabitants and was known as a land of fogs and snakes, it was a favorite stopping place for sailors because of its nearness to Lima and its abundance of cherimoyas, oranges, bananas, and other tropical fruits which provided a welcome change from the salt meat and stale bread of a long cruise. Forty or more vessels were normally to be found in the protected anchorage behind the volcanic island of San Lorenzo on which was located the Protestant burying ground, and the port was a clearinghouse for Pacific gossip and news from the United States. A well-built mole lessened the work required to supply a ship by providing a convenient landing for boats, making water accessible by a conduit from the canal, and offering a railway connection between the boats and the supply depot. The town itself was the most remarkable one on the coast, for there were really two towns: the new city, running along a paved main street which was parallel to the bay and lined with pool halls and pulperias for the entertainment of sailors; and the old city, clearly visible beneath the waters of the bay, which had been destroyed by an earthquake and a tidal wave nearly a century before. In other respects, too, Callao was a place of fantastic contrasts. The remains of its fortress, which had once been able to contain ten thousand men, represented a civilization which was old and European; while just outside its walls were large open pits, filled with human bones and corpses, dogs and vultures, representing a barbarism more primitive than anything Melville had seen in the cannibal isles. A similar contrast existed between the well-kept center of the town and the open abattoirs and miscellaneous filth of its outskirts. Nature and humanity each seemed at odds with itself there, and despite the notorious fogs of the winter season a child might have children of his own before he saw rainfall.

Although the *United States* had received news from home at Valparaiso, it was probably not until its crew had begun to exchange gossip with men from various vessels in the Pacific squadron, in Callao, that Melville began to hear a story which affected his meditations upon the articles of war and was to be introduced into his later account of his naval experiences and stay in his mind as long as he lived. Over a year before, a mysterious "mutiny" had occurred on board the U.S.S. *Somers,* and a midshipman named Philip Spencer, a boatswain's mate named Samuel Cromwell, and a seaman named Elisha Small had been hanged. The affair had been kept quiet until the ship reached New York in December, 1842, but had soon afterward been given wide publicity because of the mysterious circumstances surrounding the affair and because Spencer was the son of Secretary of War John C. Spencer. Almost as interesting, to the sailors of the fleet, was the report that Small (who was a great favorite with the crew) had been run up to the yardarm with the patriotic exclamation "God bless the flag!" on his lips—although a later tradition was to attribute the exclamation to Spencer and revise its wording into a tribute to his Greek-letter fraternity, Chi Psi. The secret knowledge which turned a distressing story into an obsession with Melville, however, was the fact that the Lieutenant Gansevoort who had been in charge of the court-martial was his own first cousin Guert. He could not believe that the young naval officer who had so impressed him as a boy had become the villain that he evidently appeared to be in the eyes of the common sailors of the fleet, and the puzzle doubtless bothered him through many lonely hours of his night watches and contributed to the growth of that analytic and critical attitude with which he had already begun to contemplate organized society. While in Callao, too, he had an opportunity to collect material for other meditations about trouble on the high seas, for the *John Adams* came to anchor in the bay and was boarded by men from the *United States* on the second of January, 1844. Melville probably did not go aboard the whaler, but on the main street of Callao, barely a third of a mile in length, he might easily have run across members of its crew and learned from them of the difficulties which made some of its men refugees in the hills of Eimeo while he and Long Ghost were on the beach. From such sources as these, in any case, he picked up tales that he later told in his books.

The most memorable of his personal experiences in Callao was the trip to Lima which he and his friend Norton made when their section of the starboard watch were granted forty-eight hours of liberty between December 28 and January 3. The capital city of Peru, lying less than eight miles away and five hundred feet above the harbor, was constantly visible from the decks of the *United States*. Through the clear air of the December summer its dusty mud and adobe buildings looked strangely white and impressive to the young man who was aware that they represented the earliest beginnings of European civilization in America. The long road which gradually ascended to it from the sea was in bad repair and haunted by men who would cut a sailor's throat for his jacket, but its upper end was lined with tall Peruvian willows which grew along the banks of the irrigation streams watering the fields of corn and groves of oranges and lemons on either side. Only after he entered the city did a traveler become aware of the atmosphere of corruption and decay. For more than two decades Lima had suffered from invading armies and civil strife, and after the last great earthquake of 1828 its citizens had neither the energy nor the hope to restore its ruins. Some walls still lay flat with the dust of fifteen years upon them, others crazily supported the flat roofs and sagging balconies of inhabited dwellings, and the thick adobe blocks of the Franciscan convent and the gateway to the naval school sported ornamental caps which had been twisted and tilted into architectural monstrosities. The streets were carefully laid out at right angles, but those that sloped with the ground from the southeast to the northwest had open sewers running through the middle and were alive with buzzards fighting over pieces of offal or perched in evil rows on the housetops.

Yet there was romance and grandeur in Lima's decay. A wandering sailor, catching an inviting glance from a pair of black eyes above a concealing cape or shawl, could readily convince himself that he had been an object of interest to one of the great ladies of the town who were known to go abroad in *tapada;* or he could linger in the cool of the evening along the outer edge of a tiled piazza and imagine himself telling strange stories in Spanish to the ruffled gentlemen dallying over their cigars and glasses of wine or *chicha.* The homes of the upper-class Limenos were built around courtyards with enclosed balconies projecting over the street, but almost everything else in the city was open to the inspection of a stranger. On two sides of the plaza he could walk through the arcades paved with small stones and the knucklebones of sheep and look into the open shops on one side or pause between the pillars on the other for a meal of fried fish and corn-meal cakes while he watched the lace and fringe makers or other craftsmen near by. He could visit the convent and see the religious paintings of the famous Murillo and much-talked-of statue of the black Virgin and the white Child; or he could wander into the cathedral and admire the great altar, which, though tarnished, was of pure silver, and purchase a relic of an archbishop in the crypt beneath. Or he could stroll through the open-air market where all kinds of foods and fancywork were spread out on mats and the *chola* women—who displayed more vitality than any other element in the mixed population of Peru—exhibited their dexterity in frying twisted cakes of dough on the ends of peeled sticks. No other city in South America made a deeper impression upon Melville than did Lima.

Most of the ten weeks that the *United States* remained in port, however, were weeks of pure boredom. As the flagship of the American squadron, the vessel was excessively ceremonious; and, since Melville's place for the inspection twice a day was beside his gun on the quarter-deck, he had a good opportunity to observe his officers with an eye made critical by the absence of any other interest. His attitude toward Commodore Thomas ap Catesby Jones seems to have been the friendly mixture of respect and amusement which an independent young man might naturally hold toward an elderly hero with whom he had no personal contact—not greatly different, in fact, from the attitude Oliver Wendell Holmes had expressed toward Major Thomas Melville in "The Last Leaf." He had no such feelings, however, toward his immediate commanding officer, Captain James Armstrong, who occasionally exhibited the same symptoms of inebriation for which he flogged the common sailors and was observed with some bitterness by the maintop man who later portrayed him as "Captain Claret." Melville was by no means a temperance seaman, and his one hero among the officers was Lieutenant Latham B. Avery, who had been court-martialed for drunkenness on duty earlier in the cruise but despite his failing was generally recognized as the best sea officer on board the ship. But he had begun to react with violent antagonism to anything that resembled sanctimony in high places. Toward the other officers he cultivated a defensive attitude of varying degrees of contempt and shared the common opinion that the ship's surgeon, William Johnson, was a cold-blooded butcher. His strongest feelings of dislike, however, were reserved for the two petty officers other than Jack Chase whose personalities were a constant threat to his resolution to stay out of trouble: the gunner, Asa G. Curtis, whom he considered an ill-tempered "Old Combustibles"; and the master-at-arms, John C. Turner, whom he looked upon as a bland hypocrite far more sanctimonious and dishonest than the punch-loving captain. There may have been more fear than fairness in this estimate of his noncommissioned superiors, for Melville dreaded the indignity of a possible flogging more than he dreaded anything else that could happen to him in the Navy, and the master-at-arms especially was the man assigned to search out and report all infractions of the rules.

The most exciting interruption to the tedium of these weeks occurred on January 21 when the *Constellation* (which had come up from Valparaiso) sailed for home, carrying Commodore Jones, who had been recalled. The captains of *United States* and the British frigate *Vindictive* decided to race her and each other out of harbor, and with his responsibility for the main royal Melville became an active jockey in his first "man-of-war Derby." The "Old Waggon," as the *United States* was popularly called, was known as the fastest but most ungainly sailer in the American Navy; and the men could always be brought to life by a competitive display of her surprising qualities. They won the race and returned to their anchorage the next day in good spirits, feeling sure that their ship would be the next to be called home and that she could be trusted to make a swift passage.

A long time was to pass, however, before their anticipations were justified: When their new commodore, Alexander J. Dallas, appeared on the frigate *Savannah* in the middle of February, he ordered the *United States* to Mazatlán for a supply of the Mexican silver dollars which could be used as currency in Latin-American ports. Leaving on the twenty-fourth, they spent thirty-three days on a long slow passage to the modern little city which had recently grown from a fishing village into an important port serving the mining districts of the interior. For nineteen days, between March 28 and April 16, they lay at anchor while coins were being obtained from the inland mint, but Melville did not have time enough ashore for Mexico to make any lasting impression upon him. The men all dreaded the passage back to Callao, for two years before they had been caught short of provisions by the calms and light head winds of the Gulf of Panama and had found it a miserable experience which they did not wish to repeat. This time, except for the state of their supplies, it was almost as bad. The trip lasted for fifty-one days, and its only item of interest, for Melville, was a distant sight of Point St. Helena and other landmarks he had seen before during his whaling days off the coast of Ecuador.

When they finally reached Callao on the afternoon of June 5 they discovered that Commodore Dallas had died two days before and that Captain Armstrong, as the senior officer of the Pacific squadron, had inherited the position of Dallas and would not be going home until relieved of this command. Instead of the *United States* the *Cyane* had been the next vessel ordered around the Horn, and Melville and his companions settled down to another long period of idleness in the harbor while the more fortunate crew prepared to sail. In the shake-up of command caused by Commodore Dallas' death, however, Captain Armstrong took over the flagship *Savannah,* Captain C. K. Stribling (the next in seniority) moved up to the *United States,* and Captain Holland of the flagship was assigned to the *Cyane.* Thus when Melville finally did sail for home, on July 6, 1844, it was not under the "Captain Claret" of his later story but under an entirely different officer. Yet he had spent almost eleven months under Armstrong—more than two of them on the tedious voyage to Mazatlán and nearly five idly in port with only forty-eight hours of formal liberty—and these were his most trying months in the Navy. If he was later to select the passage home as the framework for his story of naval life, he was to put into that frame his earlier annoyances and irritations and group them around a portrait of the captain under whom he had acquired these emotions.

Melville's outward-bound trip around Cape Horn had been made in the southern summer. His homeward passage would be in midwinter, and he knew, from his experience with the summer temperatures of the lower latitudes and from the stories he had heard of the Horn in winter, that he could suffer bitterly from the cold as he took his turns of duty in the high rigging. With the habitual caution which he displayed in all his adventuring, he apparently prepared for the ice and sleet of the Cape before leaving Callao by constructing the curiously quilted white canvas jacket which gave him the title for his later book and became the symbol, as he looked back on the voyage, of his distinction as an individual among the mass of men who made up the crew of a man-of-war. Such an overcoat was unofficial equipment in the American Navy but sufficiently common to be referred to casually as a "lined frock" by other sailors, and there is no reason to doubt Melville's later assurance to the skeptical R. H. Dana, Jr., that it was a "veritable garment" which he deposited upon the bottom of the Charles River at the end of his voyage. Nor is it unlikely that a young man accustomed to wearing clothes made by his mother and sisters should have attracted a certain amount of ridicule from his companions by manufacturing a garment which was more ingenious than practical, although any unusual distinction he achieved by it probably existed more in his own sensitive mind rather than in the minds of his fellow sailors. Like so many other things aboard the *United States,* Melville's white jacket existed first as a relatively insignificant kernel of reality which germinated for more than four years before it flowered into a symbol.

Whatever ridicule and discomfort Melville may have suffered because of his jacket, his voyage eastward around Cape Horn turned out to be almost as easy as his passage westward. For a week after losing sight of the cloud-capped Andes at Callao they made rapid headway toward the south, running before a stiff breeze and through a heavy sea in which the "old wagon" of a frigate half buried herself at every plunge. On the afternoon of the fifteenth, after a short period of calm, the wind changed; and, although they had to sail against it to the south and east, they made good progress until they struck the squally weather in the neighborhood of the Cape ten days later and Melville had to take in his main royal while his companions aloft reefed the topsails and stood by to take in the topgallants if the expected storm should follow. During this period of watching and waiting Melville saw the most breath-taking spectacle the ocean could offer: a full-rigged ship—the *Natchez,* sixty-four days outward bound from New York—spreading all the canvas she could carry, from skysail to water sails and from flying jib to spanker. It was a sight to take a man's heart back to the Pacific again, but all the sailors on the *United States* could do was admire the boldness of the New Yorker and hope for a change of wind in their own favor. As on Melville's own outward voyage, the gale held off for three days before striking on the twenty-eighth and forcing the frigate to lay to for six hours under nothing more than its storm staysails until the wind abated and shifted. They rounded the Horn without seeing the Cape or even any sign of Staten Land and reached the harbor of Rio de Janeiro on August 16, where they had the satisfaction of overtaking the *Cyane,* which had required a week longer to make the passage and was not yet ready to sail northward.

For eight days, without any unusual incident and without shore leave, they lay at anchor in the bay of Rio in company with a half dozen other American war vessels, half as many more belonging to Great Britain, a French frigate, a strange Dutch paddle-wheeled "steamer of war," and a number of merchant ships. There was news from home for many of the men, but probably none for Melville, whose letters were then resting in Honolulu. Yet he had undoubtedly written home from Callao, for his family had not yet begun to make inquiries about him as they had about his cousin Thomas, who had gone whaling at about the same time and had not been heard from since, and he could begin the last six-thousand-mile stretch of his long voyage with every expectation of finding a warm welcome awaiting him at the end of six or eight more weeks of naval life.

Once again, on the morning of the twenty-fourth, the *United States* began its voyage with a race, against three American ships and a French sloop, and once again "the Old Waggon" demonstrated her speed, heaving to in the middle of the next afternoon to collect letter bags from her two nearest rivals before proceeding homeward before a good breeze. Before they sighted the North American continent its crew had to fight squalls and calms and give a sea burial to the captain's cook and a seaman, and Melville had the final dramatic experience of assisting in hauling down the royal yards and close-reefing the topsails during a storm; but by October 2 they were eating fresh cod from Massachusetts fishing boats and on the next day made land, were welcomed by the pilot boat, and dropped anchor before sunset off the Boston Navy Yard. Half the men, whose term of service had expired, were discharged and put ashore that evening. The rest, including Melville, were obliged to wait until Captain Stribling could clear their discharges with the secretary of the navy. Lieutenant Guert Gansevoort, however, was stationed on the receiving ship *Ohio* while recovering from the strain of his court-martial for the hanging of Philip Spencer, and the Melville family was able to get word that Herman had arrived and might be expected home at any moment. Herman himself was ready to bid good-bye to his friends and put the Navy behind him forever. He tossed his remarkable white jacket overboard (he later called himself "a great fool" for doing so) and on October 14 drew his pay and began a new phase of his life. The recoil from his restless youth was complete. His mind was ripe for a new kind of adventuring, but his body was disposed to settle down.

5
Settling Down

I

WHEN MELVILLE reached his home in the familiar village of Lansing-burgh he found that the inevitable changes of four years had brought a lessening of the strain under which his family had been living. The country as a whole had recovered from its financial depression, money was no longer tight, and if his mother's circumstances were still difficult they were not desperate. Gansevoort had apparently regained his energetic brilliance if not his health and was on his way home from a long and active political tour during which he had stumped Tennessee, Kentucky, Ohio, and western New York for the presidential candidacy of James K. Polk and the admission of Texas to the Union—gaining for himself the reputation of a fiery Tammany Hall orator and a solid party man, although the antagonistic Horace Greeley described his speeches as being more devoted to "gas and glory" than to genuine issues. His younger brother, Allan, had belied a temperamental apprenticeship to the law by developing into a solid citizen who had settled into an office at 10 Wall Street in New York City and was promising to be the sort of son the mother always had wanted. The only one of Maria's boys who had remained at home was Thomas, now a sturdy youngster of fourteen, eager to hang on Herman's every word with an interest which brought the two brothers close together and ripened into a deep affection.

The four Melville girls had all grown up. Helen, who had been a young lady of twenty-three when her brother began his wanderings, was still living at home; but she had become intimate with the Shaws in Boston and made frequent long visits in their house, being occasionally squired about by Judge Shaw's oldest son although her greatest admirer seems to have been the judge's only daughter, Elizabeth, who had begun to visit regularly in the Melville household in Lansingburgh. Augusta, two years Herman's junior, was ready to share Thomas' admiration for their wandering brother. The earnest temperament which destined her to an inevitable spinsterhood found a practical outlet in giving Herman the serious approbation he needed, and her unquestioning loyalty, if not rewarded with the same sort of affection he gave Tom, was a grateful relief from the suggestions of misgiving which he continued to perceive in the reactions of other members of the family to his past activities and his present condition. Catherine, or Kate, just reaching young-womanhood at the age of nineteen, was, to Herman, at the most interesting age of all the sisters; and he treated her with a mixture of teasing and courtliness which Fanny, at seventeen, was too young to merit and Augusta was too serious to acknowledge in the same spirit. The returned traveler, however, with some money in his pocket and no pressing demands upon him, was probably too full of good humor to make many conscious distinctions within the family circle when he had so much to hear and tell about the occurrences of the past four years.

As he caught up with the family news, he learned that his favorite uncle, Peter Gansevoort, had lost his wife and had remarried two years later, giving his nephew a new aunt Susan to become acquainted with in Albany, but that there were few other extraordinary changes among his Gansevoort relatives except for the change he may himself have noticed in his cousin Guert. For Guert Gansevoort had become a man of mystery who looked the part. Nearly two years before, when the *Somers* had reached New York after its mutiny, he slipped into the home of his widowed mother looking as haggard and broken as "an infirm man of seventy" and had not recovered his spirits since. While on his way to Washington shortly afterward he had stopped overnight in Philadelphia and had confided in a cousin, Passed Midshipman Henry or "Hunn" Gansevoort, that he had practically compelled a reluctant court-martial to render a sentence of "guilty" against Philip Spencer and his associates at the insistence of Captain Mackenzie, who had told him that the court had "misapprehended the aggravated character of the offense, and that there would be no security for the lives of officers or protection to commerce if an example was not made in a case so flagrant as this." The family knew nothing of this confidence, for two days later Henry had put to sea on the *Grampus,* which had been lost with all hands in March; but Guert had assured his mother that he had done his duty and that his action "was *approved* of God," however mysterious it might appear to his fellow men, and the entire family was convinced from his words and his character that he was an innocent victim of circumstances. The formal inquiry had cleared him of legal blame but had not fully resolved the mystery of the circumstances, and the matter was a distressing puzzle to all his relatives and friends who were in a position to observe its devastating and lasting effect upon him.

Among the Melvilles, the tragic accounts of his uncle Thomas' family were finally being cast. A settlement of the long-awaited French legacy due the children of Thomas' first wife was compelling a formal investigation and report of their circumstances: three had died more than twenty years before in Pittsfield; and of the surviving three only one, Priscilla Anne Marie, was able to enjoy her estate. The oldest son, Thomas, was aboard the whaler *Oregon* but was to die before its return the following spring. Parisian born and formally christened Pierre François Henry Thomas Wilson Melville, he was the true Ishmael of the family; and his unhappy experiences, like those of Guert Gansevoort, were to arouse the imagination and form a part of the literary consciousness of his cousin Herman. The youngest surviving child of that marriage, Henry, was being cared for in Pittsfield, but would have to be legally declared insane and have a guardian appointed before the legacy could be collected. The elder Thomas was only sixty-eight, but he was nearing the end of his days and was to die within the year, leaving Herman's aunt Mary unprovided for and dependent upon her oldest son Robert, who had returned to Pittsfield. Most of the younger children were to remain in Galena and drop out of their cousin's life.

Maria and her children, for once, had little to complain of when they compared their situation with that of their most intimate relatives; and the return of Herman in good health and spirits from what his family considered the human depths of the sea was a pleasing novelty to relatives who had little reason to expect good news from beyond the horizon. From them he received an attention which he had never enjoyed before, and he apparently encouraged it by making more than one good story out of his own adventures. His life among the cannibals, of course, was the high point of his experiences, so far as the curiosity of his audience was concerned, and he could make a vivid tale of such matters as his escape from the *Acushnet,* the descent into the valley of the Typees, his anxiety after his separation from Toby, and the personal combats of naked savages who fought with painted war clubs and treated their dead enemies as "long pig." He could be amusing, too, about the simplicities of the children of nature who possessed so few civilized inhibitions and whose attitude toward such complex matters as theology and economics was so unfrustrated and direct. Surrounded as he was by the curiosity of four unmarried sisters, he could also be romantic, although the effort required him to bring to maturity an attractive child to whom he and Toby had taught a few words of English, give her the improbable name Fayaway, and endow her with strange blue eyes—perhaps in order to pique the curiosity of his sisters concerning the actual existence of a girl whose reported behavior was on some occasions like that of a savage and on others like that of a well-bred young lady picnicking on the banks of the upper Hudson.

At other times he was argumentative about the South Seas. For upon his return home he discovered that most of the political news of the Pacific region was colored by the point of view of the American Board of Foreign Missions, which had its headquarters in Boston, and that the activities of the American missionaries looked better in the newspapers than they had to a wandering sailor. He may have been perversely affected by the rabid imperialism of his older brother when he actively took the British side in the argument over Hawaii, although Gansevoort, however determined he may have been to annex Texas despite British opposition, apparently made no serious objection to Herman's defense of Lord George Paulet's activities in Honolulu. The latent antagonism which had previously existed between the two brothers seems to have disappeared from Gansevoort's mind during their reunion at the height of his oratorical success and while he was filled with optimistic expectations concerning the spoils of political victory, and Herman kept his own feelings under control until many years later when he was to recapitulate his youthful emotions in his poetry.

With so many of his recent experiences kept alive in his mind by daily conversations, it was perhaps inevitable that the young man who had once tried to publish the "Fragments" from his "Writing Desk" should have thought of writing a book. The time was ripe for a romantic but informative treatment of the South Seas. Travel literature dealing with that region had been increasing in quantity for more than a decade, and it was a well-established custom for publishers to exploit a serious interest in faraway places by books designed for a more popular audience. His family and friends, according to contemporary report and later tradition, urged him to transfer his vivid narratives to paper; and he himself had nothing else to do. At some time during the late autumn he took an unaccustomed pen in his calloused hand and began work.

Some parts of his story came as easily as his struggles with unfamiliar problems of spelling, syntax, and sitting still would permit. His memories gathered easily around such emotional attitudes as a liking to tease a sympathetic audience with curiosity or suspense and an irritation at the complacency of the missionaries and the unnecessary hardships of a seaman's life. But other parts involved him in difficulties. He had no extraordinary power of exact auditory or visual recall, and he could reproduce accurately on paper neither the words he had heard during his wanderings nor the sights he had seen. The literary conventions of the time permitted him to use stilted language in his infrequent passages of conversation, and his public was not prepared to challenge the accuracy of his Marquesan orthography; but the same conventions and the same public demanded luxuriant descriptions and a narrative made educational by accounts of manners and customs. These were demands that he could not supply entirely from memory, nor was his actual narrative sufficiently rich in incident to enable him to defy them. A full-sized book would require not only the hard work of writing but a considerable amount of research, which would be difficult if not impossible in a village of three thousand inhabitants who were mostly employed in factories. Melville needed access to a good library.

He could have found such a library in the Young Men's Association in Albany; but, with the coming of cold weather, writing could hardly have been easy in a household adjusted to an almost entirely feminine regime. In any case, he had enough money saved from his sailor's wages to support himself, with reasonable economy, for a half year or more in New York. After Christmas he accordingly joined his brothers and apparently put most of his recollections of life among the cannibals down on paper "amidst all the bustle and stir of the proud and busy city" of New York. Among the books he was able to obtain there were Charles S. Stewart's two-volume account of *A Visit to the South Seas, in the United States' Ship Vincennes, During the Years 1829 and 1830,* an anonymous *Historical Account of the Circumnavigation of the Globe* which he may already have seen in Harper's Family Library, Edward Fanning's *Voyages Around the World,* the four volumes of William Ellis' *Polynesian Researches,* and eventually (although he claimed, in the first part of his own book, that he had "never happened to meet with" it) Captain David Porter's *Journal of a Cruise Made to the Pacific Ocean in the U.S. Frigate Essex.* He may also have made an acquaintance, if he had not already done so, with Georg H. von Langsdorff's *Voyages and Travels in Various Parts of the World,* for his uncle by marriage, Captain John De Wolf, whom he had probably seen after his own return from the Pacific, had been the master of von Langsdorff's ship on one of the voyages. Stewart's *Visit to the South Seas,* however, had the most intimate family associations in Melville's mind because it recounted the adventures of the cousin Thomas who had preceded Herman into the valley of the Typees and whose fate was still a matter of anxious investigation for the family. Stewart's narrative, in fact, became so intimately a part of Melville's mind while he was writing his own book that his visual remembrance of the Marquesas was adapted to Stewart's descriptions and some of his observations on manners and customs were simply borrowed from it.

Melville's *Narrative of a Four Months' Residence among the Natives of a Valley of the Marquesas Islands* or (to give it its original, American title) *Typee: A Peep at Polynesian Life* was not easy to put together. For one thing, his actual residence had not been long enough to give him a very comprehensive peep, and he was obliged to quadruple its length in order to justify the inclusion of scenes and incidents which may have been vaguely a part of his historical consciousness but which he could describe in necessary detail only after research into the observations of others. For another, he was too inexperienced in authorship to get his whole book in mind so completely that he could anticipate its eventual length or give it any depth of imaginative coherence. The latter difficulty was to become especially evident in the labored opening chapters, which were probably written, in their final form, only after a substantial portion of the later chapters had been composed. A mixture of genuine experience, argumentative self-justification, and borrowings from other books, they contain a curious reference to a whaling crew languidly watching the spout of a whale from the deck of a vessel putting in toward land because of poor hunting and are marked by the sort of intellectual incongruity which enabled Melville to attribute the savagery of the native islanders to the influence of civilization and also to their traditional antagonism toward one another. Nevertheless, as the book grew, it revealed the engaging charm of a lively and unconventional mind and acquired the unity of a continuous narrative which involved a certain element of suspense. By summer it was sufficiently near completion to be submitted to a publisher.

In the meantime Gansevoort had been pursuing the spoils of office with the usual Melville luck. During the political campaign, of course, he had ignored any legal practice he might have acquired and in midwinter was so near bankruptcy that one of his creditors was willing to accept ten cents on a dollar in satisfaction for a judgment against him, and his trip to Washington for the inauguration in March was not productive of an immediate appointment. He was anxious for the position of first marshal of New York, an office which would have given him considerable power and paid him some nine hundred dollars a year, but his major services had been to the national party rather than to Tammany Hall and his applications were in vain. It was not until the middle of July that he received his reward—an appointment as secretary to the American legation in England which offered him little opportunity to relieve himself of the further indebtedness he had incurred to Judge Shaw during the period of waiting. He was pleased with the opportunity to travel abroad in good company, however, and arranged to sail on July 31, 1845, on the *Great Western*.

The arrangement was fortunate for Herman. According to a later report, his manuscript had been rejected by the Harpers on the grounds that it could not possibly be a true story; but Thomas L. Nichols, to whom it was shown shortly before Gansevoort's departure, expressed confidence in its success—if it could be published first in England. The question of an English copyright at that time was so ambiguous, in any case, that no American author could hope for an income from English sales unless his book was first published in Great Britain, and the suggestion that it be taken abroad was both apt and timely. The manuscript was not yet complete, but, with the promise of revisions and additions to follow, Gansevoort took the greater part of it with him for reading and criticism during the voyage.

The book could not have been in very good shape, for, despite Herman's need for money, Gansevoort waited for six weeks or more after his arrival in England before submitting a portion of it to John Murray for publication in his Home and Colonial Library. Murray surprisingly took it for the work of "a practiced writer" and, although he had some doubts as to its authenticity, asked to see the entire manuscript. In the meantime, Herman tried to adjust his work to a series of publications which were designed to be informative rather than exciting by making revisions and adding new material such as that contained in the published chapters describing a typical day in the Typee Valley, the antiquities of the community, and the social condition and general character of the natives. Before the revisions and new chapters arrived in early December, however, Murray had agreed to print the book in a two-volume edition of one thousand copies and pay the author a hundred pounds for the English copyright.

The offer was a generous one, for at a half crown a volume it meant that the author was to receive forty per cent of the retail value of the minimum edition while the publisher gambled on a popular success which would enable him to recapture his investment through half profits on a large sale. Gansevoort undertook to prepare the manuscript for the printer and by December 20 had it ready except for the eleventh and twelfth chapters, which required a further going-over, and four or five pages of new corrections which the author had sent by the last steamer and were simply handed over to the publisher. The work of preparation was over before the first of the year, and on January 3, 1846, Gansevoort was able to write his brother that the book was paid for, that he had been arranging for the discount of Murray's note, and that he was sending the sum of five pounds on account. Herman could relax in the assurance that he was well along on the way toward professional authorship, but he apparently had no money to live on between steamers.

The following month was a busy one for Gansevoort, who had to read proof on the book, rising on one occasion before six in order to work for two and a half hours before breakfast and continuing at the labor from after dinner until midnight. Washington Irving, who was then on a visit to London and knew something about the Marquesas, read most of the *Narrative* in proof sheets with optimistic expressions of confidence in its success; and an American publisher, George Palmer Putnam, found it as interesting as *Robinson Crusoe* and expressed his desire to publish it in Wiley and Putnam's Library of Choice Reading. Gansevoort prophesied a sale of five thousand copies in the United States during the first year and was so optimistic that he accepted, on his brother's behalf, half profits of the American venture rather than a royalty of twelve and a half per cent of the retail price. The final arrangement was that it should follow the English format by appearing in two volumes at thirty-seven and a half cents in paper bindings or fifty in cloth; and if Herman and Allan, in New York, investigated printing costs and began figuring Herman's possible income on the basis of Gansevoort's anticipations, they may have arrived at the round sum of a thousand dollars to be derived from the American sales. With the payment from Murray, this would be a handsome income for a beginning author; and Herman found his prospects so "gratifying" that he immediately began work on a sequel.

Gansevoort had every reason to be pleased with himself as the patron of his less brilliant brother and as the good angel of his destiny. John Murray's bellows was in good working order, and even before the first volume of the *Narrative* made its appearance on February 27, 1846, it was being "puffed" in the English periodicals. The notices which immediately followed its publication were nearly all complimentary, for although the reviewers could not avoid some doubts concerning its complete authenticity they generally recognized the vivacity of its author's mind and the graphic quality of his style. Herman was well launched. But Gansevoort, who had done the launching, was on the shoals. For while Irving and Putman were singing the praises of his brother's book they were looking askance at him as a source of serious embarrassment to the American minister, Louis McLane, who was making every effort to get rid of him. A fiery Tammany Hall orator who had earned his position by screaming "Fifty-four forty or fight!" along the length of the American frontier was, at best, a potential source of trouble to a diplomat at the Court of St. James's during the Oregon controversy; and Gansevoort had grown little if any in judgment since he had failed in the fur business as a youth of twenty-one. His public indiscretion had been brought to the attention of his superiors, but before any politic disposition could be made of him he settled the problem himself by developing symptoms of cerebral anemia and giving up his official duties. On April 3 he wrote Herman of his lethargy and his fears that he was "breaking up"; four days later he informed McLane that he was threatened with a total loss of sight; on May 4 a public announcement was made of his severe indisposition; and on May 12, at the age of thirty, he died. He was still under a considerable financial obligation to Judge Shaw, but he had paid his debt to Herman by his practical assistance in beginning a transformation of the younger brother's aimless wanderings, which he had partly inspired, into promising literature.

II

While Melville was writing the greater part of *Typee* he probably gave no particular thought to the publisher's classification into which it should fit. The book was something between fiction and fact—a good story based upon personal experience which combined the freshness and episodic quality of an oral narrative with the conventional amount of description expected by readers of the printed page. Its appearance among the more purely factual narratives in Murray's Home and Colonial Library had forced him to change its tone and make it more informative and plausible by introducing new chapters and revising portions of the original manuscript. But when he began his new book for the same Library, he knew what he was doing. It was to be a sequel to *Typee* but otherwise entirely independent of it. His emphasis would be clearly upon an "aspect of life"—that of the South Sea Islanders in a half-civilized state, as opposed to the primitive conditions he had portrayed in *Typee,* and that of the wandering sailors who met the natives on their own level. He would reserve any description of the whale fishery for later use but would achieve novelty by giving a dramatic account of his experiences on board an Australian whaler, a comic version of his life in Tahiti, and a "familiar" survey of life on Eimeo as seen from the beachcomber's point of view. Furthermore, he would avoid the appearance of exaggeration, unless it was clearly humorous, which was causing readers of *Typee* to disturb both its author and its publisher with expressions of doubt concerning its authenticity.

Clear as his purpose was, however, he was not able to make much progress on the story he was to call *Omoo* or "the wanderer." After he had revised the English proof sheets for *Typee* and Wiley and Putnam had applied for its American copyright, on February 26, 1846, he had taken a vacation and gone to Lansingburgh. There his youngest brother,

Tom, who had reached his sixteenth birthday barely a month before and had begun to show signs of manly restlessness in his feminine environment, was disturbing the family by his determination to sail the South Seas before the mast; and Herman may actually have been called home to reason with him, for he immediately wrote Gansevoort in a vain effort to arrange something which would provide a less drastic satisfaction for the boy's adventurous spirit. With money enough to relax for a while and a normal desire to see a bound copy of his first book before he plunged wholeheartedly into his second, he had prolonged his vacation by spending eight days with the Shaws in Boston, where Helen was visiting and where Herman could appear, for the first time since his childhood days, with an air of assurance. As an author who was soon to become a public figure, he had acknowledged, both at home and abroad, his family's indebtedness to Judge Shaw by dedicating the book to his brother's most consistent benefactor; and his new self-confidence was a revelation both to the judge and to his daughter, Elizabeth, who was then twenty-three and had probably been curious for several years about Helen's wandering brother. On the twelfth, he returned with Helen to Lansingburgh and awaited copies of the American edition of *Typee* which reached him, two days after publication, a week later.

The book was to be a success. The favorable notices from the English press were already beginning to arrive by steamer, and complimentary notices of the American edition were soon to appear, although anonymously, from the pens of such well-known literary figures as Nathaniel Hawthorne, Charles Fenno Hoffman, Margaret Fuller, and George Ripley, and from the yet relatively unknown Walt Whitman. The first American edition was of only two thousand copies, but it was well promoted and selling at a rate which threatened to exhaust it within a couple of months. In addition to his public review, Hawthorne spoke well of the book in private; and, in Craigie House at Cambridge, Professor and Mrs. Longfellow were charmed as they read it to each other in the evening. Some reviewers were skeptical of the author's complete veracity and others were offended by his treatment of the missionaries, but, on the whole, the objections to it were of the sort that get a book talked about and consequently read. Melville was not only well launched, but in the words which N. P. Willis had applied to James Russell Lowell several years before, he was one of the "best launched" authors of his time.

Yet he could not have had very easy sailing with his second book, which seems to have been written at intervals between interruptions of almost every possible sort. His younger brother, Tom, shipped out to the Pacific so soon after his sixteenth birthday that a close friend of the family could later make the mistake of saying that he sailed at the age of fifteen; and a month after the publication of *Typee* there arrived the disturbing letter from Gansevoort in which the older brother expressed his worries about his health and his debts and revealed his apprehension of approaching death. John Wiley, the senior member and American manager of the publishing firm which brought out *Typee,* was worried about the raciness of the book and also about the serious criticism of the missionaries; and instead of simply bringing out a new edition from the original plates, he was insisting that the author revise and rewrite sections of it—a procedure which not only involved Melville in problems of judgment but made extra demands upon his time for proofreading and also cut into his anticipated profits. John Murray in England continued to be disturbed by the skepticism of reviewers and was pressing the author for documentary evidence of the fact that he had actually visited the Pacific, and other letters from England kept the entire Melville family distressed about Gansevoort's condition. On May 13 President Polk declared that a state of war existed between the United States and Mexico and set the village of Lansingburgh in "a state of delirium" with apprentice-boys leaving the factories by scores while the people left behind talked of nothing but the "Halls of the Montezumas." In the midst of all this excitement, Augusta was asked to be a bridesmaid in the wedding of a Miss Van Rensselaer and the Melville household turned busily to dressmaking. The atmosphere was hardly productive of easy literary composition.

Herman was sufficiently disturbed by the doubts cast upon the genuineness of his narrative to prepare an anonymous article in its defense and send it to Alexander Bradford on May 23 for possible publication in the *Morning Courier and New York Enquirer,* which had been particularly obnoxious in a review of April 17. But he remained detached from the other disturbances and reported on the Mexican excitement, locally and in Washington, in the same irreverent spirit he was using in his book to describe the relations of the sailors of the *Julia* and the authorities at Tahiti. During the early part of June, however, he became completely involved in problems unrelated to the adventures of "Omoo." For on the fourth of that month the news of Gansevoort's death reached Lansingburgh, and the family had to face not only their own shock and grief but Maria's distraction at the loss of her favorite son and their inability to meet the expenses incidental to bringing his body home for burial in Albany. Herman took over the responsibility by writing directly to the president, the secretary of state, and the secretary of war, and by getting friends to write in a successful effort to have the government pay the funeral expenses; and on June 17 he went to New York in order to await the body, which arrived on the packet ship *Prince Albert* on the twenty-sixth and was brought to Albany overnight for a funeral from the home of Peter Gansevoort on the afternoon of the following day.

During his stay in New York Melville had been further disturbed by the skepticism of Evert Duyckinck, Wiley and Putnam's editor, concerning *Typee;* and the sadness of his mission was probably deepened by a discouraging fear that his own promising career might be cut short by the growing opinion that he was a romancer rather than a historian of his own experiences. On the night of July 2, however, his spirits rose again when he received a copy of the Buffalo *Commercial Advertiser* dated the day before which contained a letter from Richard Tobias Greene asserting that "the true and veritable 'Toby' " was alive and "happy to testify to the entire accuracy of the work" in the parts describing the adventures in which he had participated. Melville immediately wrote to his former companion and on the next day composed a gloating letter to Duyckinck, proposing that the communication from Toby should be widely circulated and that a sequel to *Typee,* dealing with his friend's later adventures, be incorporated in the yet-unpublished second edition of the book. Within a week he was in New York, where he collected an advance of a hundred and fifty dollars (which was almost twice as much as the first edition earned) from his publishers, listened carefully to Wiley's criticisms and suggestions for revisions, and made plans to go to Buffalo for a full account of Toby's adventures. During the two weeks following his departure from New York on the evening of the fifteenth he was a busy man, visiting Buffalo and getting Toby's full story (along with a lock of his hair), writing up the "Sequel," and returning to New York on the twenty-seventh for an overnight stay and a discussion of the finished plans for the revised or expurgated edition of the book which was published in the early fall. He also found time to sell "The Story of Toby" to John Murray for fifty pounds and to try to persuade him that an expurgated edition might be profitable in England. *Omoo* could have made little progress during June, July, or August.

The next three months, however, were months of steady, efficient, and happy work. The departure of Tom had given him a room of his own in which he could write without interruption from early morning until the approach of darkness, and the arrival of Elizabeth Shaw on the last day of August for a two-months' visit enlivened the household and gave Herman someone new to impress. His imagination worked more freely with real materials than it had in his first narrative, and he was able to preserve his role of the adventurous hero with less of the sharp alternation between facts and fancies than had been characteristic of his first book. The greater part of *Omoo* was neither exactly fact nor pure invention: it was a convincing narrative of what might have been had the runaway Melville been a little more bold and a little more carefree than he actually was. If he had been more active in the mutiny on board the *Lucy Ann,* he might have played the role he attributed to himself on the *Julia* and, consequently, really would have been sent in irons aboard *La Reine Blanche* and kept in the native calaboose as long as he indicated. Or, if he had stayed for two months instead of two weeks on the island of Eimeo, he could have had experiences very much like those he described. He had developed a practiced yarn spinner's unwillingness to let his audience suffer from the inadequacies of the material from which his stories were made, and his consideration for readers accustomed to Smollett, Captain Marryat, and the early Dickens pervaded his book. He not only improved upon his own adventures but resurrected the real characters in the story from the shadowland of memory and painted them in bold strokes of comedy or villainy. Dr. Long Ghost, in particular, stalked and scampered through the written pages as though he had stepped out of an illustration by George Cruikshank rather than Melville's recollections.

But an exaggerated re-creation of his own experiences could not provide Melville with all the material he needed for his book. As he had killed off two entirely fictitious members of the *Julia*'s crew in order to paint a strong picture of conditions leading up to the mutiny, so he borrowed from other books—especially the *Polynesian Researches* of William Ellis —details and incidents which would make his writing vivid and satisfy the kind of curiosity which made people buy travel books. He confessed to his publisher that he had borrowed from his experiences in the Marquesas the native dance which he transferred to the village of "Tamai," but he did not at any time confess the extent of his indebtedness to written sources for such matters as the details of the bullock hunt, the observations and encounters described during the journey to "Partoowye," and most of the scenes and incidents associated with that village. He seems to have been obliged, in fact, to scrabble hard through his source material during the late fall, for the evidence suggests that he had to work twice through the *Polynesian Researches* in order to extend his own book to its proper length. Without the unconscious help of the missionary, William Ellis, *Omoo* might never have been finished.

Yet *Omoo* was more severe on the missionaries than *Typee* had been, for, as Evert Duyckinck wrote his brother George, Melville owed them "a sailor's grudge," which he paid off in his accounts of Tahiti. He was not willing to pay it off, however, at any considerable expense to himself, and on the day after Thanksgiving he brought the completed manuscript to New York and left it there for criticism while he went up to Boston for a ten-day visit with the Shaws. The criticism was apparently severe, for after picking it up on December 8 he wrote Duyckinck for advice (addressing him as a friend rather than as a reader for Wiley and Putnam) and spent two days meditating revisions of his remarks concerning the missions and the conditions of the natives. The result was that he decided to reject three of the earlier chapters entirely and begged Duyckinck "to pay particular attention" to eight others which he wanted to retain in one form or another. The questionable chapters were those numbered thirty-three and thirty-four and forty-five to fifty in the original version of the book, and, of these, the first and the last two seem to have bothered him especially. Since the book finally proved too strong for the agitated conscience of John Wiley and was actually published by the Harpers, it is impossible to determine the extent to which it was expurgated before publication and whether the three early chapters (originally numbered five, seven, and seventeen) were really suppressed. But some changes were evidently made, for Melville's references to the questionable sections do not apply precisely to the chapters bearing those numbers in the printed book. His tender regard for a publisher's sense of the proprieties proved unnecessary in dealing with the Harpers, and a week before Christmas he signed an agreement for the publication of *Omoo* at half profits with the privilege of bringing it out first in England.

Arrangements were made for sending the manuscript to press promptly after the holidays, and on December 30 Melville was able to write John Romeyn Brodhead, of the American ministry in London, asking him to serve as his agent and promising to send by steamer on February 1 the proof sheets from which the English edition was to be printed. During the interval he may have begun another story of his South Sea adventures, using some of the impressions derived from his experiences in whaling; but, if he did, he was obliged to put his efforts aside at the end of January in order to go to New York, look over the proof sheets for *Omoo,* write a Preface (which he dated January 28, 1847), make preliminary arrangements for the American copyright, and send the completed work and his power of attorney to Brodhead. After some delay in the English customs, the sheets reached Brodhead on February 20 and were immediately delivered to John Murray. Murray expressed himself six days later as being much pleased with the new book, which he found "full of talent and interest," although lacking the novelty of *Typee.* He offered £150 for it—two-thirds by note eight months after the date of publication, April 1, and the remainder by check four months later. But Melville, as always, was anxious for cash, and the final arrangement was for £144–3–4, of which Melville drew £140 on March 31, allowing his agent the odd sum for expenses. The Harpers brought out the American edition within a few weeks after the English publication, giving the author an advance of $400.00, and by early May Melville was in a fairly prosperous condition. He had received more money from his new book than his friend Duyckinck was to receive for a whole year of weekly editorial contributions to the new periodical, *The Literary World;* he had good expectations from the revised editions of *Typee;* and he had an opportunity to earn a small sum by lecturing on his South Sea adventures and from occasional contributions to his friend's magazine.

But, curiously enough, at the time he was anticipating this prosperity and actually expecting more from *Omoo* than he ever got, he was making an energetic effort to find some other means of livelihood. For when he took up his pen immediately after sending off the proof sheets of *Omoo* it was not to begin work again on his third book but to try to get a government job as a clerk in the Treasury Department at Washington. On February 3 he wrote his politically influential uncle in Albany, Peter Gansevoort, saying that he had already "obtained several strong letters from various prominent persons here to the most influential men at the seat of government" and requesting an additional letter to Senator John A. Dix. The next day, without waiting to hear from his uncle, he set out for Washington, where he made a favorable impression upon General and Mrs. Dix but found that the new loan bill provided fewer new offices than the rumors in New York indicated. His hopes were crushed and all he got out of his trip was a sight of the Senate in action and the feeling of wholehearted contempt for politicians of which he was to make literary use later.

The most probable reason for Melville's abortive attempt to obtain a salaried job at precisely the time when he might normally have been expected to be most enthusiastic about continuing his literary career was that he was thinking of getting married. Soon after he had returned from his visit to the Shaws during the preceding December he had ordered an expensive copy of James Andrews' elaborately illustrated *Floral Tableaux,* possibly as a Christmas present for Elizabeth, and if he did not become formally engaged to her during this visit his intentions were almost certainly known by the time of his next trip to Boston in early March. After all his experience with the Melvilles' improvidence, Judge Shaw could hardly have looked with enthusiasm upon his only daughter's financial dependence upon a young man who was both a Melville and an author; and Herman may have thought it wise to have both a substantial amount of cash on hand and a steady job before proposing a wedding date. Marriage, in any event, would involve furnishing if not buying a house, and he could not undertake to do that and also expect to live on his publishers' advances until he could finish another book. His immediate prospects were hardly substantial enough to sustain a cautious man's hopes of marital happiness, and, under the circumstances, he was willing enough to settle down on the federal government if the occasion permitted.

When the occasion failed, however, he was ready to take up literature again with at least an external show of enthusiasm, writing to his English publisher that if *Omoo* succeeded he would immediately follow it up with something else; and on July 30 he allowed the Lansingburgh *Gazette* to announce that he had in preparation another book of adventures in the South Seas. A review of J. Ross Browne's *Etchings of a Whaling Cruise* and Captain Ringbolt's *Sailor's Life and Sailor's Yarns,* which he had written for the *Literary World* of March 6, after returning from Washington, had given him ideas for a new work. For Browne's book had dealt in detail with life on board a whaling vessel, deriving narrative continuity from the voyage itself, yet had failed to achieve any of the romantic interest which Melville had so successfully introduced into his books and which he also associated with whaling. He could go ahead with what he had half promised at the end of *Omoo* and what some reviewers of that book were led to expect—an account of a whaling cruise through the southern Pacific and off the coast of Japan. He would have to depend heavily upon literary sources, but the essence of his book would be derived from his own experiences and it would not be wholly different from its predecessors. He could also set up housekeeping in New York City at a relatively modest expense, for Allan had been courting a Bond Street beauty named Sophia Thurston, and the two brothers had thought of buying a house large enough for themselves and their brides and for their mother and four sisters. Such an arrangement would provide their mother with the companionship of her sons, enlarge the social opportunities of the unmarried daughters, give Herman a secure place in which to write, and perhaps save money for them all. The young author had definite plans, if not a regular job, when he arrived in Boston on the first of June to settle the date of his wedding.

III

However definite Melville may have been able to make his plans sound as he discussed them with his prospective father-in-law during the first week of June, 1847, he was uncertain in his mind about his new book and finding it difficult to focus his attention upon it. Although a record has been preserved of less than a quarter of his book purchases through Wiley and Putnam and only slightly more of those made through the Harpers, a fairly good indication of his interests may be found in the fragmentary material which has survived. When he first began charging books against his *Typee* account in the late summer of 1846, they were of the sort that were most probably intended as gifts: Cowper's *Poems* on August 28, perhaps as a delayed birthday present for Augusta, and Martin F. Tupper's *Proverbial Philosophy* in September. His next purchases, of December 12, were partly of the same sort: *The Recreation: A Gift Book for Young Readers* might well have accompanied the *Floral Tableaux* to Boston as a gift to Elizabeth's younger brother, Sam. But his purchase at the same time of Bayard Taylor's *Views Afoot* and the annual English "year book of adventure" *Curiosities of Modern Travel* may have reflected his own desire to keep informed of what was popular in his own literary field, and when he bought Waddy Thompson's *Recollections of Mexico* on December 30 he was certainly indicating more interest in the Mexican War than he had shown at its outbreak. At some time during the year his uncle Herman, whose financial troubles had evidently aroused such sympathy that his namesake tried to cheer him up by dedicating *Omoo* to him, gave him a copy of Ephraim Chambers' curious *Cyclopaedia: or, an Universal Dictionary of Arts and Sciences* (which had been published in 1728); and early in the following spring he picked up, in a secondhand bookstore, a volume of selections from Burton's even more curious *Anatomy of Melancholy* without noticing at the time that it had once belonged to his father. When he began to think of his own new work, his interests were clearly divided among such different subjects as popular travel literature, contemporary political events, and somewhat antiquarian literary curiosities.

Such varied interests would naturally have been encouraged by his growing friendship with Evert Duyckinck, whose library at No. 20 Clinton Street was well stocked with "old books" that he enjoyed lending to a sympathetic reader, whose brother George was traveling in Europe and writing home about current events, and whose numerous friends were given to animated conversation on literature and politics. Yet at the time that he picked up his copy of Burton, on April 10, 1847, Melville seems to have been determined to restrict his reading almost entirely to books that would be useful to the literary project to which he had committed himself after his disappointing trip to Washington and his visit to Boston in March. His first orders against his new account with the Harpers were for a copy of Webster's Dictionary (which was his new publishers' standard of orthography), three volumes of Pacific voyages (Benjamin Morrell's *Narrative of Four Voyages,* Thomas J. Jacobs' *Scenes, Incidents, and Adventures in the Pacific Ocean,* and Charles Darwin's *Journal of Researches . . . during the Voyage of HMS Beagle around*

the World), and three unnamed volumes of the Harpers' Family Library
(which included a considerable amount of travel literature). A week
later he spent twenty-one dollars, or almost three times the amount of
the balance due him in January, with Wiley and Putnam for the six
volumes of Wilkes's account of *The U.S. Exploring Expedition in the
South Pacific,* and on May 7 he added Reynolds' *Voyage of the U.S.
Frigate Potomac* to his growing library by a purchase from the Harpers.
At the time that he bought most of these books he may have been engaged in writing the adventurous opening chapters of his new story and,
not yet having planned to settle in New York where a good library would
be available to him, was simply investing in the material necessary for
filling out the bare outline of his remaining adventures as a whaler.

He had good reason to continue writing along that line, for the first
edition of some three thousand copies of *Omoo,* which had made its
appearance by the first of May, was selling out rapidly, a new printing
was being planned, and, according to literary gossip, its success was
"carrying off" large quantities of *Typee.* Both books were soon to be
vehemently attacked by religious journals with some assistance from the
Whig newspapers, but Melville seems to have been less sensitive to
suspicions of prejudice than he was to charges of romancing; and he let
John Wiley worry about the unsuccessful attempt to please Mrs. Grundy
with the revised edition of *Typee* while he accepted the compliment of a
translation of that book into German and enjoyed its increased American
sales. He could not have put much uninterrupted work on his new book
after settling upon August 4 as his wedding day, however, for although
he was back in Lansingburgh by the tenth of June, getting his mother's
garden in shape by hoeing the young corn and tomatoes, he returned to
Boston in early July for the social affairs that necessarily preceded an important wedding in the Athens of America. There he met Richard Henry
Dana, Jr., whose *Two Years Before the Mast* had affected him very much
as his own story had affected his brother Tom; and he reached New York
on the eleventh in high spirits, ready once more to talk over plans with
Evert Duyckinck (who had lost the editorship of the *Literary World* on
the first of May) and to meet professionally with Duyckinck's friend,
Cornelius Mathews, who had recently taken over the comic weekly
Yankee Doodle.

As a result of the meeting, after some discussion of a possible article
on the sea serpent and of a woodcut of Buena Vista Alley in the July number of *Yankee Doodle,* Melville undertook to do a series of humorous
articles on General Zachary Taylor; and he composed at least several of
his nine "Authentic Anecdotes of 'Old Zack' " (which were to appear
in seven installments from July 24 to September 11) between July 14

and 19, when he collected $150.00 from Wiley and Putnam and left for Lansingburgh. At home he accompanied his mother on a hasty visit to his uncle Herman in Saratoga County, where they spent the nights of July 21 and 22, and completed all but perhaps one of his spirited satires while his sisters fluttered over preparations for his wedding. As descriptions by a born and bred Democrat of a prospective Whig candidate for the presidency, the articles were surprisingly good-natured; for they made the general seem like a character from the Knickerbocker History of New York and evidently disappointed Evert Duyckinck, who, after dining with Melville at the Astor House on July 31, tempered his customary admiration for his friend's writing by observing that he was "cheerful company but not very . . . original and models his writing a great deal on that of Washington Irving." In New York he collected a balance of $16.71 due him from Wiley and Putnam on his *Typee* account and received a statement from the Harpers showing that he had $294.59 coming to him from *Omoo* in addition to his advance of $400.00 and his book orders of $24.20. Although he could not call himself well-to-do, he was prepared for a honeymoon free from financial troubles when he took the overnight boat for home in order to spend his twenty-eighth birthday with his family before escorting his mother and two of his sisters, Helen and Fanny, to Boston by train on August 2.

The wedding day was unusually pleasant for Boston in August. The bride received the present of a Bible from Herman's aunt Lucy, who was much better acquainted with Elizabeth than she was with her nephew, and Communion from the Reverend James Freeman Clarke. The groom took a walk and discovered a four-leaf clover which was to remain in his mind for over forty years as a happy augury of the occasion. Various other Melvilles and friends of the two families gathered for the ceremony, which was performed by the Reverend Dr. Young; and the reception provided more cake than the thirteen-year-old Samuel Shaw, buttoned up in a new blue jacket, could eat. Afterward the couple departed by train for the northern terminus of the railroad and a leisurely trip by stage and boat through New Hampshire and Canada.

Their wedding journey, aside from the normal physical discomforts of traveling, was apparently an entirely happy one, with stops at Concord, Center Harbor, Conway, and Mount Washington before continuing into Canada. Montreal pleased Elizabeth with its foreign air, and with the convents, cathedral, and government buildings they visited two weeks after the wedding; but Quebec struck her as cold, forbidding, and comfortless, and its general appearance and military atmosphere reminded Herman of a man-of-war. The chateau in which they were staying, although it offered the best accommodations in the city, depressed her with its rambling structure and tawdry decorations, and the English officers who made up most of the company at table were disturbing in their lack of refinement. It was raining, moreover, during most of their stay, and they were forced to inspect the Plains of Abraham between showers, miss seeing the falls of Montmorency, and drive themselves to see the Indian village of Lorette only by their determination to see as much as possible before they left. They were not sorry to leave Canada and hurry home, going by stage through the scenery of Vermont and taking an overnight canalboat from Whitehall to within an hour's ride by cars to Lansingburgh, which they reached on August 28. The tribulations of the last night, sitting on the crowded deck and bobbing her head at every cry of "Low bridge!" until the chill and damp forced her into the cramped and suffocating "Ladies' Saloon" below, left Elizabeth a little shaken and vague about the day of the month, even after a day of rest and recovery. But neither she nor Herman seemed to have any worries about the future as they waited for Allan to find a proper house in which they could all move after his wedding in September.

The fashionable marriage of Allan and Sophia, on the evening of September 22, impressed the Melvilles' Pittsfield cousin Priscilla as being less certainly the outcome of an "ethereal" love bearing them *"upward, towards a heavenly Paradise"* than was Herman's and Lizzie's; but it did mark the end of Maria's long exile from the metropolis and the beginning of an opportunity for Herman to develop the intellectual qualities which had been awakened in him in Honolulu and of which he himself had been conscious since he returned home and commenced writing. The house which the two brothers obtained was at 103 Fourth Avenue, in the neighborhood of the Duyckincks'; and Margaret and Evert Duyckinck made themselves the hospitable center of one of the several coteries which were then engaged in making New York the rival of Boston as the literary capital of the United States. Melville was welcomed as a regular member of the group, and Duyckinck was also impressed by the kindness and "softness" of Augusta in comparison with the New York literary ladies who shared her admiration for her brother's work. The household arrangements promised to be happy, and Herman, with no chores to do and with a lawyer in residence to attend to his business affairs, was free for the first time in his life to cultivate a routine which would lead to a professional efficiency in composition.

During the first bustle of settling down, however, Melville probably did more reading than writing. The furniture from Lansingburgh was moved down and distributed, Elizabeth had the furnishings of her own room sent from Boston, and Allan and his bride put their living quarters in order while the ex-adventurer of the cannibal isles entertained himself with the works of other voyagers whose experiences he was trying to make his own. On the evening of October 6, he accompanied Duyckinck to the brilliant opening of the new hall for the Art Union, where he met William Cullen Bryant and an assortment of other literary men and artists; and he apparently began to develop the habit of dropping in upon his friend for a brief call when he was out walking. Despite having two rooms to themselves and perhaps more formal privacy than they were accustomed to, neither Herman nor Elizabeth found it easy to become adjusted to their new routine, although they were both so conscientious in their efforts to do so that they were willing to spare only a few days in order to spend Thanksgiving with Elizabeth's parents in Boston.

The routine, as it was finally worked out and described by Elizabeth in a letter to her mother two days before Christmas, permitted Herman six uninterrupted hours a day for writing. The family had breakfast at eight, after which Herman took a brief walk while Elizabeth hurried to straighten out his room so that he could have four peaceful hours before luncheon at half past twelve. Another walk of at least an hour, with Elizabeth, followed; and two more hours of writing occupied his time until the dinner bell sounded at four. After dinner they had an hour or so together in their own room, where Herman often tried out his day's composition by reading it aloud before taking a turn downtown for a glance at the papers in a public reading room and perhaps a bit of masculine conversation before his return at seven-thirty or eight. His eyes permitted him to do little work of any sort, reading or writing, by candlelight; and the whole household usually gathered in the parlor during the evening for conversation, cards, or family reading until they all retired at ten.

There must have been times when Herman thought that he needed only a tot of grog before breakfast and a hammock to stow away in order to feel himself back on the U.S. frigate *United States* with its long fasts between crowded meals, its congregated living enlivened by a free dogwatch, and its contrasts between solitude in the maintop and supervised conduct below. But Elizabeth, in strange and wholly unaccustomed surroundings, was the one to become most restive; and her account of the routine may have actually been an exaggeration based upon the normal feelings of a homesick girl on the eve of her first Christmas holiday away from her brothers and parents. Her sole housekeeping responsibilities during the long hours of Herman's morning labors were for her room, and when he returned to his desk in the afternoon she had nothing to do except make herself "look as bewitchingly as possible" to meet him at dinner. The entire household revolved around Maria, and Elizabeth's position was that of no more than a satellite revolving around Herman. The occasions which required her to take a more planetary position in the

social life of the Melvilles offered her no recreation, for her tastes were
plain and the politeness of Herman and Allan's friends—not to speak of
Mrs. Melville's old acquaintances—was almost more than the daughter
of the chief justice of Massachusetts could endure. She grew "sick and
tired" of the afternoons spent in returning calls which led only to more
calls that had to be returned. Even the prospect of a trip to the opera with
Herman and Fanny to hear Ferdinando Beneventano in *Lucia di Lammermoor* on Christmas Eve, although it meant her first visit to a place of
public amusement in the three months she had spent in New York, left
her listless. Nevertheless, she kept a bright face toward her husband, who
was beginning to suspect that she needed entertaining, and with more
understanding than might be expected of a young bride encouraged him
to keep his mind on his work.

Under such circumstances Herman had little positive intellectual development. His brief evening visits to the reading room or to the Duyckincks'
home stimulated his mind without giving him an opportunity to work
off that stimulation; and the occasional full evenings that he spent in
company at his friend's house were likely to be devoted to such practical
matters as the failure of *Yankee Doodle* to pay either its editor or the
contributor of the "Old Zack" articles or to the possibility of starting a
new weekly newspaper which he, Mathews, and Duyckinck talked over
on the evening of October 23. A new friend, Dr. Augustus Kinsley Gardner, with literary interests, a store of curious information, and an original
inquisitiveness about medical and other scientific matters, was perhaps the
most stimulating of all the young author's acquaintances at the time; and
he, with other literary lights that flickered in the Duyckinck circle, kept
Melville's mind in a state of excitement too strong to be relieved in a
simple whaling story.

But the routine had to be preserved. Elizabeth had a small income for
personal expenses derived from a wedding gift of three thousand dollars
placed in trust for her by Judge Shaw, but Herman's financial situation
was once again growing precarious. Two months after his marriage he
drew a bill of exchange upon his father-in-law for two thousand dollars to
be used for the purchase of the New York house, but only half the amount
was actually devoted to that purpose. John Murray had written him
bluntly on December 3 that he had not yet made expenses on the first
two books and consequently indicated that the author could have no
immediate expectations of a share in their "profits." He had only $154.36
coming to him on the first of the year from Wiley and Putnam and only
$102.63 due him a month later from the Harpers. Before his new book
appeared it was not impossible that he might fall in arrears for his share
of the household expenses or be embarrassed by interest payments and

ground rents. Under the circumstances, the least he could do was to restrain the impulses toward mental give-and-take which normally accompany intellectual growth and put all of his energy into his book while keeping a working schedule comparable to Allan's in his new office in Wall Street.

The result was that by the beginning of 1848 Melville had a large intake of new ideas and intellectual energy but only a restricted outlet for their expression. Circumstances and his own conscience combined to bottle up his mental activity and cause it to ferment in the curious but not unnatural way which was to be revealed in the slow growth of his new book—a growth which was less a reflection of the development of a professional author than of the progress of an individual in the world of the mind. Without the stimulus which New York continued to provide, it would not have occurred; but without the restraints placed upon that stimulus, it would not have been so clearly revealed in a single book. The long work which was eventually to be called *Mardi* was to have literary faults in plenty and was to be a puzzling disappointment to most of its contemporary readers. But it was also to become one of the most interesting of all documents in the life of a man who changed, in the course of three short years, from a popular writer exploiting the novelty of his own experiences into one of the most stimulating inhabitants of the complex world of the nineteenth-century mind. If Melville had at last succeeded, perhaps better than he desired, in settling down, he settled under conditions which forced his intellectual growth.

6

The World of the Mind

I

MELVILLE COULD have done little coherent work on the book which was
to become *Mardi* when, on the last day of March, 1847, he promised his
English publisher a sequel to *Omoo*. But he was certainly making preparations to fulfill his promise when he began to collect a personal library of
voyage literature ten days later. His critical reading of J. Ross Browne's
Etchings of a Whaling Cruise in the light of his own literary accomplishment was an undoubted challenge to him; and if he had any doubts of
his ability to meet that challenge the long review of *Omoo* in *Blackwood's
Magazine* for June (which anticipated a continuation dealing with a
whaling cruise to Japan) encouraged him to let his home-town newspaper announce that he was actually "preparing for the press another book
of adventures in the South Seas." None of his early plans seems to have
been for a book which would be, in any way, more intellectual in quality
than *Typee* or *Omoo* had been. He simply hoped to put together a

spirited series of adventures which would be partly based upon his own experiences and partly derived from the volumes he was collecting.

When he began systematic work upon it in October he had not changed his plans. He described its relation to *Omoo,* during the latter part of that month, precisely as he had earlier described the relationship of *Omoo* to *Typee*—that is, as a continuation of the preceding story, yet wholly independent of it. He evidently had made fairly definite narrative plans by this time, for he hoped to be through with the book before the end of the following spring, or by autumn at the latest, and was primarily concerned with the form in which it should be published. The Harpers had succeeded in selling *Omoo* at a higher price than Wiley and Putnam had charged for *Typee,* with a corresponding increase in profits; and Melville hoped that Murray might do the same with the English edition of his third book, publishing the first edition at least in an expensive format and perhaps reprinting it in the cheap Home and Colonial Library form later. His reasons for the suggestion were entirely economic. He gave no indication that his book would be an inappropriate addition to Murray's collection of factual narratives; and five months later, when his plans had changed radically, he wrote that *Mardi* had first been undertaken as a bona fide continuation of *Omoo.*

The first important change in his plans apparently occurred during the last two months of 1847, for on New Year's Day he wrote Murray that the design he was then pursuing clothed his whole subject in new attractions which included all that was romantic, whimsical, and poetic in Polynesia. He was still on the verge of claiming that it was an authentic narrative but, on second thought, merely called it a continuous one. Although some of the early chapters were later revised, or even written and inserted in their entirety, he had probably progressed at this time through the straight adventure sections of the finished work and was becoming involved in the romantic rescue of the fair maiden, Yillah, and the flower allegory with which he decorated his poetic account of a hero's Endymion-like pursuit of an ideal which was half symbol and half dream. Yillah, as a character, was inspired by the heroine of one of the most popular German romances of the time—La Motte-Fouqué's *Undine,* which Lemuel Shaw had borrowed from the Boston Athenaeum during the preceding March. She may not have acquired her name and her flower symbol, however, until after Melville had purchased Philip P. Cooke's *Froissart Ballads* on December 2 and read Cooke's poem "To My Daughter Lily" after being reminded in *Undine* by the Proem to that volume.

One reason for the new development, of course, was the simple fact that he was accustomed to spinning his yarns out into a continuous line of adventure which was basically true, and without the guiding power of memory his invention got out of hand and began to approach fantasy. But the major reason why his fantasy took the form it first did was that his only consistent partner in intellectual communication during his cold winter of writing in a fireless room was Elizabeth. Her interest in flower symbolism formed a private bond between them, and, with the natural tendency of the imagination to work along some line of communication, Herman addressed perhaps more of his book than he realized to the girl who shared his hopes for it, kept his inkwell filled and his paper in order, and prized the hour at the end of the day when he would read the result of his labors aloud to her. The gently enthusiastic Augusta also became the confidante of his efforts, and the genuine interest of the two girls (who alone, apparently, among all his friends and relations, knew precisely what he was doing that winter) led his invention through the romantic allegory which he substituted for personal experience as the narrative thread on which he strung the incidents of his book.

How much of the "meaning" of *Mardi* was determined by Herman's intimacy with Elizabeth, of course, cannot be discovered. But much of it evidently was. He and his fiancée had probably read both *Undine* and its companion piece, *Sintram and His Companions,* together before their marriage; and the continued allegory of the story was made up of suggestions derived from these two German romances, from Spenser's *Faerie Queene,* and from Elizabeth's books of flower symbolism. As a romantic heroine and the object of an adventurous quest, Yillah resembles the heroines of Keats's *Endymion,* Shelley's *Alastor,* and Byron's *The Island;* but the details of her watery background, her rescue from a heartless old man, and her mysterious disappearance make her more akin to the sentimental German's water sprite than to the fair maidens of the English poets. The flower symbolism of the quest shows that Melville conceived of it as a search for pure and ideal happiness during which the searcher was beset by the attractions of sensuality personified by the cold and heartless beauty of a haughty female resembling the seductive Acrasia of the *Faerie Queene.* And the contrast between the two characters— Yillah and Hautia, ideal and temptress—was the sort of contrast that Spenser liked to draw in such allegorical representations as Fidessa and Duessa or the true and the false Florimel. But the hero of Melville's romance, like La Motte-Fouqué's Sintram, was pursued by the symbols of death and revenge as well as by the temptations of sensuality; and, although there are Byronic and Coleridgean overtones of crime and retribution in this pursuit, the whole pattern of "the pursuers and the pursued" appears to be derived from the two romances which Melville read at a time when he was peculiarly susceptible to the sort of sentiment they reflected.

A number of incidental passages, such as an early comment upon the strength of the marriage bonds and a later allusion to Elizabeth's pregnancy, indicate that Melville was communicating more to his bride than he ever expected the public to understand. But he was reading too much and his mind was developing too rapidly during the early part of 1848 for him to be content with sentiment—even of a high moral sort. The whimsicalities of Robert Burton had probably already begun to creep into his manuscript by the time he decided he needed a complete edition of the *Anatomy of Melancholy* on February 8, 1848; and at about the same time he began to borrow the works of Sir Thomas Browne and Rabelais from Duyckinck's library, delighting his friend with such a display of interest in "old books." The new stimulation which came from reading of this sort, channeled as it was into the narrow outlet of his own writing, inevitably caused the book to overflow the boundaries of ordinary coherence or simple fantasy. He had a lot of time for meditation during his walks, during the evening gatherings of the family when he had a literary license to stay out of the conversation, and during the long hours set aside for repose; and his meditations often seem to have taken the form of what he might say if he were a "crack'd archangel" in prose or a pursuer of vulgar errors like Sir Thomas Browne, an avid collector of antique lore like Burton, or a man of grotesque and sardonic exaggerations after the fashion of Rabelais.

Other reading added strength and variety to these meditative impulses. He had bought a membership in the New York Society Library from the absent George Duyckinck on January 17, 1848, and on the same day withdrew Louis de Bougainville's account of *A Voyage around the World* made some eighty years before and Davis Hartley's empirical *Observations on Man: His Frame, His Duty, and His Expectations* with a volume of notes and additions translated from the German of Herman Andrew Pistorius. On the eighteenth, he bought for his personal library an edition of Shakespeare and one of Montaigne from John Wiley, and on February 8 obtained from the same source a copy of Defoe's *Roxana* and Coleridge's *Biographia Literaria,* in addition to the complete edition of Burton's *Anatomy of Melancholy.* To these he added on June 22 a copy of Cary's translation of Dante's *Divine Comedy* (to which he had probably been attracted by an introductory note to Philip P. Cooke's translation of the Ugolino story in the *Froissart Ballads*), and at some undetermined time during the year, James Macpherson's *Fingal, An Ancient Epic Poem* (which particularly impressed him by its melancholy and pathos) and Roger L'Estrange's version of Seneca's *Morals by Way of Abstract.* Other important literary acquisitions of the period are unrecorded, but he evidently had at hand while writing *Mardi* at least one additional major source of information about the whaling industry, Frederick Debell Bennett's *Narrative of a Whaling Voyage Around the Globe,* and his book reveals a general if perhaps secondhand interest in philosophy and philosophers ranging from Aristotle to Spinoza, Priestley, and Kant.

He could not express the thoughts inspired by such reading in the character of his sailor hero, especially since the review in *Blackwood's Magazine* (which seems, in various ways, to have made a profound and lasting impression upon him) had found fault with *Omoo* because of the glaring inconsistencies existing between the character of a common sailor and one who displayed the literary sophistication of Melville; and so, in a spontaneous impulse to enlarge the outlet of his own mind, he changed the plan of his book once more by creating four fictitious characters who could relieve him of his artistic inhibitions. For the most important of these he wrapped Burton's Democritus Junior in "a voluminous robe," gave him Sir Thomas Browne's philosophical interest in vulgar errors and desire to pursue reason to an "O altitudo," and called him Babbalanja the talking philosopher. Another was a venerable antiquarian with a long braided beard, Mohi, a living encyclopaedia of miscellaneous information such as that collected by Ephraim Chambers, some of the voyagers, or William Ellis whose *Polynesian Researches* had contributed so much to *Omoo.* A third was a wan, romantic, long-haired poet, resembling Burton's "Inamorato" and sardonically called "Yoomy, or the Warbler," who interpreted the flower allegory and often served, with Mohi, as a foil for Babbalanja's philosophical observations. The fourth (or the first, in the order of their introduction) was King Media, who belied his royal estate and his position as a demigod by normally taking a plain common-sense point of view in the discussions which arose and who mediated the eccentricities of his companions. With these as vehicles for the expression of his unassorted ideas, Melville let his hero lose most of his character as a sailor, take on the mythological name Taji, and fall as far into the background as the requirements of first personal narration and a continued allegory would permit.

These were not the first entirely fictitious characters to be drawn by Melville's pen, for the Norseman Jarl and the Islanders Annatoo and Samoa in the early chapters of adventure appear to have had no basis in reality, but they were the first to whom he gave distinctive minds and individual modes of expression; and one of the most significantly personal revelations made by the author of *Mardi* may be found in the fact that he abandoned the characters created for physical action as soon as he developed a new group with active minds. Melville was losing interest in action supplemented by attacks upon bigotry and social abuse. Instead, he was beginning to indulge in speculative fancies, rhetorical exercises for their own sake, and whimsical representations of conflicting points of view. His book had taken flight from even the most tenuous of contacts with the solid ground of his physical experiences and was completely caught up in the whirl of his overstimulated but repressed mind. When it became a fantasy, a romance designed not to inform but entirely to entertain, he might have described it in the words of Robert Burton by saying that although he had just cause to point at "particular species of dotage that men might acknowledge their imperfections and seek to reform what is amiss," yet he had "a more serious intent" of helping his readers avoid melancholy. In his solitary naïveté Melville aimed his third literary effort at a larger and more popular audience than his first two books had found.

Mardi had certainly taken on its uncontrolled, fantastic, and almost final character by March 25, 1848, when its author offered to supply Murray with the American proof sheets by the middle of July at the fanciful price of £150 for the first edition plus half profits of all future editions after expenses had been paid. The proposal to consider the advance payment to the author as an expense to be met before profits were figured (rather than as an advance against the author's share of the profits) might have strained the patience of a less friendly publisher than John Murray, but Melville was probably too self-centered in his financial problems and too typically an author by this time to consider the implications of his demand. His letter actually indicates little more than his naïveté and his evident determination that *Mardi* should be a popular book. In describing its virtues to Murray he spoke of it as an out-and-out romance in which he exercised the freedom and invention of a poet in dealing with rich material never before used in a work of fancy. As a story wild enough, although with a meaning too, it would demonstrate the actuality of *Typee* and *Omoo* by contrast. It did not occur to Melville that Murray was averse to publishing fiction of any sort, nor did he know that influential pressure was being brought on the English house to drop him from the Home and Colonial Library on the grounds that his books were not of the sort that "any mother would like to see in the hands of her daughters"; and it is good evidence of the American's high prestige abroad that Murray, in the light of his experience with the earlier books, his publishing policy, and the increasingly uncertain state of the copyright, should have remained willing to consider his book after receiving his preposterous letter.

In his enthusiasm for taking flight into the nebulous region of his whimsical fancies, Melville was making *Mardi* a preposterous book too. But he was also suffering from diversions which occupied his spare time, interfered with his writing schedule, and caused him to lose what little coherence he could achieve by meditation during the intervals between his stints at the desk. Elizabeth's brother, Lemuel Shaw, Jr., arrived in town on Thursday, January 27, and had to be entertained and shown the sights. Herman and Allan together took him to the top of the Trinity Church steeple on Friday morning and gave him a fine over-all view of the city, and that evening the family entertained a second Boston visitor in the person of Edmund Dana. On Saturday Herman took another day off from his work in order to show his young brother-in-law the spectacular new aqueduct bridge over the Harlem River before turning him over to Allan in the evening for "a great Democratic war meeting in Tammany Hall." Their activities for the next few days of what Elizabeth called a "very dissipated week, for us" are not on record, but Allan's mother-in-law on Bond Street entertained them on Wednesday evening, keeping them out "quite late," and on Thursday they went to a party and on Friday to hear *Lucrezia Borgia* at the Astor Place Opera House. Herman felt the strain of these interruptions of his normally quiet life, for, as Elizabeth wrote her mother, if he did not get a full night's rest or indulged in a late supper he did not "feel bright for writing the next day, and the days are too precious to be thrown away." Since neither cared much for parties, they resolved to return to their schedule as soon as Lemuel departed; but an elaborate Valentine party, given by Anne Lynch for a large group of artists and literati with individual Valentine verses composed by Bayard Taylor, tempted them out on the fourteenth, and Duyckinck's records of a long evening at whist and a visit of inspection to a new ship called the *Hermann* in March indicates that Melville did not settle completely into his old routine.

He continued optimistic about the "book in hand," however, for he was persuaded that more than one London publisher was making "very liberal offers" for it, and a proposal had been made to translate it immediately into German. *Omoo,* like *Typee,* had already been translated; and *Typee* had been issued in Dutch as well. His reputation was spreading, and in early March he felt sufficiently assured to try out a few chapters of *Mardi* on Evert Duyckinck, who wrote his brother George that it would "be ahead of *Typee* and *Omoo*" in "the poetry and wildness of the thing." It was the optimism inspired by what he considered the eagerness of English publishers for his work, the signs of a growing reputation on the Continent, and Duyckinck's interest in the chapters he had seen, perhaps, which caused him to write his curious letter to Murray in the latter part of the month. But there was some uncertainty in his mind, too, which caused him to explain himself too nervously and too much.

For it was just after he had pointed with pride to his ardent flight from dull commonplaces, apparently, that he began seriously to bring his work under control and devote more attention to a serious "meaning" which would make it different from the "dishwater" of a circulating library. He seems to have realized that his voyage into "the world of mind," as he put it in a chapter possibly written in early April or while his letter to Murray was still fresh in his mind, had been "chartless" and "though essaying but a sportive sail, I was driven from my course, by a blast resistless; and ill-provided, young, and bowed to the brunt of things before my prime, still fly before the gale." Yet he had striven hard "to keep stout heart"; and he had reached a decision: "So, if after all these fearful, fainting trances, the verdict be, the golden haven was not gained;—yet in bold quest thereof, better to sink in boundless deeps, than float on vulgar shoals; and give me, ye gods, an utter wreck, if wreck I do."

The depths into which he eventually plunged, as might have been expected of a young man whose most persistent opinions had hitherto dealt with the evil influences of missionary civilization upon a primitive people, were religious in their implications. He had already made a veiled attack upon institutionalized religion and the priestly profession in the religious allegory of the chapters dealing with the island of Maramma, representing the simple perceptions of the human heart as being superior to all orthodox teaching and hence intolerable to it. Through his characters, he had gone even further than he had dared to go in his own proper person by allowing his philosopher to disavow Christianity (symbolized as the religion of Alma) and by attributing to his poet the disillusioning discovery that the highest religious authority dwelt in an almost complete symbolic darkness. Later he had permitted Babbalanja to discover and impress his companions with a kind of primitive Christian morality in the writings of the "antique pagan" Seneca, but he made it clear that his philosopher found no real religious illumination; and, on the whole, his comments upon religious matters in the chapters written before his determination to go "sailing on" into deeper waters were little more than generalized expressions of the carping, uncertain primitivism he had displayed in *Typee* and *Omoo*. It is impossible to tell whether they reflected some positive belief based upon a philosophical attitude or whether they were merely negative criticisms based upon his empirical observations of religious institutions in operation.

Melville himself probably could not have told at the time, and he certainly did not take his plunge into positive opinions with any great enthusiasm. Before he did so, in fact, he returned to the fantastic satire of Thomas Taylor's translation of *The Six Books of Proclus on the Theology of Plato* which he had started in an earlier chapter on the gods of

Mardi and devoted several other chapters to attacks upon philosophical gibberish and ontological hairsplitting. He also digressed long enough to allow later readers to date the composition of this section of his manuscript when he "recited at length" a parody of the last will and testament of John Jacob Astor which had appeared in the New York *Herald* for April 5 and so amused Evert Duyckinck that he had commented upon it in a letter to George. Other digressions were to be inserted in this part of the book before it was published, but, in the early spring of 1848, Melville was anxious to fulfill his promise to give his book meaning and bring it to a rapid conclusion. The result was a section which—for modern readers, if not for the author's contemporaries—proved to be one of the most impressive parts of the Mardian allegory:

As his poet, his antiquarian, and especially his philosopher began to brood upon death, time, and eternity with a melancholy awareness of the impersonality of theology and the gloominess of religious doctrines, they were greeted by an aged messenger from the island of "Serenia" who held out to them the flower symbols of victory, immortality, and love. In their search for happiness the travelers had not planned to visit this relatively unknown land where the inhabitants pretended to "the unnatural conjunction of reason with things revealed" by trying to base their "social fabric" upon "the idlest of theories" that they could follow the simple teachings of Alma or Christ. Urging them to "judge not Alma by all those who profess his faith," however, the old man persuaded them to listen to his exposition of the philosophy of Serenia. Men's faculties are God-given, it held in essence, and Christ was not a religious authority but a means of opening unto men their own hearts for the purpose of discovering happiness on earth rather than in Paradise. "But think not we believe in man's perfection," he added:

> "Yet, against all good, he is not absolutely set. In his heart, there is a germ. *That* we seek to foster. To *that* we cling; else, all were hopeless!"
>
> "Your social state?"
>
> "It is imperfect; and long must so remain. But we make not the miserable many support the happy few. Nor by annulling reason's laws, seek to breed equality, by breeding anarchy. In all things, equality is not for all. Each has his own. Some have wider groves of palms than others; fare better; dwell in more tasteful arbors; oftener renew their fragrant thatch. Such differences must be. But none starve outright, while others feast. By the abounding, the needy are supplied. Yet not by statute, but from dictates, born half dormant in us, and warmed into life by Alma."

Such "fine," familiar, but "impracticable" poetry eventually impressed the four companions of Taji as representing the highest wisdom the world had to offer. When they were made to realize that Serenia offered them a practical compromise between reason and revelation which subjected reason to the dictates of the heart but to no dogmatic authority, they gave up their pursuit of the will-o'-the-wisp of perfect happiness and one of them, Babbalanja the philosopher, formally accepted the substitute state of emotional and intellectual serenity.

The achievement of such wisdom was not extraordinary. A belief that human beings were guided by innate moral ideas or sentiments represented the characteristic and widespread compromise made by the early nineteenth century between the empirical and the neoplatonic traditions in philosophy; and the notion that the existing social order should be improved, but not completely changed, by the application of simple Christian principles was a part of most of the American reform movements of the time. Had Melville gone to Harvard as a student instead of to the Pacific as a sailor, this solution of philosophical problems would have been systematized for him before he was introduced to the problems it resolved; and it was to remain an active scheme of reference in his mind, perhaps because he had been obliged to work it out for himself—at first, as he indicated fourteen years later, by a process of "revulsion from the counting-room philosophy of Paley." In its religious implications, it was at complete variance with the Calvinistic dogmas of corrupt human nature which formed a part of the theology of the Dutch Reformed Church in which he was reared; but it corresponded closely to the ideas inherent in a serious letter of advice which Allan had received from his mother many years before, and it was probably a mature expression of all that the Melville boys had been seriously taught to believe.

The philosophical compromises of an earlier generation, however, satisfied the intellectual energies of Herman no better than they satisfied most of his thoughtful contemporaries. Nor did they satisfy the demands of the romantic quest in *Mardi* which had to be, by convention, as indeterminate as that of Endymion or Alastor. The book went on after its major philosophical character stopped, and its hero, Taji, was allegorically exposed to the flowery temptations of a Spenserian bower of sensual bliss before he was finally abandoned to a sort of vaguely Byronic perdition as he fled with "eternity in his eye" and the symbols of retribution behind him "over an endless sea."

II

Elizabeth wrote her stepmother that the new book was "done" on May 5, 1848, and that a copy for the press was "in fair progress." She herself was busy making the copy, which Herman looked over and punctuated, and they expected it to be printed and the proof sheets en route to England before the end of June. Herman planned to stick to his work of supervision and proofreading until after the English edition was out and the American edition was actually on the booksellers' shelves; but they thought that everything would be finished and they would be free to visit Boston in July or perhaps August. In the meantime, they looked forward to a period of freedom. Augusta was planning to go to Albany within a few days to visit the Van Rensselaers, and Herman was expecting at any moment to go to Westport to welcome Tom home from his first voyage, see that he was regularly discharged and paid, and bring him back to New York, since Tom knew nothing of the family's removal from Lansingburgh. They were even ready to receive a visit from Elizabeth's youngest brother, Sam, and show him the sights they had earlier shown Lem.

But Elizabeth was not yet acquainted with her husband's literary habits. Both *Typee* and *Omoo* had bulged a bit with late additions and afterthoughts inserted into the original manuscript, and *Mardi* offered infinitely more opportunities for such insertions. Furthermore, although the over-all plan for the book was that of an allegorical voyage through the world, as symbolized by the archipelago of Mardi, the real world of current events was curiously absent from the manuscript of whimsical satire, poetic allegory, and philosophical abstractions which Elizabeth was copying. Yet the real world was pressing far more imperialistically into the consciousness of everybody, during the spring of 1848, than it had been while Herman was expressing his opinions of the French and the English and of the American missionaries in his earlier books. The United States was still in the process of bringing home its troops from war with Mexico, and the Melvilles' enigmatic cousin, Guert Gansevoort, had redeemed his naval career by heroism at Vera Cruz. The problem of Anglo-American relations was still an uneasy one, with the Oregon controversy fresh in people's minds and with the prospect of further imperialistic conflicts growing out of the current war. Internally, the country was being torn by factional strife in anticipation of the political conventions of the late spring and early summer and the presidential election in the fall: the slavery question was causing the Democratic party to split apart into antislavery "Barnburners" and proslavery "Hunkers," and a highly vocal group of "Conscience" Whigs were threatening to add their strength to a growing new party of "Free-Soilers." In Europe, the French Revolution of 1848 had broken out, and all New York had been set agog by the reports of it brought by the *Cambria* on the morning of March 18 and kept excited by the further reports and counterreports which followed on each successive steamer. George Duyckinck was sending firsthand accounts of events in France by letter to his brother Evert, and at precisely the time Melville was supposedly finishing up the last chapters of his book new excitement was created by the dispatch printed in the *Morning Courier and New York Enquirer* of May 1 concerning the "Great Chartist Meeting" in England and the "six points" demanded by the reform "Charter" as reported by the London *Times*. It was no time for a man to rest comfortably in a state of serenity or pursue a romantic quest "over an endless sea."

During the month of May, however, Herman resisted the pressure of the times and devoted himself to his nearly finished manuscript as completely as circumstances would permit. Tom got back safely from his voyage; and although the two brothers, with a new bond of common experience between them, had much to talk about, the older was probably preoccupied with his own affairs while the younger tried in vain to get a job in New York, grew quickly restless, and decided to go to sea again. His mother protested, but Herman, perhaps remembering his own feelings under similar circumstances, tried to help him get a berth which would lead to advancement and a responsible seafaring life. The copying did not go as rapidly as Elizabeth had originally hoped, but when she wrote her mother about it again on June 6 she expected to be through within a couple of days and was willing to consider the idea of returning to Boston with Sam, although she hated to leave her husband and half joked of being "afraid to trust him to finish up the book" without her.

She had more reason to fear than she perhaps realized, for she could hardly have been aware of the activity going on in Herman's mind as he proofread and punctuated the copy she was preparing. The political situation was becoming increasingly intense. News from abroad indicated that the revolutionary movement was spreading from France into other countries, and the movement toward reform in England was growing. A tumultuous Democratic convention in Baltimore, in the latter part of May, resulted in the nomination of Lewis Cass for president, and the dissatisfaction of the antislavery Democrats threatened to disrupt the party. Most of Duyckinck's friends allied themselves with the antislavery faction, but Allan Melville, as a member of Tammany Hall, remained regular and became a candidate for the New York Assembly in opposition to a Whig and a Free-Soiler. Herman was probably more inclined to listen to the political discussions that swirled around him than to take an active part in them. Yet he had the interest of a firsthand observer in the operations of international foreign policy and a disillusioned dislike for American politicians and their demagoguery. With the somewhat Olympian attitude of a man who had recently ascended to philosophical heights, he also had a notion of what he might say if people would just listen to sense. He itched, in short, to discourse at large upon current affairs; and before him lay a manuscript which could readily absorb such a discourse, and perhaps be improved by the addition of journalistic interest. Whether he waited for Elizabeth to get safely to Boston or not, he certainly, at some time during the early summer of 1848, took up his pen again and began to give *Mardi* a large extra bulge.

In part at least the bulge represented an outburst of irritation at the rhetorical chauvinism which was one of the dominant characteristics of American politics at this particular time—an irritation which Melville had probably been feeling and repressing ever since he had returned from the South Seas, disillusioned by imperialism, and discovered that his brother Gansevoort was making his political reputation by screaming "Fifty-four forty or fight!" England he recognized as being domineering and bellicose enough, but the American willingness to invite an armed conflict with the mother country, which was particularly common among the Democrats, he considered both absurd and intolerable. The United States had gained its independence and won the War of 1812 less by its own strength than by the force of circumstances, he insisted; and although some of the circumstances he recounted were major factors in history, others (such as his suggestion that the British were defeated during the Revolution by the geography of America rather than by its people, or his hint that the American naval victories of the War of 1812 were all won by superiority of tonnage and man power) merely indicated the intensity of his irritation at those of his countrymen who did not realize "that true grandeur is too big for a boast." Melville obviously had little patience with the Anglophobes who liked to believe that England was growing old and beginning to decay, that it was about to be crushed by the weight of its internal debt, or that the United States and other nations had grown too powerful for a country weakened by colonial responsibilities: the British Empire, he observed, sometimes refused an opportunity to expand because it valued new territory less than the good will of its neighbors; and somehow, like an "obstinate old uncle," it "persisted in flourishing, in spite of the prognostications of the nephew nations." His opinions were hardly of the sort that could be freely expressed and patiently heard either in his family circle or in the circle of his literary friends.

When he allowed the fictitious characters of his book to leave Europe and visit America, the evidence of his antichauvinism became increasingly pronounced. They were greeted by an imaginary statue of liberty iron-ically inscribed with the declaration that in this republican land all men were born free and equal except the members of the tribe of Ham, and their first sight on shore was of an expansive and obviously expansible Temple of Freedom (symbolic of both the Capitol and the Union) over which a slave with the red stripes of the lash on his back was engaged in hoisting a flag—"correspondingly striped." Within the temple, the mem-bers of the United States Senate ("all chiefs of immense capacity:—how many gallons, there was no finding out") were demonstrating their states-manship by dipping into the subterranean pork barrel. On the floor a buzzard-beaked lunatic representing Senator William Allen of Ohio, chairman of the committee on foreign relations and currently a supporter of Lewis Cass, waved hands full of headless arrows as he screamed a crazy defiance of England on the Oregon question—which had actually been settled before Melville went to Washington in search of a job, al-though the territorial status of the new section was still being discussed. Outside the temple, the voyagers discovered another parodox of the land of equality when they witnessed a scene which showed that, although any man might insult the chief executive of the republic with impunity, the American president actually had more power than a constitutional monarch. If Melville had so far abandoned the guiding philosophy of Robert Burton at this stage of his book as to point at one "particular species of dotage that men might acknowledge their imperfections and seek to reform what is amiss," he was asking his boastful countrymen to look beneath the surface of their free institutions and see what these really meant.

One of the most interesting sections of *Mardi,* in fact, is Melville's out-right attack upon what he considered the institutional illusion by means of a "mysterious scroll" which was read to the "sovereign kings" of America and violently denounced by them. In it he scoffed at the tendency of each generation to consider its own hour as the beginning of the last scene in the last act of the world drama, surveyed history to show that republics had flourished and passed away in Rome as well as in France and England, and advanced a theory of American history which was not to be discovered by formal historians until nearly a half century later. The boasted freedom and happiness of America were not the products of the country's wisely ordained institutions, but the institutions themselves were heritages of an earlier period and were preserved by the geographical fact of a frontier which made political freedom and a considerable amount of equality possible. Whether America would follow the historical pattern of European republicanism could only be determined in the future: the "wild western waste" could not be "overrun in a day. Yet overrun at last it will be; and then, the recoil must come." In the meantime, Melville offered his countrymen a social philosophy which was a mundane version of the ideals of Serenia. Man was imperfect: "For evil is the chronic malady of the universe; and checked in one place, breaks forth in another." His social state also was imperfect, for "Poverty is abased before riches, all Mardi over; any where, it is hard to be a debtor; any where, the wise will lord it over fool; every where, suffering is found." Thus true freedom was more social than political, and its real felicity was of a man's own individual getting and holding; for, while great reforms were needed, bloody revolutions were nowhere required. It was silly to believe that the age of strife was over, yet people did have within themselves the inherent moral power to exercise some control over their own destinies: if Americans would restrain their meddlesome impulses in European affairs and refrain from a grasping imperialism in their own hemisphere, they might find that, in the course of time, they could peacefully cross the equator and take the Arctic Circles for their boundaries.

Melville was by this time reaching a stage in his intellectual development which involved him in a conflict within himself. When he indulged in abstract thought, he was capable of positive belief in an ideal which may not have been entirely satisfactory but which was nevertheless genuinely attractive because of the feeling of serenity it gave to his restless mind. On the other hand, when he looked at the everyday realities of the world, he was inclined toward criticism, skepticism, and even cynicism. When he tried to apply the philosophy of Serenia to his analysis of conditions in America, he had difficulty in reaching any really optimistic expectations based upon the inherent goodness of man, and the last words of his mysterious scroll were more negative than positive in the hopes they held out for the future. Yet even they expressed more optimism than he really felt, for when he turned to the South, in a bitter indictment of slavery and of the opinions associated with John C. Calhoun, he was gloomily prophetic of civil war and unwilling to suggest a remedy for the situation or try to read the "hieroglyphics" of the future.

Much of Melville's skepticism was the result of a sailor's view of the seamy underside of the world's pretensions. Some reflected a residue of antagonism toward an older brother whose comet-like brilliance had left star dust still lingering in his family's eyes. Some was nothing more than the cynicism of a disappointed office seeker whose irritations were being kept fresh by too much political talk around him. Yet not all of it could be attributed to such unhappy causes, for this section of *Mardi* records the maturing of penetrating intelligence and a sharply realistic mind. Melville's comments upon such varied matters as the English handling of the Chartist movement, the contemporary famine in Ireland, the implications of the new French Revolution, and American imperialism in Mexico and the Caribbean reveal a shrewd and well-informed intellect and often a broad sympathy and understanding. Although he expressed himself in his own exaggerated version of the grotesque symbolic imagery and the suggestive nomenclature associated with the recognizable passages of political allegory in Spenser's *Faerie Queene,* his selection of a symbol was often imaginative and his aphoristic comments were both pointed and suggestive. The political section of *Mardi* was more intellectually mature than anything he had yet written.

It was also evidently written under less pressure than that which affected other portions of the book. For Melville fulfilled a promise to Lizzie by joining her in Boston on July 12, where Judge Shaw entertained for them with a party of about thirty guests on the following evening and Richard Henry Dana, Jr., brought together a group of his friends for an evening with Herman at the Parker House four days later. The visit lasted only for a week or so, but after his return to New York Melville was willing to quit work on a fine day to picnic with Duyckinck at Fort Lee or on another occasion with the ladies of his family. Although a later report is certainly false in saying that he spent the summer at Pittsfield, where the poet Longfellow and his family were boarding with Robert Melville, he may possibly have taken the August vacation he promised Elizabeth by running up to the Berkshires; and, in any case, he seems to have been willing to divert himself with social affairs and novels and to have made no attempt to follow the strict routine he had pursued during the winter months. Yet he did not quit writing. Yoomy's vision of the consequences of the gold rush, which appears near the end of the section of political allegory, could hardly have been composed before the first accounts of deserted towns were published on September 14 or perhaps before the colorful account of the rush itself which was printed in the New York *Daily Tribune* for September 16. In all likelihood, he kept doing something with his manuscript until within a couple of weeks of the time he received a preliminary agreement for its publication from the Harpers on November 11.

One of the things that he evidently attempted to do with his manuscript before he turned it over to his publishers was to contemplate it from the superior point of view of a professional critic. Looking at his work before he had time to rest from his labors, he found it, frankly, not so good. For the Abrazza episode near the conclusion of the book was apparently composed after the political allegory and was introduced into the book because Melville felt obliged to explain his waywardness to the public very much as he had explained it in his apologetic and protesting letter to Murray during the preceding March. He put his excuses in the form of a dialogue contained in a long chapter of philosophical discourse concerning critics and an ancient Mardian author named Lombardo and the composition of his great, curious, and crazy "Koztanza." "When Lombardo set about his work, he knew not what it would become"; Babbalanja explained. "He did not build himself in with plans; he wrote right on; and so doing, got deeper and deeper into himself." Produced by "a sort of sleep-walking of the mind" and with only an initial regard for the unities, "the Koztanza lacks cohesion; it is wild, unconnected, all episode." But so was the world itself—"nothing but episodes; valleys and hills; rivers, digressing from plains; vines, roving all over; boulders and diamonds; flowers and thistles; forests and thickets; and, here and there, fens and moors. And so, the world in the Koztanza." Melville was not only amplifying his letter to Murray but anticipating the critical disapproval he was already beginning to expect. Yet he did not mean to give the impression that writing was simply an uncritical outpouring of any author's mind: "Oh! could Mardi but see how we work," he exclaimed, "it would marvel more at our primal chaos, than at the round world thence emerging."

Although Melville's representation of the world was neither well-rounded nor free from the signs of primal chaos, it began its formal emergence from the obscurity of his upstairs room with the signing of a final agreement with his publishers on November 15. The contract provided for the customary delay of American publication for four months in order that the book might be brought out first in England, and for an advance to the author of $500.00. Herman needed the money badly. He had overdrawn his account with the Harpers on August 1 by $256.03 and on the ninth of the same month had received from Wiley and Putnam only $114.89. His first publishers had disappointed him by their manner of handling *Typee,* and ten days after receiving his statement from them he had given John Wiley written notice that at the end of sixty days he planned to take the book out of his hands. From the summary of his accounts made for him by Allan on November 13, he learned that the American sales from three editions of his first book had been 5,753 copies, from which he had gained only $686.46, or considerably less than he had expected. Transferring the copyright to the Harpers would strengthen his credit with his new publishers, of course; but it was hard, as he observed in *Mardi* at about the time he received his account from them, to be a debtor. Yet despite his financial needs, his third book was slow in making its appearance. The Harpers evidently spent some time debating the format before they decided to publish it without illustrations and in the inexpensive style of *Omoo,* and it was not until January, 1849, that he wrote the brief, defiant Preface in which he expressed once again some of the sentiments he had put in his letter to John Murray ten months before. He took Elizabeth to Boston, where she wanted her first child to be born, on the second day of the new year and hurried back to New York, where he and Augusta, on January 27, finished reading proof on what they had begun to call Herman's "Koztanza." The "child of many prayers"—and of many delays—was at last becoming a book.

Other delays, however, threatened. Melville wrote a hurried letter to Murray the next day before taking an overnight boat to Boston on the twenty-ninth in order to be with Elizabeth, and Allan forwarded the corrected proof sheets to England a week later. But Murray had no enthusiasm for publishing a "romance" and liked neither the current state of international copyright nor the high value his author placed upon his new work. Accordingly, John R. Brodhead, who continued to act as Melville's agent, took the work to Richard Bentley who, on March 3, accepted it and agreed to give its author the aristocratic distinction of being paid in guineas instead of pounds—and to pay him two hundred of them as an advance against his share of the profits. Bentley was apparently both nervous about a book that had been in the hands of another English publisher and willing to make up for any time lost in negotiations, for he proved his ability to hold his own in the fierce competition which characterized the piratical days of his trade by proposing to get out a book of more than a thousand pages two weeks after he had agreed to publish it. *Mardi* apparently made its first appearance on or about March 17 in an edition of three volumes which sold at a half guinea each. It was probably the first "three-decker" novel by an American published in England and one of the most expensive American books to be issued by an English press. Such a method of publication was not designed to make Melville a widely read author, but it would enable the publisher to make a profit if he disposed of his first edition of a thousand copies. The speed with which the whole business was handled took the Harpers completely by surprise, and although the first volume of their edition was ready by the end of March, *Mardi* did not make its formal appearance before the American public until April 14.

In the meantime, Melville had nothing to do in Boston but rest and—until his son Malcolm was born on February 16—wait. The interest in old books which he had acquired in New York and his own flights into rhetorical prose and experiments with hidden meanings while writing *Mardi* had left him hungry for the deeper substance and sensitive to the rarer flavors of literature, and while he rested he read. His nerves were naturally stretched on tenterhooks during this period of waiting for his first child, through the weeks of Elizabeth's slow and difficult recovery which followed, and until the appearance of his most ambitious literary work; and, although he occasionally found release in hearing Emerson lecture on "Mind and Manners in the Nineteenth Century" or Fanny Kemble read *Macbeth* and *Othello,* most of his tension found its escape in the imaginative perception of his reading. During all of his intellectual experiences at this time, however, his emotions were too tight for cynicism. He was "agreeably disappointed in Mr. Emerson," into whose written works he had "only glanced" once while browsing in Putnam's bookstore; for instead of the "transcendentalisms, myths, and oracular gibberish" which he had been led to expect, he found him "quite intelligible" and even on second thought was sure that "this Plato who talks through his nose" was an "uncommon" if not actually a "great" man. Abstractly, he could not approve of the "insinuation" he found in Emerson's discourse "that had he lived in those days when the world was made, he might have offered some valuable suggestions." But granting that he might be called a fool, he was the sort of fool that Melville would like to be. "I love all men who *dive,*" he wrote Duyckinck. "Any fish can swim near the surface, but it takes a great whale to go down stairs five miles or more; and if he don't attain the bottom, why, all the lead in Galena can t fashion the plummet that will."

Melville was not talking particularly of Emerson in the last words, he explained, "but of the whole corps of thought-divers, that have been diving and coming up again with blood-shot eyes since the world began." And one of the greatest of these thought-divers, he discovered during these days of unusual leisure and intense perception, was Shakespeare. Fanny Kemble had set all Boston talking about Shakespeare, and Melville, with his own edition in "glorious great type" and plenty of time for thoughtful study, "made close acquaintance with the divine William" for the first time in his life and found him "full of sermons-on-the mount, and gentle, aye, almost as Jesus." Such remarks as these shocked Duyckinck with their seeming irreverence, but Melville, who had read Spenser before he became interested in Shakespeare, believed that all men were somehow muzzled "in the Elizabethan day" and was finding in the dramatist hints of his own deepest and often unclarified thoughts. His surviving marked copies of the plays reveal the sincerity of his enthusiasm. He found the essence of Montaigne dramatized in the character of Hamlet, and in *King Lear* he discovered a passage which suggested an idea which was to germinate and bear fruit later: "The infernal nature," he commented in the margin, "has a valor often denied to innocence." His attentiveness was such that he could find the most profound implications in the most casual remarks, for one of the passages he scored in *Much Ado About Nothing* was Leonato's observation to the effect that "there was never yet philosopher, That could endure the tooth-ache patiently"—an observation in which he found significances that turned it into a major argument against transcendental philosophy two and a half years afterward when he became deeply concerned with the relative trustworthiness of different kinds of knowledge. It was Melville's good fortune, at a time when all his circumstances combined to make him a sensitive and thoughtful reader, to have his attention directed to the one author who could justify his sensitivity yet allow him to pursue his thoughts in terms of people rather than abstract ideas. Shakespeare gave him the most important direction he received during his journey in the world of the mind.

The heightened interest in literature which Melville acquired during these anxious weeks in Boston led him into more extensive reading than he had ever done before, and despite his financial difficulties he ordered through John Wiley a set of British Essayists for $18.00 and a thirty-seven-volume Classical Library from the Harpers for $12.23, in addition to a copy of Lamb's *Specimens of English Dramatic Poets* which was to introduce him to and stimulate his interest in Shakespeare's contemporaries. He also began to order Macaulay's *History of England;* and he picked up in a Boston bookshop the English translation of Pierre Bayle's historical and critical *Dictionary,* planning, as he wrote Duyckinck, "to lay the great old folios side by side and go to sleep on them through the summer, with the Phaedon in one hand and Tom Brown in the other." But a raging financial toothache made its imperative entrance upon his plans for a summer of philosophical reading. His expenses were large both before and after he brought Lizzie and Malcolm home, with a temporary nurse, Mrs. Sullivan, on April 10; and although he evidently talked the Harpers into a new advance of $200.00, he must have received it with the warning that his account was so heavily overdrawn that, even if *Mardi* proved a success, he would have to produce another book before he could expect any further income from his publishers.

And as April wore on it became evident that *Mardi* was not going to be a success. Evert and George Duyckinck (who had taken over the *Literary World* together on October 7, 1848, shortly after George's return from Europe) were puffing the book for all they were worth, and the *Home Journal* went out of its way to be friendly; but the Boston *Post,* which normally approved the writings of a known Democrat, damned it as "not only tedious but unreadable"—"Rabelais emasculated of everything but prosiness and puerility." The first English reviews were either lukewarm or almost entirely bad. The *Athenaeum* had taken the lead by writing that "among the hundred people who will take it up, lured by their remembrances of 'Typee,' ninety readers will drop off at the end of the first volume; and of the remaining nine will become so weary of the hero when for the seventh time he is assaulted by the three pursuing *Duessas* who pelt him with symbolical flowers, that they will throw down his chronicle ere the end of its second third is reached—with Mr. Burchell's monosyllable by way of comment." The *Literary Gazette* and the *Critic* tried to be kind, but the *Examiner* called it "a transcendental *Gulliver*, or *Robinson Crusoe* run mad"; and the best that *Bentley's Miscellany*, the organ of his own publisher, could say was that *Mardi* was a book "which the reader will probably like very much or detest altogether, according to the measure of his imagination." In a letter to his father-in-law, written less than two weeks after his arrival home, Melville spoke of the reviews in the *Examiner* and the *Literary Gazette* as though he considered them favorable and referred to the attacks in the London *Athenaeum* and Boston *Post* as "matters of course" which were "essential to the building up of any permanent reputation—if such should ever prove to be mine." The critics were dunces for seeing nothing in his new work. "But Time," he added, "which is the solver of all riddles, will solve 'Mardi.'"

Nevertheless, he was deeply worried, and Elizabeth revealed as much on April 30 when she wrote her mother to assure her of Malcolm's health and her own recovery. "I suppose by this time you are deep in the 'fogs' of 'Mardi,'" she began cheerfully, but continued with increasing evidences of anxiety: "—if the mist ever does clear away, I should like to know what it reveals to *you*—there seems to be much diversity of opinion about 'Mardi' as might be supposed. Has father read it? When you hear any individual express an opinion with regard to it, I wish you would tell me —whatever it is—good or bad—without fear of offense—merely by way of curiosity." By this time both she and Herman knew that he would have to write a new book immediately and that it could not be a step beyond *Mardi*, as he had hoped, earlier in the month, that his next work might be. If young Malcolm were to be supplied with the substance necessary for his "improving daily in size and intelligence," his father would have to bring his own intellectual improvement to a stop, control the "certain something unmanageable" within him, and come down to the level of popular ground in his writing. The new book could contain neither flowers nor philosophy. It had to be entirely different.

III

During the months of May and June, 1849, Melville practically dropped out of sight. The first Astor Place riots against the English actor Charles Macready on May 7 caused him to join Washington Irving, Duyckinck, Cornelius Mathews, and forty-three other well-known citizens in signing a petition urging Macready to continue his performances despite the opposition of the chauvinistic followers of the American actor Edwin Forrest; and on the twenty-fifth of the same month he purchased two Episcopal prayer books from the Harpers in order that the family might prepare themselves for the christening of Allan's infant daughter, Maria Gansevoort, who had been born in New York two days after the birth of Malcolm in Boston. But his own son went unbaptized while papa wrote. The nature of his new book was described in a letter to Richard Bentley on June 5—"a plain, straightforward, amusing narrative of personal experience—the son of a gentleman on his first voyage to sea as a sailor—no metaphysics, no conic-sections, nothing but cakes and ale." It was based upon his "own observations under comical circumstances" and would be somewhat shorter than *Typee* and ready for publication in two or three months or possibly less. He had conquered the "something unmanageable" in him which had caused him to write *Mardi*, although he assured his English publisher that his previous book, "in its larger purposes," had "not been written in vain."

The Harpers in the meantime were bringing out a new edition of the revised *Typee*, which had been formally transferred to them on April 28 and for which a new copyright had been requested on May 25, and Melville may have had to look over the proofs. But this time he permitted no interruptions to interfere seriously with his work. The book was finished, with all the author's customary last-minute enlargements and insertions, by the end of June, and an agreement was signed on July 2 for its publication by the Harpers with an immediate advance of $300. Although its title was eventually changed from *My First Voyage* to *Redburn: His First Voyage,* apparently no other revisions were made, and the book was promptly sent to press. Bentley had lost money on *Mardi* and was disturbed by a recent decision by the House of Lords that no foreigner could hold a copyright in Great Britain, but he nevertheless offered £100 for the manuscript he had never seen. The offer was for only two-thirds as much as Melville had asked, and the value of the book had been increased by the additions which made it as long as or a trifle longer than *Omoo* and therefore publishable in two volumes. Yet the author had no choice but to accept it gracefully, as he did on July 20, promising the sheets within two or three weeks and saying nothing more about the form of publication despite his earlier inclination to blame the failure of *Mardi* partially on the fact that it had not been put forth in a manner "admitting of a popular circulation."

The amount promised by Bentley was less than the author's debt to his American publishers before he received his new advance, but Melville knew, before he got the bad news, that a single book would not get him out of his difficulties. He must have begun another as soon as he signed the agreement for *Redburn* and while laboring over the proof sheets of the first worked steadily at the second, with no time for indulging himself in the luxury of planning its progress. Words were his only stock in trade, and he was being subjected to a forced sale in an effort to stave off bankruptcy. Words poured from his pen at an average rate of nearly three thousand a day in spite of the galleys of proof, household interruptions, and hysteria outside. The proofs of *Redburn* dragged through the greater part of August, while Melville wrote. Both of the babies were teething, and one of them was in the hot adjoining room. But Melville kept at his desk. The blue cholera, which had become epidemic during the murky days of early June, raged as the death toll in New York mounted in late July from one hundred to two hundred to three hundred a day and the city was described as a charnel house. People refused to eat fish, vegetables, and fruit, and those who had places of refuge left town; but Melville, whose August vacation had been a pattern of his life since childhood, stayed in his room and continued to write. By the end of August his second book of the summer, seventy-five pages longer than the first, was finished, and in early September he was reading copy for the printer. His industry and his return to the factual material of his successful early work—for *Redburn* was based upon his first experiences at sea while on a merchant ship to Liverpool, and *White Jacket* upon his voyage home from the Pacific on a man-of-war—restored his good standing with his publishers, who, on September 13, agreed to advance him $500 for his new work and delay its publication until he could go abroad and arrange favorable terms for its appearance in England. In four months he had paid for his indulgence in the intellectual growth revealed in *Mardi* and had become a tired and somewhat bitter man.

For Melville was emotionally inclined to despise the products of his forced labor. "When a poor devil writes with duns all round him, and looking over the back of his chair—and perching on his pen and diving in his inkstand—like the devils about St. Anthony," he wrote Duyckinck at the end of the year, when the first of the two books had become a commercial success, "—what can you expect of that poor devil?—What but a beggarly 'Redburn!' " Although he obviously thought better of *White Jacket* and its aggressive "man-of-*warish*" style than he did of his "little nursery tale" (as he described the two books in a letter to Richard H. Dana, Jr., on October 6) he linked them both together in a deprecatory allusion in another letter written during the following May and never put them in the class of his other works. Neither represented any peculiar experience that set him apart from other writing men, as *Typee* and *Omoo* did, and neither made the sort of demands that *Mardi* had made upon his growing intellect and conscious invention. They had no egoistic values that he was ever able to recognize, and in his own mind they could not be dissociated from the finger-cramping drudgery of their composition.

Yet in each of them Melville had written far better than he knew and far better than he could have written without the experience gained from *Mardi* and from the period of perceptive reading which followed. The most striking new quality which appeared in his work for the first time in *Redburn* was that of fictitious character creation which produced something like living people. Most of the characters in the book, of course, had originals on the *St. Lawrence* of Melville's youthful voyage. But when they were brought to life in his memory they were transformed —not by an exaggeration of their eccentricities, as John B. Troy had been transformed in *Omoo,* but from within. The captain, who most nearly resembled the characters in Melville's earlier books, was changed from a Swede to a Russian and lost all trace of his Scandinavian origin. The sailor Jackson acquired the Shakespearean depth and subtlety which perhaps inspired Joseph Conrad later to write *The Nigger of the Narcissus.* And the young narrator himself became entirely unlike the relatively mature Herman Melville who had actually shipped before the mast for a summer's voyage, taking on a youthful naïveté which later readers have found more deeply touching than his creator would have thought possible. In part, the emotions aroused by Wellingborough Redburn are the result of the style which Melville practiced when he set himself determinedly against the rhetoric of *Mardi* and adopted the flat, coördinate sentences of a child's artless narration—especially in the first part of the book, before the author's determination faded with the curious effect that Redburn appears to have suddenly grown up. But in larger part, perhaps, these emotions reflect the imaginative sympathy of Melville's affection for Tom, who had gone to sea as a boy of sixteen and had been followed by the experienced imagination of an older brother who dedicated *Redburn* to him while he was away once more on a voyage to China. Having learned to project his thoughts into the crudely fictitious character of Babbalanja, Melville had gone further and had acquired the ability, without realizing it, to project both his thoughts and feelings into the more human fictitious character of Redburn; and his success was so great that most readers since have been convinced that the thoughts and feelings were those of his own first voyage.

A second new quality which appeared in his "little nursery tale" was a social purpose which affected the author's imagination and became an integral part of his invention. The cholera, which first aroused panic in New York while he was writing the book, had been a topic of conversation since the preceding December. It had been brought to America by the packet ship *New York* from Le Havre, and its spread, at first, was chiefly among the immigrant population whose living conditions were recognized as offering a favorable opportunity for its development. Melville had seen the even worse conditions of the Liverpool slums, and, although his own ship had not been an emigrant vessel, he had an opportunity to know from sailors' talk or from more recent newspaper accounts what conditions were like on board such hellholes. The scourge then raging in New York and spreading to other cities as far west as St. Louis was an imperative argument for reform if people could only be made aware of the particular species of dotage that kept them from seeing the relationship of cause and effect, and Melville's desire to make them see it was not confined to the one chapter in which he imagined the outbreak of cholera on shipboard and the panic which followed. His description of the Liverpool slums from which the emigrants came contributed to his social purpose, and his imaginary portraits of individual characters in the steerage of the *Highlander* were designed to make his readers perceive the humanity of those nameless people who were being blamed for a plague which actually flourished under conditions brought about by the inhumanity of their betters. An American law had been recently passed restricting the number of emigrants that could be crowded into a given amount of space, and an English law fixed the amount of food which should be provided for each traveler. But humanity was required for the enforcement of the laws and for the provision of decency and convenience. And humanity rarely softened the hard lot of the emigrant.

In *Mardi,* Melville had urged that Americans wash their hands of European affairs and refrain from crossing the Atlantic barrier "by manifesto or army." But in the humanitarianism of *Redburn,* his isolationism disappeared. Waiving "that agitated national topic, as to whether such multitudes of foreign poor should be landed on our American shores . . . with the one only thought, that if they can get here, they have God's right to come," he explained his own new attitude: "For the whole world is the patrimony of the whole world; there is no telling who does not own a stone in the Great Wall of China." Mankind, when moved by selfishness and greed, was not only unconscious of its best interests but recreant to the claims of natural sympathy and Christian charity: "We talk of the Turks, and abhor the cannibals; but may not some of *them*, go to heaven, before some of *us?* We may have civilized bodies and yet barbarous souls. We are blind to the real sights of this world; deaf to its voice; and dead to its death. And not till we know, that one grief outweighs ten thousand joys, will we become what Christianity is striving to make us."

Melville's notion that any man might own a stone in the Great Wall of China—his new feeling for the collective oneness of humanity—provided the imaginative quality which made *White Jacket*, like *Redburn*, a better book than its author realized. For the narrative events of that hurriedly written story followed Melville's own experiences less closely than did those of any of his other autobiographical volumes. It is true that he had come home from Callao on a man-of-war and that he had made for himself a white jacket, and it is also true that Melville included in his story a number of incidents which were a part of his naval experience although they did not occur on the voyage home. Yet his experience had never included such matters as the running out of grog and the unofficial substitution of Eau de Cologne, Fourth of July theatricals off Cape Horn, a lieutenant's profane countermanding of his captain's orders during a gale, a sailor's report of the theft of his "dunderfunk," shore leave in Rio de Janiero and a review by the emperor of Brazil, a ruthless amputation by the ship's surgeon, a narrow escape from flogging, a massacre of the sailors' beards, or a fall overboard. The comic episodes in this list were all derived from James Mercier's *Life in a Man-of-War, or Scenes in Old Ironsides*—a book which Melville kept at hand while writing *White Jacket* and used not only as a source for entire scenes but as a means of jogging his memory and stimulating his invention very much as he had used Ellis' *Polynesian Researches* for *Omoo*. Others were derived from naval tradition and fleet gossip, from Smollett's *Roderick Random*, from Nathaniel Ames's *A Mariner's Sketches,* and from *Tales of the Ocean and Essays for the Forecastle,* by S. S. Sleeper or "Hawser Martingale." The material with which his imagination played was derived more from other men's experiences than from his own.

But an intense and perhaps largely unconscious imagination unified his memories and his gleanings around the emotional attitudes he had acquired in the Navy and the broad humanitarianism he had begun to display in *Redburn.* His resentment of the brutality of naval practices was made purposeful by the same method he had just been using to open people's eyes to the "real sights" of a steerage full of emigrants: he created dramatic scenes and situations which were moving because they were emotionally, although not historically, true. The "man-of-warish" style which he recognized in *White Jacket* was there because in his new book he had found the power to place himself in the midst of imaginary events and see them through the eyes of humanity. His new perceptions of what he was later to call the broad "significances" of particular objects or incidents made his man-of-war a better representation of the world than his Mardian archipelago had been. For in *Mardi* he had dealt in ideas which he had brought to a focus in symbols, whereas in *White Jacket* he began to make his particulars so suggestive that they appeared emblematic. A reader may find many ideas of self-sustained nobility bodied forth in Jack Chase, of punch-drunk authority in Captain Claret, of insidious evil in the bland master-at-arms, or of individual isolation in the person of White Jacket himself. Some of these ideas are there because of the fullness of mind that Melville brought to bear upon the hasty composition of his book. Others are there because words happily put together out of a fullness of mind often have the capacity for more meaning than their maker consciously puts in them. To a certain extent in *Redburn* and to a greater degree in *White Jacket,* Melville succeeded in making his readers become partners in the act of literary creation.

Of all this, however, Melville was unaware. He knew only that his "confessions of a sailor-boy" made a book acceptable to his publishers and that his account of "the world in a man of war" was a manuscript which might be valued highly. He had applied for a copyright on the former on August 18, although it was not to be published in America until after the English edition appeared in late September, and he hoped that he could take the proof sheets of the latter to England and sell them in person for enough to pay for his trip and have as much left over as he had been paid for *Redburn.* His father-in-law evidently approved of the plan, for on September 3 Judge Shaw obtained from Edward Everett letters of introduction for Herman to Samuel Rogers, Richard Monckton Milnes, and Gustave de Beaumont, and two days later wrote to Charles Sumner and Richard Henry Dana, Jr., for others. Dana obliged with a letter to Edward Moxon, and various New York friends, including Thomas Powell, also gave him notes to their European acquaintances. Arrangements were made for Elizabeth and Malcolm to spend an indeterminate period of time in Boston, and Herman engaged passage on the packet ship *Southampton* which was due to sail on October 8. He tried to persuade Duyckinck to go with him, promising a grand but economical tour of the Continent as far south and east as Rome, but was probably too busy to be greatly disappointed when he failed. The proofs of his new book had to be corrected, his son had to be baptized, tentative plans for his itinerary had to be made from guidebooks once used by George

Duyckinck and from Dr. Gardner's published memoirs of his student days in Paris, and his collection of letters had to be looked over and supplemented. He also had to give some thought to the next book he planned to write.

IV

For Melville's debt to the Harpers stood at $1,332.29 after he received his advance on *White Jacket,* and he could not have justified a prolonged trip abroad merely on the grounds that he was obliged to act as his own literary agent for a book he had already written. He was going to collect material which would be useful to him in the future. Since his whaling experiences had not worked out very well in supplying material for *Mardi,* he evidently believed that he had exhausted the interesting incidents of his own life; and, like the later Mark Twain who was so much like him in his approach to the problems of literary invention, he was bound to have some new experiences which could either be worked up in an autobiographical pattern or be used to give substance to fiction. His success with the semifiction of *Redburn* and *White Jacket* may have been encouraging, despite his insistence that they were not the sort of books he wanted to write, for he had recently picked up a worn copy of the *Life and Remarkable Adventures of Israel R. Potter* and was playing with the notion of serving up the story of this Revolutionary patriot and exile against a background of local color that he might become acquainted with on his trip. The *Literary World* had recently been printing a translation of an article by Philarete Chasles, who had talked with an American (probably Thomas Gold Appleton) who claimed to have seen the journal on which Melville's South Sea books had been based, and Melville was acutely aware that such a journal would have saved him a considerable amount of trouble and expense in collecting the reference books that he actually used to supplement his memory of details. On this trip, he planned to keep one.

Whatever Melville's hopes may have been for his voyage, its start was not auspicious. Captain Robert H. Griswold of the *Southampton* postponed his sailing two days before he decided to brave a cold and violent storm, and then, after Melville had gone shivering aboard, the captain was forced to send his passengers ashore for another twenty-four hours while he waited for a favorable wind. It was not until shortly after noon on Thursday, October 11, that Herman was able to wave good-bye to George Duyckinck and his brother Allan, feel the release of the anchor from the mud of North River, and know that the tugboat was at last taking him through the Narrows and toward the open sea. But out of sight of land, with the ship running beneath double-reefed topsails and half a gale blowing from behind, the voyage began to look more promising. Captain Griswold was a sociable man and a fancier of literature who recognized Melville as his most distinguished passenger by providing him with a comfortable stateroom by himself and giving him the run of the ship. There were enough whist players in the saloon to provide him with recreation until seasickness broke up the party, leaving an ex-sailor free for a good night's sleep and energetic enough to get up betimes and renew his youth by climbing to the masthead and recalling his early emotions as he looked out over the unchanging ocean. The burdens of authorship slipped from his mind, and he found that even reading was "hard work."

Talk was easy, however, for a man who had been bent over his desk for five solid months. And the *Southampton* provided, in addition to its captain, two stimulating conversationalists—the young German philologist, George J. Adler, to whom he had been introduced by George Duyckinck before going aboard; and Dr. Franklin Taylor, a cousin and traveling companion of Bayard Taylor who had composed a Valentine for Melville at Anne Lynch's party in February. Adler was a particularly stimulating companion for a man who had tried without success to get an introduction to Carlyle before going abroad. He was "full of the German metaphysics," Melville recorded in his journal on the second day out after hearing him discourse on Kant, Swedenborg, and similar subjects; and that evening they walked the deck "till a late hour, talking of 'Fixed Fate, Free will, foreknowledge absolute,' etc." His philosophy was "Coleridgean," Melville observed with reference to his acceptance of the divine nature of the Scriptures without believing them to be either infallible or all-revealing, and he evidently probed deeply and carefully into his new companion's mind. For the creator of Babbalanja carefully put down in his little book the next morning: "He believes that there are things *out* of God and independent of him,—things that would have existed were there no God: —such as that two and two make four; for it is not that God so decrees mathematically, but that in the very nature of things, the fact is thus." Here was the sort of deep-diving talking companion of whom he had dreamed but whom had never before met. Adler became his favorite companion on shipboard, in London, and in Paris; and from him Melville probably acquired the amateurish enthusiasm for metaphysics and the interest in epistemology which was to affect his thinking and much of his writing for nearly a decade.

When Taylor got his "sea legs" the talk sometimes turned to travel, and on the afternoon of October 15 he and Melville "sketched a plan for going down the Danube from Vienna to Constantinople" and thence to Athens, Beyrouth, Jerusalem, Alexandria, and the Pyramids—an expedition Melville thought could be made at "a comparatively trifling expense" because of Taylor's experience with "cheap European travel" and knowledge of German. But he learned before the end of the voyage that Taylor was in worse financial shape than he was, and, as a result, his philosophical conversation was more immediately fruitful than his talk of the Near East. Captain Griswold and a young passenger named Mc-Curdy occasionally joined the three new friends for an evening of literary discussion over mulled wine, champagne, or whisky punch; and with cards in the saloon, moonlight for a walk on deck, and a copy of *The Pickwick Papers* to fall back on when other recreation failed, the night watches passed pleasantly enough for a man who had been accustomed to the hardships of the forecastle and gun deck.

The days, too, were good for an active man who needed to flex his muscles. The weather was frequently wet or cloudy, but the packet ship could sail more magnificently than any other vessel Melville had ever been on. He spent much of his time running about in the rigging—to the admiration of the other passengers, one of whom had a copy of *Omoo* in her possession and looked at him speculatively over its pages—and even induced Adler and Taylor into the maintop for a morning of conversation in memory, perhaps, of Jack Chase and the pleasant hours recalled in the unpublished book he had in his stateroom. Between his exhibitions of agility he tried his hand at shuffleboard and found a number of incidents to record in his journal. A crazy man had jumped overboard on the third day out, and Melville had been struck by the "merry" expression on his face as he refused to catch the ropes thrown to save him and sank with "a few bubbles." Another crazy passenger from the steerage, suffering from delirium tremens, tried to pick a fight with a steward. But most of his fellow voyagers were normal and not particularly interesting. The voyage provided one novel experience for Melville, however, when the captain called his attention to the corposant balls on the yardarms and mastheads. "They were the first I had ever seen," he noted in his journal, "and resembled large, dim stars in the sky."

But despite the agreeable change involved in being at sea again, Melville was homesick. He missed "Orianna," his "faerie queene" Elizabeth; and Malcolm's baby words, "Where dat old man," came frequently into his mind. He was delighted when, at the end of nineteen days, they saw their first land bird and headed into the middle of the Channel. It was not until two days later, however, that they made land; and they did not reach Dover until November 5. By this time, Melville, Taylor, and Adler had impatiently decided to go ashore at once instead of continuing to London by sea, and at daybreak they were beached at Deal by an independent English boatman who refused to take them to Dover but left them free to walk eighteen miles to Canterbury and breakfast. They found a tumble-down inn, however, open at Sandwich, where they refreshed themselves, visited a castle, and took the cars for the remaining two-thirds of their journey. In Canterbury, they saw the sights, spent the night, and started a cold ride in exposed third-class cars for London the next morning.

The London lodging houses were crowded, but before the afternoon was over the three friends had secured a room apiece, at 25 Craven Street, for a guinea and a half per week and had sallied forth to the Queen's Hotel to inquire about the arrival of their ship friends and their baggage. Learning nothing of either, they took refuge in the crowd attending M. Julien's inexpensive promenade concerts and spent the evening listening to a popular rendition of Mendelssohn's "Symphony in A Minor," "Home Sweet Home," and a "Cossack Polka." Melville was naturally anxious to learn whether *Redburn* had been published on schedule, and, after relieving his mind by stopping at a bookstore and refusing to pay a guinea for a copy, he spent part of his time in the theatre reading room looking over the reviews. *Bentley's Miscellany* had treated it quite well, but he was more interested in *Blackwood's* "long story about a short book." It seemed "very comical" to him, as he hurried through the review, "in treating the thing as real." "But the wonder," he added in his journal, "is that the old Tory should waste so many pages upon a thing, which I, the author, know to be trash, and wrote it to buy some tobacco with."

He had a hundred badly needed pounds of "tobacco money" coming from Richard Bentley in payment for his "trash," however, which he was anxious to collect as soon as he could get a change of clothes from his trunk. The three friends spent the next day at the East India dock, getting their baggage through the customs, and the evening in the shilling gallery of the Royal Lyceum Theatre. There they saw Madame Vestris and her husband, Charles Mathews, in a play and an extravaganza by J. R. Planché; but Melville was less impressed by the performances than by the gallery as an inexpensive sanctuary where a lonely stranger could mix unobtrusively with "quite decent people" and enjoy a mug of porter sociably poured from a coffeepot. During the following morning he called upon Bentley and Murray and, finding them both out of town, turned his attention to sight-seeing, which was a secondary object of his trip.

Art galleries and historical points of interest filled a substantial part of his days, and the theatre occupied most of his evenings. But the most important impressions he gathered were those of the effect of the great city of London upon a wandering stranger from another land. In general he saw the metropolis as Dante's "city of Dis"—cloudy with smoke and fog, black with grime, and infernal in its effect upon the forlorn masses of humanity who thronged its dark streets and squalid lanes. Within it were strange contrasts. On Friday, November 9, he made his way into Cheapside to witness the "most bloated pomp" of the Lord Mayor's Show and on Saturday, with the help of a fire officer, pushed his way through the cellars and antilanes to the back of the Guildhall where a mob of beggars received the remains of the banquet. "A good thing might be made of this," he observed in his journal. He was, of course, to make a good thing of this—and of his impressions of the London Bridge and the "city of Dis," of his visit to the Royal Lyceum Theatre, and of the dinner party he attended in the Inns of Court before he sailed for home. He also went to a considerable amount of trouble to gather other material which might be of use to a literary man, climbing into the dangerous gallery of the notorious Penny Theatre (which frightened his companion, Adler), attending the burlesque court referred to as the "Judge and Jury" which was held at a tavern in Bow Street, and rising early to buy standing room on a housetop and witness the hanging of George and Marie Manning and the behavior of the "bruitish" mob which formed a part of this "most wonderful, horrible, and unspeakable scene."

In the meantime, Bentley's return to town, by appointment, on November 12 brought Melville's mind back to his main business. He accepted a note for £100 at sixty days in payment for *Redburn* and was offered twice that amount for the privilege of printing a thousand copies of *White Jacket* despite the state of the copyright and the fact that Bentley had time only to look at the title page. But the publisher could not give him an advance, and the author, needing cash, had to peddle his manuscript. Murray looked at the proof sheets but found that the book "would not be in his line." Henry Colbourn turned down the proposition to publish it, presumably with an advance, on the same terms offered by Bentley, and Melville gave up the hope of seeing Italy. Longmans were not willing to offer acceptable terms. John Wiley's London agent, David Davidson, relieved his immediate anxiety by getting Bentley's note discounted, encouraged him to try other publishers, and introduced him to David Bogue. But Bogue declined the book, "alleging among other reasons, the state of the copyright question." Mr. Chapman of Chapman and Hall and H. G. Bohn both gave him short shrift. That night of Saturday, November 24, he sat in his room and thought of his dead brother, Gansevoort, "writing here in London, about the same hour as this—alone in his chamber, in profound silence—as I am now." He spent the rest of the night in "one continuous nightmare till daylight" before he could turn over and nap until ten o'clock, when he arose and got lost in the fog while searching for a cheap place to breakfast. Religious services in both Westminster Abbey and St. Paul's helped him through the "foggy, melancholy, sepulchral day," which he brought to an end by dinner with the secretary of the American legation and a "fine fellow" named Stevens with whom he hoped to "recover" himself "in the companionship and conversation of mortals."

Melville attributed his purgatorial night and the bad day which followed to the effects of "a cup of prodigiously strong coffee and another of tea" taken just before leaving a dinner party given by Joshua Bates at East Sheen. There he had also consumed "an indefinite quantity of Champagne, Sherry, Old Port, Hock, Madeira, and Claret" and had talked with George Peabody about Gansevoort, of whom the generous American merchant had spoken "with much feeling." But the nine-mile drive home in Peabody's carriage should have made him ready for sleep had he not been tense with disappointment as well as with stimulants. He had been well entertained in London. J. M. Langford had invited him to the theatre on the evening of November 19, taken him into the critics' box, and, two days later, entertained him at supper with Albert Smith, Tom Taylor, and several other sociable "young fellows." Murray had shown him through his portrait gallery of famous authors, presented him with guidebooks, and on Friday, November 23, had him to dine with the famous Lockhart and other dignitaries. Abbott Lawrence, the American minister, had received him kindly and invited him to a dinner which he could not attend because of his engagement with Murray. David Davidson had given him a good dinner and taken him to the American Bowling Saloon (where Melville's Honolulu experience stood him in good stead) before he had supper with Langford. Edward Moxon had told him intimate stories of Charles Lamb and presented him with copies of Lamb's works. Lord John Manners had put Bentley's establishment in a dither by calling for him there and leaving a note enclosing letters to Monckton Milnes and Lady Elizabeth Drummond; and the Duke of Rutland, although leaving the city for Belvoir Castle, had sought his address from the American minister. Such was the treatment that a successful author might well take as his due. Yet it made Melville critical, defensive, and ill at ease in his inability to receive it gracefully. Aware of the shabbiness of his cheap room on the fourth floor of a common boardinghouse, he left word with the servant that he was "out" to callers; and he was acutely self-conscious about his unfashionable green coat, which aroused amusement on board the *Southampton,* attracted attention on the London streets, and caused people to stare in church, but which he could not afford to replace. It was the contrast between the social and the financial rewards of literature, combined with homesickness for Elizabeth and "Barney," that made him feel like a spiritual Robinson Crusoe as he wrote up his journal on the Sunday afternoon following his bad night.

But he was determined to visit the Continent despite his inability to get any advance on *White Jacket*. His dinner so restored him that he was able to call on Mrs. Lawrence and find the minister's wife, in contrast to his first impressions, "very pleasant." The next morning he found that he could get Murray's note cashed, deposited £40 for Allan to draw upon, and visited the British Museum. With his pocket full of gold sovereigns shoveled out by his banker, he could repay Davidson for his courtesy by taking him to dinner at the Mitre in Fleet Street and pack his little portmanteau in preparation for taking an inexpensive cabin passage on the *Emerald* for Boulogne the next morning. After spending the night in the French port he took a third-class car to Paris and found a room at a hotel on the Rue de Rivoli while he sought for his friend Adler and looked up the lodging house of Madame Capelle, on the Left Bank, with whom Dr. Gardner had stayed during his student days.

He found Madame Capelle at 12 and 14, Rue de Bussy, on Thursday and engaged an inexpensive room on the fifth floor (which supplied him with excellent "atmosphere" he was to use later) for the week he planned to spend in the French capital. Adler got in touch with him the next day, and the two friends were often together as Melville crowded his week with sight-seeing and absorbed more German metaphysics. He managed to see most of the sights—the Bourse and the Sorbonne; the Madeleine, St. Roche, and Nôtre Dame; the abattoir, morgue, and Père-Lachaise; the Louvre and the Luxembourg; the Hôtel de Cluny, the Hôtel des Invalides, and the Museé Dupuytren; the Bibliothèque Royale and Galignani's Reading Room; the boulevards and public monuments; and, at the end of the week, Versailles. He obtained a twenty-five-sou admission to the Palais Royal on his second evening in town, and he and Adler attended the Opéra Comique. Twice, however, their queue was "cut off" before they were able to get into the Palais Royal when Rachel was playing, and Melville was "bitterly disappointed" at failing to see the great French actress. Paris pleased him with its many places of interest and with the inexpensiveness of its good food and wine. But he was homesick in the midst of his activity and determined to see more of the Continent before going back to London to complete his business. He spent the night of Thursday, December 6, in Adler's lodgings, enjoyed a final long conversation on metaphysics, and took the early morning train for Brussels.

Like most travelers, he found Brussels dull, after Paris, and was glad enough to take a train for Cologne the next day. Unable to get a morning boat up the Rhine as he had anticipated, he spent the morning visiting the cathedral, the museum, and other churches including St. Peter's, where he saw a Rubens' "Descent from the Cross"; and he topped off a good German dinner with an afternoon devoted to wandering through the old town, reading about the scenery and history of the Rhine, and writing up his journal. His slow night boat to Coblenz was cold and miserable, putting him ashore in the darkness of five o'clock in the morning for five hours of sleep before he went about his sight-seeing. The fast boat he took down the river the next afternoon was also too cold for comfort on deck, and he saw only the most famous scenes along the river which he unenthusiastically observed was "not the Hudson." But he was, as he put it in his journal, *"homeward-bound! Hurrah and three cheers!"* After attending the theatre and spending the night in Cologne, he arose at five o'clock in the morning, reached Brussels twelve hours later after a brief stop at Aix-la-Chapelle, took "a horrible long dreary cold ride to Ostend," booked a second-class passage on a waiting steamer for Dover, and "went down into a dog-hole in the bow, and there sat and smoked, and shivered and pitched about in the roll of the sea" from midnight until he landed at five the next morning.

From Thursday, December 13, until Christmas Day he remained reluctantly in London. When he arrived at his old lodgings in Craven Street, dirty from travel and with a week's growth of beard, he found the chambermaid wide-eyed over a letter delivered by a gentleman in a coach and sealed with a coronet. It was from the Duke of Rutland, inviting him to visit Belvoir Castle in January. But he was "homeward-bound" and conscious that Malcolm was "growing all the time." Letters from Lizzie and Allan, which he found at Bentley's, gave him "the blues most terribly" and made him feel "like chartering a small boat and starting down the Thames instanter for New York." A glass or so of punch with dinner and a new batch of cheerful letters delivered from the legation raised his spirits, and after reading them over again, in the mellow atmosphere of the "Edinburgh Castle," he was ready for a long night's sleep and a new interest in business.

Melville's fifteen days on the Continent had been economically managed, so, with the prospect of only a short stay in London before him, he made his first item of business the purchase of a new overcoat to take the place of the green one which had been playing the devil with his respectability. The new coat and a haircut so impressed him, apparently, that he dressed again in order to pay calls on other English people to whom he had letters of introduction—Samuel Rogers, the aged poet; John Foster, the literary editor of the London *Examiner* and the biographer of Goldsmith; and a friend of Evert Duyckinck's, Mrs. Daniel, at the College of Surgeons. The last was the only one he found in, and he spent the afternoon making tentative arrangements to go home on the packet ship *Independence* and writing letters before seeing Charles Kean in Douglas Jerrold's *The Housekeeper*. Still enjoying his new appearance of respectability, and hoping to make his final arrangements about *White Jacket* the next afternoon, he wound up his day by leaving the theatre at nine o'clock in order to buy a new pair of pantaloons before going to bed.

Saturday morning he spent searching the bookshops until he found copies of Rousseau's *Confessions* and of *Knight's London,* which he wanted, and killing time until he went home and "rigged" for a one-o'clock call on Bentley who was expected to come up from Brighton that day. He was not expected and the publisher had not arrived, but he was asked to come back at four and by six he was back in his room writing "Hurrah and three cheers!" once more in his journal. Bentley had not only purchased the book for the £200 he had first proposed but had offered to divide profits on all editions after the first 1,000 copies and had agreed to pay him in advance by a note at six months. The note, he was "almost certain," he could cash at once; and "this," he observed, "takes a great load off my heart." His trip was justified, and he was cheerful enough, while waiting for evening "tea" with Mrs. Daniel and her daughters, to read over the Duke of Rutland's cordial invitation and wish he could accept it. On Sunday, after attending St. Thomas' Church and hearing the Reverend H. Melvill deliver as excellent a discourse as he had heard "from an 'orthodox' divine," he spent several hours sitting before the fire, smoking cigars, and debating with himself:

> Would that One I know were here. Would that the Little One too were here. I am in a very painful state of uncertainty. I am all eagerness to get home—I ought to be home—my absence occasions uneasiness in a quarter where I most beseech heaven to grant repose. Yet here I have before me an open prospect to get some curious ideas of a style of life, which in all probability I shall never have again. I should much like to know what the highest English aristocracy really and practically is. And the Duke of Rutland's cordial invitation to visit him at his Castle furnishes me with just the thing I want. If I do not go, I am confident that hereafter I shall upbraid myself for neglecting such an opportunity of procuring "material." And Allan and others will account me a ninny. I would not debate the matter a moment, were it not that at least three whole weeks must elapse ere I start for Belvoir Castle—three weeks! If I could but get over *them!* And if the two images would only *down* for that space of time.—I must light a second cigar and resolve it over again.

His final resolve, long after dark and after a lonely dinner, was "irrevocably" what it had been at first: he would book a passage on the *Independence* and miss his chance. A steamer would get him there faster, but the extra hundred dollars was more than he could afford. Somehow he would have to "weather" the month that the sailing vessel would take.

Actually, he weathered the week before sailing without any trouble. He called on Stevens Monday morning, made his arrangements with Captain Fletcher of the *Independence,* got Bentley's note, and spent the afternoon in the National Gallery and the evening in bookshops and in doing such incongruous chores as mailing his refusal of the Duke of Rutland's invitation and taking a pair of pants out to be altered by a tailor. Tuesday was a miserable rainy day and the British Museum was closed, but Melville was able to occupy his time buying a map of London in 1766 in preparation for his story of Israel Potter, browsing in bookshops, buying presents, and making arrangements with Davidson for cashing Bentley's note. At six he dined with Bentley (whom he had begun to like very much) in company with the journalist Robert Bell and the comic writer and well-known caricaturist, Alfred Henry Forrestor or "Alfred Crowquill," who invited him to see the pantomime rehearsal at the Surrey Theatre two evenings later. On Wednesday, after a day in bookshops and the British Museum, he dined with Bentley's cousin, Robert Francis Cooke, in Elm Court in the Temple, which he found a veritable "Paradise of Bachelors" and a good source of literary material he was later to use. Breakfast with Samuel Rogers and another interview with Bentley (who gave him some free books) started off another day which was mostly spent with Cooke on a tour of London clubs and the new Houses of Parliament with an unusual opportunity to examine the frescoes in the House of Lords. He missed his engagement at the Surrey Theatre but got behind scenes "a little" and dined that evening with Robert Cooke's brother, "a barrister with a quizzical eye" and a good taste in companions, at the Erechtheum Club in St. James's Square.

His last three days in London were even busier: a visit to a Mr. Cleves in the Temple on Friday morning and a tour of its various places of interest, final arrangements for sailing, last-minute shopping, and dinner with Davidson filled the first. Packing and getting his luggage to the ship, cashing Bentley's note, and obtaining a letter of credit for America took up most of Saturday; and the day was brought to a close with a splendid dinner at the Erechtheum Club in the company of Cooke, his old publisher John Murray, the painter Charles Robert Leslie, and such literary figures as Charles Knight, Richard Ford, and Peter Cunningham. On Sunday morning he had breakfast again with Samuel Rogers, Barry Cornwall and his wife, and Alexander William Kinglake. London had treated him well; and, with his new clothes, money in his pocket, a good supply of books in his baggage, and a letter of credit for £180 in addition to the £40 he had deposited for Allan, he had no feelings of despondency or apology. He spent his last night in London in the company of Captain Fletcher and some of his prospective fellow passengers, devoted Monday morning to additional shopping and a visit to the Reform Club, and took an afternoon train for Portsmouth, where he spent the night, and embarked on the *Independence* early Christmas morning.

The voyage took longer than the month he had anticipated, but, except for a few notes on stories told by Captain Fletcher and on his reading, it went unrecorded; for during the first five days of favorable weather nothing happened and Melville decided that he would "keep no further diary." He meditated *The Confessions of an English Opium Eater*, which he had read with fascination during the last busy days in London, read in Rousseau's *Confessions*, browsed in Boswell's *Johnson* and in an old folio of Sir Thomas Browne which he had purchased, and read some of the plays of Ben Jonson. Something, perhaps, really did happen on the voyage; but Melville himself could not have realized it until he got home and began to plan his next book.

7

Second Growth

I

LOADED WITH BOOKS for himself and presents for his family, Melville disembarked from the *Independence* on February 1, 1850, without realizing that he was entering upon the crucial year and a half of his entire life. He was stimulated by his trip and eager to get home and settle down to work. The store of observations carefully set down in his journal would be useful for the new novel he had in mind—the story of an American exile in England and Paris—which would be a departure from his customary method of semiautobiographical writing. His adventurous years had been largely exploited, and if he was to continue upon a literary career he would be obliged to use his own experiences for merely incidental material while inventing or borrowing the narrative substance of his stories. For his immediate purpose he had the tale of Israel Potter, whose crude little biography he had purchased some time before, and notes on material that he was to incorporate into his own later book on the strange history of that forgotten patriot. Had he promptly carried out his evident intention of becoming an historical novelist, he might have achieved at once a minor but unquestioned place in American literature. However, something else happened. He wrote a book which failed to fit into any conventional classification, which turned his mind in a direction that led to temporary oblivion, and which eventually forced the world to recognize him as one of the major writers of the nineteenth century.

Except for the activities of one brief period, which represented the social high point in Melville's life, the physical events of these eighteen months were remarkably commonplace. Within a reasonably short time after his return from Europe he settled down at home to an even more severe working regime than he had adopted for *Mardi,* and by March 7 he was apologizing to Evert Duyckinck for not using his concert tickets

on the evening before because he had been "shut up all day" and consequently "could not stand being shut up all the evening." Instead, he
put on his "green jacket" and strolled down to the Battery to watch the
stars. His star-gazing, however, was that of a man whose eyes did not
permit him to work at night; for although an occasional dinner party with
good company at the Duyckincks' could bring him out in public, he devoted himself to his desk so conscientiously that on May 1 he could write
Richard Henry Dana, Jr., that he was "half way" in a new work.

But the new book was not the story of the American exile which he
had been meditating. Dana had evidently suggested that Melville do
for the whaling industry what he had just done for the naval service in
White Jacket and what Dana himself had done for the merchant marine
in *Two Years Before the Mast,* for Melville described his work as a
"whaling voyage" along lines that anticipated Dana's suggestion. "It
will be a strange sort of book, tho', I fear," he added; "blubber is blubber
you know; tho' you may get oil out of it, the poetry runs as hard as sap
from a frozen maple tree;—and to cook the thing up, one must needs
throw in a little fancy, which from the nature of things, must be ungainly
as the gambols of the whales themselves." Yet, lest Dana expect another
Mardi rather than a realistic account of two years before the try-pots, he
added: "I mean to give the truth of the thing, spite of this."

He may have had several reasons for changing his original plans. The
voyage home from England, made cheerful by the prospects of rejoining
his family, refreshed his memories of the sea and perhaps reminded him
that he had by no means exhausted the incidental material of his own
life as the substance of literature. Upon his return he learned that his
despised "nursery tale" *Redburn* had sold surprisingly well—more than
four thousand copies by February 16, according to his royalty statement
from the Harpers—and that *White Jacket* promised to do even better.
Both books aroused favorable comment. *Redburn* reminded George Duyckinck's friend Joann Miller of Defoe and "greatly charmed" her friend
Rosalie Baker. The *United States Magazine and Democratic Review* had
hailed it as a new triumph by "the most captivating of ocean authors"; and
Holden's Dollar Magazine had authenticated the Liverpool scenes in a
review presumably written by Charles F. Briggs, who had made the
same sort of trip and spoke with some public authority. *Holden's* review,
in other respects, was not especially favorable; but Elizabeth had news
from Boston that her father's friend, Amos Nourse, liked the book, and in
Philadelphia the popular *Graham's Magazine* found it equal to Defoe in
its realism and superior in its "deviltry" and "raciness." He had to wait,
of course, for comments upon *White Jacket;* but he had hardly stepped
from the deck of his sailing vessel in New York before an enthusiastic

review from the London *Athenaeum* was ready for the next Cunard steamer. "Mr. Melville's sea-creatures, calms and storms, belong to the more dreamy tone of 'The Ancient Mariner,' " announced the *Athenaeum,* pointing out his distinction from other sea writers, "and have a touch of serious and suggestive picturesqueness appertaining to a world of art higher than the actor's or the scene-painter's." With all his many faults, the reviewer concluded, "Mr. Melville possesses, also, more vivacity, fancy, colour and energy than ninety-nine out of the hundred who undertake to poetize or to prate about 'sea monsters and land monsters'; and we think that, with only the commonest care, he might do brilliant service by enlarging the library of fictitious adventure."

The last suggestion may have aroused genuine satisfaction in Melville when it came to his eyes, for it was exactly in accord with his new plan. In fact, it is not impossible that the plan crystallized around this suggestion and around James Fenimore Cooper's *The Red Rover.* Melville mentioned the new edition of Cooper's book in a review which Duyckinck printed as "A Thought on Book-Binding" in the *Literary World* for March 16—probably having requested it during the evening party of February 27, when Melville's wit was more impressive in an atmosphere of lively company and brandied peaches than it later appeared to be in cold print. Insignificant though the note itself is, it nevertheless indicates that Melville had been interested in Cooper's avowed effort to free the sea novel from the influence of Smollett by giving it a certain legendary flavor. Some of the incidents by which Cooper strove to give his book this quality were of particular interest: the mystery of the officer in command of a vessel, whose unconventional behavior caused his superstitious crew to mutiny in the belief that he was an emissary of the devil; the sinking of the ship in the ominous presence of a blowing whale; and the almost supernatural appearance, in the middle of the ocean, of the staring-eyed corpse of a man last seen the day before. Such material as this was the stuff of romance, although the romance was tempered by occasional bits of comic realism exemplified by the agent who talked generous generalities while taking a penny-pinching advantage of a man's anxiety to serve on board his ship and by a psychological realism in its stress of the Red Rover's strong-minded personal dominance over his crew. If such stuff entered into Melville's early calculations at all, it is evident that his new book was planned as something not unlike the work later published as *Moby Dick.*

In any event, whether the narrative plan of *Moby Dick* was definitely formed at this time or not, he began writing the first chapters of that book soon after his return from Europe. His brother-in-law, Samuel Shaw, who was then a freshman at Harvard, had visited him soon after his arrival and had taken back to Boston Melville's presents to the Shaw family and a letter to Sam's mother saying how much the returned traveler had enjoyed the visit of "that interesting young Collegian." But it could not have been long afterward that Melville sat down in the privacy of his study and described his heathen harpooner Queequeg, in the fourth chapter of *Moby Dick*, as being "just enough civilized to show off his outlandishness in the strangest possible manner." "He was," mused the successful author from the vantage point of his thirty years, "an undergraduate."

Almost from the beginning Melville's progress on his new book may be traced, through the uneventful months that followed, more readily than that of any earlier work. He had received the last of the proofs for the American edition of *White Jacket* by March 6, and within a few days had finished reading them and was free to devote himself entirely to writing—probably with highly stimulated energy during the first week of April when he learned that the first edition of four thousand copies had been promptly sold out and that the Harpers were planning to issue a fifth thousand in the middle of the month. By the seventeenth he was far enough along in his story to realize that he would need more reference books than he had at hand, and he applied for membership in the New York Society Library, from which he drew on April 29, five days after his certificate was delivered to him, William Scoresby's volumes on the *Arctic Regions* and the *Northern Whale Fishery*. His report to Dana on the first of May that he was "half way in the work" was perhaps excessively optimistic as a reference to the amount actually composed, but he felt secure in his rate of progress and on June 27, although by this time he certainly anticipated an interruption of his labors, he offered it to his English publisher, Richard Bentley, as a manuscript which would be available "in the latter part of the coming autumn." "The book is a romance of adventure," he explained, "founded upon certain wild legends in the Southern Sperm Whale Fisheries, and illustrated by the author's own personal experience, of two years and more, as a harpooner."

The hiatus in the steady progress of the book was a result of the success of *Redburn* and *White Jacket*. For Melville was at last getting a glimpse of enough prosperity to enable him to afford the luxury of becoming dissatisfied with living and working conditions in the crowded house on Fourth Avenue. Allan and Sophia were expecting their second child, none of the Melville girls had yet married, and a household consisting of a widow, two wives, three babies, and four spinsters would provide an impossible environment for a writer who was just hitting his stride and was anxious to keep up with the public demand for his work. With Malcolm still teething, Elizabeth dreaded the approach of hot weather; and she did not, in any case, relish the idea of her baby becoming fretful within hearing distance of her mother-in-law, who was growing increasingly formidable as Allan developed into the solid citizen she expected a son of hers to be. Although they first thought of a house of their own in the city, they eventually concluded that the country would be better suited to Elizabeth's simple tastes and to the demands of Herman's profession, and their minds turned to the Berkshires and to the village of Pittsfield, which had long been associated in Herman's mind with peace and relaxation. When he wrote Bentley that "circumstances" made it "indispensable" that he should be paid for his new book on the date of acceptance rather than upon publication Melville was thinking of using the money to get his family through a winter of independent existence.

Accordingly, in the middle of July, he returned to the familiar countryside for a brief visit with his cousin Robert and aunt Mary during which he intended to investigate the possibility of settling with them for the remaining part of the summer while he made arrangements for a permanent move. The old family house was more run-down than he remembered it, but it was still commodious and hospitable. As chairman of the "Viewing Committee" of the Berkshire Agricultural Society, Robert had to make a rambling trip of several days, by wagon, through the southern part of the county; and he persuaded Herman to go with him to ghostwrite his report (which was published in the local *Culturist and Gazette* on October 9) and perhaps to see what other villages might have to offer in the way of farms for sale, since the Melville place had already been promised at the end of the season to the Morewoods, who were spending the summer near by. The two cousins left on the morning of Thursday, July 18, and were to be gone for about a week. But Herman was impatient to get home. He deserted the wagon at Stockbridge on Saturday night and returned to Pittsfield by train with a brilliant idea in his head. The Berkshire hills were full of literary lights, and he would add to the galaxy by giving a house party, before the family home was sold, to his friends Evert Duyckinck and Cornelius Mathews and as a host perhaps outshine the friend who had so often dazzled him with distinguished company. Aunt Mary could look after Malcolm while Lizzy also enjoyed herself with more sprightly companions than she was accustomed to having in New York.

Within ten days he had gone to New York, persuaded his friends to come, and moved his wife, son, and sister-in-law to Pittsfield. Duyckinck and Mathews were to follow on Friday, the second of August, arriving late in the evening and putting up overnight in the local hotel since their proper entertainment was conditioned upon the departure of two strangers who were boarding with Robert at the time. Whatever plans Melville had in mind for their entertainment, though, he could hardly have anticipated the whirl of activity which followed during the next ten days when both he and his company fell into the hands of older and more energetic summer residents. The momentum began to develop when Duyckinck and Mathews met David Dudley Field on the train coming up and fell in with his plan to get up a party to climb Monument Mountain on the following Monday. In the meantime, the equally energetic Mrs. J. R. Morewood, the neighbor whose husband was to purchase the Melville house, had been making her own plans. Clad in a linen duster and equipped with transportation, fishing equipment, and bait, she arrived on Saturday afternoon to take the entire party to Pontoosuc Lake, where she and Lizzie (who had not yet caught on to Berkshire summer fashions and was dressed for a garden party) made the party hilarious with their incongruous boating costumes. Sunday was a day of gossiping and lounging in preparation for the strenuous activities of Monday.

Early in the morning the three men were up to take the train for Stockbridge and were joined at the station by the Melvilles' literary neighbor, Dr. Oliver Wendell Holmes, with a shiny rubber bag in his hand and a mind loaded with mischief. Field met them in Stockbridge and transported them to his expansive "cottage," where they all took a practice run up a hill near by while waiting for the other members of the party —Nathaniel Hawthorne, the oldest man in the group, who, at the age of forty-six, had just achieved his first great literary success with *The Scarlet Letter;* Hawthorne's publisher, the plump, jovial, curly-whiskered James T. Fields, with patent-leather shoes on his feet and his new bride on his arm; and young Harry Sedgwick, the only male present who had not written a book but who inevitably would and who, as a proper representative of the Stockbridge aristocracy, arrived on horseback after the others had gathered. The party of ten, including Mrs. Fields and Miss Jenny Field, punned and jolted their way in wagons to the mountain and scrambled and sparkled their way upward. As they approached the top they were caught by a summer thundershower which drove them into the shelter of the overhanging cliffs, where Holmes uncorked champagne and passed it around and around in a silver mug. When the sun came out, they climbed the short distance to the summit. There Melville found a projecting rock which resembled the bowsprit of a ship, scrambled out to the dizzy end, and began to pull on imaginary rigging. Holmes affected the symptoms of vertigo and declared himself "epigastrically affected" by the height. Hawthorne peered around for the great carbuncle about which he had written a story thirteen years before. Mathews, who had planned in advance to rise to the occasion, produced a copy of William Cullen Bryant's poems, adjusted his glasses, and, for the honor of New York, rendered the blank verse legend of the Indian maiden who had thrown herself over the cliff. The New Englanders politely mentioned Longfellow, of whom Mathews had been severely critical but who shared with Bryant the honor of being the most highly paid American poet at the time. It was growing too late for literary conversation, however, and the party started downward for the wagons and dinner at Field's.

The midday dinner included turkey, roast beef, and ice cream, "well moistened by the way," and lasted for three hours. Holmes apparently spent much of the time perversely riding Mathews' literary hobby concerning the greatness of all things American; for after the conversation had touched upon the monstrous sea serpent recently reported in New York harbor and upon Mr. Henry M. Payne of Worcester, Massachusetts, who had just issued a public challenge to scientists from the rest of the world to match wits with him, the little doctor offered his opinion that within twenty years the United States would be regularly growing men sixteen or seventeen feet high "and intellectual in proportion." The effect of climate upon growth and genius was a subject of old debate and, since it influenced theories concerning the future of American poetry, a lively one. The company ignored such topics of contemporary gossip as Stephen Girard (whose will provided for the establishment of a college in which no clergyman would be allowed to set foot) and the spirit-rappings induced by the Fox sisters of Rochester, and perhaps even Jenny Lind and the last-minute confession of the homicidal Professor Webster of Harvard, while they carried on a high-spirited argument which went so far as to introduce "a remarkable bullock at Great Barrington" as evidence. Perceiving the sharpness of Holmes's irony and of the division between the Bostonians and the New Yorkers, Melville, who had a claim on both cities, came to Mathews' rescue in defense of Americans against Holmes's more serious assertions of English superiority. The line of his defense is not recorded. But in an essay on Hawthorne, written within a few days of the debate, he argued that America should prize, cherish, and glorify her writers because "they are not so many in number as to exhaust her good will." In it Melville called himself a "Virginian" and quoted a "hot-headed Carolina cousin" as saying that "if there were no other American to stand by, in literature," he would swear that "Pop" Emmons' monument of epic dullness was "not very far behind the *Iliad*." "Take away the words," Melville explained, "and in spirit he was sound."

It was a great day, and five of the group—all of the men except Holmes, Melville, and their host—left a record of it. But the day was not over. Before the dinner party was finished, Joel T. Headley (who shared with Melville the distinction of being "the most talked of author of the moment") appeared and escorted them on a tour of Stockbridge's second natural curiosity, the Ice Glen. There in the slippery darkness of the late afternoon—where it was so damp and chilly that ice was popularly supposed to last through the summer—Hawthorne outdid his play acting of the morning by calling out in fear of the dark while Fields provided a less calculated amusement for the entire party by his panting efforts to keep a protective eye on his two prize authors, Hawthorne and Holmes, who were both under contract for new books. When they came out again on the peaceful fields of the Housatonic, they were ready for a quiet tea at their host's. On their way back or during the teatime, while Duyckinck was being cross-examined by Miss Catherine Sedgwick who had dropped over to see the lions, Melville and Hawthorne each had time to realize that he did not want this meeting to be the last. Before the older writer made his departure, in time to get back to Lenox before dark, he invited the younger to spend several days in his cottage.

The Pittsfield group had to wait for the ten o'clock cars, and, in the light of later events, it is not difficult to guess their thoughts as the train puffed its slow winding way through the night. Duyckinck alone could have looked back on the day with unqualified satisfaction. Mathews probably was reviewing its events with reference to the way he would treat them in a series of articles for the *Literary World*—a series in which he mischievously attempted to have the last word with Holmes by attributing to "the Town Wit" in all seriousness some of the statements Holmes had made satirically in his attack upon the "little man with glasses." Holmes was more irritated by Mathews than he had revealed and may have already started turning in his mind some of the couplets he was to use nine days later in a Yale Phi Beta Kappa poem. For the latter part of his *Astreae: The Balance of Illusions* turned the theory of climatic influences cleverly against New York by representing poets as giving up their "Strength from the mountains, freedom from the seas" as soon as they entered its foggy and commercial atmosphere, and it was also sarcastic about any "scholar" who would yield to the uniform standard of orthography such as that set up by the Harpers. But it was particularly vicious in its comments upon "the scholar's ape" of "the pseudo-critic-editorial race" which he represented by a "small creature" swollen "to alarming size" with "an eyeglass, hanging from a gilded chain" and tapping his leg as he puffed, patronized, put on airs, and hissed such words as "provincial" and "metropolis." Melville, more sensitive and perceptive than any of them, may have divided his thoughts between his new acquaintance, Hawthorne, and his own contribution to the dinner-table conversation—with perhaps an occasional glance at Holmes and a moody thought of the "Bostonian" flunkeyism to which he would refer and then excise from the essay he was soon to write. But they were all tired, and it was with relief that they found the conductor agreeable to the notion of stopping the train at the bridge near the Melville home, where all three New Yorkers—now that Robert Melville's strange boarders had left that morning—could stumble into bed.

The indefatigable Mrs. Morewood had wanted to plan a picnic for the following day, but Duyckinck had put her off because he had brought with him the proof sheets of Wordsworth's posthumous masterpiece, *The Prelude,* and was anxious to get out a review by the time of its American publication. Thus, until Headley came over from Stockbridge for dinner, they had a day of leisure which Melville evidently used to get acquainted with the writings of the new friend on whom he planned to pay a brief call in the near future. His aunt Mary had given him a copy of Hawthorne's *Mosses from an Old Manse* when he started out on his tour with Robert nearly three weeks before, but he had paid it no attention. Now he read the book with mounting excitement, for he not only was personally attracted to the man but found in his stories unmistakable evidence of the American genius he had defended at the dinner table the day before. The arrival of Headley may have interrupted his reading before he finished the volume, but he could have started meditating that evening an essay which would express his genuine enthusiasm for the work and also confound the Bostonian preference for Englishmen by justifying the New York attitude with references to a born and bred New Englander. It was a project which Duyckinck, who had long been one of Hawthorne's admirers, would have encouraged; and Melville certainly talked over his literary plans and prospects with his friend at that time, for the latter wrote his brother George, on the following day, that "Melville has a new book mostly done—a romantic, fanciful and literal and most enjoyable presentment of the Whale Fishery—something quite new."

But, after that Tuesday, there was little prospect of any leisure for composition. On Wednesday they had planned a drive over to Lebanon to see the Shaker settlement and call on some of Duyckinck's friends in the fashionable hotel, and they made the trip as scheduled with Herman driving his wife and friends in a spanking two-horse carriage while Allan Melville (who had come up Monday night) followed behind with the expectant Sophia in a sedate wagon. On Thursday Duyckinck had to rise at five in order to get a letter off to his wife before the four gentlemen set off at eight to pay a morning call upon Hawthorne in Lenox (where they were hospitably treated to a couple of bottles of champagne), keep an engagement with Headley at the hotel (where they were "saluted" with "a volley of bottles at the dinner table"), and drop in on Dudley Field (where their refreshment was not recorded) in the afternoon. On Friday the undiscourageable Mrs. Morewood had planned a twelve-mile drive and a picnic. But to Duyckinck's delight, early Friday morning, it rained just enough to keep a party from eating on the grass, and the picnic was postponed for another twenty-four hours. His first impulse was to take the next train back to New York, but, instead, he wrote his wife that he had reasons of which she would approve for prolonging his visit beyond the intended week and staying on until Monday. Since his only anticipated activities were the picnic, which he would have been glad to avoid, and a vaguely planned trip to witness the religious services of the Shakers on Sunday, which he did not make, his major purpose for staying was probably that of getting Melville's essay to take back with him for the next issue of the *Literary World*.

Thus the essay, which appeared in two installments on August 17 and 24 under the title "Hawthorne and His Mosses," would naturally have been undertaken during that Friday of expected leisure. But it would not have been easy going. The irresistible Mrs. Morewood had come over before the day was half gone and planned a costume party for the evening; and Duyckinck had received a note from his friend William Allen Butler saying that he and his wife expected to be in Pittsfield between trains at three o'clock in the afternoon. Although Melville could hardly have been the mysterious stranger with a luxuriant beard who joined Duyckinck at the station and whisked Mrs. Butler out of the cars in a vain effort to persuade her and her husband to stay over for the masquerade, he could not have remained unaffected—either in the house or in the barn—by the bustle around him as the wagon was got ready for Duyckinck's use and the womenfolk scurried around looking for costumes and making other preparations for the party. In any case, his essay was apparently still unfinished when he and Allan had to get into their waiters' costumes and prepare cobblers for the refreshment of their evening guests. The party was a success and the evening made memorable by an audacious pun from the respectable Allan—"an awful pun," according to Mathews' account, "portentous, ill-timed, rude, unseemly, mean, inhospitable, villainous, and so complicated in its scoundrelism as to cause the sudden and violent ejection of its maker out of a back door into the door-yard grass at midnight." The whole party, however, was able to see Captain Taylor of the "Pittsfield Artillery"—who was, most probably, the unsuccessful abductor of Mrs. Butler—safely into his buggy and off to his village domicile with nine rousing huzzas.

The next morning the inevitable Mrs. Morewood showed up with a char-à-banc and extra horses from the village livery stable, a great hamper of food, and a spirited determination that the Melville party and a considerable number of others should see the beautiful Gulf Road and the countryside to the west. They did, spending the entire day in the jaunt. In the midst of all this activity, probably during the Sunday of peace which brought it to a close, Melville's essay got finished and copied; and the two editors of the *Literary World* went into conference with their author on the spot. They evidently decided that the marks of its origin were too strong upon it, for Melville altered the copied manuscript in order to attribute it to "a Virginian spending July in Vermont" and removed from it his sneer at Boston and some of its anti-English nationalism while carefully disguising any other signs of its connection with a New York critic. Duyckinck took it with him when he and Mathews caught the train for New York Monday morning, leaving their friend free to return to his "mostly done" book.

For a month Melville had little to do except write. The arrival of another couple of paying guests disturbed the intimacy of the family on August 15, but privacy was to be had in the hot attic, where Melville found an old fowl-stained desk which he cleared away and made his own. Duyckinck had sent him a dozen bottles of champagne and a box of cigars after his return to the city, but Hawthorne was busy entertaining his mother-in-law and trying to drive himself through *The House of the Seven Gables* and there was no one else in the neighborhood whom Melville was eager to cultivate. On the third of September, however, he paid his promised visit to Lenox, during which he and Hawthorne drove Mr. Tappan over to Pittsfield and had dinner at the Melville home. It was the first chance the two men had had to become closely acquainted, and Melville found a good listener to whom he could talk philosophy, literature, or adventure without reserve. Hawthorne at least welcomed the companionship, and Mrs. Hawthorne was not at all sure but that she thought their guest "a very great man." He was, in any case, "very agreeable and entertaining"—"a man with a true warm heart and a soul and an intellect—with life to his finger-tips—earnest, sincere and reverent, very tender and *modest.*" Neither she nor her husband suspected that he was the author of the anonymous article in the *Literary World* which represented the most enthusiastic praise Hawthorne's work had yet received, and neither knew how important Hawthorne's influence was to be upon the new book then supposedly being completed. But when Melville left on the morning of the seventh, he and Hawthorne were mutual admirers and genuine friends.

The activities of Melville's next five weeks permitted little if any time for writing. He had selected the Brewster place, adjoining the Melville homestead, as his country estate and had found that he could buy the quaint old house, together with other buildings and a hundred and sixty acres of land, for sixty-five hundred dollars. The purchase would require another loan of three thousand dollars from his father-in-law (from whom he had already obtained two thousand at the time he thought of buying a house in the city), the exhaustion of his current account with his publishers, and a note for fifteen hundred dollars in anticipation of the royalties expected from his new book; but it would give him greater independence than he had ever possessed before and, on the whole, could be considered a sound investment. Judge Shaw and his wife came to Pittsfield on September 10, approved the move, and settled down for a short term of court at Lenox. The purchase was made on the fourteenth, and the new landowner planned to return to New York and manage the moving while his sister Helen, who had come up to see the Shaws, remained with Elizabeth and the ailing Malcolm.

In New York, Allan's wife had not yet recovered from the arrival of her second daughter on the fifteenth, and Augusta was also ill in bed, where she was cherishing the praises of Herman she had seen in letters from the Hawthornes to Duyckinck—especially the comment, "the freshness of primeval nature is in that man." The problem of packing and moving under such conditions was not an easy one; but Melville found time to attend a dinner party given for Sir Edward Belcher, young Bayard Taylor, and himself, on the twenty-first and was back in Pittsfield four days later with the expectation of being followed by his possessions and some of his womenfolk (for his mother and sisters had decided to move with him) about the end of the month. During the first week in October he was "as busy as man could be" sawing and hammering and moving furniture in an effort to keep up with the directions of from two to a half dozen females who were having their first chance in three years to re-arrange their living quarters. When Sunday provided him with a respite, he spent the day walking over his acres, admiring the apples in his orchard and the contrasting brilliance of the red maples and the young green pines in his woodland. Although he had no intention of becoming a commercial farmer, he had corn to harvest for his horse and pumpkins for his cow; and he expected to be out of doors, except when called in to execute new decisions about the furniture, for another month. By the sixteenth, however, the house was in comfortable order for the winter and Malcolm was able to run around freely, and there was nothing to keep him from dividing his time between his book and his harvest or woodpile.

II

The stimulating events of early August had a profound effect upon Melville's new book when he returned to its composition after the departure of his guests and meditated its progress during his physical labors in the autumn. For although Duyckinck had described it as being "mostly done," it still lacked copiousness in its treatment of the whaling industry; and Melville evidently intended to extend its length after his usual fashion as soon as his technical library was complete. He already had on hand when he began his work Frederick D. Bennett's *Narrative of a Whaling Voyage round the Globe* and J. Ross Browne's *Etchings of a Whaling Cruise,* and he had borrowed from the New York Society Library on April 29, 1850, William Scoresby's *Arctic Regions* and *History and Description of the Northern Whale Fishery*. He had also ordered at about the same time Thomas Beale's *The Natural History of the Sperm Whale,* but Putnam's had been obliged to import the book from England and it had not arrived until July 10, shortly before he went to Pittsfield, and he had hardly had time to look at it. Since the portion of Melville's own work which had reached a "half way" point at the time of his letter to Dana on May 1 could have contained nothing derived from Scoresby, and the part seen by Duyckinck could not have included much if any material from Beale, it seems most probable that he had been engaged upon a narrative which he expected to supplement in various places rather than upon the progressive composition of the sort of book he later published.

A careful study of the sources of the finished work bears out this conclusion, showing that he interpolated one distinctive chapter, "The Advocate," in his early sourceless narrative and did not begin to draw regularly upon Beale and his other sources of technical information until he reached chapter thirty-two, entitled "Cetology." It is quite evident, however, that when he began to rework his manuscript for the purpose of introducing technical information and description he did not merely add to its substance as he had done in his previous books and as he had started to do in this one. Of the seventy-four chapters which may be described as representing the central section of the finished work, all but twenty-two contain material based upon published sources of information—much of it from Beale—and some of the twenty-two are so intimately linked with chapters influenced by Beale that they must necessarily have been written after their author had access to the *Natural History*. Occasional allusions which have nothing to do with whaling also show that his revision amounted to more than his customary insertions of new material: the reference in chapter seventy-eight to an occurrence at Niagara Falls on June 25, 1850; the identification of "this blessed minute" in chapter eighty-five as "a quarter past one o'clock P.M. of this sixteenth day of December, A.D. 1851" (which seems to be a printer's error for the year before); and the use in chapter ninety of an anecdote which appeared in the *Literary World* for June 29, 1850. Melville may have salvaged large sections of the work in progress, but when he took it up again after the departure of his friends he not only began to enlarge but substantially to rewrite his book.

For this reason, in order to understand what was going on underneath the visible surface of his life, it is necessary to look somewhat closely at the new parts of the book itself in an attempt to uncover the intellectual and emotional stimuli which kept him working at it for another full year and which later affected his whole career as an author. Nothing that had ever happened to Melville in his travels was more important than the activities of his mind between August, 1850, and August, 1851, as he sat before his desk in the privacy of a locked room. Although these activities are recorded in his book, they are revealed there only obliquely; and it is impossible to recognize them at all unless the book is considered in relation to the literary tradition of which it was a part—that is, unless Melville's own work is examined against the background of works by other writers who were in his mind at the time he planned and wrote his own story.

These writers were almost all romantic poets and novelists or earlier writers seen through the eyes of romantic essayists. There seems to be little reason to doubt that in undertaking to write *Moby Dick* Melville, having almost exhausted the autobiographical materials around which he had constructed his successful early books, planned to make his new story a dramatic romance that combined the characteristics of a romantic novel with those of a Shakespearean tragedy. His cast of characters and his description of the work as a romance both indicate the general type of fiction he was planning to produce; and such early hints as his reference to Ahab as "a mighty pageant creature, formed for noble tragedies" and his allusion to the "tragic graces" to be woven around "meanest mariners" anticipate the stage directions, the dramatic form of certain chapters, and the soliloquies in high style which are visible evidences of his calculated intent to dramatize and poetize his fiction.

The romantic tradition in which Melville conceived and began *Moby Dick* is revealed by the opening section of the book itself and by the type of fiction which predominates in the lists of books he brought back from

Europe or borrowed during the first few months after his return. In general, he bought Gothic and borrowed transcendental romances. Both had in common a considerable element of mystery and either a hero or a villain driven by some intense emotion—often a desire for power—which kept the entire plot moving. Melville's Captain Ahab, in his early appearances, could have stepped from the pages of either. In his "greatly superior natural force" of brain and heart, in his "queer" state of being neither sick nor well, in his mysterious but somehow extraordinary past, this "grand, ungodly, god-like man" belongs in the tradition commonly called Byronic because Byron—most typically in his verse drama *Manfred*—so perfectly gathered up the strands of romantic mettle, moodiness, and mystery and wove them into an individual pattern which was enormously popular among early nineteenth-century writers and readers alike. Melville evidently intended to follow this pattern and, by drawing a popular type of romantic hero through the curious incidents and "wild legends" of the whale fishery, produce something quite new and entirely different from the realistic story by J. Ross Browne which he had reviewed three years before.

Melville may not have been conscious of one considerable obstacle to his success. The author who had composed the "Old Zack" articles and had made such sport of the Irish captain of the head in *White Jacket* possessed too much humor to take his Byronism straight. The humor is evident enough in *Moby Dick*—in the account of Ishmael's first acquaintance with Queequeg, in sardonic turns of phrase and frequent examples of verbal playfulness, and in the occasional tall stories succinctly slipped into the narrative. Like Thomas Carlyle, Melville could take romantic moodiness seriously but not with entire solemnity; and of all the novels he read during the gestation of his own, Carlyle's *Sartor Resartus* was the one which seems to have made the greatest impression upon him and which was to be most frequently reflected in his writing. Carlyle's manner was to become particularly evident in Melville's use of Scoresby's *History and Description of the Northern Whale Fishery,* which he obtained soon after reading *Sartor Resartus,* for he dipped into it and brought out the raw material of his own book with the same sort of Shandean humor that Carlyle exercised upon the various paper bags from which he extracted the autobiographical and philosophical writings of Professor Diogenes Teufelsdröckh of Weisnichtwo. Scoresby, in *Moby Dick,* was variously Captain Sleet, an Esquimau doctor Zogranda, a famous authority on smells named Fogo Von Slack, and Professor Dr. Snodhead of the College of Santa Claus and St. Potts. The elaborate bibliographical classification of whales and their kindred in the first of the intermediary chapters (where Scoresby is introduced under the first of his comic pseudonyms, Charley Coffin) is entirely in that vein of humor, and the vein is abundant throughout that section. Had something not happened to Melville's original design his humor would have considerably modified the book's high romantic tone.

The dramatic influences upon *Moby Dick* are less clearly traceable from a precise knowledge of the author's reading, but Melville is known to have begun rereading Shakespeare in a new edition with large print and with a new enthusiasm after hearing Fanny Kemble render the part of Lady Macbeth in February, 1849. He had also brought back from England two plays of Shakespeare and editions of Ben Jonson, D'Avenant, Beaumont and Fletcher, and Marlowe. He was even then caught in the net of Shakespearean idolatry and by the middle of 1850 explicitly shared the tendency of such romantic critics as Lamb and Coleridge to despise the "popular" aspects of his genius and admire him primarily as a profound and subtle literary artist who was to be seen at his best in the "dark characters of Hamlet, Timon, Lear, and Iago." How much he actually knew of Lamb's and Coleridge's Shakespearean criticism, however, is not indicated by external evidence. Duyckinck, who was a great admirer of both writers, certainly interested Melville in Lamb before he called on the English publisher Moxon and received Lamb's *Works* and Talfourd's *Final Memorials* of Lamb as a gift; and Melville's markings in the latter of these indicate an interest in Coleridge which may have led to the reading of other works than the *Biographia Literaria* he is known to have acquired in 1850. Insignificant though this may be, it nevertheless touches up a curious resemblance between Melville's anticipatory references to Ahab as a character who, "dramatically regarded," has "a half-wilful overruling morbidness at the bottom of his nature" and Coleridge's statement, in his famous essay on *Hamlet,* that "one of Shakespeare's modes of creating characters is to conceive any one intellectual or moral faculty in morbid excess, and then to place himself . . . thus mutilated or diseased, under given circumstances." Melville made the resemblance even more striking by adding: "For all men tragically great are made so through a certain morbidness. Be sure of this, O young ambition, all mortal greatness is but disease." Later Ahab's disease was to become more malignant and to be more carefully diagnosed.

But at the beginning Melville gave no indication that his mysterious, queer captain was anything more than an ominous character set up for a bad end by the "ambiguous, half-hinting, half-revealing, shrouded sort of talk" of the water-front prophet Elijah and by the clearer insistence of the squaw Tistig that "his name would somehow prove prophetic." Other characters were almost as ominously queer: the tattooed cannibal harpooner, Queequeg, who was evidently designed to play some major part in the story before he took his "last long dive"; and the tall sailor Bulkington with land-scorched feet, an outcast whose tragic fate and "stoneless grave" were foreshadowed by a formal address to his immortal spirit. The other notable outcast, Ishmael, was of course destined by his role as narrator to survive his companions' fate; but at least one other member of the crew, the little Negro Pip, had the finger of death put upon him from the very beginning. Of the mates, the chief officer Starbuck was created for trial by conflict, a man with a spirit to be bent but not broken; and the others were characterized with reference to strife, the happy-go-lucky Stubb being described as "neither craven nor valiant" and the little Vineyarder named Flask as a man of "ignorant, unconscious fearlessness." These, with the Gay Head Indian Tashtego and the gigantic African Daggoo, constituted the crew of the *Pequod* formally introduced in the first thirty-one chapters, although Melville referred incidentally to others such as the gray Manxman and Dough-Boy the steward and placed certain shadowy figures in the hold to be brought above decks later.

If *Moby Dick* had been published serially and Edgar Allan Poe had been alive to review the whole book from the logic of its first installments, as he had successfully reviewed Dickens' *Barnaby Rudge,* he would have had few qualms about anticipating the progress of the narrative. He would have guessed that Melville was preparing for a conflict of wills between a bizarre master and a steady though superstitious mate, a plot of dramatic violence in which the heathen harpooner was to play an active role, and a resolution of the action by catastrophe rather than victory. If he recalled his Bible sufficiently well to know that "king Ahab of old" had been killed by an arrow from "a bow drawn at a venture" and had read Joseph C. Hart's *Miriam Coffin,* Owen Chase's *Narrative* of the sinking of the *Essex,* or any of several other stories that might have been called to his mind by contemporary newspaper accounts of the *Ann Alexander,* he might even have expected to find the catastrophe caused by the very white whale of which Ahab so queerly inquired at the end of chapter thirty-one.

But except for the importance of the white whale, hinted at in only the last hundred words of the opening narrative, the concluding section provides a situation quite different from that toward which the book appeared to be moving at its beginning. Although it contains a minor clash between master and mate which the former does not force to an issue, the officers and crew are completely under Ahab's control. Queequeg has become indistinguishable in importance from Tashtego and Daggoo. Bulkington has disappeared entirely with no more of an accounting than may be explained by a revision of the early proof. Pip has gone mad, but has not preceded anybody before the heavenly throne. The narrator Ishmael has been so completely replaced by the omniscient author that an

Epilogue is required to explain his survival. The dramatic conflict is between Ahab and the white whale who is no longer a piece of machinery but a character with a personality and a strange suggestiveness of his own, between Ahab and the great ocean which hides the object of his mad search, and between Ahab and Ahab during a rare moment of humane weakness. The narrative has passed through the seventy-four central chapters like a straw through the surface of water in a glass, and the two segments appear disjointed fragments of the same substance, contiguous but not continuous with one another. Although these incoherences are not so great that an ingenious critic, determined to find some mysterious perfection in every admirable work of art, cannot explain them away, they are evident enough to suggest that something unexpected happened to the book during its composition—something which would have infuriated such a literary artisan and student of craftsmanship as Poe.

What may have happened can be inferred from a consideration of the crucial point at which the second growth of the book began and of Melville's recorded activities at that particular time. The first of the narrative chapters in the central section of *Moby Dick* is the thirty-sixth, "The Quarter-Deck," and the first of such chapters which actually contains materials derived from Beale's *Natural History of the Sperm Whale* is the forty-first, entitled "Moby Dick." The two are intimately related by the close parallelism of the explanations they offer concerning Ahab's attitude toward the white whale and by a continuity of narration which suggests that Melville's separation of them by the four intervening chapters in dramatic form was an arbitrary act of arrangement having nothing to do with their actual order of composition. The two seem to have been conceived together and written successively. In the second of these Melville was clearly referring to his source book while he wrote, for he borrowed from it some specific testimony concerning the ferociousness of the sperm whale (which Beale, incidentally, did not accept) and followed the *Natural History* in misspelling the name of one of the witnesses by writing "Olassen" for "Olafsen." This chapter in its present form thus could not have been written before July 10, 1850, and was probably not composed until after Melville had returned from his agricultural inspection on the twentieth and had spent the next three weeks in a trip to New York and in the entertainment of his visiting friends in Pittsfield. On the other hand, since both it and its twin are essentially preliminary to chapters forty-two and forty-four and to the main development of the narrative which follows, they are not likely to be late insertions introduced into the early part of the book as afterthoughts. They most probably date from the time Melville began to tinker with his story shortly after his friends departed on August 12 in their fond belief that the book was "mostly done."

This means, of course, that the second growth of *Moby Dick* began immediately after Melville had written his essay on "Hawthorne and His Mosses" and while he was still under the powerful influence of his stimulating conviction that the literature of America could rival that of England. For this essay was more than a generous tribute to a fellow author and a mischievous continuation of a dinner-table controversy over the present state and future prospects of American genius. It was a serious contention that an American writer with the intellectual capacity of Hawthorne could reach, through the medium of narrative prose, the heights of excellence achieved by Shakespeare; and in its serious insistence that Hawthorne had already approached these heights, it was a confession that the author of *Mosses from an Old Manse* possessed some extraordinary power of appeal to him at that special time. Melville had previously read some of the same author's *Twice-Told Tales* and possibly *The Scarlet Letter* without any great enthusiasm, and after the publication of *Moby Dick* he rarely saw him again except on business—although he enjoyed these later visits, bought his books, and, on one occasion, tried to interest Hawthorne in important literary business. The excitement and enthusiasm aroused in him by Hawthorne belonged entirely to the period in which he was reworking *Moby Dick*.

At the beginning of this period, at least, there is no doubt of the genuineness of the excitement and enthusiasm. In the *Mosses from an Old Manse* Melville discovered some stories with a "mystical depth of meaning" and a "profound, nay appalling" moral and others "shrouded in a blackness, ten times black." He found a man capable of mountainous heights of "humor and love" and depths "immeasurably deeper than the plummet of a mere critic." In this "still, rich utterance of a great intellect in repose," he decided, "Shakespeare has been approached": "Not a very great deal more, and Nathaniel were verily William." In the concluding section of the essay, written after an interruption of twenty-four hours or more, he added: "To what infinite height of loving wonder and admiration I may yet be borne, when by repeatedly banqueting on these Mosses I shall have thoroughly incorporated their whole stuff into my being,— that, I cannot tell. But already I feel that this Hawthorne has dropped germinous seeds into my soul."

The explanation of Melville's curious enthusiasm may be readily found in his preoccupation with Hawthorne's "blackness," in his appreciation of Hawthorne as a master "of the great Art of Telling the Truth" which Shakespeare had practiced only "covertly and by snatches," and in the particular stories and sketches that made the most profound impression upon him. Two of the last provide especially good illustrations of the thoughts by which Melville could be deeply moved at this time: "Earth's Holocaust," discussed in the first part, had as its "profound" and "appalling" moral the teaching that even if the follies and affectations and all the vanities and empty theories of the world could be utterly destroyed they would be re-created by the "all-engendering heart of man"; and "Young Goodman Brown," described in the postscript as being as "deep as Dante," taught the ambiguity of appearances, hinted that goodness might be merely a disguise for Satanism, and ended with the representation of a desperate and bewildered young man allegorically crying for "Faith." Either of these deserves the description Melville gave to the second—"a strong positive illustration of that blackness" which so attracted him in both Shakespeare and Hawthorne. The first declared something that the onetime primitivist, the admirer of the noble savage and the denouncer of civilization, had begun to suspect: that man is not innately good but may have the source of the world's evil in his own nature. The second sympathetically portrayed the agony of a young man faced with that belief. The ambiguities of *Mardi,* the increasing tendency to portray such inherently vicious or weak characters as Bland in *White Jacket* and Jackson and Harry Bolton in *Redburn,* and the strong impressions made by the "sane madness of vital truth" in *Lear* and the "great thoughts" in *Hamlet*—all culminated in Melville's excited willingness to accept the black moral of "Earth's Holocaust" as "Truth" and in his sensitive appreciation of the tragedy of "Young Goodman Brown."

Melville, in short, began to revise his romantic narrative of the whale fishery at a time when his reading of Hawthorne's stories and his meeting with their author had just served as a catalytic agent for the precipitation in words of a new attitude toward human nature which his mind had held in increasingly strong solution for some years. Such an experience, like that of a religious conversion, is exciting and stimulating to a high degree; and in his state of excited stimulation Melville was not content merely to feed new raw material into his story, as he may have originally planned, in order to give it a comfortable bulge and enable his English publisher to bring it out as a three-decker. He was emotionally obliged to put into it some of the force of his new philosophical convictions, and he could hardly have avoided thinking of it, in the secret recesses of his mind, as a possible medium through which these convictions could reach Shakespearean heights of expression. The book became, in its essence if not in its superficial design, a different one from the romance he had planned.

Just how the essential imaginative quality of the book revised itself at this critical point may perhaps be revealed by an examination of two short passages from "The Quarter-Deck" and the "Moby Dick" chapters which have often been recognized as crucial in the interpretation if not in the writing of Melville's drama. In the first, Ahab explains himself:

> All visible objects, man, are but as pasteboard masks. But in each event—in the living act, the undoubted deed—there, some unknown but still reasoning thing puts forth the mouldings of its features from behind the unreasoning mask. If man will strike, strike through the mask! How can the prisoner reach outside except by thrusting through the wall? To me, the whale is that wall, shoved near to me. Sometimes I think there's naught beyond. But 'tis enough. He tasks me; he heaps me; I see in him outrageous strength, with inscrutable malice sinewing it. That inscrutable thing is chiefly what I hate; and be the white whale agent, or be the white whale principal, I will wreak that hate upon him.

In the second, from the chapter "Moby Dick," which is so intimately related to "The Quarter-Deck" in its opening lines and in its content, Melville has the narrator explain Ahab to the reader:

> Ahab had cherished a wild vindictiveness against the whale, all the more fell for that in his frantic morbidness he at last came to identify with him, not only his bodily woes, but all his intellectual and spiritual exasperations. The White Whale swam before him as the monomaniac incarnation of all those malicious agencies which some deep men feel eating in them, till they are left living on with half a heart and half a lung. That intangible malignity which has been from the beginning; to whose dominion even the modern Christians ascribe one-half of the worlds; which the ancient Ophites of the east reverenced in their statue devil;—Ahab did not fall down and worship it like them; but deliriously transferring its idea to the abhorred white whale, he pitted himself, all mutilated, against it. All that most maddens and torments; all that stirs up the lees of things; all truth with malice in it; all that cracks the sinews and cakes the brain; all the subtle demonisms of life and thought; all evil, to crazy Ahab, were visibly personified, and made practically assailable in Moby Dick.

What, we may ask of this examination, do these passages signify concerning the imaginative growth of Melville's book?

In the first place, they signify that Melville modified but did not renounce his conception of Ahab as a romantic hero. The captain became less a conventional man of mystery, driven by obscure but powerful impulses, and more like the "half prophet and half fiend" Arbaces in Bulwer-Lytton's *The Last Days of Pompeii*—a man whose superior intellect induced him to practice "goetic, or dark and evil necromancy," instead of "theurgic, or benevolent magic," in his efforts to divert Nature from her "ordinary course" and control the hearts of men. For the Ahab of these new passages was led by his "dark imagination," like Arbaces, beyond the "appointed boundaries" of the ordinary human understanding and "into the land of perplexity and shadow"; and a note on a blank page in one of Melville's volumes of Shakespeare seems to indicate that he was aware of Bulwer's characterization of misguided greatness and may have reflected upon it while considering the "snatches" of dark truth he found in Shakespeare's tragedies.

This Ahab also belongs to the race of "demonical," or demon-possessed, characters discussed by Goethe in the autobiography, *Poetry and Truth,* which Melville had recently purchased in London. But his nearest prototype—the literary hero whose meditations his were made to resemble almost to the point of parody—was the hero of Carlyle's *Sartor Resartus* who believed that "all visible things are emblems; what thou seest is not there on its own account; strictly taken, is not there at all: Matter exists only spiritually, and to represent some Idea, and *body* it forth." Indeed, the Ahab who appears here had many resemblances to the Teufelsdröckh whose "strong inward longing shaped Fantasms for itself" and drove him toward them: he too had come to feel that the Universe, whether hostile or indifferent, was "rolling on . . . to grind me limb from limb"; he too had heard the words "Behold, thou art fatherless, outcast, and the Universe is mine (the Devil's)" and had replied with his "whole Me," "*I* am not thine, but Free, and forever hate thee!"; and he too came out of his "Baphometic Fire-baptism," as Carlyle had called it, as "a specter-fighting Man" whose "Indignation and defiance" against "things in general" was "no longer a quite hopeless Unrest" but something with "a fixed center to revolve round" and whose tendency to "eat his own heart" did not disguise the fact that he had "a certain incipient method" in his "madness."

But these passages also show that if Melville retyped his romantic hero he retained and made unexpectedly productive use of the dramatic method of creation which Coleridge may have taught him. The reappearance of the Coleridgean language in such words as "morbidness" and "mutilated" in the second quotation indicates that Melville was still thinking of Ahab as a sufferer from some mental disease. In modern terms, he would have been suffering from a "transference neurosis." In the terms of such a contemporary psychologist as Hawthorne's college instructor in "mental science," Thomas C. Upham, who had prepared the *Outlines of Imperfect and Disordered Mental Action* for the Harpers' Family Library, he would have been a good illustration "Of disordered Judgment in connexion with obstinacy of Belief"—that is, of those persons who "attach themselves to a particular object" or "seize upon a particular opinion" and "hold it with a tenacity which neither life nor death can separate" and which makes out-of-place and ridiculous "all appeals to their feelings, to their sympathies, to their common humanity." "Leviathan," Upham had incidentally added of such appeals, "is not so tamed."

Melville's representation of his condition, however, was more literary. Ahab was like Carlyle's Teufelsdröckh, in the passages quoted above, a transcendentalist who had not achieved the Everlasting Yea of optimism although he had passed from depression to defiance. He was a super-ambulatory rather than inactive case of the disease which the transcendental Coleridge, looking into his own mind, diagnosed as Hamlet's: a man with a "craving after the indefinite," who "looks upon external things as hieroglyphics," and whose mind, with its "everlasting broodings," is "unseated from its healthy relation" and "constantly occupied with the world within, and abstracted from the world without—giving substance to shadows, and throwing a mist over all commonplace actualities." Had Ahab's morbidness remained as ill-defined as it was when Melville first mentioned it, the measure of the drama in *Moby Dick,* like that in Byron's *Manfred,* would have been only the power of the author's rhetoric. By translating it from temperamental moodiness into a describable mutilation of the intellect, Melville gave his book an internal dramatic force which was genuinely Elizabethan in its power and which, incidentally, could sustain a humor that would have destroyed the dramas of Byron.

The third signification of these passages is that they had implicit within them "the pervading thought that impelled the book"—one that Hawthorne might readily have recognized and praised (as Melville said he did, in a letter of November, 1851) although we do not have the words in which he identified it. For Melville moralized his drama by making it a parable after the "germinous" fashion of Hawthorne's stories. Quite clearly, Ahab's "Fire-baptism" was in the name of the devil, not in that of the Holy Ghost. His spirit of defiance led not to the spiritual triumph of Teufelsdröckh but to the destruction of himself and of the *Pequod* and all its crew save one. In the language applied to his Biblical prototype, "king Ahab of old," it was a "lying spirit" which led into the path of undirected vengeance a man who had done evil in the sight of the Lord. The teaching of the parable was that same black "Truth" which had been struggling into Melville's consciousness for years and had been brought to recognition by his excited reading of Hawthorne's *Mosses from an Old Manse:* the human heart engenders its own evil, men seek or can be led to seek their own worst fate, the noblest appearance of heroic manhood may be but a pasteboard mask. It was a "Truth" which went contrary to all Melville's early assumptions, it was opposed to all he had been taught that he ought to believe, and it was one which all the obscure censors of the mind had resisted. But it is always a relief, in the familiar phrase, to "face the worst and get it over with," especially when someone else knows that you have done so. When *Moby Dick* was at last finished and Hawthorne had read it, Melville wrote: "A sense of unspeakable security is in me at this moment, on account of your having understood the book. I have written a wicked book, and feel spotless as the lamb."

The feeling of security was slowly and painfully achieved, however, and all the surviving evidence concerning Melville's activities during the year of unexpected delay in bringing his book to an end bears witness both to the severity of his labors and to the strength of his impulse to seek an additional outlet for his intellectual and emotional energy through direct communication with Hawthorne. In December of 1850, while his cow was dry and his wife and young son were away on a six-weeks' visit to Boston, he described his routine to Duyckinck: rising at eight, he fed his stock, ate his breakfast, and started a fire in the room in which he locked himself up and wrote without interruption until two-thirty. At that time his family had instructions to knock on the door until he was forced to stop, do his afternoon chores, and have his dinner, after which he rigged the sleigh and drove his mother or sisters to the village for recreation and mail. Unable to work at night—although he would sometimes skim over some large-printed book or squint with one eye at the paper while he wrote a letter—he spent the evening "in a sort of mesmeric state" in his room while his mind raced with thoughts of the work in progress or of other books he would like to write in the future. It was a routine which allowed almost as much time for unemployed thought as for thoughtful writing; and his mother and sisters, knowing nothing of the normal state of excitement produced by intellectual activity which outruns its physical expression, may have begun to fear that winter that Herman—like his father, during the last weeks of life, before him—was "peculiar."

But the son was experiencing the excitement of creation rather than of desperation. His mind was swirling with new ideas and old memories. In the early fall he had received a letter from his former companion, the Long Ghost, written from California; and, somewhat later, a shipmate from the *Acushnet*, Henry F. Hubbard, had stopped by to see him with a report of what had happened to the voyage and the crew after Melville's desertion. If either of the two old friends had heard reports from the second voyage of the *Acushnet,* they might have discussed another dramatic chapter in the history of that ill-fated ship: the loss of a boat from the attack of a furious whale and the rescue of one of its crew, picked up hours afterward and miles away, swimming through an empty ocean. There was also "a sort of sea-feeling" about the snow-covered country. Melville looked out of his window in the morning as he would out of the porthole of a ship. His room seemed a ship's cabin, and as the wind shrieked at night he almost fancied that there was too much sail on the house and had to resist the impulse to "go up on the roof and rig in the chimney." It was easy to work—but not to work calmly—under such circumstances.

After the return of Lizzie with Malcolm in early January, if her later recollections may be trusted, the pressure of Melville's creative energy mounted until he extended his period of fasting and writing to include the last hour of good daylight. He felt the need of relief through conversation with some understanding spirit, however, and on the afternoon of January 22 hitched up the sleigh and drove over to Lenox in an effort to persuade the Hawthornes to pay him a visit at Pittsfield. But Hawthorne was busy finishing his own new book, *The House of the Seven Gables,* and Melville got only a supper of cold chicken and a gift of the *Twice-Told Tales* for his trouble. Back to his intellectual solitude, he was rudely impatient with Duyckinck when his friend asked him, in February, for contributions to *Holden's Dollar Magazine* and for a daguerreotype portrait to be published in that popular and well-paying periodical. "I am not in the humor to write the kind of thing you need," he explained shortly without attempting to "bore" his friend with his better reasons; and he had too much "intensified vanity" for the common distinction of having his "mug" engraved for the public. Yet he continued to want the companionship of Hawthorne and on March 12 drove again to Lenox and talked him into coming over, with his daughter Una, to Pittsfield for an overnight visit on the following day. Kept indoors by a spring snowstorm, the two friends talked of their first meeting the summer before, of their mutual friends in New York, and of the thoughts that crowded the younger man's brain; for Hawthorne had finished his book while Melville was still wrestling with his, and each realized that it was Melville's enthusiasm which had kept their friendship from hibernating during the winter.

When the snow melted and the Berkshires began to show signs of approaching spring during the next two weeks, Melville took time to escort his boyhood companion, Eli James Murdock Fly (who had become a confirmed invalid), as far as Springfield on his way from Greenbush to Brattleboro; but generally he continued to be too busy writing to get abroad during the daytime. Nevertheless, he paid another visit to Hawthorne on April 11, enriching his friend's poorly furnished cottage with a bedstead and a clock, and afterwards took another day off to read *The House of the Seven Gables*—a book which he found full of "genialities" but also full of the same tragic perception which had so impressed him when he read the *Mosses from an Old Manse*. Hawthorne was an enigma who appeared to lack the normal vitality of a red-blooded writer yet possessed the tough spiritual vitality of a hero who would try to tear through the web of fate. Melville saw him as a quiet version of the hero of Carlyle's *Sartor Resartus,* whispering rather than shouting the "thunder" of his everlasting "No" in defiance of a universe which threatened to crush the individual ego beneath its heavy material weight. The enigma was fascinating, for Melville was feeling the same pressure and had no inclination to confine his response to a whisper. His failure to finish his book on schedule had got him into financial difficulties, and when he was finally driven, late in April, to ask his publishers for another advance he met with a refusal—a refusal which forced him to borrow $2,050 at nine per cent in order to pay off his note to Brewster. Furthermore, the inevitable revolutions of the universe were, as a matter of literal fact, bearing down on his creative activity and suppressing it: with the arrival of May he had to stop writing and plant his corn and potatoes if he wanted to get his family—which was due to increase in October—through the next winter.

Frustrated by the processes of nature, pressed by the march of the seasons, and exasperated by the conflict between his financial and creative necessities, he took advantage of a rainy day that kept him indoors during the planting season and let the turmoil of his mind overflow in a long letter to Hawthorne. It was a rambling and not altogether coherent outburst, filled with the perplexities that beset a man who had been brooding over the peculiar intellectual attraction exercised by his friend, over the contradictions between ideal or moral "truth" and the visible truth of consciously perceived facts, and over the conflicts between philosophy and everyday reality. It was also charged with his emotional distress at his inability to make his book come out right as a practical job:

> In a week or so, I go to New York to bury myself in a third-story room, and work and slave on my 'Whale' while it is driving through the press. *That* is the only way I can finish it now,—I am so pulled hither and thither by circumstances. The calm, the coolness, the silent grass-growing mood in which a man *ought* always to compose,—that, I fear, can sel-

dom be mine. Dollars damn me; and the malicious Devil is forever grinning in upon me, holding the door ajar. My dear Sir, a presentment is on me,—I shall at last be worn out and perish, like an old nutmeg-grater, grated to pieces by the constant attrition of the wood, that is the nutmeg. What I feel most moved to write, that is banned,—it will not pay. Yet, altogether write the *other* way I cannot. So the product is a final hash, and all my books are botches.

But the story was once more, as it had been almost ten months before, approaching completion. His "whale"—for he had begun to refer to it as an account of a particular animal rather than as a presentment of the "whale fishery"—was "in his flurry" and would soon be finished up "in some fashion or other." "What's the use," he asked, "of elaborating what, in its very essence, is so short-lived as a modern book?" If he should write the Gospels in the nineteenth century, he would die in the gutter; and he was trying to reconcile himself to the "fame" of going down to the next generation of posterity as a "man who lived among cannibals" and then being forgotten. It was the letter of a man who was trying to escape the excitements of intellectual activity and creative emotion and find sanctuary in the belief that his hopes were all vanity and vexation of spirit.

By the fourteenth of June he was actually close enough to the end to return the reference volumes he had borrowed from the New York Society Library in April of the year before. But his publishers were enlarging their plant, the printers were behind schedule, and the city was too hot and uncomfortable for good work. Before the end of the month he was back in Pittsfield, feeling some relief from pressure. The "tail" of the book was "not yet cooked," but he did not expect to be busy very long; and he had enough leisure to rest his eyes by working around the farm, construct a few "shanties of chapters and essays" which would hold his book together more firmly, and add footnotes to completed chapters which he was reading in proof. Although it was "only half through the press," he wrote Hawthorne, he could look forward to talking "ontological heroics" over a bottle of brandy with his friend in the near future; and he was in sufficiently good spirits to make a joke of "the hell-fire in which the whole book" had been "broiled" and to reveal its "secret motto": *"Ego non baptiso te in nomine*—but make out the rest yourself." Five weeks were to pass, however, before Melville could write Richard Bentley, to whom he had sold the English rights for one hundred and fifty pounds, that he was passing "the closing sheets" of his new work through the press and would be able to forward a printer's copy "in the course of two or three weeks." And it was to be two and a half weeks longer before he was completely free from entertaining relatives and gathering hay and sufficiently far ahead in his proofreading to bring Hawthorne and his New York friends together for another entertainment like the one of the year before. The finished proof sheets were not to be bundled up and sent to England until September 10, and it was not until after the proof sheets had been sent that he settled upon *The Whale* as his English title and decided to inscribe the book to Nathaniel Hawthorne "in token of my admiration for his genius." But when Evert Duyckinck, on his second visit to Pittsfield, wrote his first letter home on the morning of August 7, 1851, he might have repeated with literal truth what he had so mistakenly written exactly one year before: "Melville has a new book mostly done."

How well he had written Melville did not at the time know. Acutely aware of the way in which he had put his book together and of the nervous strain it involved, he may not have begun to realize its essential coherence until both Sophia and Nathaniel Hawthorne wrote him of its success. Replying to Mrs. Hawthorne on January 8, 1852, he expressed his amazement that a woman had found "any satisfaction" in *Moby Dick* and explained the phenomenon with the theory that her "spiritualizing nature" enabled her to see things that other people did not see and to refine them until they became "things, which while you think you but humbly discover them, you do in fact create them for yourself." "At any rate," he added, "your allusion for example to the 'Spirit Spout' first showed to me that there was a subtle significance in that thing—but I did not, in that case, *mean* it." Of the book in general he wrote: "I had some vague idea while writing it, that the whole book was susceptible of an allegorical construction, and also that *parts* of it were—but the specialty of many of the particular subordinate allegories, were first revealed to me after reading Mr. Hawthorne's letter, which, without citing any particular examples, yet intimated the part-and-parcel allegoricalness of the whole."

Melville was neither the first nor the last writer between Isaiah and Thomas Mann to have such an experience. It is, in fact, a normal one for an author who uses the kind of symbolism found in *Moby Dick*. For a symbol is an imaginative bridge between the general and the particular which may be crossed in either direction; and Melville, having tried without much satisfaction in *Mardi* the method of expressing a general conception in a specific image, had gradually slipped into the practice of letting his mind play around concrete details until they were made luminous with suggestive implications. Part of this was conscious and fairly obvious, as in the short chapter called "The Pipe" in which Ahab tosses the conventional symbol of peace into the sea. Part of it was a mental habit, built up while dealing with "the world in a man-of-war" in *White Jacket,* which had grown upon him more than he knew. It was the energetic burgeoning forth of this habit of mind in every phase of his writing which was the important result of his intellectual excitement while writing *Moby Dick.* The story which he wanted to sell, the whaling details which he wanted to exploit, and the dramatic vigor and heroic characterization with which he wanted to demonstrate the potentialities of American literature—all of these became the material substance that attracted the impulses of his more abstract thought as he brooded upon such questions as the origin of evil, the validity of intuitive perceptions which contradicted common experience, and the mysterious nature of man. Although the meaning of his calculated fable was that of his general observation, in a letter to Hawthorne, on the validity of the transcendentalist's experience— "But what plays the mischief with the truth is that men will insist upon the universal application of a temporary feeling or opinion"—it was a meaning to which he had committed himself with the enthusiasm of a recent convert rather than one which he had accepted with settled conviction. Thus the major "truth" revealed by the book was itself speculative, and its cold morality was humanized by Melville's admiration for Ahab's vigorous heart and his sympathetic awareness that he himself might have made the same intellectual error. He had compared Hawthorne with the hero of *Sartor Resartus* because Hawthorne had denied intellectually the validity of those appearances which Carlyle's hero had defied emotionally; and he had found in himself a tendency to shout his defiance of the universal illusion even while denying its reality. He was temperamentally closer to the passionate Carlyle than to the intellectual Hawthorne, and thus his attitude toward the seagoing Teufelsdröckh who became the hero of his own book was ambiguous. Intellectually he condemned him. Emotionally he identified himself with him. And some of the dramatic effectiveness of the book comes from the divided attitude which enabled Melville to portray a hero with a tragic flaw and to do so without a feeling of superiority.

He was never, of course, to be made aware of the full power of his creation, for it was not until a generation after his death that his book began to have the same effect upon his readers that his fabulous white whale had upon its pursuers, provoking responses ranging from studied indifference to neurotic obsession. But by the time he wrote Hawthorne his discouraged letter of June, 1851, he was conscious that the book was having a profound effect upon himself as its author. He had been unfolding within himself at regular intervals since the beginning of his development and had "now come to the inmost leaf of the bulb" so that "shortly the flower must fall to the mould." He had been going through a period of artistic development far greater than anything he had ever experienced before. Financial need and commitments to his publishers had prevented him from giving up his original design of a romantic but literal present-ment of the whale fishery. But as he worked at it he discovered that he had unwittingly begun to use materials that made their own structural de-mands because of their own peculiar and unanticipated qualities. The inherent dramatic power of the reconceived Captain Ahab was too great to be matched by the opposition of any individual or individuals among the officers or crew. Such a conflict might do for an episode like "The Town-Ho's Story." But Ahab demanded a more worthy antagonist. The white whale which may have been originally intended as a piece of ma-chinery—a wedge of dissension between captain and mate, or the arrow of fate from a bow drawn at a venture—began to dominate the narrative; and that was why the author's allusions to the book, at the very time that he was writing out his technical descriptions of whaling, came to be refer-ences to his story of "the whale" rather than "the whale fishery." The sweep of the drama became too broad and its intensity too great to be presented through the medium of a bystanding narrator, and Melville was forced into an omniscience which made new and severe demands upon the literary craftsmanship of a habitual spinner of pseudo-autobio-graphical yarns.

Furthermore, "the prevading thought that impelled the book" was one not only at odds with the author's earlier beliefs but at odds with the pervading thoughts of some of the greatest literary minds of his day—with those of Emerson, in whom Melville had become interested the year before; with those of Carlyle, whose book had made such a considerable impression upon his own; and with those of the great Goethe, whose autobiography he was reading with thoughtful regard to this particular point at the time he was writing. Nor, as his chapter on "The Whiteness of the Whale" indicated and his next novel *Pierre* would prove, was Mel-ville wholly and absolutely convinced that the great "Truth" of his parable was true at all. His struggle in *Moby Dick* was a struggle to master the art of reconciling a calculated plan with an independent organic growth, old habits with new techniques of literary craftsmanship, and an unwilling skepticism concerning the goodness of man with his will to believe in man's inherent nobility. Not only the book but its author had been going through a period of imaginative and intellectual second growth, and his allusion to the hell-fire in which his book was broiled was a reference to his growing pains. Although he was to try, in the years that followed, to repeat the popular successes of his earlier books, his interest in literature and philosophy was never again to be as relatively superficial as it had been before he wrote *Moby Dick*.

8

Misdirections

I

THE INTERRUPTIONS through which Melville pursued his white whale during the summer of 1851 were more stimulating than distressing, however much he may have agonized over his book at the actual time he was working on it. A visit from Judge and Mrs. Shaw, and from Allan, during the first week in July was probably restful, for Melville was on close sympathetic terms with both his father-in-law and his younger brother. But young Sam Shaw, who had just finished his second year at Harvard, brought more energy into the Melville household than Herman liked. He arrived on July 22 for two weeks and was joined by his cousin Samuel Savage at the end of the first week. Elizabeth enjoyed their stay and was willing to "let them do just as they please and take care of themselves"; but Herman undertook to wear down their spirits by walking them up a mountain on August 2, and for months afterward his favorite derogatory adjective was "sophomorean." Exactly what he thought of them is not a matter of direct record. But he had not forgotten them when he began his next book.

At the moment, however, his primary desire was to see them on the train to Boston and his house filled with more agreeably stimulating guests. He had written the Duyckincks to come up any time after August 5, and, on the day before taking the boys up the mountain, he had ridden over to see Hawthorne and invited him to bring Julian over for a few nights at Arrowhead while the New Yorkers were there and Sophia and Una were away from Lenox. He was planning another house party such as he had held the summer before at Robert's, but without the little bantams, Mathews and Holmes.

Evert and George Duyckinck arrived on the afternoon train of August 6, bringing with them "a fat cask and a couple of demijohns" which Allan had sent as tokens of his regret at not being able to accompany them, and they were able to have an evening of talk before falling into the hands of the now-indispensable Mrs. Morewood. Melville was reserved about his whaling book except to say that arrangements for its publication by the Harpers had been "concluded" and it was not available to another publisher. Yet Evert Duyckinck was probably reassured about his "inward misgivings" concerning "the probable effects of a second visit to Berkshire," and on the next morning their activities went into full swing. They found Mrs. Morewood—with her sister, a young lady from England, another from Cincinnati, and a poet named J. E. A. Smith in tow—already prepared for a picnic and delighted to have an extra wagon-load of companions. On the following day, however, the three men avoided feminine company by hitching up a barouche and pair, skirting their neighbor's house, and driving over to see Hawthorne—who was relieved to discover that his guests had packed a lunch for the trip and who produced his last bottle of champagne for the occasion. They spent the afternoon in talk and in a visit to the Hancock settlement of Shakers and got back by moonlight to the little red cottage, where Hawthorne's unpredictable housekeeper, Mrs. Peters, managed a quite respectable supper. Julian was particularly delighted by the expedition and decided that he loved Mr. Melville as much as he did his father, mother, or sister.

Mrs. Morewood took over again on Saturday with a musical party and gave them their "marching orders" for Monday, when she had decided that they would all take the train for Williamstown and climb Mount Saddleback or Greylock on an all-night excursion. In the interim they corrected their omission of the year before by attending the Sunday religious services of the Shakers at Lebanon. Evert Duyckinck, shocked by the enthusiasm and the gross language of the glassy-eyed preacher, found it "a ghastly scene." But the less conventional Melville was probably more impressed by the contrast between the crude impulsiveness of the preacher and dancers and the cool sophistication of the large audience made up of "city fashionables from Columbian Hall." The contrast represented not only two ways of living but two ways of thinking. The Shakers were uncultured and ignorant, and they were violators of conventions because they believed in the primacy of their inner impulses. But were the contemptuous onlookers, who could pay the rates of Columbian Hall, any better for their calculated suppression of the impulses in their hearts? The fable of *Moby Dick* provided an answer for such a question, but the problem still remained unsettled. Here it was, alive again, before the author's eyes.

If any serious meditations were aroused in Melville's mind by his visit to the Shakers, they were overwhelmed by the activity and gaiety of the next three days. Allan Melville and his wife came up for the ascent of Saddleback, Augusta Melville went along instead of Elizabeth (who was expecting her second child in October), and Mrs. Morewood replaced her poet with a clergyman in keeping her full party of five. They took the eleven o'clock train to North Adams, where they hired wagons to pull them to within three miles of the final steep ascent to the seventy-foot observatory on the top. A half tumbler of Port around helped them recover from their climb, and Melville was expert enough with an ax to get a roaring fire going, before which they could dry themselves out after a cold supper of ham and Heidsieck. The observatory provided a one-room sleeping story, and the party stretched out on quilts and buffalo robes. But the unsuppressible Mrs. Morewood remained gay until after midnight, feeding the company brandied cherries and shocking Duyckinck by her comments concerning his position "alongside of the English lady" until he began to mutter "Sleep no more, Morewood has murdered sleep." Augusta sat upright in a corner, until daybreak, counting the rats that ran over the covers, and only Allan was able to snore peacefully away and get a good night's rest. It refreshed him enough to talk down the sheriff on a trumped-up charge of arrest in North Adams the next morning, but no one was in proper condition to take an interest in Mrs. Morewood's proposal to make up a fishing party after they arrived home Tuesday afternoon.

She managed to get George Duyckinck to join her boating party on Lake Pontoosuc for Wednesday, but Evert was trying to resist her "maelstrom of hospitality" (as he called it in a letter to his wife) and compromised on accepting an invitation to a *"quiet* card party in the evening" which he fervently hoped would not involve champagne and dancing until daylight—since he and his brother had to leave at five o'clock in the morning. Herman was apparently able to get them off, however, driving them ten miles to Stockbridge to take the train. George had enjoyed himself thoroughly, whether Evert had or not, and Herman had rivaled Mrs. Morewood in being the life of the long-sustained party. He had not only played the host, done the driving, and cut the wood for their picnic fires; he had entertained the whole group by reading aloud a manuscript poem by Smith when they were all shower-bound in a hayloft during the first expedition, and, on Greylock, he had shinned up a tall tree and called the scattered climbers together with his loud and enthusiastic halloos. Bentley had notified him, shortly before his visitors arrived, that he would buy his whaling book; and, although he had not yet reached a formal agreement with the Harpers, the last parts of the manuscript were out of his hands and going through the press. He had only to look over the final proofs, make the necessary last-minute changes, and send them off to England before becoming a free man. He had every reason, for the while, to be in good spirits.

He was, as a matter of fact, in unusually good spirits when he conceived his next book amid the jumbled impressions which survived in his mind from July and early August. The "certain silly thoughts and wayward speculations," into which "the Fates" plunged him before the proof sheets for *The Whale* had crossed the ocean, were different from any he had ever experienced before. His half-amused irritation at sophomoric impetuousness, his feeling of satisfaction at being the hospitable master of his own house and country estate, his delight in the local meadows from which he could see the heights of old Saddleback, his pleasure in the joyous energy of civilized rural society, his awareness of the great gap between simple impulsiveness and supercilious conventionality, and possibly even his recent discovery of priggishness in so good a friend as Evert Duyckinck—all these swirled around in his mind in a procreative chaos. Shaping these disordered thoughts and his speculations concerning what might be done with them, perhaps, was his annoyed recollection of the frank disbelief of the British reviewer of *Omoo* in *Blackwood's Magazine* in the existence of any person in America who could sound so much like a landed gentleman as "Herman Gansevoort of Gansevoort." Such skepticism revealed an English ignorance of one aspect of American life which, romantically portrayed by a novelist, would have some of the charms of novelty that Melville had exploited in his books on the South Seas. Certainly he felt some obligation to his feminine readers, like Sarah Morewood and Sophia Hawthorne, whom he did not expect *Moby Dick* to please. For the ladies, he would serve up "a rural bowl of milk"—as he was to call his new book in a letter to

Mrs. Hawthorne—and, for the English, he would make the bowl as aristocratic as possible.

There seem to be no reasonable grounds for doubting that Melville, when he began to write the book which was to be called *Pierre,* was planning to turn out a genuinely popular story, touched by the strange mystery of the Gothic romance yet full of the "genialities" he had so admired in *The House of the Seven Gables.* Hawthorne had worked a similar vein with great success, and Melville had no reason to suppose that he could not do likewise. His setting, a New York manorial estate before the time of the rent wars, would be a novel departure from the ordinary paths of life familiar to most of his readers. An idyllic atmosphere and an archaic language, such as Hawthorne used in the dialogue of *The Scarlet Letter,* would keep it from degenerating into realism. And in such a book he could explore at will "the truth of the human heart" which Hawthorne had said was essential to a good romance. All occasions seemed to conspire with him for a happy outcome. His neighbor and friend had led the way; a reading public was ready for what he had to give; and the inspiration was bubbling in his recent impressions. For once, he would not have to borrow or buy a book from which to get material: he could draw upon his own family background and his boyhood impressions of fact and legend.

During the first two months of composition, at least, the words seem to have come easily from Melville's pen. He did his autumn chores and entertained the Shaws in mid-September with so little worry about lost time that he could take a day off to drive to Lake Pontoosuc on the last Friday in the month and on the next Thursday escort three of his sisters to a plowing contest and take a long walk with them and Mrs. Morewood afterward. His second son was born on the afternoon of October 22, and although the father may have been jittery enough, while recording the event, to give the town clerk the name of his own mother rather than that of the child, he does not seem to have been nearly so tense as he was during the similar period which intervened between the birth of Malcolm and the publication of *Mardi.* He was spending much of his time in the woods with ax, wedge, and beetle, getting in his winter's supply of fuel; and he was too actively engaged in practical affairs to brood very much about his writing or anything else. When Duyckinck sent him a newspaper account of the actual sinking of the *Ann Alexander* of New Bedford, by a sperm whale, he was spontaneously enthusiastic: "Ye Gods! what a Commentator is this Ann Alexander whale. What he has to say is short and pithy and very much to the point. I wonder if my evil art has raised this monster."

The strange gaiety in the early chapters of *Pierre*—which was eventu-

ally to appear hectic in the light of what followed—was originally, perhaps, nothing more than the awkward geniality of casual writing. The
nearest Melville had ever come to a hereditary country estate was his˙
uncle Herman's new ground at Gansevoort or the poverty-stricken farm
of his uncle Thomas and cousin Robert in Pittsfield. His own mother,
it is true, was a matriarch; but she would have been scandalized beyond
words at any suggestion that she possessed any of the coy whimsicality
portrayed in the mother of Pierre Glendinning. And the young sweethearts, Pierre and Lucy, haunted by a dark mysterious face, were the
creatures of pure if slightly satiric romantic fancy. Melville's imagination
was inclined to crystallize around the substance of his own past, and he
raked up as many memories as he could for his new story; but they were
peripheral rather than central to his invention, and he had to strain his
rhetoric in an effort to hold his materials together. It was his first narrative wholly conceived in the third person, too, and so made new technical
demands upon him.

At some time in late November or early December he became worried. When Mrs. Morewood came back from the city to spend Christmas
in the Berkshires she heard that since she had left in November he had
become so "engaged in a new work as frequently not to leave his room
till quite dark in the evening—when he for the first time in the whole
day partakes of solid food." Such discipline was more severe than any
he had adopted while writing *Moby Dick,* and his kindhearted neighbor
was convinced that "he must therefore write under a state of morbid excitement which will soon injure his health." But Melville cheerfully
admitted that he was probably "slightly insane," continued to shock
Mr. Morewood by his religious views and irreverent language, and succeeded in giving Sarah the impression that he "cares very little as to
what others may think of him or his books so long as they sell well." Yet
she felt "strangely" attached to the whole Melville family and had them
over for Christmas dinner.

Actually, Melville had been casting his accounts and finding that
they added up to a serious need for a new book by spring. He had drawn
drafts upon Bentley as of three and six months from the date his English
publisher was due to receive the proofs of *Moby Dick* and, after discounts
and other expenses, had received only $703.08 in cash to see him through
the winter. Shortly afterward Allan had drawn up a summary of his
earnings as an author, revealing that he had averaged only about $1,200.00
for each of his first six books; and on November 25 he had received a new
statement from the Harpers, showing that, although *Moby Dick* had sold
1,535 copies in less than two weeks after publication, his account was still
overdrawn by $422.82, which had to be paid before he received any

returns from the American edition. From the averages, his prospects looked poor.

Furthermore, it was not at all certain that *Moby Dick* was going to be received better than *Mardi* had been. The earliest English notices, with the exception of an enthusiastic review in *John Bull* and a favorable one in *The Leader,* were not encouraging; and American opinion varied. The *Home Journal* was loyal, as usual, but the supposedly dependable *Literary World* was wavering—at least to the extent of objecting to its vein of moralizing in "the run-a-muck style of Carlyle" and its appearance of violating and defacing some of "the most sacred associations of life." Neither of the Duyckincks liked what Melville had done to the book in its revision. While Evert was publicly objecting to its stylistic and intellectual heterodoxies and to Captain Ahab as being "too long drawn out," George was privately groaning over the tediousness of the whaling material. But Melville would have been pleased to know that Longfellow bought a copy as soon as it appeared in a Cambridge bookshop, read it all evening, and described it in his journal as "very wild, strange and interesting." Hawthorne, after writing enthusiastically to the author, took Duyckinck gently to task for not doing justice to it in his review; and at least two ladies, Sophia Hawthorne and Joann Miller, liked it very much.

But there was no promise that it would have the popular success of *Typee* and *Omoo.* On the contrary, in January, 1852, some important signs may have been pointing in the opposite direction. *Harper's New Monthly Magazine* for the preceding month had shown all the enthusiasm that might be expected from an organ of his own publishers, but a severe attack in the January number of the *Democratic Review,* accusing the author of *Moby Dick* of imposing upon the public out of his "immeasurable vanity," must have hurt him severely. It is not surprising that he should have grown tense over the new work in preparation. Furthermore, his household routine was also upset; for, just after Christmas, Elizabeth decided that her looks belied the real state of her health and that she needed to go "home" in order fully to recuperate from her confinement. Although he had been too busy to accept an invitation to attend a memorial dinner for James Fenimore Cooper before Christmas and had written a letter about Cooper instead, Herman escorted her to New York and spent a few days with Allan before he saw his wife and baby safely on their way to Boston, where she was to remain until February 12. He was too busy to see as much of Duyckinck as he usually did on his visits; but he probably took time to check up on a few city scenes he planned to use in *Pierre* and certainly talked over his literary business with Allan—who soon afterward, in preparation for negotiating a contract for the new book, asked the Harpers for a special statement of his brother's account on the first of February. Back in Pittsfield, Herman settled down to complete his job as quickly as possible.

At this time Melville may really have thought that he was preparing the "rural bowl of milk" which he promised to Mrs. Hawthorne in a letter written from New York. The mysterious face which haunted Lucy and Pierre was that of a dark girl who believed herself to be Pierre's illegitimate sister, and Pierre, half intuitively convinced of her claims and half persuaded by the empirical evidence offered by a concealed portrait of his father, accepted her as such. The experience of a wayward servant girl named Delly, however, made him realize that his mother could never accept the dark Isabel into the family or endure any scandal in her world of proprieties. Accordingly, after brooding too much if not too precisely upon the event, Pierre yielded to a burst of sophomoric impulsiveness and, without explanation either to his mother or his fiancée, announced that he had married the stranger and thus given her the Glendinning name. To his innocent surprise, Mrs. Glendinning hysterically refused to accept Isabel as a daughter-in-law either; and he left for New York, taking his supposed bride and the outcast Delly with him. The trustful and devoted Lucy was to join them later, pursued by Pierre's cousin, Glen Stanley, who was in love with her, and by an indignant naval officer who was her brother. Running through the story was the extraordinary collection of mysteries to which Melville called atention by giving it a subtitle "The Ambiguities": the conventionally romantic mystery of Isabel's origin; the mystery, both to himself and to his associates, of Pierre's peculiar behavior; the mystery of love, which might be either destroyed or strengthened by shock; the mystery of virtue, which could not always be pure and practical at the same time; and the mystery of knowledge, which Melville had already tentatively explored in his chapter on "The Whiteness of the Whale" in *Moby Dick*. There were enough ambiguities in the book to arouse the curiosity of anybody, on any intellectual level.

Melville evidently intended to represent Pierre's New York ménage as a sort of cultured Shaker establishment in which the inmates, surrounded by transcendental "Apostles," lived a life of highly emotional celibacy while practicing the arts instead of agriculture. From it could have emerged, at the end, either an explanation of the more superficial mysteries and a happy conclusion or a tragedy of unresolved misunderstandings. Pierre was a sophomoric Ahab, getting himself and others into trouble by following his transcendental intuitions, but there was not much in the satiric amusement with which he was characterized to require a tragic fate for him or his friends. Following the fable implicit in *Moby*

Dick, Melville could either have nipped him in the bud, as he had blasted Ahab in full bloom, or have merely knocked the dew off his innocence. There was nothing in his rural bowl of milk which would necessarily cause it to turn sour.

But there was, as usual, a ferment in Melville—especially after he began to cut himself off from normal communication and live for long hours of the day entirely in his book. Unlike Hawthorne, whose precedent he thought he was following, he did not decide in advance upon the truth he wanted to represent and select precise symbols through which he would express it. Each of his intellectualized books was a voyage of exploration, chartless in *Mardi,* ambitiously calculated in *Moby Dick,* and without preliminary soundings in *Pierre.* Much of the calculated intellectual design of the whaling story was repeated in the tale of New York. The pattern of *Hamlet* was more clearly displayed in the later book, and so was the conflict between transcendental and empirical knowledge. But in seeking out what Hawthorne had called "the truth of the human heart," Melville began to dive beneath the surface of formal dramatic or philosophical conflicts. He may have pursued a great philosophical question in *Moby Dick;* but in the depths, as he hinted to Hawthorne in late November, when he learned that his friend had understood the meaning of that book, was bigger game. "So, now, let us add Moby Dick to our blessing, and step from that," he wrote. "Leviathan is not the biggest fish;—I have heard of Krakens."

Thus Melville had apparently begun to dive deeply into the "significances" of his romance at about the time he began to apply himself intensely to it. Its implications, he discovered, were potentially larger than those of the preceding book. He was still interested in the relative values of the transcendental and the empirical theories of knowledge— the inspired impulse as opposed to practical common sense—and less inclined than he had been in *Moby Dick* to dismiss irrational impulsiveness as mere insanity. Yet if a man without common sense was not mad, what was the true nature of the force which impelled his irrational behavior? Was Pierre really "noble" in his absurd attempt to give Isabel the Glendinning name without disillusioning his mother? Or was he the victim of sexual attraction and a perverse fascination which he elevated into an illusion of nobility because he could not face their real nature? Was his impulse suprarational or subrational? Did it come from heaven? or from hell? Such questions as these led Melville into a more searching, if less conclusive, exploration of the truth of the human heart than Hawthorne had ever attempted.

By the time he was little more than a third of the way through his book, Melville had become aware of some of the regions he would have to explore if he followed "the endless, winding way" of "the flowing river in the cave of man," careless of whither he might be led and reckless of where he might land. Had Isabel been "a humped, and crippled, hideous girl," Pierre would not have been so enthusiastically inspired in his devotion to the ideal of absolute justice. "Womanly beauty, and not womanly ugliness, invited him to champion the right." Yet at the beginning Melville apparently planned to recognize Isabel's physical attractiveness only as a subordinate quality, admitted frankly in an effort to keep Pierre from seeming impossibly "perfect" and "immaculate." It was, he said explicitly, one of the "mere contingent things, and things that he knew not," which helped contain the "heavenly fire" of his enthusiasm within his human "clay."

But Melville was also consciously and contemptuously aware of the superficiality of the ordinary novel in its attempts "to unravel, and spread out, and classify, the more thin than gossamer threads which make up the complex web of life." He recognized the impossibility of "systematising eternally unsystemisable elements," but he was determined to dive deeper beneath the surface than custom demanded; and, before he was half through his story, he wove the "contingent" attraction of Isabel into the main theme of her appeal to Pierre. In doing so, he clearly intended to represent his hero as sublimating his primitive feelings toward the mysterious stranger. Not having grown up in a natural relation to him, she was "forever unsistered from him by the stroke of Fate," Melville wrote, "and apparently forever, and twice removed from the remotest possibility of that love which had drawn him to Lucy." Yet she was "still the object of the ardentest and deepest emotions of his soul"; and, "therefore, to him, Isabel wholly soared out of the realms of mortalness, and for him became transfigured in the highest heaven of uncorrupted Love."

There was nothing, in the middle of the nineteenth century, very extraordinary about this. Only a decade before a respectable young man of Melville's own age, James Russell Lowell, had launched his literary career with a volume of verse which reflected a genuine attempt to sublimate his primitive feelings in precisely the same way. This analysis of Pierre was no more than an attempt to represent the high-minded young transcendental hero as some such characters, in real life, represented themselves. Nor was Melville's obviously satiric attitude toward his hero necessarily an indication of disapproval toward his transcendentalism. Even when he scolded Pierre, he did so in the sort of language used by the transcendental Carlyle toward people who had not yet seen the full light: "Well may'st thou distrust thyself," he wrote, shortly after this analysis, "and curse thyself, and tear thy *Hamlet* and thy *Hell!* Oh! fool, blind fool, and a million times an ass! Go, go thou poor and feeble one!

High deeds are not for such blind grubs as thou! Quit Isabel, and go to Lucy!" Whether such language was to be read as an ironic parody or to be taken seriously was something for the reader to decide.

For the major calculated ambiguity of the novel was the moral behavior of its hero. Was it morally right or wrong for Pierre to have followed his notion of achieving absolute justice, granting, perhaps, that his methods reflected an immature judgment? Melville thought he was supplying materials for a debate, on a high plane, between the transcendentalist and the exponent of common sense. He had traveled too much in the South Seas and too little in conventional literary society to make the egregious Victorian assumption that moral problems were primarily related to sex; and he may have assumed, if the matter crossed his mind at all, that he could touch upon the "contingent" attraction of Isabel to Pierre without confusing the higher moral issue. At any rate, the imagery of light and darkness he so consistently used was adopted solely for its philosophical implications. In his deliberately ambiguous novel, the symbolic darkness of Isabel may have stood for Melville's peculiar notion of "black" truth or for the more conventional darkness of error; but it did not stand for impurity. Isabel was originally imagined with only a romantic and incidental resemblance to the dark temptress in *Mardi:* she did not attempt to hold Pierre in any sensual bower of bliss. It was not until Melville reached the last quarter of the book that he began to dwell seriously upon her sensual attractions.

In fact, Melville seems to have kept his prospective readers fairly well in mind until after he had returned from New York in January, 1852, feeling under pressure to complete his book and perhaps somewhat sorry for himself. He had committed himself to delivering the manuscript; he knew that he would have difficulty in doing so; and Elizabeth, simply by nervously talking too much, was placing him under some extra and unnecessary strain. She had disturbed Mrs. Morewood by saying that although Sarah had "some good" in her, she had no "real character" or "fixed purpose in life." And she undoubtedly disturbed him, whether he would admit it or not, by spreading the report all along her circuitous route to Boston that her husband was ruining himself with overwork. She was certainly not helping his situation by going off while his other faithful copyist, Augusta, was spending the winter in New York with Allan and the once-more-expectant Sophia, who needed her worse than Herman did at the time she agreed to stay. Under the circumstances, Herman had to accept and keep the services of his sister Helen, despite the fact that she had been invited to visit the Custises in Brookline, where a certain Mr. George Griggs also lived. Mrs. Morewood had freely hinted that his New York friends thought him crazy, and the most intimate of them, Duyckinck, had commented upon *Moby Dick* like a missionary on *Typee* and had reprinted the review in the *Dollar Magazine*. Furthermore, under pressure, he began to draw more directly upon his own immediate experiences, displaying through the medium of Pierre an exaggerated version of the author's toils by combining the long hours he was currently working with the mental frustrations he probably suffered while writing *Moby Dick*. Hawthorne had moved away in November, and he had no outlet for his emotions except through his manuscript. He turned reckless in the concluding sections of *Pierre,* but, at that, he left unexpressed most of the normal feelings of a man in his circumstances—feelings that might readily have been introduced into what had become a story of impotent striving against economic circumstances, priggish society, unadmitted biological demands, and the waywardness of creative inspiration.

Instead he tried to keep his sense of humor. After drawing a caricature of Pierre as a cold but unconquerable author, doubly shod and with hot bricks under his feet, coated and overcoated and cloaked over all, with a biscuit available in case of hunger and a basin of cold water and a towel for his brow when outraged nature made him feverish during the course of eight unmoving hours, Melville stepped back and looked at the scene: "A rickety chair, two hollow barrels, a plank, paper, pens, and infernally black ink, four leprously dingy white walls, no carpet, a cup of water, and a dry biscuit or two. Oh, I hear the leap of the Texan Comanche, as at this moment he goes crashing like a wild deer through the green underbrush; I hear his glorious whoop of savage and untamable health; and then I look in at Pierre. If physical, practical unreason make the savage, which is he? Civilization, Philosophy, Ideal Virtue! behold your victim!" However much Melville may have drawn upon his own experience and emotions for his hero, he kept him, not too sympathetically, a sophomore.

Yet there was no humor in an earlier scene in which Pierre, newly come to his city lodgings, rhetorically expressed Melville's own thought that the "contingent" attraction of Isabel might be the real one: "If to follow Virtue to her uttermost vista, where common souls never go; if by that I take hold on hell, and the uttermost virtue, after all, prove but a betraying pander to the monstrousest vice,—then close in and crush me, ye stony walls, and into one gulf let all things tumble together!" In seriously suggesting that Pierre had not been sublimating but had merely been rationalizing his primitive feelings, Melville was winding his way through the "cavern of man" into a dangerous region. It was all right to suggest that an ideal of "uncorruptible Love" might lead a man astray, for transcendentalism was not generally treated with reverence—especially by New Yorkers—in 1851. But sex was. And a hint that Platonic love might be the disguise for something more corruptible than even ordinary love was something Melville should have known would prove nerve-racking to his readers.

Nevertheless, writing with perhaps more introspective knowledge of the nature of human clay than cautious regard for literary success, Melville made his hint clear:

> "Yes" [Isabel had said, with reference to her feeling about her mysterious life], "it is all a dream!"
>
> Swiftly he caught her in his arms:—"From nothing proceeds nothing, Isabel! How can one sin in a dream?"
>
> "First, what is sin, Pierre?"
>
> "Another name for the other name, Isabel."
>
> "For Virtue, Pierre?"
>
> "No, for Vice."
>
> "Let us sit down again, my brother."
>
> "I am Pierre."
>
> "Let us sit down again, Pierre; sit close; thy arm!"
>
> And so, on the third night, when the twilight was gone, and no lamp was lit, within the lofty window of that beggarly room, sat Pierre and Isabel hushed.

Such a conversation as this, amid the soft-spoken delicacies of the Victorian novel, was a clear and reckless defiance of the sort of priggishness Duyckinck had displayed in his objection to the violation of "the most sacred associations of life" which he found in *Moby Dick*. It was probably something more than a coincidence that on February 14—perhaps the very day Herman gave Allan instructions concerning the contract for publishing *Pierre,* which the younger brother signed six days later— Melville canceled his subscription to the *Literary World.*

This recklessness drove Melville to the very end (for the book apparently did not go to the printer until sometime in March) as he went "deep, deep, and still deep and deeper" in his efforts to "find out the heart of a man" while he let both his literary and his commercial judgment go hang. He had gone too deep to come up with a conclusion based upon the explanation of superficial mysteries; and, although he probed into Pierre's dreams and attributed to him the fainting fits he remembered seeing his mother go through when she was under great stress, he would not or could not resolve the innermost mystery of his hero's behavior. A tragic conclusion became the only one possible, and, in working it out, Melville piled up almost as many corpses as had to be carried from the stage in *Hamlet:* Pierre murdered Glen Stanley and was thrown into a dungeon in the Tombs, Isabel brought him a vial of poison and inadvertently revealed to Lucy that she and Pierre considered themselves brother and sister rather than husband and wife, Lucy dropped dead of shock, Pierre drank the poison, and Isabel found enough left in the vial to enable her to fall lifeless across her champion's no-longer-beating heart. Illuminated by a light thrust into the cell by a squat-framed, asthmatic turnkey, Lucy's brother Fred held her fair form in his arms, while a faithful friend, Charlie Millthorpe, knelt over Pierre, clasping his dead hand through the covering of Isabel's ebon hair. For once, Melville had outdone his "divine William."

Yet even after reading proof on the finished book and taking a vacation, with Elizabeth, in Boston, Melville was curiously unwilling to face the fact of what he had done and persistently thought of the book he had intended rather than the book he had written. Sending the proofs to Bentley on April 16, he took issue with his publisher's refusal to meet his terms (on the grounds that he had lost money on all of the earlier books) by insisting that this time he had written something different and better designed for success. He described his "new book" as "possessing unquestionable novelty, as regards my former ones,—treating of utterly new scenes and characters;—and, as I believe, very much more calculated for popularity than anything you have yet published of mine—being a regular romance, with a mysterious plot to it, and stirring passions at work, and withal, representing a new and elevated aspect of American life." He thought it might be more advantageously issued "anonymously, or under an assumed name" such as "By a Vermonter" or "By Guy Winthrop" and optimistically trusted "that on the new field of production, upon which I embark in the present work, you and I shall hereafter participate in many not unprofitable business adventures."

Of all the "ambiguities" involved in *Pierre,* perhaps one of the most puzzling is suggested by this letter telling Bentley what to find in the book which accompanied it. The reception of both *Mardi* and *Moby Dick* had left him with little respect for the penetration of reviewers, and he may have expected his publisher and his readers alike to overlook some of the implications of his psychological probings. The book also got somewhat out of hand, for he told Bentley that it was a hundred and fifty pages longer than the one he had originally proposed, and he may have written more significantly than he knew at the time—just as he had done in the three works which immediately preceded it. Or he may simply have misjudged his market by abandoning (as Hawthorne was accused of doing) the "hearty and wholesome tone" of English fiction and following "a bastard French school" which was concerned with "the analysis and dissection of diseased mind and unhealthy and distorted sentiment." For the new division into books and chapters which Melville adopted for *Pierre* resembles that of Mme. de Staël's *Corinne,* which he had heard curiously discussed on his trip abroad, which had been published by Bentley in a translation by Isabel Hill, and which he had obtained from his English publisher and brought home with him. The mysterious background of Corinne was not unlike that of Melville's Isabel, and the contrast, in each book, between a dark musical temptress and a fair and wholesome good angel named Lucy was remarkably similar. Melville may have innocently believed that in *Pierre* he was writing precisely the sort of book that Bentley wanted.

It seems reasonably clear, in any event, that Melville did not intend to write the "impure" book which his critics denounced. In spite of temptations, Pierre's New York ménage was maintained in a state of true Shaker celibacy. Furthermore, it was never clear that the supposed husband and wife were actually brother and sister. On the contrary, the peculiar evidence by which Pierre was convinced of his relationship to Isabel was of a sort which the author did not take seriously. A raging toothache, he had written Hawthorne out of his recollections of Shakespeare, was enough to demonstrate the "nonsense" of Goethe's transcendental dictum: "Live in the all." There was "some truth in" the "feeling" of being at one with the universe, he had added in a postscript: "But what plays the mischief with the truth is that men will insist upon the universal application of a temporary feeling or opinion." The fable of *Pierre* and the fable of *Moby Dick* were the same. The spirit which impelled Melville's sophomoric hero to live in a transcendental "all"—a realm of absolute rather than relative justice—was a "lying spirit." It whispered to betray.

But within the fable of *Pierre* was an implication more distressing to a man of Melville's temperament than anything in *Moby Dick.* If he was right in his analysis of the truth of the human heart, it was not impossible that the spirit had whispered in his hero's sensual rather than his transcendental ear. If human beings were misdirected by their subrational impulses and not by their philosophical errors, they could not protect themselves by keeping their feet on the ground and their heads out of the clouds. There might be no good results from any search for truth. The very will to believe might be man's tragic flaw. "Something must occupy the soul of man," he had written, quite early in his novel; "and Isabel was nearest to him then." In the light of his later speculations, such a commonplace observation, carelessly drawn from his own emotional temper, could have had almost unendurable implications. How many of them Melville was to face during the months and years to come is a mystery. It was to be a long time, however, before he gave up his pursuit of philosophy.

Whatever else Melville's letter to Bentley reveals, it shows that at the time he was determined to stress the genialities of his book and ignore its distressing implications. Bentley himself may never have caught them. Reading the proof sheets in the light of the letter, he might have been willing to believe that the author's tone was predominantly "hearty" and only incidentally "French." But he was probably shrewd enough to know that sensitive Victorian readers would not gather that impression from the book itself. It was, he decided, a bad risk.

II

Melville took Elizabeth to New York with him in the middle of April, 1852, in order that she might have a vacation from the children while he read the last pages of proof on *Pierre* and got the book off to Bentley. He was so anxious to dispose of it that he sent off proofs made from type rather than wait for the plates to be stereotyped, and, despite his insistence that it would be more popular than his other books, he offered it outright to his English publisher for £100. The Harpers, to whom his indebtedness had been reduced to less than a hundred and fifty dollars by the sale of 471 additional copies of *Moby Dick* and the continued sale of his other books, had given him an advance of $500 in February and had agreed to publish the new work on a royalty basis. But he had labored too hard over it and needed a change of occupation. Before it was finished he had evidently decided to take his farming more seriously, and one reason for his haste in getting off the proof sheets, perhaps, was that he wanted to be free for spring plowing and other work around home.

In any case, he obtained a hired boy named David, spent May and June entirely out of doors, and so improved his property that the assessed value of his buildings was increased by twenty-five per cent that summer. When the first of July came and the crops were laid by, the whole Melville clan gathered at Arrowhead—Maria and all the girls, and Allan and his family from New York. It was at this time that he built the northern piazza about which he was to write later. It may have been this summer, too, that his mother began to bombard him with other suggestions for household improvements which so irritated him that they lurked in his mind until his annoyance found a disguised expression in "I and My Chimney" three years later. But Judge Shaw, although he doubtless shared his wife's hopes that the farm would flourish, continued to look upon his son-in-law as a literary man rather than a farmer. He was to hold court in Nantucket in July and had persuaded Herman to go with him, promising an excursion to Martha's Vineyard and the Elizabeth Islands after the sessions had closed. The trip was to be a vacation for the young man who had been driving himself so ruthlessly for nearly a year, but the shrewd old judge was going to see that Herman met some of the New Bedford and Nantucket whaling characters who might have interesting tales to tell.

After seeing the family settled down for the summer, Melville left for Boston on July 3 and three days later took the cars for New Bedford. There he and the judge were met by a prominent local lawyer, John Clifford, who had them to dinner and accompanied them to Nantucket on the afternoon boat. The business of the court, as it turned out, required only about two hours the next morning, and they were free to spend the afternoon driving out to Siasconset and making a tour of the island. They met Thomas Macy, who gave Melville a copy of Obed Macy's *History of Nantucket,* and spent the evening with William Mitchell, the astronomer, and his daughter Maria, who was a year older than Herman and a celebrated astronomer in her own right. One of the strongest impressions Herman gained of the island was of the patience of its women— those whose husbands were away at sea and also the widows, of whom there were two hundred and two by Obed Macy's count. Maria Mitchell, watching the skies from her chill terrace in the northern air, may have been a lasting part of that impression; for many years later, after she had become a distinguished professor at Vassar, his mind was to turn backward and brood upon the possible emotions of such a devotee to Urania. Another person whom he met, during a series of calls and visits the next day, certainly made an enduring impression upon him: Captain Pollard, who had been the master of the ship *Essex* when it was attacked and destroyed by a whale, was quietly living on Nantucket as "a nobody" to the islanders, but to the author of *Moby Dick* he was "the most impressive man, tho' wholly unassuming, even humble," he had "ever encountered."

On the morning of Friday, July 9, they took the boat for Martha's Vineyard, where they remained through Sunday, traveling over the island and visiting Gayhead and the Indian territory. A sailboat on Monday gave them a pleasant trip to Naushon, where Mr. Swain, the baronial owner of the whole wild island, had invited them to spend the night and where Herman saw Hawthorne's new book, *The Blithedale Romance,* in the hands of one of the other guests. Tuesday they spent making their way to the mainland at Falmouth, crossing the Cape to Sandwich, and returning to Boston on the Cape Cod Railroad. Herman had enjoyed the excursion, and Judge Shaw was pleased that his literary son-in-law had been so "extremely glad to see" the many people he had met as well as the places he had imagined but had never before looked upon. Before getting back to his farm, Melville spent a day with the Shaws and another day with his cousins in Brookline. He returned to Pittsfield on Friday, and Sam Shaw, who had been visiting at Arrowhead in Herman's absence, left for Boston before he arrived.

At home, Melville found awaiting him his own presentation copy of *The Blithedale Romance,* which he acknowledged in a letter to Hawthorne on July 17; and a few days later he received through the mail an interesting document from John Clifford. For on one of the evenings at Nantucket, when the conversation had turned upon the women of the island, the lawyer had drawn upon his own professional experience of ten years before to tell the strangely affecting story of Agatha Robertson —a Quaker woman of Falmouth whose sailor husband had deserted her after two years of marriage, leaving her to overcome poverty and bring up their daughter. After seventeen years he returned and gave his wife financial assistance without telling her that he had contracted a second, bigamous marriage; and still later when his second wife had died, he urged his original family to move with him to Missouri. When they refused, he married another time, with Agatha's knowledge but without her reproaches. Clifford had learned the story after Robertson's death, when he was called upon to assist in discovering the truth in order to settle the estate. To the author of *Pierre,* who had turned Lucy Tartan into just such a character in the concluding sections of his book, the situation offered an opportunity for "a story of remarkable interest." His creative eye saw it as "a skeleton of actual reality to build about with fulness and veins and beauty."

But the "spontaneous" and "very great" interest it aroused in Melville did not come, as Clifford thought, so much from a desire to make literary use of it as from a "very different consideration"—perhaps from the proof it offered that he had been representing the genuine "truth of the human heart" in Lucy's unconventional behavior. Yet he could not help turning the subject over "a little" in his mind "with a view to a regular story to be founded on these striking incidents." It was all "instinct with significance"—even to the shawls, emblems of secrecy, which Robertson (or, as Melville called him, Robinson) sent home to Agatha and his daughter after his second wife had died. On his trip, Melville had collected a number of "tributary items" in the form of observations which could be worked significantly into the story: an innocent lamb "placidly eyeing the malignity of the sea" which could be introduced as "having poetic reference to Agatha and her sea-lover, who is coming in the storm," and such things as a decaying mailbox and the remains of a wreck, almost covered by sand, which could be given a similar poetic or symbolic "significance." Captain Pollard perhaps might sit as a model for Agatha's father as "a man of the sea, but early driven away from it by repeated disasters" and hence "subdued and quiet and wise in his life."

Such a meditation upon the raw material for a story is a revealing one because it shows Melville consistently crossing the bridge of symbolism from the particular image to the general implication and because it shows that the images were tied together in his own mind by a certain unity of origin in his own experience: "these things do," he wrote, "in my mind, seem legitimately to belong to the story; for they were visibly suggested to me by scenes I actually beheld while on the very coast where the story of Agatha occurred." It is also significant because it shows how active his creative impulse was at a time when he had little if any external stimulus to write.

For at the time he put this meditation on paper, on August 13, 1852, Melville's potatoes were flourishing better than his literary prospects. Bentley, presumably pleading the state of the copyright, had refused to publish *Pierre;* and the best arrangement which could be made for an English edition was an issue of the American sheets under the imprint of the Harpers' London agent, Sampson, Low, Son, and Company, which was to appear in November. To a man who had derived more than half of his literary income from England and had been hoping for "many not unprofitable business adventures" there in the future, the situation was, to say the very least, uninspiring. On the other hand, *Pierre* had been published in America less than two weeks before, and the reviewers had not yet had time to express their opinions of it. The earliest newspaper notices that could have come to the author's attention had not been unfavorable, and he had no reason to suspect, yet, that it would disappoint "his hopes and expectations" of success which he had confided in Judge Shaw. The thought of a new book, to Melville, in the middle of August, would normally have been nothing more than an attractive idea for his fancy to play with. He had neither hope nor desperation to attach him to his desk.

Furthermore, he had neglected to provide himself with the customary literary inspiration of his friends. He had not asked the Duyckincks back to Arrowhead for a third visit that summer, Hawthorne was gone, and he had put himself outside the circle of local literary lights by his refusal to collaborate in their production of *Taghconic; or Letters and Legends about our Summer Home,* which they were busy getting ready for the press in August and September. A forlorn attempt to seek out G. P. R. James in Stockbridge had failed in late July because the English novelist's "people" had been too distant to tell him that James was eating an open-air dinner only a mile from the house at the time he called. There was as much gaiety as usual at the Morewoods', in which young Sam, back for another visit, participated while Herman evidently did not. If he spent the early days of August at Arrowhead, he could hardly have avoided missing his companions of the preceding years.

But whatever the general tenor of his thoughts, he certainly remembered Hawthorne while he meditated the Agatha story and hesitated over his own impulse to write it. The suggestions for its development were all in a letter to his friend which he sent, with Clifford's document and an inscribed copy of *Pierre,* on August 13. "But, thinking again," he wrote of his own impulse, "it has occurred to me that this thing lies very much in a vein, with which you are peculiarly familiar. To be plump, I think that in this matter you would make a better hand at it than I would.—Besides the thing seems naturally to gravitate towards you." The impulse to create a story was strong in him, but he was more impelled to create by deputy than to commit himself to another long hard winter in his study.

Melville may actually have spent part of early August with his brother Tom, who appeared in Boston on the tenth of the month and spent several weeks with the Shaws while waiting for a berth as mate on a ship. Mrs. Shaw could not avoid contrasting the two brothers, finding Tom completely "rational" with "nothing extravagant in his views." Yet she liked Herman "much" and was inclined to feel that "he only needs money." When her husband was scheduled to hold court in Lenox on September 20, she went with him four days in advance for a long week end at Arrowhead, where they found everybody well and in good spirits and where Herman entertained them with a long drive through the country. Malcolm distinguished himself as a farmer's boy by picking up three barrels of potatoes, and his Melville grandmother had settled down, at the end of the summer, to bossing the hired hand. After the court convened, the Melvilles and the Morewoods went over to Lenox to have dinner with the Shaws; and on September 24, Elizabeth, accompanied by Augusta Melville and Mr. Morewood, rode over on horseback for another visit. Mrs. Shaw was brought completely up to date on the Pittsfield situation and wrote young Lemuel that "the farm in time will yet flourish."

By this time the reviews of *Pierre* were getting into print, and they were unanimously unfavorable. The author's friend Duyckinck of the *Literary World* was one of the few to read it carefully and summarize it accurately, but he was carried away with indignation. After correctly presenting Pierre's motives in pretending marriage with Isabel, he exclaimed: "He is battling for Truth and Right, and the first thing he does in behalf of Truth is to proclaim to the whole world a falsehood, and the next thing he does is to commit in behalf of Right, a half a dozen most foul wrongs. The combined power of New England transcendentalism and Spanish Jesuitical casuistry could not have more completely befogged nature and truth, than this confounded Pierre has done." "The most immoral *moral* of the story, if it has any moral at all," he continued, "seems to be the impracticability of virtue; a leering demoniacal spectre of an idea which seems to be peering at us through the dim obscure of this dark book, and mocking us with this dismal falsehood." Duyckinck—who was beginning to object consistently to any sort of psychological probing and had held up the "large, healthy, observing eye" of Charles Dickens as a model to Hawthorne in a review of *The Blithedale Romance*—objected as strongly to the "supersensuousness" found in *Pierre* as to the transcendentalism. It disturbed the "sacred facts" of family relationships with "sacrilegious speculations": "Mrs. Glendinning and Pierre, mother and son, call each other brother and sister, and are described with all the coquetry of a lover and mistress. And again, in what we have termed the supersensuousness of description, the horrors of an incestuous relation between Pierre and Isabel seem to be vaguely hinted at." Duyckinck came nearer than anyone else to understanding what Melville was trying to do and of all Melville's literary acquaintances, perhaps, was the one most likely to be appalled by what he understood.

By the end of September Melville seems to have been avoiding literary company. He attended an anniversary celebration of the Pittsfield Young Ladies' Institute on the last day of that month and heard his uncle Peter's friend and neighbor, Alfred Billings Street, read a poem; but he hurt the feelings of the poet, who was also a friend of Augusta, by failing to seek him out and speak to him afterward. "Oh Herman, Herman, Herman truly thou art an 'Ambiguity,'" protested his uncle ten days later. Yet when G. P. Putnam and Company circularized him on October 1 with an inquiry concerning his willingness to contribute to the new magazine they were planning, his favorable response indicated that he had no serious thought of giving up his profession of authorship. He had no definite plans of his own, but he continued to meditate the Agatha story he had given Hawthorne. "The probable facility with which Robinson first leaves his wife and then takes another," he suggested to his friend on October 25, "may, possibly, be ascribed to the peculiarly latitudinarian notions, which most sailors have of all tender obligations of that sort. In his previous sailor life Robinson had found a wife (for a night) in every port." Remorse for his desertion of Agatha could have come to him only after he had been ashore long enough for "his moral sense on that point" to become developed. It does not seem to have occurred to Melville that he might have been viewing the story with too "large" a realistic eye for contemporary respectability. Yet he was feeling discouraged. "If you find any *sand* in this letter," he added in a postscript, "regard it as so many sands of my life, which ran out as I was writing it."

In the meantime, the reviews of *Pierre* were taking such a tone that the book did not even have a *succes de scandal:* only 283 copies were to be sold during the first eight months of publication, an average of less than two sales for each of the 150 copies sent out for review. The opinion of the *Southern Literary Messenger* that it had better be left "unbought on the shelves of the bookseller" was successfully communicated to the public by critics who thought that "the details of such a mental malady as that which afflicts Pierre are almost as disgusting as those of physical disease itself" or who thought that "Herman Melville has gone 'clean daft.' " His family—although not so contemptuous of his *high faluting* romance" as was his disappointed and spiteful brother-in-law, John Oakes Shaw—had some inclination toward the latter opinion. In the election of a Democratic president, Franklin Pierce, in November, they saw their chance to get Herman into some easier and more profitable occupation. A foreign consulship, they thought, would be ideal for a man who liked to travel; and Herman's mother, convinced that her son was "very anxious" for such a post, busied herself with plans for keeping up Arrowhead with the assistance of the girls, who would look after the children while Lizzie went abroad with her husband.

Such an arrangement could hardly have been a happy one for a man who got as lonesome for his children as Melville always did when he traveled, and it became wholly impracticable as soon as he learned that his wife was expecting another baby in May. He went with Lizzie and the boys on November 22 to Boston, where he stayed until December 13 without setting any political machinery in motion. Instead, he decided to turn his hand once more to literature. For at some time during the visit he went out to see Hawthorne in Concord and talked over the Agatha story with him in person. His friend was seriously expecting a good political appointment, uncertain of his willingness to undertake the work which had been urged upon him (although, before the election, he had been planning "a new romance"), and doubtless aware that Melville was more fascinated by the material than he was. They parted with Hawthorne urging Melville to write the tale, and soon after the latter got back to Boston he decided to do so and to begin as soon as he got home. Accordingly he wrote Hawthorne to send all the material to him, including any suggestions for its treatment that he might have, and asked permission to use at least the name of the Isle of Shoals, where Hawthorne had recently spent a vacation and where he had kept a careful journal of his observations.

Elizabeth—whose "very delicate constitution," according to Herman's aunt Lucy Nourse, required "frequent relaxation, to enable her to get along comfortably with her numerous cases"—remained in Boston with Stanwix for several weeks after her husband and Malcolm returned to Pittsfield. And there, back in the familiar vacuum caused by Lizzie's absence, Melville took up the pen which had occupied him during the preceding two winters. *Pierre* had not ruined his literary standing, for he was one of the first two "Young Authors" publicized by the new *Putnam's Monthly* in a series of essays which discussed Melville in the February number and warned him to "stay his step" from the "edge of the precipice" over which he was tottering. Its author felt that a man of his "peculiar talents, which may be turned to rare advantage," should "diet himself for a year or two on Addison, and avoid Sir Thomas Browne"; but the editor had seemed interested in whatever he might have to offer, and the English publisher who had refused his book had afterwards invited him to contribute to *Bentley's Miscellany*. His sister Helen, after spending a few days at Arrowhead in early February, 1853, wrote Mrs. Shaw that everybody was well and that Lizzie was "remarkably active and cheerful." Herman was not causing any great worry in the family even though he was working steadily enough for his mother to believe that he had a new book "now nearly ready for the press" on April 20.

He probably did not become "so completely absorbed by his new work" as to worry his family seriously until after March 21, when he received the distressing account from the Harpers which showed that the royalties from *Pierre* had paid off little more than ten per cent of the advance he had received and the earnings of almost three hundred dollars from his other books still left him $298.71 in debt to his publishers. Dollars once again damned him to the sort of concentrated effort which made the family feel "anxious about the strain on his health" and more determined than ever before to get him a job. Herman himself may have realized by this time that the Agatha story, however "instinct" it might be with poetic and psychological "significance," was not instinct with enough narrative continuity to lend itself to his customary method of writing. But he could hardly have realized how difficult it was for the particular inventive quality of his own mind to "do justice to so interesting a story of reality" in the form of a book which would sell as a novel. For his empirical imagination developed normally around a consciousness of experience, and his unifying experience with this material was that of collecting it and becoming aware of its significance rather than that of participating in the story itself. He could dramatically fancy himself— "so mutilated or diseased"—having the experience of Ahab or even of Pierre. But he could only understand, not share, the weakness of Robertson; and, as his later writings were to show, he was entirely external to the patience and endurance which fascinated him in Agatha. The "old Nantucket seaman" who seems to have been foremost in his thoughts when he talked to Hawthorne in November or early December was the only character who could have given the tale a narrative and dramatic unity of the sort Melville's mind could have worked with, yet he was merely one of the "contributary items" in it. The problem of doing both poetic and practical justice to this story would have been almost as hard for Melville to solve as the problem of justice to Isabel was for Pierre. Whether he bogged down or simply gave out in his efforts, the "new work" seems not to have been "made ready for the press"; and, in April, its author fell in with the family's plans to get him a political job.

How much Hawthorne may have known of Melville's difficulties is uncertain, but the campaign to rescue him was evidently begun early in the third week of April when the new consul to Liverpool was on his way to Washington in an effort to get Manchester included in his domain. Allan Melville saw him as he passed through New York, and together they planned the strategy of doing something for Herman. Their plan was for Allan to collect letters of recommendation for the consulship at Honolulu and forward them to Hawthorne, who would see that they were placed in the proper hands and, at the same time, exercise such personal influence as he possessed through his friendship with President Pierce. Allan at first seems to have placed most of his hopes upon Hawthorne's influence; but he wrote to his mother, who was then visiting in Albany, to have Peter Gansevoort get letters from influential acquaintances while he himself undertook to obtain recommendations from the local district attorney, Pierce's friend Charles O'Conor, and a neighboring lawyer, Edward C. West. He was apparently sensitive about his brother's genuine need for a remunerative job—which he justified to West on the grounds that Herman was overworked—and made clear to his mother that there would "be no necessity of any further explanation of the cause of his friends wishing to obtain such a position for him except to get him away from writing for a time, and a change of labor."

The letter to the elder Mrs. Melville was handed to her just as she was getting on the stage for Lansingburgh, but as soon as she arrived in the village she sent a letter back to her brother which summed up the official family attitude toward Herman. "A change of occupation," she wrote, was "necessary" for him, although his dislike for "asking favors from any one" had caused him to postpone making any efforts in his own behalf until he had become so preoccupied with his new work "that he has not taken the proper and necessary measures to procure this earnestly wished for office." Then, in phrases which were to be echoed and re-echoed by the family for years, she continued:

In my opinion, I must again repeat it Herman would be greatly benefitted by a sojourn abroad, he would then be compelled to more intercourse with his fellow creatures. It would very materially renew, and strengthen both his body and mind.

The constant in-door confinement with little intermission to which Herman's occupation as author compels him, does not agree with him. This constant working of the brain, and excitement of the imagination, is wearing Herman out, and you will my dear Peter be doing him a lasting benefit if by your added exertions you can procure him a foreign consulship.

Melville regularly drove himself too hard while writing his books, but some of the unusual anxiety his family later remembered feeling about his health in the spring of 1853 was not genuine. It was partially the recollection of a story spread abroad because of Allan's belief that an overworked author had better political chances than an unsuccessful one and exaggerated because of Maria's conviction that it was somehow more respectable for a Melville to suffer from mental strain than from misjudging his talents or his market.

Peter Gansevoort immediately obtained letters from Justice Amasa J. Parker of the New York supreme court and Chancellor G. L. Lansing of the state university. Both dealt with Melville's health, and when they reached Hawthorne, forwarded with West's letter touching upon the same subject, they almost put the new consul for Liverpool in the position of a man engaged on a medical rather than a political mission. Uncle Peter, however, persuaded Edwin L. Croswell, editor of the *Albany Argus,* to write to Caleb Cushing on the grounds that "Herman has always been a firm Democrat" as well as a man with an overworked brain; and Edwin's brother, Sherman Croswell, wrote directly to the president. But before receiving Edwin Croswell's letter, Attorney General Cushing, as the president's political adviser, had written to the Pittsfield bookseller and publisher of the *Sun* concerning Melville's politics. Coming the day after Croswell's letter, the reply from Phineas Allen, Jr., did little to encourage the preferment of a fellow townsman. So far as Allen knew, Melville had "not taken any part in politics since his residence in Pittsfield," had "not attended the polls," and had not "made any public expression of his political opinions." Nevertheless, Cushing indicated to Hawthorne that he was "warmly in favor" of Melville's appointment to a consulship, and Pierce, while making no promises, seemed sympathetically disposed.

In the meantime, General Dix had suggested to Allan that the New York Democrats had already received their share of spoils and had implied that Herman might have a better chance if supported by fellow residents of the state of Massachusetts. Allan accordingly wrote to Judge Shaw in Boston, and the judge, some days later, dutifully wrote to his friend Cushing, to whom he was already indebted for assistance in keeping his son John in his position as clerk in the Boston Custom House. On May 4 Hawthorne was back in New York, pointing out that consular jobs were the responsibility of Secretary of State Marcy rather than the attorney general and bringing news that the Honolulu position would not be available to Melville although Antwerp (which had been Allan's alternative selection) might be. Further scurrying around produced letters to Marcy from John Cochrane, newly appointed surveyor of the Port of New York, and Azariah C. Flagg of Albany, who was then in New York City, and also a letter to Pierce from John Van Buren—all of them representative of the Barnburner faction of the Democratic party. But Uncle Peter either could or would not obtain further documents; and Judge Shaw apparently was not informed of the new developments, for an open letter of recommendation sent by Richard H. Dana, Jr., on May 10 and letters to Marcy from H. W. Bishop and Samuel D. Bradford two weeks later dealt specifically with Honolulu. The whole business was ineptly handled: the Honolulu appointment was actually given to a New Yorker, and the Antwerp post was left unfilled until late October. But both went to active politicians.

How much Herman really knew about the campaign in his behalf is uncertain. It seems highly improbable that his uncle Peter, whose devotion to "Typee" was genuine, would have confined his efforts to the two days following Maria's first appeal if his favorite nephew had really "earnestly wished for" the office; and it is inconceivable that Judge Shaw should have been so casual and uninformed in his efforts at assistance if either Herman or Elizabeth had been actively interested. Peter Gansevoort and Judge Shaw were both planning to go abroad in June and were to meet some of the friends Herman had made on his trip; and the Shaws were certainly in close touch with Arrowhead, for Elizabeth was expecting her confinement in May and her parents were more than normally concerned about her condition. Her first daughter, Elizabeth, was born on May 22, and Herman notified her family. He reported that she was "very well" in comparison with her situation after the birth of Stanwix; but, although the receipt of the letter evidently reminded Judge Shaw to speak to Bishop and Bradford about writing to Marcy, Herman seems to have said nothing to his father-in-law about his plans or expectations.

The first recognizable echo of Herman's voice in any of the documents connected with the campaign, in fact, occurred in a letter from Judge Shaw to Caleb Cushing, written from New York on June 14, after he had talked to his son-in-law and just before he sailed for Europe. Cushing had made a "confidential" report to Shaw that the best Melville could hope for was "one of the less lucrative consulates in Italy, say Rome," and Shaw had passed the news on to Allan on June 8. Before Allan answered the letter, Herman had come to the city to see his uncle Peter off on the *Atlantic* and was planning to remain at least until his father-in-law departed on the *Arabia* three days later. Dollars and cents were on his mind. "There can be no consulship in Italy, not even Rome," Allan wrote Shaw, "where the fees would amount to enough to make it advantageous for Herman to accept a position there." After his own talk with Herman, Shaw could be equally firm and definite in his reply to Cushing: "I am satisfied, that such are Mr. Melville's circumstances, that he could not with propriety take a consulate, the emoluments of which, would not be sufficient to meet the expenses of a family, at a foreign station, which would be necessarily large." There was nothing more, as Allan wrote Shaw, to be said on the subject. When Herman was allowed to have his say, there was no further nonsense about his going abroad, with or without Elizabeth, while the children remained behind at Arrowhead.

The Melville imagination probably was overstimulated during the spring of 1853. But Herman's was not so excited that he could contemplate accepting a job which would not enable him to keep his family with him and keep them in comparative comfort. He may have been overworked and discouraged about his literary prospects. A better teller of tales than he liked to admit to himself, he had been seriously misdirected —according to the judgment of the reading public—in his attempt to write a romantic novel of situation and in his unconventional interest in the psychology of the peculiar situation he considered romantic. His interest in feminine patience and determination was a much greater misdirection in that such a subject failed entirely to provide him with the sort of narrative, either personal or dramatic, which his talent required. The story of Pierre had been a failure, and the story of Agatha had apparently not even been conceived. But Melville was willing and able to work, and, as a professional author, he still had prospects. He had not yet taken advantage of the opportunities offered by the magazines.

9

Magazine Writer

I

MELVILLE seems to have been in no hurry to settle down to work for the magazines during the summer of 1853. Instead of sticking to his desk, he played an active but not a leading part in the social activities of the Berkshires. On the Fourth of July, while Peter Gansevoort and Judge and young Lemuel Shaw were dining with his friends the Cookes in London, Herman was attending a celebration on the public square in Pittsfield where he heard some complimentary remarks on himself and the Melvilles from the presiding officer. Allan and his family spent most of the summer at Arrowhead while various of Allan's in-laws boarded from time to time in the village, and Sam Shaw, no longer an undergraduate, made his customary visit in late July accompanied by Miss Elizabeth Dow. Richard Lathers, who was married to Allan's sister-in-law, was one of the New York visitors with whom Herman discussed books over cider made from his own apples, but there was no exciting literary house party at Arrowhead. Mrs. Morewood was not her usual energetic self that summer, but her husband had begun to find Melville more companionable than he had at first expected, and the two men made a quiet excursion to the top of Mount Greylock. Later, during the second week in August, he went with the artist Darley and a number of other gentlemen upon a trip of exploration to the Dome of Taconic and the region thereabout, but, on the whole, the summer was not very stimulating.

September was a more exciting month. Catherine, the first of the Melville girls to find a husband, was married on the fifteenth to John C. Hoadley, who had moved from Pittsfield to Lawrence, Massachusetts, the year before; and Helen became engaged to George Griggs, a lawyer in Brookline, who was another friend of the family. Judge Shaw returned home from Europe and hurried to Arrowhead with his wife for an overnight visit before opening court in Lenox on September 20. Three days later he was back at Arrowhead for another visit. Elizabeth and her family were flourishing. She had developed no complications after her third confinement, the baby was healthy and active, and Malcolm had begun attending school in the little white schoolhouse across the railroad tracks by Dr. Holmes's summer place. Even Maria admitted, in a letter welcoming her brother Peter back home, that Herman was "looking remarkably well."

When he began writing again, it was apparently without any strain. He was not going to attempt anything ambitious, and, for the first time since his marriage, he was free from financial troubles. When he had bought the New York house he had used only half of the $2,000 he had borrowed from Judge Shaw for that purpose, and he seems to have preserved the other half intact through all his difficulties as a sort of emergency fund, not quite his own, upon which he steadfastly refused to draw. Since he had taken up farming seriously, the fund had begun to grow. The advance he had received from *Pierre,* according to the evidence provided by the Pittsfield tax rolls, went into the bank and stayed there; and during the next year, without any income from his books, he added another five hundred dollars to his balance. He had been a good enough farmer, perhaps, to indulge himself as an artist by filing away or destroying the Agatha material when it proved intractable; and he was certainly confident enough about the future to feel that he would be better off at Arrowhead than in a foreign consulate paying less than $2,500 a year.

Nevertheless, the Agatha theme of nonaggressive but unshakable patience continued to haunt his mind. His first magazine story, "Bartleby, the Scrivener. A Story of Wall-Street," which was published in *Putnam's Monthly* for November and December, 1853, gave some indication of the sort of secret power which he conceived as existing in quiet stubbornness. The story was supposedly based upon a certain amount of fact, and the fact may have been either some anecdote concerning a lawyer's clerk or the unfortunate condition of Melville's friend Adler, who had developed such a severe case of agoraphobia that he was to be confined in the Bloomingdale Asylum in October. Or it may have been simply the murder of Samuel Adams by John C. Colt, twelve years before, to which allusion was made in the story. But the essence of the story was distilled from Melville's literary meditations. For the young scrivener, with a whim stronger than his employer's will, was a man whose mind was made up just as Lucy Tartan's had been made up when her mother had tried to remove her from Pierre's New York apartment. Like Agatha, he was uncomplaining, yet was unmoved by considerations that might normally stir a person to action. And like Jackson, in *Redburn,* he exercised an influence which could not be rationally explained. In the power of his quiet resolution and independence lay one of the mysteries of humanity.

Melville could not penetrate the mystery with any psychological explanation, but in his next story, published in *Harper's Magazine* for December, he found a symbol which suggested his analysis of it. For in the story "Cock-a-Doodle-Doo!" a character like Bartleby reappeared in the person of Merrymusk—a calm, proud, silent ex-sailor who lived with an invalid wife and four sickly children whom he supported by hard work. Like Bartleby, he would not gabble; and also like Bartleby, he and his family with him died in a state of pallid malnutrition. But there was no secret about the strength which maintained the Merrymusk family in their reserve. They owned a Shanghai rooster, "more like a Field-Marshal than a cock," who "was of a haughty size, stood haughtily on his haughty legs," and whose crowing was like the singing of Signor Beneventano in *Lucia di Lammermoor*. He "irradiated the shanty" in which the family lived with "a strange supernatural look of contrast." And his crowing inspired his humble owners. It imparted pluck and gave "stuff against despair." Literally, they died of it, and the cock died with them. Melville interpreted the humble patience which fascinated him as an expression of pride, and, as such, it struck a strong responsive chord in his own being.

But such magazine pieces as these, serious at the core but surrounded by a jollity of style and manner, could not completely occupy Melville's mind. When his harvest was over and his winter's supply of fuel was cut—and when Elizabeth had taken the baby to Boston on another Thanksgiving trip—he once more set about writing a book. This time he would get back to the sea, as the reviewers of *Pierre* had demanded; and on December 7 he obtained from the Harpers an advance of $300 for a work on "Tortoises or Tortoise-Hunting" which he optimistically intimated would be ready in January. The book was never delivered, but the steps he took toward its production are perhaps indicated by the series of sketches called "The Encantadas or Enchanted Isles" which were to appear in *Putnam's Monthly* from March through May in 1854. Primarily, they seem to have been steps taken in an effort to arrive at some sort of central narrative. He had visited the Galápagos Islands, of course, and had seen the giant tortoises for which they were famous; but he had experienced no significant adventures there, and one of his first jobs was that of gathering material which would supplement his own observations. He found such material in Captain David Porter's *Journal of a Cruise Made to the Pacific Ocean*, which he had used for his additions to *Typee*, in James Colnet's *A Voyage to the South Atlantic and Round Cape Horn into the Pacific Ocean*, in James Burney's *Chronological History of the Discoveries in the South Sea or Pacific Ocean*, in Captain Cowley's *Voyage round the Globe*, and probably in some other yet unidentified work.

These provided him with the sort of descriptive and anecdotal material which he normally inserted into his books in order to pad them out to the proper length, but none gave him the narrative framework he needed.

The Agatha theme of patient endurance, however, was still in his mind; and he may not have wanted to tell a tale of adventure so much as one which would enable him to make use of the "significance" with which his material was "instinct"—the barren loneliness of the Galápagos, the strange currents which made them almost unapproachable by ordinary navigation and caused them to be called "the Enchanted Isles," and the emblematic potentialities of the slow but long-lived tortoises. The one story connected with the islands which he developed at some length, either from some unidentified written source or from some tale he had himself heard in the Pacific, was of a *chola* woman who had gone to Norfolk Isle with her husband and brother to hunt tortoises and had been left as a sort of female Crusoe after her companions were killed in a fishing accident. Through the character of Hunilla, in the eighth of his sketches, Melville at last managed to get his admiration for a strong patient widow into print.

Whether Melville had hoped to let the Hunilla story carry the narrative burden of his book seems impossible to determine. It lacked incident, and he lacked invention. At some time before the publication of his sketches he seems to have thought of developing the narrative, as he had done in *Mardi,* by the use of calculated allegory. For the published sketches were all introduced by quotations from Spenser, and his selection of passages to be quoted shows that the poetry of Spenser over which he pored was all related to the unwritten story of Agatha. Most of it dealt with the theme of patience—the ninth canto of the first book of *The Faerie Queene* in which the Redcrosse Knight withstands despair, the tenth canto in which he is healed of his hurt by the leech called Patience, and the "Visions of the Worlds Vanitie" in which an emblematic array of patient little creatures destroy others many times their size. The other Spenserian quotations came from passages which were complementary in theme—the last canto of the second book of *The Faerie Queene* in which Sir Guyon overthrows the bower of bliss, and the section of the "Mother Hubberds Tale" in which the Fox and the Ape grow weary of their lot and begin to seek their fortunes far abroad. Melville had also read Wordsworth's "Resolution and Independence" and parodied it in "Cock-a-Doodle-Doo!" And by that he had been reminded of Chatterton, whose "Mynstrelles Songe" provided another epigraph for the *chola* widow sketch. Of all the verse quotations he used, only a single stanza from Collins' "Dirge" for *Cymbeline* has no observable connection with the ideas that haunted his mind after he had meditated the story of the patient

Agatha and her wandering husband. Bartleby, Merrymusk, and Hunilla were all products of the same ferment which stirred him to reread Spenser.

Melville's first attempts at magazine fiction were embarrassingly successful. The public reception of "Bartleby" seems to have been almost wholly favorable, and its author's disappearance on his tortoise hunt was probably a disappointment to the editor of *Putnam's,* Charles F. Briggs, who was not so fortunate in some of the other contributions he received from his "young authors." Nor could Melville have worked very happily upon his book. For only three days after he had received his advance from the Harpers a fire had destroyed the entire establishment of his publishers, causing an estimated loss of a quarter of a million dollars in their stock of unbound books alone. Their stereotyped plates, stored in underground vaults, were saved, but there seemed to be little prospect of their being able to publish a new book in January or for months thereafter. It was therefore possibly by request from *Putnam's* and certainly with no expectations from the Harpers that Melville turned over the first four sketches of "The Encantadas" to Briggs for publication in his magazine for March, 1854. They aroused enough editorial enthusiasm for advance news of their appearance to get abroad, and a paragraph in the New York *Evening Post* for February 14 welcomed the author of *Typee* and *Omoo* back "from that uneasy sleep, during which his genius was disturbed by such distempered dreams as Mardi, and frightful nightmares like the ambiguous Pierre." In the Pacific, "under the pilotage of Melville," the *Post* promised, "all readers will be sure" of being refreshed by "fountains of pleasure and delight."

Could this be the Harpers' book? The publishers were not too harried by the reconstruction of their plant to overlook the most favorable publicity one of their authors had received in several years. And it was probably in reply to some such inquiry that on February 20 Melville sat down to express his "concern" that the promised work, "owing to a variety of causes," had not been ready in January. "In no sense," he assured his publishers, would they "lose by the delay"; but he reserved specific explanations until he arrived in New York a few weeks later, when he promised to call and inform them "when these proverbially slow 'Tortoises' will be ready to crawl into market." He probably made a special trip to the city in order to make his explanations and attempt to preserve the light tone of his letter. His efforts seem to have been acceptable but not satisfactory: he was evidently not required to return the advance payment, but, although he continued to write for Harpers' magazine, the firm did not bring out another of his books until twelve years had passed.

Melville drove himself less hard than usual during the early months of 1854. "The Encantadas" was probably mostly done by January 6, when he gave his copy of Chatterton to John C. Hoadley, and he had diversions at home which tempted him out of the upstairs study where his work gave him an excuse to take refuge from the women and children. His uncle Thomas' daughter Priscilla had moved in with him for the winter, but Tom was at home in January and the two brothers always had a lot to talk about. Helen was married to George Griggs on January 5, and for a week or more the house was full of wedding guests, including Hoadley, who was a poet as well as a brother-in-law and close friend. The Morewoods were spending the holidays at Broadhall, and, all in all, the midwinter season was almost as active as that of midsummer.

Magazine writing was fairly profitable, too. *Putnam's* paid five dollars a page, and, although it was printed in double columns of small type, "Bartleby" was worth $85 and "The Encantadas" was to bring in $150 more. *Harper's* did not pay quite so well, but it would take easily written sketches and was a dependable source of supplementary income. Almost all of his earnings from writing could go into the bank, where his balance grew by another $500 over the winter, and he did not have to suffer the strain of putting all his time into the speculative enterprise of a single book. With Helen and Kate gone, the household seems to have been further thinned out during the late winter by the departure of Fanny and her mother for a long visit in town; and, although there was always a strain involved in keeping children indoors through a long New England winter, the family seems to have survived the season with less tension than usual. When the winter proved to be unusually prolonged, Cousin Priscilla wrote Lemuel Shaw on March 27, with her customary emphases: "*We—that is*—Lizzie, Augusta, Herman, the little folks, and myself are driven to the necessity of being *very* amiable, and *obliged* to play the agreeable for mutual entertainment *within* doors." They were all "becoming rather weary of winter quarters." "But," she added, without realizing that it was a family convention to worry about Herman at this time of year, "we are all in the enjoyment of very robust health."

And Herman, relaxed in the approval of the magazine-reading public, was also violating a family convention by preserving his amiability while continuing to write without much inspiration. As the Spenserian quotations used in "The Encantadas" show, he had been attempting to stimulate his flagging invention not only with allegory but with complementary or contrasting themes, and he continued to do so during the later winter months. To follow his Galápagos sketches, he sent *Putnam's* two contrasting descriptions of what he called "The Two Temples"—the first dealing with the vain attempt of a poorly dressed man to gain admission to public worship in a fashionable new church, and the second describing an agreeable experience, of the same travel-stained stranger, in finding refuge in the shilling gallery of the Royal Lyceum Theatre in London. Far worse criticisms of the church had been a commonplace in American radical literature for more than two decades, but they had not appeared in popular magazines. Recognizing a satire upon the new Grace Church in New York and knowing better than to offend its congregation or the clergy in general, Briggs rejected the contribution, just as he had used his editorial pencil upon some amplification of the figure of the cross on the ass's back in the Hunilla story in "The Encantadas." But he was apologetic for his editorial discretion. He praised the "exquisitely fine description" and "pungent satire" in the article and reported that James Russell Lowell had said of the edited figure that it "brought tears into his eyes, and he thought it the finest touch of genius he had seen in prose." On the next day, May 13, George Palmer Putnam himself wrote Melville, asking whether the objectionable "point" of "The Two Temples" could be removed and expressing a desire to print the author's portrait in the magazine. Both publisher and author of course knew that the article had little interest without its point, but the former's politeness kept the rejection from giving offense and assured Melville that he genuinely wanted "some more of your good things."

His next contrasting sketch, "Poor Man's Pudding and Rich Man's Crumbs," dealing with his observations of the Lord Mayor's feast in London and the poor who ate its remains, had already gone to *Harper's* for publication in the June issue. But he had something for Putnam and probably sent in a substantial part of it in response to his tactful letter. The London material in the two sketches had been the by-product of his meditations upon his European journal as a source of material for his "Revolutionary story of the beggar," Israel Potter, which he had at last decided to "serve up." Potter's own "sleazy gray paper" story of his adventures provided the sort of narrative thread which Melville had so much difficulty in weaving for himself, and he could supplement it with suggestions drawn from another book "printed for the author" in 1806— Nathaniel Fanning's anonymous *Narrative of the Adventures of an American Naval Officer*. He had never before successfully borrowed a story, but he had proved in "The Encantadas" that he could successfully compose fine bits of ornament without having a story of his own on which to hang them. With the rather clearly defined interests of magazine readers in mind, he could write a full-length book without getting so personally involved in it that he was led astray by his own thoughts.

Israel Potter; or, Fifty Years of Exile was one-fifth completed by June 17, 1854 (when its dedication, to the Bunker Hill monument, was dated), and began its appearance as "A Fourth of July Story" in *Putnam's Monthly Magazine* for July. It could not have been a difficult book to write. For, having found a dependable narrative, Melville decided to indulge in "very little reflective writing" and compose a light adventure story containing "nothing of any sort to shock the fastidious." He made Israel a native of the Berkshires in order to open the book with a more general description of his own neighborhood than he had used in "Cock-a-Doodle-Doo!" And when he got his hero abroad, he used him primarily as a connecting device for sketches of historical characters—George III, Horne Tooke, Benjamin Franklin, Ethan Allen, and, especially, John Paul Jones. The first three historical characters had appeared in Potter's own *Life and Remarkable Adventures;* Ethan Allen was arbitrarily introduced on the basis of material freely adapted from his own *Narrative;* and Jones appeared very much in the character given him by Fanning, although Melville also drew upon the standard *Life* based upon Jones's own papers and the account of his raids on the British coast given by Captain Alexander S. Mackenzie in the biography he published shortly before taking command of the *Somers.* The use of Fanning as a primary source for his sketch of Jones was unfortunate, for the officer who had once been kicked out of the cabin, across the main deck, and down the hatchway by his commander did not give Jones the sort of character which would arouse sympathy. But Melville was in an antagonistic mood toward popular heroes. His emphasis upon the sly penny-pinching wisdom which Parson Weems admired in Benjamin Franklin was hostile; and while the captive Ethan Allen was portrayed as a heroic figure, his heroism, like that of Jones, was not entirely admirable. The author of *Israel Potter* found nothing in his sources to inspire him to treat his material in any way other than that of the "magazinist," and one of the most suggestive passages he found in Fanning's *Narrative* was a rather silly reference to the moon's emotions which Melville made even sillier in his description of the fight between the *Serapis* and the *Bonhomme Richard.*

Yet as he approached the end of his story, Melville could not keep his creative mind entirely detached from it. He had introduced Israel as a man who was "brave-hearted" and something of a "dare-devil" but who nevertheless "evinced, throughout many parts of his career, a singular patience and mildness"; and this introduction, at first, seemed less a positive characterization than an apology for the inconsistencies of a character who did not hold together as an imaginative unity. Yet in one of the later chapters, when Israel found himself inadvertently on board a British vessel with which his own ship had become entangled in the night, the American sailor tried to worm his way into a British mess with all the unaggressive stubbornness of Bartleby the Scrivener. That the theme of patience had not entirely disappeared from Melville's mind is also indicated by his comparison of the lower guns of the *Serapis* to "the sea-worm called Remora"—an emblem of patience recalled from the stanza of Spenser's "Visions of the Worlds Vanitie" which he had used in part as an introduction to the fifth sketch of "The Encantadas." He did not develop the theme in *Israel Potter*, but it affected the story he had originally conceived as a story of a "beggar." Patience, interpreted as a form of pride, had caused him to observe in "Poor Man's Pudding" that "the native American poor never lose their delicacy or pride"; and it now made him take care that "Israel, the American," although reduced in his later years to the physical degradation of a European pauper, should not be allowed to descend "to actual beggary."

There was only a residual element of imagination in the incidental significance Melville gave to the character of Israel Potter, but his treatment of Ethan Allen was more positive. His prolonged attention to the personality of John Paul Jones—that "devil in a Scotch bonnet" who slipped into British harbors like evil into the human heart—seems to have alerted his mind to the significance he found "instinct" in the captive hero of Ticonderoga. "Though born in New England, he exhibited no trace of her character," Melville meditated after drawing his picture of a Yankee Samson among the Philistines: "His spirit was essentially Western; and herein is his peculiar Americanism; for the Western spirit is, or will yet be (for no other is, or can be), the true American one." His pride raged like a wild beast, and he was the complete antithesis of patience. "For, besides the exasperating tendency to a self-assertion which such treatment as his must have bred on a man like him," the now-thoughtful Melville continued as he approached the end of his book, "his experience must have taught him, that by assuming the part of a jocular, reckless, and even braggart barbarian, he would better sustain himself against bullying turnkeys than by submissive quietude." He was right in the course he pursued, and there is perhaps something more than an intentional significance in his return to America on a quarter-deck while Israel lingered for forty-five summary years in the murky "City of Dis" which the awakened author described from the memories recorded in his London journal: Melville may have failed to take advantage of his opportunity to develop the theme of patient endurance because he had lost his fascinated admiration for that quality in human nature. The imaginative impetus he received from the Agatha story had at last died out.

Melville's mind, however, was of a sort which could not remain passive. The imaginative and intellectual alertness which found its way into the concluding chapters of *Israel Potter* colored the three otherwise simple stories he had written in the spring or early summer of 1854. The two companion pieces that appeared in *Harper's* for July and August, "The Happy Failure" and "The Fiddler," may have had reference to the ease he had found in writing his unambitious magazine pieces. The first dealt with an old man who for ten years had worked on an invention and found room for kindness in his heart only after his device had failed. The second told of an even happier failure in the person of a violin teacher who had once been an infant prodigy, but who, having been "crowned with laurels," had become content with "a bunged beaver" and the knowledge that he still possessed his genius although it was no longer accompanied by fame. Each probably made use of real characters who had been a part of the author's past—the first drawing upon his uncle Thomas and the old Negro Tawney who had lived in Lansingburgh, and the second alluding to Joseph Burke who had been a successful child violinist in Britain and America before settling into obscurity in Albany. But, coming at this particular time in Melville's life, they were more than fanciful character studies, remotely based upon real people. For two years his imagination had dwelt upon pride expressing itself in patient humility. In the concluding part of *Israel Potter,* he had asserted the superior effectiveness of its expression in the "peculiar Americanism" of Ethan Allen. But he did not admire the pose of "a wild beast." He was turning away from the theme entirely, and these two stories took their emotional life from a revulsion which continued throughout that winter.

A similar emotion was revealed in the more intense story of "The Lightning-Rod Man" which was published in *Putnam's* for August. Like the other two, it had a factual basis in Melville's own experience; for family tradition, at least, relates it to an interview he had with a hair-raising salesman during the aggressive lightning-rod campaign put on in Pittsfield during the autumn of 1853. But the significance implicit in the incident may have been suggested to Melville by Cotton Mather's *Magnalia Christi Americana,* which represented a thunder stroke as an arm of God's providence, reaching forth in wrath against particular individuals. The narrator in the story threw the salesman bodily out of the house with the "impious" confidence "that the Deity will not, of purpose, make war on man's earth." But "the Lightning-rod man," Melville observed, "still dwells in the land; still travels in storm-time, and drives a brave trade with the fears of man." Fear, like ambition, was a form of pride; and Melville seems to have been trying to make himself believe, in the spring of 1854, that a man was best off when he was free from both.

NOTE:—"The Fiddler" was included in Melville's *The Apple-Tree Table and Other Sketches* (Princeton, 1922), and its authorship remained unquestioned despite the fact that Francis Wolle, on the evidence of the *Harper's* Index, attributed it to Fitz-James O'Brien in his biography of O'Brien (Boulder, Colorado, 1944). Aside from the weak evidence of similarity in theme to "The Happy Failure," I have found no reason for questioning this attribution and believe "The Fiddler" should be excluded from the Melville canon.—L.H., 1958.

II

The summer and winter of 1854 seem to have been relatively uneventful months in Melville's life. *Israel Potter* brought him an income of almost fifty dollars a month while it was appearing serially in *Putnam's* from July until the following March, and the regularity of the payments, perhaps, removed one important stimulus to his writing. The money was not enough to live on, but with the produce of the farm, Elizabeth's income of $180.00 a year from her trust fund, and such contributions as his mother may have made to the expenses of the family, it enabled him to get along comfortably enough without lowering his bank balance. Although *Putnam's* had published "The Lightning-Rod Man" simultaneously with the second installment of *Israel Potter,* the author could hardly expect to sell the magazine additional stories while the novel was running; and he had no practical inducement to undertake a new book. The statement of his account rendered by the Harpers in October showed that nearly 2,300 copies of his earlier books (in sheets and in bindings) had been destroyed by the fire and that he was $319.74 in debt to his publishers. A new book for them would do little more than remove his indebtedness and relieve them of an inducement to reissue his earlier works, and he had no English publisher with sufficient faith to encourage him with a cash advance.

When Elizabeth and the children went to Boston on their annual Thanksgiving visit, accordingly, Herman went with them. They missed the train on the morning of Tuesday, November 26, and he had an extra day in his upstairs study—where he went "as usual," according to his mother. But he had no urgent business there. Even the appearance of *Israel Potter* in book form in early March, 1855, made no great demands upon him. He received a total of $421.50 for the magazine rights to the story and was to receive a royalty of twelve and a half per cent on the book which was published to sell at the popular price of seventy-five cents. He probably got little or nothing from the English edition which Routledge brought out at a shilling, but he had little reason for complaint. He was not doing badly, considering the small amount of labor he had put into this particular book, and the columns of *Putnam's* and *Harper's* were still open to him. He was nearer financial security than he had ever been in his life and could well have tried to persuade himself that he was "a happy failure."

But the habits of a decade are not easily broken, and Melville did not have the temperament to fiddle away at popular tunes while being simply content with a private awareness of his genius. One of the two literary products of that winter was a sketch, "The Paradise of Bachelors and The Tartarus of Maids," which appeared in *Harper's* for April, 1855, and seemed to be nothing more than an ordinary magazine piece. "The Paradise of Bachelors" was, in fact, a genial description of a London dinner in the Temple, based upon his entertainment by Robert Francis Cooke and his brother while he was in England; and "The Tartarus of Maids" was a description of a visit to a paper mill, critical enough of the boasted New England industrial system to be sharp, yet not so aggressive as to give the sort of offense which had made "The Two Temples" unacceptable to a popular magazine. But Melville put more into the second sketch than met the modest Victorian eye. For Elizabeth was expecting her fourth child in early March, and her husband, meditating on the process of gestation, slipped into his account of papermaking a little natural allegory which amounted to a genuine mockery of what Evert Duyckinck considered the "sacred" aspects of life. Taking his ease, with an active mind, he found himself disposed to violate deliberately some of the conventions he had inadvertently given the impression of violating in his earlier writings.

The impulse to defy priggishness from behind the veil of allegory, however, was only a minor amusement of Melville's leisure. It was a single flash from a mind which was once more sparkling and alert. He had recuperated his intellectual energy and had also discovered another "story of reality" which was "instinct" with narrative as well as with all sorts of other "significance." The story was tucked away in the eighteenth chapter of another forgotten autobiography, Captain Amasa Delano's *Narrative of Voyages and Travels,* which had been printed for the author in Boston in 1817 and was perhaps almost as rare as the less substantial pamphlet dictated by Israel Potter. Consisting of an extract from the journal of the ship *Perseverance,* the captain's fuller account of the incidents recorded, and a series of official documents, it was Captain Delano's defense of his action in boarding and taking the Spanish ship *Tryal* at the island of Santa Maria, off the coast of Chile, in February, 1805. The situation was one which Melville could readily understand. Captain Delano had been at sea for a year and a half but had experienced such ill luck as a sealer that his men's shares amounted to no more than twenty dollars apiece. He was having difficulty with his crew; and the *Tryal,* abandoned by her captain, was a prize which would enable him to reward his men, recruit provisions, and continue the voyage. The narrative contained accounts of misfortune, references to good men in a state of dissatisfaction and to unruly Botany Bay men, and suggestions of general desperation which were a part of Melville's own past and therefore easy for his imagination to grasp.

But Melville's attention did not dwell upon the qualities of the story which reflected the experiences he had already used in *Typee* and *Omoo*. These merely made him alive to the remarkable story of the *Tryal*. For the ship had sailed from Valparaiso, only three hundred miles to the south, two months before, carrying slaves on a short voyage to Callao. One week out, the Negroes had revolted, killed their owner and a substantial part of the crew, and compelled the captain, Don Benito Cereno, to promise to take them to Senegal. Out of water and completely cowed by seven weeks of uncertainty and terror, Don Benito had put into the supposedly deserted bay of the island and, under the watchful eye of the Negroes, had entertained Captain Delano as an unexpected visitor on board without letting him suspect the real situation. He abandoned his ship by a desperate leap overboard into the boat carrying Captain Delano away and urged the American captain to retake his vessel in the name of humanity and with the promise of a half share in its value. Two boats from the *Perseverance,* under the command of the first officer, boarded and took the *Tryal* after a severe fight, and Captain Delano learned all the earlier details of the affair during two months spent in Concepción in an effort to get a compromise settlement from Don Benito.

Here was material perfectly suited to Melville's imagination—sufficiently close to his own experience for him to realize it, yet fascinating in its novelty. It was also peculiarly appropriate to his emotional attitude at the time. In his intellectual revulsion against pride and in his temperamental inability to be a happy failure, he could feel an extraordinary sensitivity toward the proud Don Benito, reduced as he was to nervous and moral debility by the primitive violence and shrewdness with which he could not cope. The Negro who was Don Benito's absolute master while pretending to be his loyal servant seemed to possess the secret of dominance which Melville had not quite been able to penetrate in his accounts of Jackson's relationship to the sailors in *Redburn,* of Ahab's to the officers and crew in *Moby Dick,* and of the clerk's to his employer in "Bartleby the Scrivener." Furthermore, the "poetic" or symbolic significance of the material was almost inexhaustible, and it may be that one of the strongest appeals Melville found in the story was that it made the "darkness" of life visible in the primitive blacks. Captain Delano's sober defense of his actions brought together in Melville's mind more of the genuine stuff of literary creation than had found its way there since he had written *Moby Dick.*

During the winter Melville brooded it, without driving himself to write too rapidly or too much. What he put on paper was the story of

Santa Maria Bay, from the first sight of the Spanish vessel to its capture, embellished with all the significance latent in Captain Delano's narrative and with much more which his own meditations produced. He changed the name of the American vessel to the *Bachelor's Delight* and that of the Spanish ship to the *San Dominick,* doubled the number of slaves originally on the latter, and represented it as having been four rather than two months at sea. The vessel in the story was more completely a death ship, in appearance and history, than its prototype had been; and, to symbolize its character, Melville gave it a skeleton figurehead, horribly fashioned from the corpse of the owner of the slaves, with "Follow your leader" chalked below it as a ghastly joke and a warning to the surviving Spaniards. Babo, who was the ringleader of the uprising but whose son Mure acted as the guardian of Don Benito, was transformed by Melville into "a small negro of Senegal" and made the evil genius of the entire story. And for dramatic effect he created four old oakum pickers who crouched on the bulwarks, supervising the Negroes below, and a row of six Ashantee hatchet polishers who occupied the poop in the manner of savage marines. These and other changes gave the whole story a quality of suggestiveness which was rare even in Melville's work. Neither *Moby Dick* nor *Pierre* had been so completely and pervasively charged with provocative implications.

As the story of Benito Cereno was published, much of the background to the action in Santa Maria Bay was given in an elaborate document near the end which purported to be a series of extracts from the deposition made later by Don Benito. To a considerable extent it actually was a literal transcript of such a document printed by Captain Delano, but in many respects it was as much changed from the original as Melville's tale was from its source. Some of these changes were made to correspond with revisions in the body of the story. Others outlined incidents and actions merely hinted at in the account of Captain Delano's visit to the *San Dominick.* These included a prolonged calm during which half the Negroes had died, examples of terrorism which were not necessary to an explanation of conditions Captain Delano observed, and, most peculiarly, certain matters related to an invented character whom Melville called the young Marques de Aramboalaza and who appeared in the story only as a mysterious sailor seen with some bright object in his hand. From these, it would appear that the full story of Benito Cereno's voyage did not get told. Melville had more in his mind than he put on paper.

What happened to the story may possibly be inferred from a series of events which occurred in the late winter or early spring. In February, according to his wife's later memoir, "he had his first attack of severe rheumatism in his back—so that he was helpless." On March 2, his fourth child, a daughter who was named Frances, was born. And in late March, according to the implications of a note from George William Curtis, he proposed another serial novel to J. H. Dix, who had just purchased *Putnam's Monthly* and was editing it with Curtis' advice. In a letter apparently written very soon after he took over his advisory position in March, Curtis advised Dix to "decline any novel from Melville that is not extremely good," and nothing more was heard of the project. But by the middle of April Melville seems to have turned over to Dix the story "Benito Cereno" more or less in the form which was to be published. After hearing about it from Dix, Curtis wrote on April 17 that he was "anxious to see Melville's story, which is in his best style of subject," and two days later made a formal report upon it: "Melville's story is very good. It is a great pity that he did not work it up as a connected tale instead of putting the dreary documents at the end.—They should have made part of the substance of the story. It is a little spun out—but it is very striking and well done. And I agree with Mr. Law that it ought not to be lost." On the next day he returned it for publication, presumably at once, but fretted that Melville "does everything too hurriedly now."

In his hasty reading of the manuscripts forwarded him by Dix, Curtis was both blind and shrewd. He did not realize that Melville's tale of the action in Santa Maria Bay was too full and rich in its suggestiveness to be the product of hurried composition. Yet he did recognize the sketchiness of the summary of events which were supposed to precede and follow that action. Nor did he suspect that if he had encouraged Dix to negotiate for a novel, Melville might have worked the material of the documents and the conclusion into a "connected tale" which was actually summarized in the manuscript he accepted for publication. More than three months later, after Dix had paid for "Benito Cereno" but had not yet begun to print it, Curtis was still worrying about his mixed impressions. He suggested that Dix "take up" the story but also suggested altering "all the dreadful statistics at the end." "Oh, dear, why can't Americans write good stories," he complained. "They tell good lies enough, and plenty of 'em."

The answer to Curtis' complaint, in this particular case, probably is that Melville was in a state bordering upon panic. A farmer with a new baby and a stiff back was in no position to face the approach of spring with equanimity. Wanderer though he was, Melville had a strong sense of responsibility, engrained in his character since boyhood; and the sudden loss of his feeling of security was undoubtedly a shock to him. A farmer incapable of doing his spring plowing can feel more desperate than an author with a rejected manuscript, for neither extra labor nor a new judgment can provide him with a harvest once the season of planting has passed. His last magazine payment for *Israel Potter* had reached him on the day his daughter was born, he had only a single sketch available for publication in *Harper's*, and he had an unusually leisurely winter on his conscience. His difficulty was more psychological than real, of course, for he had money in the bank and hired help was not out of the question. But to a man of Melville's background and temperament—and with his relatives—the psychological difficulty was perhaps more nerve-racking than a genuine catastrophe might have been. With his publisher unwilling to encourage him to gamble on a novel, with a family of little faith in his practical judgment as a writer, and with a strong immediate need for the reassurance of an income, he probably thought it better to sell "Benito Cereno" in an incomplete form than to worry himself and everybody else with an effort to follow out its veins of fullness. Whether he worked up Don Benito's deposition and the conclusion "too hurriedly" or whether he had it on hand as a tentative part of the story, written before he realized the possibilities of a novel, that section increased the value of the tale by twenty-five per cent at the space rates paid by *Putnam's*; and he had no desire to abbreviate it by removing unnecessary or repetitious explanations or unused implications. The "statistics" of which Curtis complained may have been altered into something less "dreadful" before the story was finally published in three installments beginning in October, 1855, but the revision could not have been very great. Nor could Curtis have ever had an opportunity to realize that had he not been so hasty in his original note to Dix, he might have had the sort of "good story" he wanted and Melville might have produced another novel comparable to his best earlier work.

Melville's rheumatic back, although a lasting ailment, did not keep him literally "helpless" for any considerable length of time. Whether or not he was able to put in his own crop, he was able to keep writing; and, on June 18, Curtis found himself worrying over another provocative story. At first, his opinion was that it did "*not* pass muster," but the next day he changed his mind and reported: " 'The Bell Tower' is, after all, too good to lose.—It is picturesque and of a profound morality. It is rich in treatment, not unlike the quaint carving of the bell." He again thought that "some erasures" were necessary and felt obliged to explain his over-night conversion: "To many the style will seem painfully artificial and pompously self-conscious. But it seems to me well suited to the theme. The story has the touch of genius in it—and so—in spite of the style—it should be accepted." Somehow the story had caught him in its grip, and he continued arguing, half to himself perhaps and half to his employer: "In reading 'The Bell Tower' you must remember that the style is *consistently* picturesque. It isn't Addisonian, nor is it Johnsonese.—Neither is malmsey wine, springwater." Dix was easily persuaded and published the story, before "Benito Cereno," in the August number of *Putnam's*.

"The Bell Tower" began with three quotations "from a private MS," one of which, at least, read like an extract from a philosophical digression originally intended for the story of the *San Dominick:* "Like negroes, these powers own man sullenly; mindful of their higher master; while serving, plot revenge." In any case, his story of an overambitious architect, killed by a force he was supposed to master and his work ruined by a concealed human flaw, was intimately related to the tale of the unfortunate Don Benito who wasted away and died after being overcast by the shadow of a Negro slave. Both were stories of pride going before a fall, but in "Benito Cereno" that theme was woven into a complex pattern of suggestiveness which "The Bell Tower" lacked. Whereas the former implied unexplored depths of meaning, the latter moralized. "So the blind slave obeyed its blinder lord; but, in obedience, slew him," Melville wrote in his concluding paragraph: "So the creator was killed by the creature. So the bell was too heavy for the tower. So the bell's main weakness was where man's blood had flawed it. And so pride went before the fall." He left no questions for a reader to ask.

Yet "The Bell Tower" was, more probably than any of his other stories, Melville's commentary upon his own career. As an author, he had created such Frankenstein monsters as Captain Ahab and Pierre, who had seriously damaged his reputation even though they had not slain him as the architect Bannadonna had been slain by his mechanical creature who seemed alive. His own works had been flawed, he might well have believed, by the life's blood he had put into them. And if his own pride had not gone before a fall, he was trying to convince himself that it ought to go. He was not of a temperament to derive much creative excitement from a meticulous diagnosis of his own complaints, but neither could he write effectively without drawing upon the energy inherent in the emotions which affected him while he worked. At a time when circumstances forced him to take stock of his situation, he might, for once, have told a tale which was designed to reflect his sardonic view of his condition as a writer who had overreached his fame.

At some time during the month of June, according to his wife's memoir, Melville's troubles were increased by an attack of sciatica; and his family became so worried about the state of his health that they called in their neighbor, Oliver Wendell Holmes, who was professor of anatomy and dean of the Harvard medical school, for a consultation. The patient was well enough by the end of the month, however, for Augusta to invite Peter Gansevoort's daughter Catherine to spend a week end at Arrowhead, and he may have driven his sister over to Stockbridge to get their young cousin on the morning of Saturday, June 30, and taken her back Sunday evening. He was "seriously" ill, everybody agreed, all through the summer of 1855, but his illness was the sort which made him moody and irritable without completely incapacitating him.

In one mood, he worried about money matters, writing Dix during August in order to make sure that the new owner of *Putnam's* paid him at the proper time for his stories and to G. P. Putnam and Company about the copies of *Israel Potter* which were sold in book form. In another, he made literary capital of his troubles with an air of geniality. For Melville not only wrote the most intimately personal of all his magazine sketches that summer but composed it with such skill that Curtis, reporting on the manuscript on September 7, described it as "capital, genial, humorous," and "thoroughly magazinish"——a piece so appealing that "it would be great" if it could be squeezed into the October issue of *Putnam's*. Melville called it "I and My Chimney," and it was a genuine description of the great chimney at Arrowhead (with some details from the one at Broadhall) and an imaginary account of his defense of it against the efforts of his energetic wife to have it torn down. His references to the feminine determination to remodel and modernize his house, Elizabeth later noted, referred to his mother; but he put into the sketch many observations of his real situation at the moment—his sciatica and his feeling of age and kinship to his twisted old grapevine, and Elizabeth's efforts to take over the practical management of the farm and build a new barn. Despite the wholly imaginary "plot" in his sketch and his exaggerated representation of his age and his henpecked condition, there was a certain amount of reality in his picture of himself with his pipe in his mouth, "indolently weaving" his "vapors" and getting the reputation of being "sour and unsocial" while a houseful of women, "like all the rest of the world," ignored his "philosophical jabber" and tried to manage his affairs.

Beneath this surface was also something comparable to the biological allegory slipped into the "Tartarus of Maids." His dealings with "the master-mason"—who "had been not a little employed" by his wife "in preparing plans and estimates for some of her extensive operations in drainage"—included an examination such as might have been endured by a man who was suffering from a stiff back and sciatica, both of which were attributed to his sedentary habits while writing. Having referred to his chimney as his backbone, he arranged for "an unmolested survey" and led the examiner "to the root of the matter, in the cellar":

> "This is a most remarkable structure, sir," said the master-mason, after contemplating it in silence, "a most remarkable structure, sir."

"Yes," said I, complacently, "every one says so."

"But large as it appears above the roof, I would not have inferred the magnitude of this foundation, sir," eyeing it critically.

Then taking out his rule, he measured it.

Just what was implied in the conclusion that the chimney could be "removed" or by the later suggestion that it contained a secret compartment which might be discovered with the help of a "crowbar" (if Melville's mischievous allegory should be followed to such pedantic lengths) is uncertain. It is not improbable, however, that Herman's womenfolk wanted him to have more medical attention than he was willing to receive, and that he was irritated without being too worried to hold on to as much of his sense of humor as his literary purpose demanded.

But the bit of humor Melville derived from his situation did not lessen its seriousness. Whether or not he continued to have trouble with the aging bricks in his spinal chimney, his physical condition was such that he could not depend upon farming for a livelihood. He had offered his farm to the consideration of the commissioners authorized to select a location for an insane asylum in Pittsfield; and when two of its members appeared in town at the end of August in order to go over the ground a second time, he was perhaps seriously disappointed at their failure to select it. In the meantime he had no intention of giving up literature as a means of support. The Harpers had either begun or were planning to begin reissuing all his books which bore their imprint, and he was looking around for the substance of a new work. At five dollars a page, he had been the most highly paid regular contributor of prose to the old *Putnam's Monthly* (most of whose authors got only three dollars); and if the new regime was hesitant about publishing his contributions, it paid him in advance of publication and probably paid him as well or better. Soon after "I and My Chimney" was completed and probably before it was copied he was ordering books in his particular literary line, Robert Tomes's *Panama in 1855* and Ephraim George Squier's *Waikna; or, Adventures on the Mosquito Shore* which was published under the pseudonym of Samuel A. Bard. Neither of these provided him with the inspiration he needed, but he continued to look around. A new book was certainly on— if not in—his mind.

10

The Quest for Confidence

WHILE MELVILLE was getting better physically and looking around for a new literary inspiration, he attended what the *Berkshire County Eagle* called "a startling novelty in this region"—a "fancy dress picnic" at which Lizzie carried off the honors in the character of "Cypherina Donothing" dressed in a costume of cyphers. As a convalescent from a "severe illness," he was merely an onlooker at the festivities, but Malcolm went dressed as Jack the Giant Killer, Augusta as a market woman of olden times, Mrs. Morewood as an old lady, Mrs. Ellen Brittain as a squaw, and J. E. A. Smith as a gray friar. Most of his local friends were there, and it was perhaps while engaged in the "sad business" of "holding out against a good time" that he began to meditate the conceit that "life is a picnic *en costume*" in which "one must take a part, assume a character, stand ready in a sensible way to play the fool." He had Shakespeare's authority for the notion that all the world was a stage on which one man in his time plays many parts, and he himself was of a mind to play the melancholy Jaques. He knew that to come to life's picnic "with a long face, as a wiseacre, only makes one a discomfort to himself, and a blot upon the scene." But he had a desire to take the wind's liberty to blow on whom he pleased, speak his mind, anatomize the wise man's folly, and cleanse the foul body of the infected world if it would but patiently receive his medicine.

From the union of this conceit and this desire was to come his next book. But before he began to write it he told another story of pride going before a fall which appeared as "Jimmy Rose" in *Harper's* for November, 1855, and related how a wealthy gentleman lost his fortune, retired from the world in misanthropic obscurity for twenty-five years, and then returned to his old haunts as a pathetically and desperately cheerful cadger of free meals. He was well enough in mid-September to take his mother on "a few days jaunt" to Gansevoort and Albany, bringing home with him on the eighteenth a copy of *Don Quixote* which was not entirely unrelated to his literary intentions. During his absence Judge and Mrs. Shaw had been visiting Arrowhead, where the judge entertained himself by making Malcolm a kite and perhaps leaving it for Herman to fly. The autumn seems to have passed without any difficulties. The statement of his *Israel Potter* account, which was finally sent on October 8, showed that three editions of the book had been published and 2,577 copies had been sold by July 1, earning the author $193.27 in royalties—a figure which had to be corrected to $241.58, in view of the fact that he was to receive twelve and a half per cent instead of what appears to have been the more customary ten. Although he seems to have spent much of his time sitting on his piazza and reading, Melville was feeling "pretty well again." He was able to brave a day of howling wind and snow on October 24 to call on his cousin Priscilla (who had taken a room in the village the year before), and three days later he went to Gansevoort to help watch by the bed of his uncle Herman's wife, who died on October 29. His mother and sister Frances remained at Gansevoort to keep house for their brother and uncle, and Herman came back home for a late autumn of meditation and another winter of his customary labors at his desk.

As he sat on his northern piazza in clear weather, smoking his pipe, reading Shakespeare, and gazing off at the distant mountains, his thoughts evidently went back to another period of his life in which he had also felt helpless in the grip of circumstances—and which, incidentally, was the only period he had not yet exploited in his writings. For the scene of the book he planned was laid on the sort of Mississippi River steamer he had taken home after his fruitless trip to Galena, fifteen years earlier, and just before he had shipped to the Pacific on a whaler. A river boat, crowded with the variegated specimens of humanity who moved up and down the Mississippi, offered an admirable stage for the masquerade of life; and the "operators" or swindling confidence men supplied him with a type of character who played many roles while exposing the wise man's folly. "What fools these mortals be!" was his theme, but he called his book *The Confidence Man*.

Melville's somber recollections of his ill-adventured youth, however, did not lead him into another enterprise as deliberately reckless as that of signing up for a whaling voyage. *The Confidence Man* was almost certainly designed for serialization in *Putnam's Monthly*, which was publishing "Benito Cereno" in the last three issues of the year and was to publish "I and My Chimney" in March. The magazine had printed in May, 1855, a story called "The Compensation Office" which was not unlike the book Melville planned. It had satirized the manipulator of stocks and had made the point that the lonely wife, the high-minded clergyman, the disgusted writer, and the sorrowful maiden deserved no compensation for their miseries, because their self-centeredness had made them what Melville would have called "fools of virtue." He was not planning to stultify any representatives of society more "sacred" than these, and the novel and picturesque surroundings in which he expected to place his satire probably made him think of it as being especially "magazinish."

Certainly he did not plan the book as a novel. Like "The Compensation Office," it was a story "without any end" which could be continued as long as the boat moved down the Mississippi and new disguises could be invented for the confidence man. The river, the confidence man, and the theme provided the only continuity which ran through the book; and in an early appearance of the central character, disguised as a crippled Negro beggar, Melville had him prophetically allude to more disguises than he ever actually used. As a serial, designed for a magazine which was interested in picturesque sketches with a meaning to them, it was admirably planned: the confidence man could appear periodically in a new disguise, swindle a new group of characters or some of the same ones over again, and each time demonstrate the foolishness of mankind which could be gulled by appeals to a variety of impulses ranging from greed to goodness. It presented a cynical and melancholy view of humanity, and one of the most interesting characters in it was a peg-legged fellow who vehemently insisted that "looks are one thing, and facts are another" while trying to make his fellow travelers see the evil reality beneath the confidence man's disguise. The ghost of the commander of the *Pequod* still existed in his creator's mind; but in this book, for the first half at least, Melville was his own Ahab and the peg-legged man soon disappeared from its pages.

For once again in a book not unified by the continuity of his own adventures Melville changed his course before he had finished the work he had planned. In his last masquerade, the confidence man became a talkative figure in motley, and he remained in that role for the entire second part of the book, never becoming the "ge'mman as is a sodger" which the crippled Negro had led the reader to anticipate. The satire, instead of being directed at the gullibility of mankind, was turned against men of little faith. A misanthrope was told that the "notion of being lone and lofty is a sad mistake": men, in this respect, were "like roosters; the one that betakes himself to a lone and lofty perch is the henpecked one, or the one that has the pip." A character called Charlie Noble, who volunteered friendship and praised the press of the vine, proved to be afraid of the bottle and suspicious at heart. An Emersonian transcendentalist was shown to be cold toward humanity, and his practical disciple, ingeniously reasoning against the obligations of friendship, demonstrated how easy it was to keep "one eye on the invisible" and "the other on the main chance." But a suspicious nature offered no greater protection than a gullible one: the barber, whose very motto was "No Trust," was bilked in the end; and the book concluded with the discovery that the Biblical authority for his suspicions was not in "the True Book," which he cited, but in the Apocrypha, and with a brief scene indicating how readily a good man could be made uneasy by suspicion.

Had Melville conceived of his book as a balanced satire, playing off the material dangers of gullibility against the spiritual dangers of mistrust, he might have achieved a comedy comparable in its emotional and dramatic values to the tragedy of *Moby Dick*. He approached the delicate balance of the comic point of view early in the second part of the book when he had Frank Goodman, his man in motley, suggest that a spurious vintage might be better than no wine at all and draw an "extravagant" parallel to the effect that the society of falsehearted men might be preferable to a lone security from the wicked. Near the end, he achieved it, momentarily at least, when he had Charlie Noble argue that "there is no bent of heart or turn of thought which any man holds by virtue of an unalterable nature or will." "Even those feelings and opinions deemed most identical with eternal right and truth," he explained, "it is not impossible but that as personal persuasions, they may in reality be but the result of some chance tip of Fate's elbow in throwing her dice." There is a higher and lighter comedy in the conception of men made fools by fate and varying their foolishness from day to day than there is in the representation of men victimized by deceit—just as there is higher comedy in Shakespeare's *As You Like It* than in Ben Jonson's *Volpone*. But Melville did not have this balance in mind when he began writing *The Confidence Man,* and he did not give it a calculated balance in structure. The change of course observable in the book is more nearly explicable in terms of the author's life than in terms of his art.

Melville's worries about his health decreased while he was writing the book. Images and remarks born of his own troubles abound in the first part—the moroseness of "a criminal judge with a mustard-plaster on his back," fancies about "an invalid's easy-chair," the prescription of tincture of iron for the restoration of "lost energy," expressions of irritation at being "a gallipot" for doctors to "rinse" their "experiments into," the observation that "when the body is prostrated, the mind is not erect," an allusion to "the inglorious lockjaw" of a character's arthritic "knee-pans," references to "a crick in the neck" and to servility as a "spinal complaint," and, above all, a preoccupation with cripples. These, together with his meditations on the shortcomings of hired boys, disappeared from the latter section of the story. The attitude of the long-faced wiseacre, standing apart from life's masquerade, faded as the author's nagging worries about his illness dropped out of his mind.

The quality of detachment which Melville achieved during the winter was probably acquired by a conscious effort which was reflected in his short stories and sketches. "Jimmy Rose," written no later than September, 1855, had been an unhappy picture of the loss of human dignity under the impact of misfortune. "The Piazza," probably written not long before February 16, 1856, when he sent it to Dix and Edwards as an introductory piece for his collection of magazine tales, was of an entirely different tone. In it, Melville told the story of an imaginary adventure in late autumn, after he had recovered from his illness. While sitting on his piazza, he had noticed a flash of light in the distant mountains which could only come from a newly glazed window in that supposedly uninhabited region. Seeking out what he thought would be a princess in this distant fairyland, he discovered a wood burner's sister whose lonely amusement was to look down across the valley and think of the "happy one" who lived in the "marble" house she could see in the distance. The deceptively white house was his own, but he could not show the poor girl the "happy being" who lived there. Yet, "for your sake, Marianna," he could imagine himself saying, I "well could wish that I were that happy one of the happy house you dream you see; for then you would behold him now, and, as you say, this weariness might leave you." The story was a parable of what Melville called, in *The Confidence Man,* "the mystery of human subjectivity"; and, without resolving the mystery, it showed that by the middle of winter Melville was sufficiently free from his self-centered broodings to imagine how different his situation might appear to another person.

Related to "Jimmy Rose" and "The Piazza" were most if not all of the stories incorporated into *The Confidence Man.* The first, the "Story of the Unfortunate Man," told of a good merchant who was turned into a poverty-stricken wanderer by the inhuman behavior of a wife named Goneril, was as "black" as Shakespeare's *King Lear,* which obviously suggested it. The second, dealing with "A Soldier of Fortune," was almost as dark in its implications concerning a social order which let a murderer go free while keeping a material witness in jail until his health was ruined and he was left a cripple. The third, a retelling of Judge James Hall's tale of Colonel John Murdock, the Indian hater, was introduced by a chapter on "the Metaphysics of Indian-hating" which tried to explain such misanthropic behavior in terms of the frontiersman's experience and education. The fourth, a "Story of the Gentleman-Madman," was a retelling of the story of Jimmy Rose, with the hero of the new version merely affecting a misanthropic attitude out of sensitivity while he actually preserved his courage, made a new fortune, and reassumed his place in society as though nothing had happened. The bitterness implicit in each successive story decreased, and of the separate tales found in *The Confidence Man* only the fifth and last, the "Story of China Aster," was out of harmony with its position in the book. The longest of the separate tales, it told of a poor young candlemaker who was ruined by accepting a loan from a generous friend who afterward joined the Come-Outers and had the ungenerous side of his nature come out; and it is not impossible that it was written as a short story and inserted into the longer manuscript, as a contribution from the practical transcendentalist, when Melville felt his customary need to extend his narrative enough to make a book of respectable length.

As Melville's disposition softened during the course of the winter his reading also began to have a more humanizing effect upon his mind. For Shakespeare pervaded *The Confidence Man* as thoroughly as he pervaded *Moby Dick* and *Pierre*. The conceit of the world as a stage on which a man played various roles came from the familiar speech by Jaques in *As You Like It*, which Melville quoted, and the similar notion of a "fond pageant" showing "what fools these mortals be" was from *A Midsummer Night's Dream*. In addition to borrowing a name and the burden of a story from *King Lear*, he let his characters discuss or comment briefly upon Polonius in *Hamlet*, Autolycus in *The Winter's Tale*, and Jack Cade in *Henry VI*. *Cymbeline*, in a section from which he had taken a quotation for "The Piazza," supplied him with the name Fidele for the boat on which his action took place. But the reading reflected in these rather incidental allusions had a more profound effect upon him. "This Shakespeare is a queer man," he had Frank Goodman comment. "At times irresponsible, he does not always seem reliable. There appears to be a certain—what shall I call it?—hidden sun, say, about him, at once enlightening and mystifying." There was something of the same quality in Melville, especially in the second half of *The Confidence Man* when he had dropped the bystanding role of the melancholy Jaques and slipped into the story himself in the character of Touchstone. For when he let his confidence man drop the familiar disguises of the conventional swindlers and make motley his only wear, he began to "take a part, assume a character," and "in a sensible way to play the fool" as he had not been able to do before he reasoned and wrote himself out of his earlier despondency.

Frank Goodman, the man in motley, was a new sort of "Mississippi operator." Although a Machiavellian desire to match wits with the world remained a part of his character, he did not operate for money. He attempted to enlighten the world by serving as a touchstone to men's hidden faults. Whether he shed "the true light" his creator was unwilling to say. All the action of *The Confidence Man* was dated, like the signing of the master mason's report in "I and My Chimney," on April Fools' Day, and it was not supposed to be taken too solemnly. It was enough for Melville to have a character through whom he could discourse at large with the license permitted Shakespeare's fools or Cervantes' mad knight, Don Quixote, whose story he had brought home from Albany in September. If he was not free from worries about his health and economic prospects, he had recovered, for a while, his mental equilibrium; and he was inclined to celebrate it with exuberance.

Unfortunately for the success of Melville's high comedy, his exuberance made him careless. It is to be doubted that he knew, at times, whether he was writing ironically or enthusiastically. In a more elementary way, he was careless about identifying his speakers as they punned with ideas; and in one conversation he actually had one of the talkers inadvertently address himself. The book was too difficult to be taken lightly by readers, who have an inveterate tendency to confuse obscurity with either profundity or madness. Furthermore, not only was it incoherent in its emotional quality, but the aftertaste of its early bitterness inevitably affected the flavor of the second part of the story. Allusions to the Bible were as pervasive in the first half as allusions to Shakespeare were in the second; and Melville, with his habitual insensitivity to the reverential sensibilities of more orthodox minds, had seemed to be engaged in an ironic parody of the Sermon on the Mount and St. Paul's message of faith, hope, and charity. Against that background, even so commonplace a thing as a satire on Emerson might seem somehow sacrilegious. The loose serial construction, in general, was a mortal temptation to the author's worst faults of discursiveness. The artistic sophistication so necessary to any good comedy was simply lacking in *The Confidence Man;* and, although its readers were neither to look for nor consciously to miss such sophistication, its absence left a vacuum which they could not fill with any clear quality of understanding.

There is no evidence of any sort that Melville anticipated the failure of his new book or had any notion that it would be the last piece of prose fiction he was to publish during his lifetime. On the contrary, he seems to have been keeping a careful eye on his professional prospects. After a second reading of "Benito Cereno," just before it appeared in print, Curtis had decided that it was both "ghastly and interesting"; but he had no great hopes for the collection of stories Dix and Edwards were preparing to publish. "I don't think Melville's book will sell a great deal," he had advised them on January 2, 1856, "but he is a good name upon your list. He has lost his prestige, and I don't believe the Putnam stories will bring it up." Melville had greater expectations. Writing on January 7 for back numbers of the magazine in order that he could do his "share of the work without delay," he was vigilant to correct the tentative royalty agreement from twelve to twelve and a half per cent; and he did his proofreading and made his verbal revisions carefully. It is unlikely, too, that he would have written "The Piazza" specifically as an introductory sketch for the volume had he not been optimistic about its success.

He also varied his usual procedure during a winter's work on one book by keeping up his magazine contacts. He did a sketch of the seagoing Portuguese from the Cape Verde island of Fogo for publication in *Harper's* for March, 1856, under the title "The 'Gees," and "The Apple-Tree Table, or Original Spiritual Manifestations" for *Putnam's* in May. The latter, however, was probably written less from a desire to preserve a literary connection than from the impulse of a mind lightened by the composition of "The Piazza" and the feeling of relief at getting a book off to press. For it was another study in human subjectivity, humorously developed from a passage he had found and marked in *A History of the County of Berkshire* which he had used for *Israel Potter*. It told of "a strong and beautiful *bug*" which "*eat*" its way out of an apple-tree table belonging to P. S. Putnam in Williamstown, presumably after developing from an egg deposited many decades before. Melville related the ticking sound accompanying its emergence to the fad for "spirit-rapping" which had swept the country some years before, but primarily he stressed its effect upon the members of the household who listened to it—a man given to midnight musings on Cotton Mather's *Magnalia,* his matter-of-fact wife, his two nervous daughters, and his superstitious Irish servant. The most humorously detached of all his tales, it indicates that he preserved his ability to escape from brooding melancholia throughout the latter part of the winter; and it also suggests that, in keeping the fictitious literary character and imaginary role he had created for himself in "I and My Chimney," he was looking forward to a continued career as a "magazinist."

Although his mental state during the spring did not prevent him from writing, his physical condition kept him from doing much active farming. On April 17 he began advertising half of his farm for sale and within a few weeks disposed of it to George S. Willis at the very good price of $5,500. The eighty acres he kept included some of his woodland, his orchard and pasture, and enough cleared ground for at least a garden and a turnip patch, but not so much as to make him dependent upon hired help except in case of severe illness. He also had $8,000 in the bank, which he seems to have begun transferring to a city bank or investing in stocks —for the tax rolls show that he declared $5,000 in money for 1857 and only his customary nest-egg of $1,000 in 1858, whereas the stocks which he first listed for local taxation in 1862 amounted in value to $6,548 and his cash to $1,500. Some of that, however, may have been speculative profit, since he had a note for $2,050 to pay off on May 1, 1856. Yet, like Jimmy Rose in the years of his misfortune, he seems to have held on to his capital regardless of how difficult it was for him to make a living. At the worst, his interest and dividends, with Elizabeth's small trust fund and their garden, could keep him in genteel poverty.

Poverty could hardly have begun to threaten his peace of mind, however, until after the middle of July when Augusta had finished making a printers' copy of *The Confidence Man* and the manuscript was ready to submit to a publisher. There are no records of its reception, but it was certainly not the kind of novel that Curtis would have called "extremely good" and it did not appear serially in *Putnam's Monthly*. Dix and Edwards were even hesitant about bringing it out as a book. They had printed 2,500 copies of the *Piazza Tales,* but the 1,047 copies sold by the end of August were only about three-fifths of the number required to pay expenses; and the firm, which may have already been in financial difficulties, not only assumed that the author would get no royalties until printing expenses had been paid but evidently wanted to wait and test the "fall market" before deciding whether Melville's name was good enough to carry a doubtful book. In any event, no agreement was signed for the publication of *The Confidence Man* until October 10. During the period of delay and its inevitable nervous strain, his family once more decided that too intensive an application to literature was ruining his health and that something should be done about it.

Herman's activities of the summer, however, were not those of a man in need of any particular attention. He spent his thirty-seventh birthday with his mother and uncle Herman at Gansevoort and for the next two weeks enjoyed a holiday away from home. Allan arranged to take his vacation at the same time, and on August 7 the two brothers went to Lake George on what their uncle called "an excursion of pleasure." Their friend Daniel Shepherd, Allan's former law partner and an author like Herman, joined them on their two-day jaunt; and after their return Herman relieved the quietness of Gansevoort by spending Tuesday and Thursday at Saratoga Springs, while Allan returned for a longer stay on Lake George. En route home by way of Albany on Saturday, August 16, he stopped off long enough to call upon his uncle Peter and take a midday meal with his family before taking the afternoon train to Pittsfield. Peter was anxious for him to return for a longer visit while the American

Association for the Advancement of Science was meeting during the following week and reserved his "whole house" for his nephew, Lizzie, and the children. But for some reason—perhaps from Lizzie's reluctance rather than his own—he did not get back. He may have been worried and tired of writing, but he was neither rheumatic nor unsocial.

Elizabeth nevertheless continued to worry about him in her letters to Boston, and Judge Shaw began to turn over in his mind ways and means for breaking him of what had now become the vain habit of trying to make his living with his pen. The judge's daughter seems to have had no relish for a winter in the country with Herman shut up in his study, Mrs. Melville and the girls all away, and four small children and a big farmhouse to look after while she worried about making financial ends meet and about what she would do if her husband became bedridden. Herman was sensitive enough about the situation to be difficult at best, and, at his worst, he was probably impossible to deal with. How difficult Melville actually was, as a rule, no one can tell. He certainly was too independent to close up his house and move in upon his relatives with his large family, even if they would have had him: when he had lived with Allan and his mother after his marriage, he had always played host. He apparently was determined not to sacrifice his small claim on independence by spending the capital he had so slowly accumulated. He could be "sent abroad for his health" without losing his respectability, for that was a well-established convention in his own family and among his friends, and that seemed to be the only solution to the problem in a year when there was no political turnover to raise hopes for another government job.

Such was the solution probably pressed upon Judge Shaw by Elizabeth, who seems already to have begun cultivating her lifelong habit of worrying audibly about Herman's health and nervous condition whenever she was secretly disturbed about her own situation. The expenses of a trip to the Mediterranean and the Holy Land, which Melville had sacrificed in 1849, could be borne by the judge as a "loan" against his daughter's future inheritance—just as he had treated his advances toward the purchase of the house in New York and the farm in Pittsfield. Judge Shaw was sympathetically disposed, but, before committing himself definitely, he briefed the case in a letter to Sam:

> I suppose you have been informed by some of the family, how very ill, Herman has been. It is manifest to me from Elizabeth's letters, that she has felt great anxiety about him. When he is deeply engaged in one of his literary works, he confines him to hard study many hours in the day, with little

or no exercise, and this specially in winter for a great many days together. He probably thus overworks himself and brings on severe nervous affections. He has been advised strongly to break off this labor for some time, and take a voyage or a journey, and endeavor to recruit. No definite plan is arranged, but I think it may result, in this that in the autumn he will go away for four or five months, Elizabeth will come here with her younger children, Mrs. Griggs and Augusta will each take one of the boys, their house at Pittsfield will be shut up. I think he needs such a change and that it will be highly beneficial to him and probably restore him.

The investment—for an "outfit" and traveling expenses—in Herman's health and Elizabeth's happiness would amount to something between fourteen and fifteen hundred dollars, and the "definite plan" had to be arranged through Allan as an intermediary. But with tactful handling Herman's sensitivity could be made to blossom into enthusiasm, and all the practical details were settled well before the end of the month.

With the prospect of spending the winter in her beloved Boston while Herman was taking a wholesome trip, Elizabeth could enter with spirit into Sarah Morewood's second fancy-dress picnic on September 3. She went as "the Genius of Greylock" with a hat of bird-nests and a dress decorated with leaves and pine cones, while Augusta covered herself with leaves and flowers and little Bessie took her first part in Berkshire festivities in the costume of Bo-Peep. Augusta probably spent most of the month working on a second copy of *The Confidence Man,* for Herman was expecting to sail on October 4 and hoped to sell the book abroad although no arrangements had yet been made for its publication at home. On Saturday, September 27, he bade most of his family farewell and left for Gansevoort to deliver Stanwix, who was to stay with his grandmother, while Augusta remained behind to help close the house and get Elizabeth and the other children off to Boston. He stayed at home to talk with his uncle Herman while his mother and two of his sisters, Fannie and Kate, took Stanny to church on Sunday; and the next morning his uncle accompanied him as far as Saratoga Springs on his way to New York.

In the city, Melville was his old self. He sloughed off his four years of sensitive estrangement from Evert Duyckinck and spent the evening of October 1 with him, "fresh from his mountain" and "charged to the muzzle with his sailor metaphysics and jargon of things unknowable" as well as with good stories and lively comments upon books and people. It was "a good stirring evening," Duyckinck observed in his diary, "—ploughing deep and bringing to the surface some rich fruits of thought and experience." Melville enjoyed it, too, for he seems to have encouraged

Allan to see that Duyckinck and Daniel Shepherd (who had recently published a novel called *Saratoga, a Tale of 1787*) were made acquainted with each other as soon as possible. The only restraint upon his spirits was his failure to come to any agreement with Dix, Edwards, and Company for the publication of *The Confidence Man,* for that was possibly the reason why he postponed his sailing for a week, getting a written agreement only on Friday, October 10, and delivering the manuscript the next morning just before his departure.

The delay was not long enough to enable him to go to Boston, but it permitted him to run up to Gansevoort over Sunday in order to say good-bye once more to his mother and son before hurrying back to New York for "engagements" which prevented him from stopping in Albany. He may have had to confer with his publishers on Monday morning and make some last-minute changes in his book, for he did not go with Allan and Shepherd to call on Duyckinck Wednesday evening. But on Thursday evening he attended a farewell party given by Shepherd, with Duyckinck, Allan, and Robert Tomes (whose book on Panama Melville had bought the year before) as the other guests. They had "good talk," Duyckinck recorded, "Herman warming like an old sailor over the supper." He had got his passport, his book was at last going to be published, and over the seas lay Italy. Even the weather was wonderful —a "series of extraordinary fine days," according to Duyckinck's diary, "sunny, mellow, quiescent." On Saturday, October 11, his friends saw him off on the propeller steamer *Glasgow,* eagerly bound for Scotland, Naples, and points east.

When Melville left for Europe, he was in a state of mental excitability which his family and friends recognized but could not analyze, although it was rather clearly revealed in the unpublished manuscript of *The Confidence Man* that some members of the family had helped copy. He was still suffering from the conflict between the will to believe and the tendency to doubt which had provided the emotional tension observable in *Moby Dick* and *Pierre*. But the conflict no longer was represented by a skeptical assault on the will to believe. His skepticism had developed into cynicism, and, as a bystanding wiseacre, he had written the first part of his unpublished book from a point of view which portrayed all faith as folly. But in the second part he had shown himself to be skeptical of his own cynicism. He had no intellectual vantage point from which he could view life, consistently, either as a tragedy or as a comedy. As a writer and as a human being, he needed some sort of conviction in which to take refuge from his own moods; and he may have hoped, ironically enough, that whatever his trip might do for his health it might in some way restore his confidence.

II

The prospect of an ocean voyage, new sights, and new experiences turned Melville's thoughts into the same channels they had followed seven years before. Once again he found a fellow passenger with whom he could talk about fixed fate, free will, and foreknowledge absolute, and his only record of his passage was a reference to his metaphysical conversations. The *Glasgow* did not provide him with an opportunity to show off in the rigging, however, even if his sciatica had permitted him to do so; and his only chance to parade his nautical *savoir faire* came when the steamer was forced to lay to for sixteen hours during a North Atlantic gale. But the voyage was otherwise favorable, and within fifteen days they had sighted the north of Ireland, passed through St. Patrick's Channel, and turned into the Firth of Clyde. There, looming up through the starboard mist, Melville saw the Craig of Ailsa, which he had described with such Words-worthian wonder in *Israel Potter*. At ten o'clock at night, they dropped anchor at Greenoch, at the mouth of the Clyde, and waited for daylight to make their way through the narrow channel to Glasgow.

Scotland, as Melville began to observe it on Sunday, October 26, was a country of contrasts. The banks of the Clyde reminded him of the tow-paths along the Erie Canal, but the iron shipworks of Clydebank were like nothing he had seen before. The estate of Lord Blantyre stood opposite a mud cottage, and the city of Glasgow impressed him with its solid stone houses covered with fragile thatch and with the striking differences between the miserable poverty of the old town and the modern prosperity of the West End. He saw all the sights, including the cathedral and the university, on Monday, and on Tuesday took a river steamer and a short railroad trip to Loch Lomond (which reminded him of Lake George), returning by Dumbarton Castle where the British soldiers about the rock made him think of tropical flamingoes strangely out of place in the Scottish mist and smoke from the furnaces in Dumbarton village. That afternoon he crossed the country to Edinburgh, where he stopped long enough to visit Abbotsford and Stirling, from whence he was planning to go to London, find a publisher, and try to get in touch with Sam Shaw.

He left no record of his movements during the next ten days, but he evidently passed through Newcastle and may have gone to London to discuss *The Confidence Man* with Longman, Brown, Green, Longman and Roberts before he set out to see some parts of England that he had not visited before. He did not make any immediate disposition of his manuscript, however, in any event; and no contract was signed until March 20, 1857, when Hawthorne acted in the author's behalf, agreeing to take half profits after expenses had been paid. Yet the book should not have been hard to sell. Melville was no longer a guinea author, but he was still a good "name" among the buyers of less expensive books. Routledge had issued *Typee* and *Omoo* in 1855 in editions of 6,000 copies each, Murray had printed a fourth edition of the former book for himself in the same year, and *White Jacket* had been reprinted in 1855 and *Redburn* in 1853. *The Confidence Man,* for sale at five shillings, was not a bad offering for a publisher to place before an English public which was used to buying travelers' tales satirizing America; and the English reviewers certainly were to receive it more favorably than it was received in the United States. Its author had no reason to feel discouraged when he left the city to look at the cathedral at York and take the circuitous railway trip through Lancaster and the industrial regions of England to Liverpool.

Before leaving Glasgow Melville had been indefinite about his plans, but for some reason he apparently decided to sail directly from Liverpool to Constantinople and take in Italy on the way back. He arrived in the English port shortly after noon on Saturday, November 8, took a room at the White Bear Hotel, looked up some of the sights he had seen on his first voyage, and rather strangely waited until the next day to seek out his old friend Hawthorne. The two men had not met since one had failed and the other succeeded in getting a consular appointment, but they had not been entirely out of each other's mind. Nearly two years before, Hawthorne had suggested Melville to Commodore Matthew Galbraith Perry as a person who might be suitable to prepare for publication his notes on his voyage to Japan; and Melville had with him the address of Hawthorne's residence at that time. After taking a steamboat to the place, at Rock Ferry, on Sunday afternoon, he learned that Hawthorne had moved eighteen months earlier and would have to be located through the consulate. Melville showed up the next day, "looking much as he used to do (a little paler, and perhaps a little sadder), in a rough outside coat, and with his characteristic gravity and reserve of manner." Hawthorne "felt rather awkward at first" because of his failure to be of genuine assistance to his friend in Washington, but they were soon "pretty much" on their "former terms of sociability and confidence"; and he invited Melville to come out to Southport the next day and stay with him as long as he remained in Liverpool.

On Tuesday, shocking his friend a bit by limiting his baggage to a nightshirt and toothbrush, Melville went home with him in time for tea and found Julian "grown into a fine lad," Una "taller than her mother," and Mrs. Hawthorne in rather poor health. The next day the two friends talked—or, at least, the host listened while his homesick guest disemburdened himself of his loneliness. While they sat in the shelter of some sand hills, smoking their cigars out of the reach of a cool, strong wind, "Melville, as he always does," according to Hawthorne's account, "began to reason of Providence and futurity, and of everything that lies beyond human ken." He had "pretty much made up his mind to be annihilated," he confided; "but still," Hawthorne observed,

> he does not seem to rest in that anticipation; and, I think, will never rest until he gets hold of a definite belief. It is strange how he persists—and has persisted ever since I knew him, and probably long before—in wandering to-and-fro over these deserts, as dismal and monotonous as the sand hills amid which we were sitting. He can neither believe, nor be comfortable in his unbelief; and he is too honest and courageous not to try to do one or the other. If he were a religious man, he would be one of the most truly religious and reverential; he has a very high and noble nature, and better worth immortality than most of us.

If the reading of *Moby Dick* had not already done so, this conversation revealed to Hawthorne the explanation for the "morbid state of mind" he had noticed in his friend's writings "for a long while past"; and it was a far better diagnosis of Melville's trouble than his family and physicians had been able to make.

But Hawthorne's understanding could supply no cure, and Melville was too restless to relax in Southport and too sensitive to trouble Mrs. Hawthorne with his restlessness. He returned to Liverpool at noon Thursday, when Hawthorne had to get back to his business, and continued his inquiries among the steamers until he found that the *Egyptian,* under Captain Tate, was sailing for Constantinople on Monday and would take him as its only passenger. On Friday he had his passport endorsed at the consulate, obtained a Turkish visa, and had lunch with Hawthorne's friend Henry A. Bright and a walk through the city with him afterward. Hawthorne took Saturday off to show his friend the town and cathedral at Chester, which he considered the only place of "any old English interest" within easy reach of Liverpool, and, after agreeing to keep his trunk for him at the consulate so that he could travel with only a carpetbag, bade farewell to the lonely wanderer on a dark street corner in the rain. Melville spent Sunday packing his trunk for storage and attending church services in both the morning and evening. He was "tired of Liverpool," but his boat did not sail on schedule and Hawthorne saw him, in an anticlimactic mood, again on Monday. He had told his friend earlier of his "neuralgic complaints in his head and limbs" and on the occasion of their second parting said "that he already felt much better than in America." But he also "observed that he did not anticipate much pleasure in his rambles, for this spirit of adventure" had "gone out of him." Hawthorne thought that he was certainly "much over-shadowed" since he had seen him last but hoped that he would "brighten" as he went onward.

The *Egyptian* sailed at three in the afternoon of Tuesday, November 18, and Melville did brighten a week later, after they had passed through the Pillars of Hercules and entered the Mediterranean. The mountains on the Spanish coast were capped with snow, but the mate appeared in his shirt sleeves and a straw hat, and Melville threw open his own coat. The journals he kept on this trip were those of a conscientious traveler, supplementing with personal impressions the information contained in his guidebook, and they revealed few of the emotions so candidly displayed in his diary for 1849. But on this day he observed: "Such weather as one might have in Paradise. Pacific. November too!" Two days before Thanksgiving he was usually putting Lizzie and the youngest children on the train for Boston and reconciling himself to long weeks of separation. With a warm blue sky, the invigorating smell of salt water, and something new to see every day that he had read about in books, he had every reason to be more cheerful than he would have been at Arrowhead. He spent a day ashore at Malta, on Saturday, November 29, and reached Syra early on the following Tuesday.

"Picturesque" was Melville's constant word for Greece. The fancy dress of the people—the men wearing a "sort of cross between petticoat and pantaloons," some with embroidered jackets, and many with fine forms and noble faces—made him think of an opera spilling off the stage and all over the landscape. The streets of Syra zigzagged upward through a warren of stone houses, sometimes as steps which the native donkeys climbed, to a church with a fine view of the archipelago spread out beneath the azure sky and ermine clouds. The people were poverty-stricken and the land was rocky and worn out, looking "like life after enthusiasm is gone" in comparison with the virginal islands of the South Seas, but Melville's imagination was alive once more. On Saturday morning, as they approached Salonika, Captain Tate roused him at daybreak to see snow-covered Mount Olympus loom through the dawn while Pelion and Ossa appeared less majestically from the south. The ancient poetic associations of the Aegean shores overwhelmed him, and he was completely taken aback when the English resident at Salonika, a man not inappropriately named Duckworth, casually referred to "a day's shooting in the Vale of Tempe." The impressions he gained were to linger long in his mind, and a story of hidden arms affecting the compass of a ship, which Captain Tate told on the evening of Sunday, December 7, was later to be retold by his passenger three times in verse.

At Salonika Melville got his first vivid impressions of the mixture of races and religions which characterized the East, saw his first troop of camels, and contemplated thoughtfully the "two 'beys effendi' in long furred robes of yellow, looking like Tom cats," who came aboard with their harems and set up their tents as deck passengers to Constantinople. The ship got under way early Tuesday afternoon, passed glittering Olympus, rounded Mount Athos, and entered the Hellespont the next morning. The sail up to Constantinople was admittedly "a very fine one," but it stirred Melville to no enthusiasm, and for the better part of two days they were beset by fogs. At last the fog lifted enough for them to see the base and wall but not the dome of St. Sophia, and they were able to round Seraglio point and come to anchor on the Golden Horn. From December 12 to 16, Melville remained in Constantinople, sleeping on shipboard at first and getting lost in the maze of streets when he attempted to get around without a guide. But he saw the sights—the great mosque of St. Sophia, the indescribably magnificent view from the top of the Watch Tower, the massive city walls with "a Tower of London—every 150 yards or so," the heights of Buyukdereh from which he could catch a glimpse of the Euxine, the Seraglio, and scores of others.

Not all the sights were of a sort he remembered with pleasure. A "burnt district" seemed to haunt him, and he returned more than once to the grimy burnt column, hooped with iron and rising above a huddle of old wooden rookeries as a monument to the past fire and a reminder of what might occur again. The "Cistern of 1001 Columns"—formerly a reservoir but now a ruined yet palatial sort of Tartarus filled with boys twisting silk and flitting about like imps in semidarkness—impressed him as a "terrible place to be robbed or murdered in." The crowded bazaars were a barbaric confusion. Streets were so jammed that even the guide pushed his way through the throngs with his hands in his pockets to avoid having them picked, and visiting Europeans were warned against going abroad at night. There was a "horrible grimy tragic air" about the streets, and many of the houses were so "rotten and wicked looking" that Melville imagined a suicide hanging from every rafter in their gloomy interiors. But, in one way, the most oppressive of all the sights was that of just people—a million and a half of them, of all races, all languages, all religions, and all appearances—everywhere, swarming over the city as they had swarmed for centuries with no other purpose than to swarm. The East suffocated Melville with humanity. In such crowds, death was the only way to achieve individuality; and as he followed an Armenian funeral to a place of burial, he saw a woman with her head bent close to a new grave, calling to the dead. "This woman and her cries haunt me horribly," he wrote in his journal, and they were to haunt him for twenty years. He was "utterly used up" that night and the next morning "felt as if broken on the wheel."

On the afternoon of Thursday, December 18, he took the steamer *Arcadia* for Alexandria, passing the windy plains of Troy and stopping at Mytelene and Smyrna. In the latter port, where they remained until Tuesday, he saw the *Egyptian* and Captain Tate once more, and Captain Orpheus had Tate and another captain aboard the *Arcadia* for dinner on Sunday. The first half of Christmas Day was spent in quarantine at Syra again, and in the evening the Greek captain celebrated their departure and acknowledged the Roman holiday with a glass of champagne. They reached Alexandria on Sunday; and there Melville rode a donkey to his hotel and spent the next day making his arrangements for a passport and passage to Jaffa on Friday. He also ran across some officers from the American frigate *Constellation* and discovered that one of them was Dr. John A. Lockwood, whose brother Henry had taught mathematics to the midshipmen on the *United States* when Melville had been on board as a sailor. John Lockwood, whether Melville knew it or not, had written the series of anonymous articles against flogging which had appeared in the *Democratic Review* while the ex-sailor was writing *White Jacket*. Together, the two men with similar interests planned to spend two nights in Cairo and all day Wednesday seeing the Pyramids.

Of all Melville's days abroad, that Wednesday was to be the most impressive. Three days later, when he was writing up his journal, he was still breathless from the immensity and the mystery of the Pyramids. Approached from a distance, they looked purple like mountains, with vapors below their summits and kites sweeping and soaring around their sides. Closer, the lines of stone did not seem like courses of masonry but like strata of rocks—a long slope of crags and precipices, rising from a great ridge of sand and vast amounts of rubble. Half way to the top, they looked larger than from the bottom, precipice above precipice and cliff above cliff. Climbing one gave a man a sense of urgency. A pain in the chest compelled him to rest unwillingly, for he felt that he must hurry to the top before exhaustion caught him. At the top, the structure seemed not so high until a person sat on the edge and looked down. Then an experienced sailor, who had furled the main royal of a man-of-war in a storm, was overcome with "gradual nervousness and final giddiness and terror." After such an experience, the Pyramids loomed in Melville's imagination as "something vast, indefinite, incomprehensible, and awful."

They were as awful as death. Grass grew near the Pyramids, but would not touch them. Other ruins were ivied, but there was no vestige of moss upon these—no speck of green. Melville had breathed "the dust of ages" in Cairo, but in the desert he found the stone from which the dust might have come. They "might have been created with the creation" and "as long as earth endures some vestige will remain of the pyramids. Nought but earthquake or geographical revolution can obliterate them." Their cavernous entrances seemed to lead not to a particular tomb but to *the* tomb, and Melville shuddered with dread when an Arab offered to lead him into a side hole and thought of the main passageway as a "horrible place for assassination."

His fears were the by-products of an imagination faced with more than it could absorb. "It has been said in panegyric of some extraordinary works of man," he wrote in his journal, "that they affect the imagination like the works of Nature. But the pyramid affects one in neither way exactly. Man seems to have had as little to do with it as Nature. It was that supernatural creature, the priest." The idea of the ancient Egyptians made him "shudder." As their art had been able to evoke "the transcendent mass and symmetry" of these monuments "out of the crude forms of the natural earth," so "out of the rude elements of the insignificant thoughts that are in all men, they could rear the transcendent conception of a God." Through Moses, "learned in all the lore of the Egyptians," these "terrible" people had made their mark on religion with a "terrible mixture of the cunning and awful." The idea of Jehovah had been conceived and born "in these pyramids." Yet they had been built "for no holy purpose." Whatever dark regions of individual psychology Melville had explored in *Pierre,* whatever difficult questions he had raised in *The Confidence Man*—all faded into insignificance before the dark and difficult problem of the influence upon individual human beings of a region in which humanity was so ancient and so unimportant. Melville's concern for the problem of knowledge, which had bothered him since the beginning of his second period of intellectual growth, provided the strange emotional force that found expression in his journal. But it was no longer personal so much as historical. In its essence, it might be reduced to the question of which came first, myth or monument?

As Melville sat in the Victoria Hotel in Alexandria for five tedious days, reading a book on Palestine and meditating on Egypt and the Pyramids while he awaited the steamer for Jaffa, he did not succeed in formulating the question which bothered him. Had he done so, he might have reasoned that there had been nothing "wicked" in his suggestion that Captain Ahab had done wrong in making the white whale "the monomaniac incarnation of all those malicious agencies which some deep men feel eating in them." Nor was it really so bad to hint that Pierre had been grossly deceived in making Isabel a symbol of "uncorruptible Love." With all the curiosities of the East before him, it was neither difficult nor particularly shocking to see how mistaken people could be in their arbitrary attachments. But what of their creations? Did the expression in art of "the insignificant thoughts that are in all men" signify nothing? Might not the eternal personality of grief, exemplified by the anonymous Armenian woman in the burying ground of a dispersed race, be proof that human beings possessed something which could not be annihilated? And could this something be found in the achievements of art and the focal points of legend? Such questions as these did not arise in Melville's mind, but they put into words what he was to call those "under-formings of the mind" which explain the emotional anxiety— half eagerness and half queasiness—with which he approached and explored the Holy Land.

The exploration began with a two-day trip to Jaffa, where Melville landed on January 6, 1857, and hired a Jewish dragoman to take him by horseback to Jerusalem. An evening stop in Ramleh, made miserable by mosquito and flea bites, gave him little rest in preparation for the twelve-hour ride of the next day; and he reached Jerusalem at two o'clock in the afternoon with his eyes so affected by the glare of the bright sun and acrid hills that he could do little but rest in the Mediterranean Hotel, which was kept by a German named Hauser who had been converted to Judaism. During the next two days, however, he roamed with his guide over the hills around the city until he met a "prepossessing young man" from Boston, named Frederick Cunningham, who was as rejoiced as Melville was to find a companion and countryman in this region of strangers. Cunningham had just arrived from Jaffa with an interesting Druze called Abdallah for a dragoman, and Melville seems to have joined him for the next eight days of exploring the city and the surrounding countryside.

Their major expedition was to Jericho, the Dead Sea, and Bethlehem. Leaving the city by St. Stephen's Gate, they crossed the Valley of Jehoshaphat and passed Mount Olivet on the road to the ruined Arab village of Bethany, where the tomb of Lazarus was to be found. The country became more desolate than anything Melville had ever seen: "Stony mountains and stony plains; stony torrents and stony roads; stony vales and stony fields; stony homes and stony tombs." From the Mountains of Desolation, through which his road wound its dangerous way, he could see the high Mountain of Temptation and wonder why any fiend could be so foolish as to display a vision from there. At Jericho, another miserable village marked by ruins of the ancient city and the narrow Jordan running through banks of sand, the party camped overnight, enjoying a good dinner while they listened to thunder in the Mountains of Moab and anticipated a rain before morning. The downfall made the fertile plains of Jericho seem "mouldy," but it enabled Melville to have the novel experience of seeing a rainbow over the Dead Sea. The sea itself, within its banks of dirty brown sand strewn with salt-caked driftwood, was as bitter as Melville expected; and, after tasting it, he kept the taste of bitterness in his mouth and the thoughts of bitterness in his mind all day.

A comfortable night in the Greek monastery of Mar Saba, rising in terraces to the top of a mountain above the lower valley of the Brook Kedron and entered by a small door at the base, restored him; and the St. Saba wine took the taste of bitumen and alkali out of his mouth. Among many curious impressions of the monastery, a solitary date palm, growing midway up the barren mountain, made a lasting impression on his imagination. The way to Bethlehem led over high hills, in which the shepherds still watched their flocks as they had done centuries before, and brought them to the little town of white buildings in which Moslems now prayed with their backs toward Jerusalem. The party probably spent the night in the Capuchin monastery in Bethlehem, where a monk took them through the caves, showed them the grotto of the Nativity, and perhaps pointed out such places of interest as the Valley of the Shepherds and the pass to the Dead Sea (where Lot's wife had turned to salt), which could be seen from the high terrace in front of the building. Their return to Jerusalem was over a narrow mule track along which they hurried to avoid another rain.

Melville's notes on his trip and on his stay in Jerusalem were not so revealing as his comments on the Pyramids, but he kept enough of a record to show how much of his purpose as a traveler was later displayed in his long poem *Clarel*. His "object," he remarked, was "the saturation of my mind with the atmosphere of Jerusalem, offering myself up a passive subject, and no unwilling one, to its weird impressions." To achieve it, he walked every morning outside the walls of the city at dawn and, almost every day, would hang over the gallery above the entrance to the Church of the Holy Sepulchre in order to watch its Turkish guardians scorn the pilgrims who came to kiss the stone of the anointing. He was curious about the effects of legendary associations on his own skeptical mind and apparently fascinated by the contrasts he observed between the devoutness of believers and the contemptuous indifference of infidels. His own mind wavered over the historical problem of knowledge. Sometimes he had "little doubt" but that "the diabolical landscape of Judea must have suggested to the Jewish prophets, their ghastly theology": the "lamentable recesses" of his cave explained Jeremiah's "lamentable lamentations," and the gloomy caverns of Judea inevitably became the retreats of "gloomy anchorites." On other occasions, he wondered whether the land itself were not somehow an effect rather than a cause of its legends: "Is the desolation of the land," he asked, "the result of the fatal embrace of the Deity?" The saturation of his mind brought no answer.

No answer came during the remaining week of his stay in the Holy Land, after he left Jerusalem on January 17, in the company of Cunningham and Abdallah, to return to Jaffa. On this trip, with a letter from the patriarch, he was able to spend the night in the Greek convent at Ramleh, but with no better rest than he had found at the hotel. Since there had been a recent Arab raid on a near-by village, they joined a party led by the governor's son for the ride to Lydda the next morning and were escorted by thirty armed horsemen who cavorted around firing their pistols into every hedge. The ride across the plain of Sharon, covered with red poppies, was delightful; and they reached Jaffa in time for an afternoon swim in the Mediterranean. Another party of tourists, who had been to the Arabian city of Petra, was waiting there, and they told Melville stories of those astonishing ruins which probably made him realize that he had missed something almost as impressive as the Pyramids. Cunningham left with them for Alexandria shortly afterward, and Melville remained behind, the only stranger in Jaffa, feeling as lonely as Jonah and hopelessly confused in his journal about the day of the month.

The fleas kept him from sleeping at night, he had seen most of the sights he could take in, and he was too worn out to think much about the impressions of Jerusalem he jotted down in his journal while awaiting his steamer. But he could take an interest in people. He covertly studied the Black Jew who kept his hotel and, for the first time in all his travels, made friends with the local missionaries. Mr. and Mrs. Saunders, who were Seventh-Day Adventists from Rhode Island, living outside the wall of the city, were in such a dismal state of discouragement about their mission that they were beginning to feel it "against the will of God that the East should be Christianized." They introduced him to an elderly Englishwoman, Mrs. Williams, who had come out as a religious teacher, and to Deacon Dickson, of Groton, Massachusetts, who had sold his farm and brought his wife and four children to Palestine in order to prepare the way for the prophetic return of the Jews to Zion. They had all been influenced by the published letters of Mrs. Minot, who had tried to convert the Jews to agriculture, but only Deacon Dickson preserved any hope of making farmers or Christians out of anybody. With his Oriental beard, blue Yankee coat, and Shaker waistcoat, the deacon was a strangely Quixotic figure, who had been seen by the American consul at Beyrouth going through Jerusalem with an open Bible looking for the opening asunder of Mount Olivet and a highway for the returning Jews. "(Arch of Ecce Homo)" Melville noted parenthetically in his journal, finding in Dickson some sort of symbol of ineffectual meekness like that of an old Connecticut man he had noticed going about Jerusalem dispensing tracts. These two characters combined in his mind and were to reappear as one in *Clarel,* along with, perhaps, a Philadelphian named Warder Crisson who had been converted to Judaism, married a Jewish wife, and settled in Jerusalem. Some of the people Melville ran across on his trip made impressions upon him which were as lasting as those made by famous places.

In Beyrouth, which he reached on Monday, January 26, after sailing on the Austrian steamer *Aquile Imperiale* the evening before, he met the interesting American consul, George Wood, of Concord, New Hampshire, who not only told him the story of Deacon Dickson but also stories of Mrs. Williams, Mrs. Minot, and perhaps Lady Hester Stanhope (who also was to appear in *Clarel*). He had to remain there for a week, until February 1, when he was able to get another Austrian steamer for Smyrna. The *Smirne* was a slow boat with an unmannerly captain who cheated him on the passage money, but from it he saw Cyprus, Rhodes, the Sporades, and Patmos. Passing the last island, he wished the German Biblical critics, Niebuhr and Strauss, "to the dogs," as he was "again afflicted with the great curse of modern travel—skepticism." Looking at the barren height and feeling his spirit partake of its barrenness, he was no more able to believe in St. John's revelations than he had been able to believe in Defoe's Robinson Crusoe while off Juan Fernández. He had hoped, in spite of himself, to have some sort of simple faith restored on his trip, but too much knowledge had robbed his spirit of its "bloom" and the unattractiveness of the "ecclesiastical countries" had not been able to restore it.

Reaching Smyrna at daybreak on the morning of February 6, he was glad to go ashore for breakfast at the hotel and abandon the *Smirne* (which had given him a severe neuralgic pain in the head after five sleepless, scratching nights) and take the *Italia* out in the afternoon for a third stop at Syra and—at last—Piraeus, where they came to anchor in the moonlight at seven o'clock on the evening of Sunday, February 8. An old hack took him "straight as a die" over a good macadamized road to the comfortable Hotel d'Angleterre in Athens; and on the road, with the discomforts and disappointments of Asia behind him, he almost had his faith restored by his personal vision of the Parthenon elevated above him in the moonlight. Something was to be found in art which moved him deeply, and, at the very least, he experienced a revival of interest in the trip that still lay before him. The ruins of Athens were all that his reading had led him to expect, and he viewed them twice during his two-day stay. He also began to meet other interesting travelers, especially an American named Marshall whose business was shipping ice to all parts of the Mediterranean; and when he sailed on the *Cydnus* for Messina on Wednesday afternoon he ran across the man who had served as the guide for the author of *Eōthen*.

The trip past the coasts of Calabria and Sicily lasted only two days on a fast steamer, and in Messina Melville found Dr. Lockwood, from the frigate *Constellation,* met Captain Bell and some of the other officers, and went with Lockwood to the opera *Macbeth.* He seems to have made friends readily on his travels, and after reaching Naples on February 18 he was often able to find company. Pompeii, Vesuvius, and the ruins of Vergil's tomb, Lake Avernus, and Sorrento were among the major sights he saw, and the view from Posilipo made a lasting impression upon him —although he did not find in it the relief from pain which the name promised. He spent much of his time in art galleries, and was remarkably affected by the street scenes, especially on Saturday, February 21, when a group of tumblers blocked his way and he began to notice the merriment which characterized the Italian crowds in contrast to those of the East. They gave reluctant way to his passage, and he was cheered from the balconies for his success in getting through. He acknowledged the cheers, the waving handkerchiefs, and the general good humor with the most graceful bow he could manage and "felt prouder than an Emperor." Too many soldiers were in too many places, and Naples lived under the shadow of threatening cannon as well as Vesuvius; but a man was an individual there, not merely food for fleas and an object of robbery and assassination, and Melville began to feel better about the world. He was excited at the prospect of seeing Rome, and on the morning of Tuesday, February 24, took the diligence for the twenty-six-hour ride to the capital.

Melville remained in Rome until March 21, spending his Mondays in the Vatican and his other days among the other museums, churches, and ruins. Like many another tourist, he discovered that early spring in Rome had disadvantages which the poets failed to mention; and, although he had bought a good nine-dollar overcoat in Naples to keep himself warm, he suffered the ailments of the season. One of his eyes began troubling him within a week of his arrival and grew steadily worse until both were affected and he was suffering from such "general incapacity" that for more than a week after March 9 he could not endure the unnecessary strain of writing in his journal. During that time, he changed rooms in his hotel in order to have a fire, "prepared for being laid up," and spent almost two out of four days in his room—the last with a "singular pain" across his "chest and in back." On that day of March 15, he wrote when he was able to catch up with his journal, he "saw nothing, learned nothing, enjoyed nothing, but suffered something." Yet he drove himself out between times whenever he could. He was not going to waste Judge Shaw's money on an illness or neglect his own education.

Primarily, Melville's Roman education was artistic; and, to some degree, it came as an unfortunate anticlimax to his experiences in the East. The historical problem of knowledge and the philosophical problem of art, which had been hovering on the verge of definition in his mind, faded under the influence of the more personalized art exemplified in Roman sculpture and Renaissance painting. In Naples he had looked at bronze busts of Plato, Nero, and Seneca and had begun to think on the commonplace sameness of human appearances rather than the mystery of the artistic impulse. In Rome, as he looked upon the statue of Tiberius, he had similar thoughts. "The Dying Gladiator" showed "that humanity existed among the barbarousness of the Roman time" just as "among Christian barbarousness." But usually Melville looked less for what statues told about the perceptiveness of the artist than for what—in a term he was later to use in a lecture on Roman statuary—they "prattled" about the subject. This tendency was even stronger in his responses to paintings: he thought he detected an idealized portrait of the artist's wife in Titian's "Magdalen," and observed that Lucretia Borgia had no appearance of wickedness about her but was a "good looking dame" though "rather fleshy." Some of this interest in a portrait's "prattle" grew naturally enough out of the fact that he was informed in advance about the subject. The fascination that Beatrice Cenci held for him led him to shop for her portrait soon after he arrived in Rome and go directly from Shelley's grave to the Cenci Palace before finding his way to the Palazzo Barberini and observing that the original painting showed an "expression of suffering about the mouth" and an "appealing look of innocence" which was "not caught in any copy or engraving." But whatever the cause, his interest in art was growing more personal and less philosophical.

As he made friends with some of the artists living in Rome—notably the English sculptor, John Gibson; the American, Thomas Crawford; and the American painter, William Page—he began to take an interest in technical problems, and the journal of his visits to galleries after leaving Rome was made up almost entirely of technical observations. He met Sam Shaw on his last day in Rome, but the two relatives by marriage were not nearly so anxious to travel together as their family assumed they were, and Melville had made his arrangements for a grand tour of northern Italy. He reached Civita Vecchia by overnight venturino on Sunday, March 22, arrived at Leghorn on the French steamer *Aventine* the next day, and took the train to Florence in the afternoon. There he remained until the following Sunday, paying two visits to the Pitti Palace and three to the Uffizi (where he was so overwhelmed that he found it "idle to enumerate" what he had seen) and seeing the Duomo, the Cellini statue of Perseus, and the Palazzo Vecchio. He noted that he was "very much astonished at the wrestlers" whose statue he saw in the Palazzo, although he had himself used a similar tableau in the fight in the cutter in *Israel Potter;* and he mused upon what might be written on the subject of cafes and the peculiar young men who frequented them. But he was mostly concerned with his artistic education and before he left visited Hiram Powers and talked with him about his work.

The diligence for Bologna started at three o'clock in the morning on Sunday, March 29, and when the porter forgot to wake him, Melville had to run around the Duomo with his carpetbag and catch his ride at the gate. The way led due north across the brown and treeless Apennines which were so covered by snow in the upper regions that the travelers sometimes had to be pulled by oxen. Reaching Bologna in the morning, Melville sampled the sausage, admired the arcades, saw the sights, and visited the university. The next morning he went on to Ferrara, where he saw Tasso's prison, and crossed the Po and the Austrian frontier to Padua by midnight. The first of April was a rainy day, but Melville had recovered his health and spent the morning with a guide and an umbrella in an effort to miss as little as possible before taking the two o'clock train to Venice. The approach to Venice reminded him of that to Boston from the west, but a gondola to the Hotel Luna, near the Piazza of St. Mark, put him in a different world. On his second day in Venice he met an affable and amusing guide named Antonio, who had lost all his money in the Revolution of 1848 but was a man of the world who could not only show a visitor everything worth seeing in Venice but could tell him stories about Lord Byron and display a cynical philosophy which did provide Melville with the relief from pain he had not found on the Cape of Posilipo. He employed him for the last three days of his stay and enjoyed Venice more than any other place he had visited.

Nine hours of travel by rail and five by diligence took Melville on April 6 to Milan, where he made the customary pilgrimage to see "The Last Supper" and to the roof of the cathedral and spent a day on Lake Como. On Thursday, the ninth, he visited Novara and went on to Turin, from which he took the train for Genoa on Saturday. He remained there through Monday, but he was getting lonely, had lost track of the day of the month again, and was delighted to discover that his friends from the *Constellation* were in the neighborhood. He found Lieutenant Fauntleroy in the station early Tuesday morning as he was on his way to Arona and Lake Maggiore, and at Bellinzona, in Switzerland, he saw Dr. Lockwood on his way south. The two friends had little time for talk, however, for they were both late arriving, and Melville was due to start at two o'clock in the morning across the St. Gotthard pass. It was storming violently when he stopped at Airolo for breakfast, but parties had been waiting there for three days and they thought they could make it that day. Melville found an acquaintance named Abbott among the delayed travelers and was glad to have his company on the zigzag way upward as they skirted precipices, discussed the gods, and floundered in the snow when their horses had to turn out to make way for freight sleds coming down. They were wet through by the time they reached the summit and started down at Andermatt, but they were safely through Altdorf and into Flüelen at seven in the evening. He visited Lucerne the next day and on Friday left with Abbott for Berne and a day of restful gazing over the Bernese Alps.

Although Melville had no suspicions of the fact, he made the most profitable acquaintance of his trip on Sunday, April 19, when he ran across a New York merchant named Henry A. Smythe while dining at Soleure on his way from Berne to Basle. The two men found themselves companionable and traveled together for the next two and a half days— to Strassburg, Baden, Heidelberg, and Frankfort. On the way to the last town they encountered Abbott once more, and after an evening drive with Smythe through the city Melville bade his new friend a casual farewell and prepared to start for home. He intended to take the train for Wiesbaden the next morning but got on the cars for Mainz instead, and from there he took a boat for Cologne and, after spending a night in the city he had visited before, the railway for Amsterdam. He was cheerful despite his difficulty in finding a hotel, and when he put up at one called the "Old Bible" he began to think that "something good" might be written about it "in an ironical way." He hired a guide and visited the art gallery, where he was particularly struck by the convivial scenes of Teniers, and went on to Rotterdam the following afternoon, where he spent the night and took a boat for London. They made the mouth of the Thames early on the morning of April 26 and disembarked at St. Catherine's Wharf, and Melville took a cab for the Tavistock Hotel and spent a dreary Sunday in Hyde Park and Kensington Gardens. He made a business call to Longman's on Monday and discovered that *The Confidence Man* had been published and had received several reviews, but he seems to have made no effort to get in touch with his former friends. Instead he lay "sort of waterlogged," visiting Madame Tussaud's waxworks, the "Cock" tavern, the Crystal Palace, Richmond, and the Vernon and Turner galleries. But he was probably interested in nothing except the prospect of getting home.

In London, Melville lost track once more of the relationships between the days of the month and the days of the week; but he had made tentative arrangements for sailing on the *City of Manchester* from Liverpool on May 5, and he wanted to see Oxford and Stratford before he left. He took the train for Oxford on Saturday, May 2, made a tour of all the colleges, and found it the most interesting place he had seen in England. "It was in Oxford," he wrote, "that I confessed from the first, and with glad gratitude, my mother land." It was restful. It made him think of "old Burton" composing his *Anatomy of Melancholy,* "sedately smiling at men"; and he knew of "nothing more fitted by a mild and beautiful rebuke to chastize the sophomorean pride of America as a new and prosperous country." But he had to leave the next morning to see Shakespeare's birthplace, the New House, Anne Hathaway's cottage, and Warwick. He spent the night at Birmingham and at six o'clock Monday morning, impressed for a second time by the English industrial district, took the train for Liverpool. Paying the remaining part of his passage money, he secured his berth on the *City of Manchester,* collected his mail, saw Hawthorne for the last time, paid his respects to Henry Bright, bought presents for his family, and repacked his trunk. At ten o'clock that morning he was on the tender for the steamer, and an hour and a half later was "off for home." His mind was crowded with impressions gleaned from his travels, but he was too tired and too anxious to get back to his family to sort them out. Whether he had gained much, intellectually, from his trip, time alone could tell.

II

Critic and Commentator

I

MELVILLE LANDED in New York on May 20, 1857, with no record of his voyage home except for a few notes in the back of his journal which reveal that he spent at least part of his time meditating the literary use he would make of his travels. His mind was obviously confused with a surplus of sensations and by the lack of any consistent point of view from which to organize them. The projected book, which he thought of calling "Frescoes of Travel," reflected the confusion in that it was supposedly to be "by Three Brothers"—a poet, a painter, and a scholar or (as he decided, on second thought, to call him) an idler. Four brief notes on "Subjects for Roman Frescoes" indicated that Melville's plan was the necessity of a genuinely divided mind rather than an arbitrary device for achieving variety. For a remnant of his philosophical approach to art survived in a note suggesting an attempt to explain Pope Sixtus V and his monuments in terms of his time and the people over whom he had to rule. But the others—dealing with the Cenci portrait, the nearness of Tartarus to Tivoli, and the resemblance between the whispering cypresses in the Villa D'Este and Michelangelo's "Fates"—were all indicative of his interest in the picturesque and in the "prattle" of painting. He expected to return to his writing, but his mind was too unsettled, at the moment, to provide a solid foundation for any profitable work.

Yet his trip had been physically worth while. His health had not been entirely restored, but he was in good spirits and actually felt better after his return than at any time during his months away from home. He needed time to order his thoughts, however; and when he learned that his relatives were still anxious to prevent him from falling back into his old routine and had renewed their efforts to get him a place in the New York Custom House, he declared that he had no intention of writing any more "at present" and readily fell in with their plans.

His reception in Boston was of a sort that would almost have caused him to forget the loneliness he had felt as a tourist in such cities as Rome and Jerusalem. Shortly after he arrived, the younger Lemuel Shaw took him out to visit Harvard, where his uncle Peter's son, Henry Gansevoort, was a student in the Law School; and two days later, on May 27, Lemuel and Judge Shaw gave him a literary dinner party in the best Boston manner. Oliver Wendell Holmes and Richard Henry Dana, Jr., were among the guests, who began the meal with salmon "in the French style" and continued through mock turtle soup, spring chicken, squabs, broiled turkey, mutton chops, sweetbreads, canvasback duck, and "too many other things to enumerate." Young Henry Gansevoort, who was present, could not undertake to name the desserts in the record of the occasion he kept in his diary; but he remembered Burgundy, hock, claret, Madeira, Heidsieck, and sherry among the assortment of wines, and a number of cordials, of which anisette was the only one he undertook, vainly, to spell. "Wit circled the board, repartee flashed and humor thundered" until eleven o'clock, according to the awe-stricken young man from Albany, "when the joyous company separated." Melville must have impressed Holmes more favorably that evening than he ever had in Pittsfield, for the little doctor was then a member of the group engaged in projecting the new magazine which he named the *Atlantic Monthly,* and in August the visitor from the Berkshires was invited to become one of its contributors.

At the moment, however, Herman's decision to refrain from writing seemed well taken. His account with the Harpers was overdrawn by $352.11, and the firm of Dix and Edwards, publishers of the *Piazza Tales* and *The Confidence Man,* had been dissolved in April and its assets were being liquidated. The English publishers of *The Confidence Man* had sold barely a third of their edition of a thousand copies, and, although some notices of the book seemed "highly complimentary" to the experienced eyes of Augusta, it was not a success among the American reviewers, who found it bitter, profane, and exaggerated. Lemuel Shaw, Jr., had "dipped into it" and expressed to his brother the fear that it belonged to "that horribly uninteresting class of nonsensical books he is given to writing—where there are pages of crude theory and speculation to every line of narrative—and interspersed with strained and ineffectual attempts to be humorous." He and other members of the family probably avoided any reference to the book in Herman's presence, and their silence would have been comment enough to any sensitive author. Further writing, he knew, would upset them to no practical purpose; and when he accepted the invitation to contribute to the *Atlantic Monthly,* he did so with the qualification that he could not then name the day when he would have any article ready.

In the meantime, his family's designs on the customhouse failed and he had to make some plans of his own for the future. His mother, looking better than she had seemed in years, had come to Boston to welcome him home and visit Helen in Brookline; and, since he had returned too late to put in a crop at Arrowhead, even if he had felt able to do so, he had no pressing incentive for getting back to the farmhouse which Lizzie had got in readiness for their return. He and Judge Shaw had probably discussed the advisability of his traveling the lyceum circuit, for the subject had arisen at the dinner party, where Holmes observed that a lecturer was a literary strumpet who prostituted himself for an abnormally high fee. The occupation offered a good compromise between Herman's literary interests and his family's insistence that he give up his sedentary life. But whether or not two or three months on the road in stove-heated railway cars and hotels, absorbing what Holmes on another occasion called the "still, sad odor of humanity," would have been good for Herman, his absence from home in midwinter would have been bad for Elizabeth and his decision involved more complex considerations than would be required of a man who lived in the city. It evidently was made, though, before he left Boston about the middle of June, for as soon as he had paid a few calls in Albany and escorted his mother home he placed an advertisement in the *Berkshire County Eagle* offering Arrowhead and its eighty acres of meadow, pasture, woodland, and orchard for sale.

There were no good takers of the offer even after it was also inserted in the Pittsfield *Sun* on July 16, but Melville decided to go ahead with his lecturing anyway. Very few of his fellow countrymen were able to make a living by writing books which people would pay to read, but a considerable number managed to support themselves from the proceeds of a single short manuscript delivered with animation before audiences who were willing to pay for the privilege of seeing a live author. September was a month of decisions. Melville had to determine what should be done about the stereotype plates of the *Piazza Tales* and *The Confidence Man,* which otherwise would have been sold at public auction by the printer who had formed a firm to take over the assets of Dix and Edwards; and he also had to decide upon a subject for his lecture, arrange his itinerary, and begin working on his manuscript. The plates were withdrawn from the sale and held in hopes of a better price later. The lecture subject eventually settled upon was "Statuary in Rome." Whether he had expert advice upon its choice or whether it was his own inspiration, it was not an altogether happy one for a man whose forte was taletelling rather than criticism.

Yet the lecture which he eventually worked up was a significant revelation of his attempt to order his thoughts on art—to achieve the confident point of view necessary before his recent experiences could fall into a proper perspective. The fragmentary newspaper reviews show that he made little use of the technical knowledge he had gained during the latter part of his trip. Instead, he spoke as a layman who believed that "art could be enjoyed without the artist's skill" just "as the beauties of nature could be appreciated without knowledge of botany." His lay view, however, was extraordinarily philosophical; and he found in his "Roman statuary" evidence of the unchanging quality of "what went to make up the basis of human character," although certain virtues might be more highly prized in one age than in another. Somehow, he seemed to imply, art was a rationalization of instinct, which had the power of preserving certain human values against the assaults of time; and he dared hope that the "heroic tone peculiar to the ancient life"—and preserved in its statuary— was "not wholly lost from the world, although the sense of earthly vanity inculcated by Christianity may have swallowed it up in humility." He was still struggling with the problem of the relationship between art and myth which had excited his imagination as he wrote up his journal after his visit to the Pyramids, but he had not yet solved or wholly clarified it. Furthermore, he knew that such notions would have little appeal to a lyceum audience, and most of his manuscript was devoted to gossipy comment on his personal experiences and his impressions of what "these statues confessed, and, as it were, prattled" of matters was not recorded in history.

The lecture platform, in fact, was probably the worst place Melville could have found from which to develop his ideas of art. For his primary impulse was toward the sort of criticism which would develop some philosophical theory of art and its relation to the problem of knowledge and the history of mankind. But the seekers after culture who could be expected to pay to see the man who had seen the statuary of Rome wanted commentary and other prattle. His lecture wavered between his impulse to please himself and his desire to please his audiences, and it did little to satisfy his mind at a time when he needed to think deeply—and perhaps suffer some of the creative turmoil which his family dreaded—if he wanted to profit intellectually by his trip. He had certainly made little progress, at the time he wrote it, toward the sort of confidence a man gains from a firm point of view.

But, after committing himself to the platform, Melville had little time for sustained thought. He had to establish himself as a lecturer. At the beginning, he could do nothing but take whatever engagements he could get, hoping that reports on his performance and the appearance of his name in the newspaper list of available speakers (which was usually published in October as legitimate news) would bring him invitations from which he could pick and choose. His first appearance was for charity in Lawrence, Massachusetts, where John C. Hoadley arranged for him to try out his talents for the benefit of the poor. A heavy rainstorm kept the audience small and left the poor only thirty dollars better off for his effort, but the local newspaper responded to charity with kindness and gave him a favorable and almost enthusiastic review. On the next day, November 24, he traveled to Concord, New Hampshire, and repeated the performance for a fee of thirty dollars. Elizabeth had accompanied him to Boston, where they enjoyed a Thanksgiving dinner with her parents two days later, and they remained for another week in order that Herman might earn a forty-dollar fee and a certain amount of prestige by lecturing before the Mercantile Library Association in Tremont Temple. The newspapers covered this appearance thoroughly, and their comments were generally favorable, although the *Daily Journal* suspected that "the larger part of his audience would have preferred something more modern and personal." He had two other engagements before the end of the year—one in Montreal on December 10 and another in New Haven on December 30—for the standard fee of fifty dollars, and he had been obliged to turn down an invitation to speak in Malden. His net earnings for the period were not much more than a hundred dollars, but he had managed to get a good start on his new occupation while working into his itinerary visits to the Shaws in Boston, his mother in Gansevoort and Saratoga Springs, and his uncle Peter in Albany. He was certainly not leading a solitary life any longer, and, on the whole, neither he nor his family had reason to be displeased with his beginning.

For the new year he was able to arrange what was almost a professional circuit, with appearances in Auburn, New York, on January 5, 1858, Ithaca two days later, Cleveland on January 11, Detroit the next night, Clarksville, Tennessee, on January 22, and Cincinnati and Chillicothe on February 2 and 3, before returning via Pittsburgh, Washington, Philadelphia, and New York. His western newspaper critics were more severe than those of the East, and some of them were obviously more interested in the South Sea adventurer than the critic of Roman statuary. The reporter for the Cincinnati *Daily Commercial*—which had announced him in advance as the author of *Moby Dick* "through whose five hundred weird pages 'all thoughts, all passions, feelings and delights,' chase each other 'like shadows o'er the plain' "—was especially inclined to see him in his early role:

> Mr. Melville is rather an attractive person, though not what anybody would describe as good looking. He is a well built, muscular gentleman, with a frame capable of great physical exertion and endurance. His manner is gentle and persuasive, while a certain indefinable sharpness of features, with small twinkling blue eyes under arched brows, and a rather contracted and rugged forehead, indicates the spirit of adventure which sent him roving a sailor's sturdy life. His face still glistens duskily with the Polynesian polish it received under the tawny influences of a Southern sun, and his voice is as soft and almost as sweet, barring a slight huskiness proceeding from a cold, as the warbling of winds in cocoa groves. His style of delivery is earnest, though not sufficiently animated for a Western audience, and he enunciates with only tolerable distinctness.

Actually, although the cold which affected his enunciation in Cincinnati and almost completely dispirited him in Chillicothe was partly responsible for his lack of effectiveness, none of the reviews indicated that he was able to work up much animation over Roman statuary. He was to deliver the lecture three times after his return—for the small fee of twenty dollars at Charleston, Massachusetts, on February 10, and for his regular fee of fifty in Rochester, New York, on February 18 and in New Bedford five days later—but it was not a very great success. He had tried out a "more modern and personal" discourse called "The South Seas" before his Auburn audience at the beginning of his tour, and he decided to make that the mainstay of his next season.

Financially, Melville had not done badly for a beginner. He had taken in $355.00 on his tour, of which about $200.00 was above expenses; and, of his $645.00 from fourteen paid engagements, his clear gain was $423.70.

It was better than writing unsuccessful books, and, despite his Ohio cold, he seemed to thrive on the hardships of midwinter traveling and probably enjoyed visiting so many of the places that he had first seen as a young man. When he visited Peter Gansevoort on his way from Rochester to Boston and New Bedford, his uncle found him "stalworth, in excellent health and very fine spirits"; but a month later, while he was visiting his mother in Gansevoort, he was laid up by another attack of severe "crick in the back" and, according to Elizabeth's memoir, "never regained his former vigor and strength." But at the time his ailment seemed only temporary, and he spent a normally active summer, entertaining George and Evert Duyckinck and exchanging visits with the Morewoods, walking with Elizabeth and her brother Samuel, who paid them a visit in August, and persuading George Duyckinck to take a three-day buggy trip in the mountains during September. George got the impression in July that he was "busy on a new book" but made no reports on its supposed progress, although he did observe, on September 17, that Melville was "as robust and fine looking as Evert, but somewhat impaired in health by an affection of the spine brought on by too many hours of brain work day after day, following a life of great bodily activity." Two days later, however, Judge Shaw wrote young Lemuel that Herman was as well as he had seen him in years and that the "four children are, or it appears to me, greatly improved, in appearance and conduct." Elizabeth, too, was "quite well" that summer, and the entire family seems to have been relaxed and at ease.

During the fall, however, Melville was ill again; and Judge Shaw, after learning that his daughter and her family were not planning to spend their customary Thanksgiving holiday with him, evidently suspected financial worries. On November 8 the judge sent Herman a check for a hundred dollars to help him through the winter. It was welcome, for, although Melville spent much of November and early December in correspondence designed to arrange an efficient lecture tour, his success was less than he anticipated. The Yonkers Library Association paid thirty dollars to hear him on the South Seas on December 6, and while in New York for this engagement he tried in vain to get another that he might fill at about the time he expected, by Duyckinck's arrangement, to address the New York Historical Society on February 7. Pittsfield recognized his prominence, however, by paying his standard fee for an appearance on December 14, and the Mechanic Apprentices of Boston engaged him to appear in Tremont Temple on January 31. The hall was not more than half full, even at the low price of twenty-five cents a ticket, but the newspaper reports were favorable and the lecturer had the unexpected delight of having his brother Tom suddenly appear after a long voyage.

The two hastened off to Gansevoort to visit their mother, and Herman made his appearance in New York the following Monday evening in fine fettle and put on the best performance of his career. The crowd was not large, but the newspapers were complimentary, and young Henry Gansevoort was enthusiastic. "It was in Cousin Herman's true vein," he wrote his sister Catherine: "He was emphatically himself, and the lecture was to me like a quantity tied together of his vivid and colloquial sketches (always too short) told under the inspiration of Madeira after dinner or drawn forth by some proper association elsewhere. He should be invited to deliver it at Albany." A handsome, hundred-dollar engagement in Baltimore the next night, reported with flattering fullness by the press, did nothing to destroy his good humor. And when he got back to Pittsfield and found a warm letter from his old frigate-mate, Edward Norton, confessing that his real name had been Oliver Russ and that he had called his first son "Herman Melville Russ" without knowing that the name was to become famous, he must have felt more satisfaction than he had experienced in several years. Not only was he appreciated but he could pay his taxes out of his earnings and leave some money behind for Elizabeth while he took the road again for his second Midwestern tour, which was to last for only a couple of weeks.

He had only four engagements—Chicago on February 24, Milwaukee the next evening, and Rockford and Quincy, Illinois, on February 28 and March 2—but the first three cities were paying him fifty dollars plus expenses, and he had arranged his trip so that he could spend three nights with his blind friend William Cramer (who was publishing the *Daily Wisconsin* in Milwaukee) and probably visit his aunt Mary and her family in Galena. But his good spirits did not carry over to his audience, and professionally his trip was a failure. The newspapers in Chicago were critical, and those in Rockford were damning. "Lecturing is evidently not his forte," observed the *Republican* of the latter city, "his style as well as the subject matter being intensely 'Polynesian' and calculated to 'Taboo' him from the lecture field in the future"; and the *Register* indignantly protested that "no man has a right to set himself up as a lecturer at $50 per night, who cannot for one minute take his eyes from his manuscript." The *Daily Wisconsin* carried the only favorable report on his performance that he received on the entire trip. Cramer seems to have been determined to convince his fellow townsmen (who had missed the lecture in such numbers that Melville was only the sixth most popular speaker in a series of ten) that they had stayed away from something better than the audience could have reported. Melville never lectured west of Flushing, Long Island, again.

On March 16 he wound up his season by delivering both of his lectures at Lynn, Massachusetts, at the bargain rate of $30.00 each, thereby bringing up his total earnings to $518.50. But even though most of his engagements had paid his expenses in addition to his fees he probably cleared little more than he had during the year before, when he was only a beginner. He had not been a good provider, and Judge Shaw was growing worried about the financial security of his daughter and her family. The judge had reached the age of seventy-eight and was preparing to make his will, and he may have broached to his son-in-law, at the time of the lectures at Lynn, the idea of canceling all of Herman's indebtedness to him in return for a deed on the Arrowhead property, which Shaw, in turn, would present to Elizabeth. At any rate, Herman returned home and arranged for an exchange of deeds of discharge, on April 18 and 23, with George Willis (who had bought part of the property), which would keep the title of the estate above reproach. He also, somewhat defiantly, began writing professionally again and on May 18 submitted "two Pieces" to an unidentified magazine with instructions to the editor that "in case of publication" he might, if he pleased, send him whatever they should be worth. Five days later, Henry Gansevoort reported seeing him in New York "looking well and hearty" but without giving any indication of his business.

Melville's air of restlessness and defiance at this time was even evident to such strangers as the two Williams College students, Titus Munson Coan and John Thomas Gulick, who began their spring vacation by making a literary pilgrimage to Pittsfield on Wednesday, April 20. As the sons of Hawaiian missionaries, they were not uncritical of the author of *Typee*, but one of them at least was sufficiently homesick to be eager to hear of the South Seas. Instead, they heard a lonely man pour out his philosophy and theories of life in a "full tide" of monologue. "The shade of Aristotle," Coan wrote his mother, "arose like a cold mist between myself and Fayaway"; and Gulick recorded in his journal that "the ancient dignity of Homeric times afforded the only state of humanity, individual or social, to which he could turn with any complacency" and disapprovingly noted his host's opinion that "what little there was of meaning in the religions of the present day had come down from Plato." Young Coan was genuinely puzzled by Melville's "air of one who had suffered from opposition, both literary and social," and was inclined to explain it by the "contradiction" between the gypsy and the studious element in the nature of a man who refused to talk about his adventures and appeared "to put away the objective side of life and shut himself up in this cold North as a cloistered thinker."

Gulick, who obviously had not read Melville's books with the "rapture" admitted by his classmate, was less charitable in his description:

He has a form of good proportions, is about five feet nine inches
in height, stands erect and moves with firm and manly grace.
His conversation and manner, as well as the engravings on his
walls, betray a little of the sailor. His head is of moderate size
with black hair, dark eyes, a smooth pleasant forehead and
and rough heavy beard and mustache. His countenance is
slightly flushed with whiskey drinking, but not without expression. When in conversation his keen eyes glance from over
his aquiline nose. Though it was apparent that he possessed a
mind of an aspiring, ambitious order, full of elastic energy and
illuminated by the rich colors of a poetic fancy, he was evidently a disappointed man, soured by criticism and disgusted
with the civilized world and with our Christendom in general
and in particular.

Yet he was sufficiently impressed by his visit to read *Omoo* later in the
year, working it into a spare day or so between Ruskin and the newly
published *Origin of Species;* and if the two young men differed in charity, they agreed in the opinion expressed by Coan when he wrote that
Melville's attitude seemed "something like that of an Ishmael."

Such young visitors could, of course, have known nothing of the
emotions that they themselves may have stirred in a famous author by a
pilgrimage which made him aware of his fame at the very time that he
was engaged in legal formalities which were an admission of his inability
to make a living. Nor could they have known that his enthusiasm for
"the ancient dignity of Homeric times" represented the reaction of a
"reader of old books" to the discovery of an audience after a lonely winter
of looking into Chapman's Homer, which Duyckinck had given him the
preceding fall. Least of all could they have suspected, if Melville misled
John Gulick by offering them bourbon and branch water for refreshment,
that he was hospitably willing to share one of the two black bottles he
was carefully saving in an otherwise empty cellar and was perhaps secretly
embarrassed at not being able to follow the proprieties by offering them
a glass of wine. Coan also got the impression, either from Melville himself or from his inquiries concerning the way to Arrowhead, that "with
his liberal views he is apparently considered by the good people of Pittsfield as little better than a cannibal or a 'beach-comber' "; but their reports were so filled with misapprehensions that the only thing clear from
them is that Melville was at odds with himself and revealed it with his
usual willingness to "discourse on all things sacred and profane" whenever he thought he had a sympathetic audience.

The "Pieces" which Melville submitted to a magazine five weeks after this visit were undoubtedly in verse, and the "book" of which George Duyckinck had received a hint the summer before may have been a volume of poems he had been quietly planning. But during the summer of 1859 he made no secret of his activities. When on July 6 he addressed a rough parody of Marlowe's "The Passionate Shepherd" and Milton's "L'Allegro" to the New York lawyer and novelist, Daniel Shepherd, inviting him to come over and share one of the bottles of his "Mountain-Dew," he referred to "poet-problems, fancy-fed" in so casual a way that his verse writing seems to have been a matter of common knowledge. Exactly what poems may have survived from this period is unknown, for their author later pretended that he sold his manuscripts to a trunkmaker and none was published at the time. But among the poems left unpublished at his death were many which were intimately associated with Arrowhead, and some of these appear to have been written while Emerson (whose *Poems* Melville received as a present from Samuel Shaw in 1859) and Robert Herrick (whose *Hesperides* he acquired in September) were fresh in his mind. "The Little Good Fellows," "Madcaps," "Butterfly Ditty," "A Way-side Weed," and "The Cuban Pirate" are all suggestive of Emerson and some of them may echo Herrick, and they have survived, perhaps not very significantly, in a manuscript which Melville prepared late in life somewhat according to the plan he was to make for his first volume of poems. Among the miscellaneous poems also left in manuscript, "Falstaff's Lament Over Prince Hal Become Henry V," "In the Hall of Marbles" (which the author labeled as "Lines recalled from a destroyed poem"), "Pontoosuc," and perhaps "Fruit and Flower Painter" also contain Emersonian phrases and cadences; and although it is impossible to tell, of course, which particular poems in any group were written directly under Emerson's influence and which represented a manner that became habitual, there is evidence enough to indicate that Melville's early efforts toward becoming a poet were affected by the cryptic manner of his transcendental contemporary.

Other poems surviving in manuscript may be associated with this period more positively because of their content. "In the Pauper's Turnip-Field," for example, was almost certainly written at a time when Melville had a turnip patch and when he was brooding over the imminent technical "loss" of his property; and "Always With Us!" is of the same time with its expression of the same irritation with the same crows for cawing at him from the same dead hemlock. Both belong to the autumn of 1859, when the poet was digging his turnips after the robins had left for the South and he himself had turned over to Judge Shaw the deed to his real estate. "Stockings in the Farm-House Chimney" was also probably written at Arrowhead while the four children to whom it referred were young, and another Christmas poem, "To Tom" in its original version, was written either in 1859 or more probably in 1860, when Herman knew that his brother's ship was "on the torrid deep" at that time of year. Among the other verses which have close associations with Arrowhead, the dream "In the Old Farm-House" is also related to "Falstaff's Lament" and may be of this time, but the "Inscription" which its author designed "For a Boulder near the spot where the last Hardhack was laid low By the new proprietor of the Hill of Arrowhead" could have been composed as early as 1850, when Herman bought the place, or during any of the years of his serious farming. Others have no particular reference to time, but so many of his poems refer to country life that it seems doubtful whether much of Melville's early verse was actually destroyed.

How much of it survived in its original form, however, is another question. His poems were copied and perhaps recopied as they were preserved, and the poem to Tom (which was the only one of this group printed by Melville during his lifetime) was completely rewritten before it appeared addressed "To the Master of the 'Meteor.'" The most likely representations of his early work are the lines "Suggested by the Ruins of a Mountain-Temple in Arcadia," "Puzzlement," "The Continents," "The Dust-Layers," and "A Rail Road Cutting near Alexandria in 1855," which were preserved in a folder of Egyptian and Greek "Travel Pieces" with the comments "Rejected" and "Looked over March 23 '90" noted upon it. "The Great Pyramid" is so close to his journal that it, too, could have been preserved unchanged. Other such pieces may have been adapted by Melville in his old age for the "Fruit of Travel Long Ago" section of his *Timoleon* volume, for which these were evidently "looked over," or they may have been incorporated into longer poems. But, in either case, they may have been changed as drastically as were the verses to Tom or the lines "Suggested by the Ruins of a Mountain-Temple," which evidently became transmuted into the more finished poem, "The Ravaged Villa." The only other "travel" poem which might be singled out as possibly being an unchanged survivor from this early date is "Trophies of Peace," a poem seemingly inspired by his second trip to Illinois and the memories it aroused of the prairies as he had seen them at harvest-time in 1840.

But whatever verse Melville was writing during the latter part of 1859, he was not devoting himself to it with a clear conscience. Lecturing was still his only prospective source of income, and he forced himself to another attempt on the subject of "Travelling: Its Pleasures, Pains, and Profits." He gave this lecture for the first time on November 7 at Flushing and was presented with a bouquet of lovely flowers but only thirty dollars in cash. When no other engagement materialized, he took Bessie to New York for a week and while there borrowed—perhaps with literary intentions—Vasari's *Lives of the Most Eminent Painters, Sculptors, and Architects* and Luigi Lanzi's *History of Painting in Italy* from Evert Duyckinck. He also talked about Herbert's *The Temple* with George, who found him "moody." But Mrs. Sarah Morewood corrected that impression by explaining that he was ill, and Augusta, who also saw him in the city, reported that he was "feeling stronger" than he had been. Judge Shaw, however, made his usual shrewd diagnosis that Herman's physical and mental difficulties bore some relationship to his financial situation and obtained a twenty-five-dollar lecture engagement for him in Danvers, Massachusetts, for February 14. He was also probably instrumental in getting him a more profitable date in Cambridgeport a week later. But these were all. The lecture attracted little attention, and his total earnings for the season amounted to only $110. It was an amount to make a husband and the father of four children moody, and when he stopped by Duyckinck's in late January to borrow some volumes of British essays for winter reading he was complaining of the "mealy mouthed habit of writing of human nature of the present day" which "would not tolerate the plain speaking" of Dr. Johnson, who did "not hesitate to use the word *malignity.*" He had enough surplus cash to lend the town of Pittsfield $600 on March 1, 1860, and had some income from his investments. But with no earnings he seems to have felt not only ill but useless. Soon after his brother Tom reached home on the *Meteor,* on April 28, he decided to go with him on his next voyage around Cape Horn and perhaps around the world. Herman's Mediterranean impressions had never been organized, but he still hoped to find himself in travel.

The *Meteor* was to sail from Boston within a month, and Herman's decision to sail on her involved him in intense preparations. Judge Shaw put his financial affairs in order by canceling his notes for $5,500 in return for the deeds of the Pittsfield property (which he then deeded to Elizabeth) and accepting the six-hundred-dollar note which Herman held from the town of Pittsfield as a settlement of the informal loan of some $1,400 which had been spent on the Mediterranean trip. The amount of this note he also turned over to Elizabeth for the purpose of building a new barn which she and Herman had been planning, and the net result of the settlement was that of clearing him of all indebtedness, except for something over two hundred dollars to his publishers, by putting his real property in his wife's name. It was less trouble than making a will.

Of more serious concern to Herman, however, was the problem of his poems. He had written enough for a volume, and although he realized that "of all human events, perhaps, the publication of a first volume of verses is the most insignificant," he was anxious to get them in print and out of his mind. He and Elizabeth devoted most of the first two or three weeks following his decision to putting them in order. They had to be copied, corrected, and arranged; and some instructions had to be drawn up for Allan, who was commissioned to find a publisher, and for Evert Duyckinck, who was asked to read them over in advance of publication. Their arrangement was in numbered divisions, and he hoped that they might be brought out by Appleton or Scribner rather than the Harpers. But otherwise his instructions were largely negative. He cared nothing about royalties or profits, active promotion, or an English edition, and merely wanted prompt publication with no references to "the author of 'Typee,' 'Piddledee,' &c. on the title-page." His whole attitude, in short, was that of an author who had reconciled himself to being his only reader but who could no longer endure to read himself in manuscript. Lizzie realized the situation well enough to conquer her private uncertainties and encourage him concerning their merits, Duyckinck was genuinely pleased to see him active again, and Allan was, as usual, willing to handle the practical arrangements; therefore, Herman was able to leave with the feeling that his literary affairs were in good hands.

Before the ship sailed the two brothers, Tom and Herman, looking almost as much alike as identical twins, had an ambrotype taken for the family collection of photographs; and their ship sailed, after several days of unexpected delay, on May 28. Herman anticipated "as much pleasure as, at the age of forty, one temperately can" from the voyage, which would take him twice through the tropics to San Francisco and then, according to plan, to Manila and into the section of the Pacific through which he had pursued the White Whale in his imagination but had never visited in actuality. He hardly could have anticipated being seasick the first night out and having an unsettled stomach for the first three weeks, but it was exciting to see the Southern Cross once more and to climb out on the flying jib boom for a magnificent sight of the full-rigged clipper riding the swells behind him. He enjoyed playing chess each evening with Tom, with pieces made for them by the carpenter while they were in the doldrums, and he luxuriated in the unhurried reading of Hawthorne's recently published novel, *The Marble Faun*, and of Chapman's Homer, the *Songs* of Bérenger, Schiller's *Poems and Ballads*, the Bible, and the collection of quarterlies, magazines, and other volumes he took with him. He had worse weather rounding the Horn than he had ever experienced before, and one sailor was injured and another killed in the process; but there was a warm if cantankerous stove in the captain's cabin which was physically more comfortable than a sodden white jacket had been in his youth, although hovering around it gave him an opportunity to feel the mental distress aroused by the accidents and the narrow escapes of other sailors. Tom took the *Meteor* right through the Strait of Le Maire between Staten Land and Tierra del Fuego, and Herman had a fine view of the "horrible snowy mountains, black, thunder-cloud woods, gorges," and other aspects of their "hell-landscape" as well as "the horrid sight of Cape Horn" itself when the mist lifted just before sunset on the evening of August 8.

On more peaceful days he watched the haglets and other sea birds which pursued the ship without ever lighting upon it, and on one of these days he probably composed and gave to Tom "The Admiral of the White"—a ballad telling the story of a shipwreck caused by a compass deflected by a collection of arms in the cabin. He had first heard this story in the Mediterranean and now associated it with the pursuing haglets. For Tom had taken a set of his brother's works with him on his previous voyage, and on this, as Herman recalled later, listened during moonlight nights to a whole "cable-length" of his verse. One day in the Pacific they spoke a whale ship and Tom sent Herman over in a boat for an hour's gam and a renewal of memories. He may also have written other retrospective poems on the voyage—"The Maldive Shark," which he had first described in *Mardi* and of which he may have been reminded by a stanza he marked in Schiller's "The Diver," and perhaps some of the poems dealing with the children and Arrowhead. For Herman, as usual on his trips, was often homesick and revealed as much in his affectionate letters, carefully calculated for the understanding of the children. In these he not only described his own experiences but commented upon theirs— especially upon the girls' habit of picking the wild strawberries (which was the subject of "Madcaps" or, as he first called it, "Wild-Strawberry Hunters")—and before the end of the voyage made a drawing of Arrowhead with himself coming home behind Charlie in the carriage and Elizabeth and the girls out in the road to welcome him. By the time the *Meteor* came to rest at the Vallejo Street wharf on October 12, he was ready to trade all the sights of San Francisco for one glimpse of Pittsfield.

He convinced himself that the trip had done him little good and arranged such a trade within a week. Tom evidently discovered soon after he arrived that he would not be able to get a cargo for Manila and the Orient and would have to wait within the Golden Gate for some time before getting anything for any destination. Herman decided to return home at once by steamer. The local newspapers had welcomed his coming and were suggesting that the citizens of San Francisco might take advantage of his appearance by inviting him to lecture, but he gave them no chance to show their hospitality by putting money in his pocket. Instead, he took enough out for a steamer ticket to New York, wrote Elizabeth by Pony Express on the nineteenth of his intention to return, and sailed on the twentieth for Manzanillo, Acapulco, and Panama. After crossing the Isthmus to Aspinwall and spending one night on land, he boarded the *North Star* on November 5 and reached New York one week later—four days before the *Meteor* found a cargo and sailed from San Francisco to Falmouth. His family were disappointed that the voyage had not been effective in restoring his health, and he was disappointed that no arrangements had been possible for the publication of his poems. But Scribner had agreed to bring out Edmund Clarence Stedman's *Lyrics and Idylls* and also *The Poems of General George P. Morris* in 1860, and another volume of verse was more than they were willing to undertake. His new start at writing, like his lecturing and his voyage with Tom, had been a misadventure; and he had nothing much to do except settle down once more into his familiar, if not particularly happy, routine.

II

Sarah Morewood was delighted to have the Melvilles remain as neighbors during the cold weather, but Lizzie probably missed the easy winter in Boston which she had anticipated. Somewhat apologetic, perhaps, about upsetting her plans, Herman advertised for a woman to do cooking and general housework, but advertised in vain. Arrowhead itself seemed to be turning into a misadventure. Melville visited in Albany and Gansevoort during the early days of February, but most of the time he seems to have stuck closely at home without society, exercise, or the prospect of any occupation other than the writing which his family constantly feared. To prevent it, Allan decided in mid-February that his brother should be sent to Italy as the American consul at Florence although the position paid only five hundred dollars a year.

Before attempting to interest Herman, apparently, Allan consulted George Griggs and Judge Shaw. The judge had been confined to his room because of age and illness all winter, but he agreed that Herman needed to be shaken out of Arrowhead and devoted his convalescence to correspondence for that purpose. The assistance of Alexander Rice, the United States congressman from Boston, was obtained, and letters from various sources began to descend upon Senator Charles Sumner. After the inauguration of Abraham Lincoln, a group of Pittsfield citizens drew up a formal recommendation to the new president for Melville's appointment, and a few days later, under the leadership of John Hoadley, a similar group in Lawrence followed suit. Herman began to take a belated interest in the affair himself and on March 18 went to Albany to consult with

Peter Gansevoort before going on to New York, where Alexander W. Bradford wrote a private letter in his behalf and joined another group of influential citizens in a group recommendation to the president. Herman himself wrote to Thurlow Weed and to Richard Henry Dana, Jr., and the latter modified his general rule against political recommendations enough to speak of him highly in his "regular correspondence" with Sumner. On March 22 the now-active applicant went to Washington, where he attended the second levee in the White House, shook hands with "Old Abe," watched the Senate in session, attended a party with Dr. Nourse, visited the uncompleted Washington monument, and spent a considerable amount of time sitting on a park bench. It was six days before he accomplished the main purpose of his visit, which was to see Sumner, whom he found friendly and willing to recommend him "most cordially" for the consulship at Geneva, Glasgow, or Manchester, since the post at Florence had been filled the day before.

He was not able to press his business to a conclusion, however, for a letter calling him home arrived before he fully made up his mind to accept the proposed recommendation for Glasgow; and he reached Pittsfield on March 29 to find Elizabeth packed and ready to go to Boston, where she had been summoned by a telegram informing her of her father's serious illness. Judge Shaw was dead before she reached his side, and Herman had to follow immediately after her, through an early April snowstorm which delayed trains, for the funeral. He evidently left Elizabeth with her mother and returned to Pittsfield at once to look after Bessie and Fanny, for Stanwix was with his aunts and grandmother in Gansevoort and Malcolm seems to have already been away at boarding school. While Elizabeth remained in Boston until the end of May, he began to read poetry systematically. Within a year and a week after April 9, 1861, when he acquired editions of Shelley and Spenser, he is known to have purchased the poems of James Thomson, Tennyson, Thomas Hood, Tom Moore, James C. Mangan, Robert Ferguson, Heinrich Heine, Kirke White, Matthew Arnold, William Collins, and Thomas Churchill, in addition to the works of Isaac D'Israeli and the *Essays,* first and second series, of Emerson—all of which he read and marked. It was a miscellaneous collection representing the activity of a man who had not been completely discouraged by his failure to get his first volume of poems printed but was not yet sure of what he himself wanted to do in verse.

Some of his uncertainty was the natural consequence of the outbreak of the Civil War, which began with the attack upon Fort Sumter on the morning of April 12 and President Lincoln's call, three days later, for seventy-five thousand volunteers to suppress the insurrection. Soldiers began to drill on the cattle showgrounds at Pittsfield, and Herman's own name was on the militia roll; but, at first, the war seems to have struck him most forcefully through his interest in the sea. For his own ship, the *United States,* was destroyed in the Norfolk Navy Yard at the outbreak of hostilities in order to keep her from falling into Confederate hands, and a month after he had gone to Boston in the latter part of May to bring Elizabeth back to Pittsfield he visited New York and, on July 1, took Evert Duyckinck out to the Navy Yard—possibly in order to inquire about a commission or to see whether his own experience could be of any other use to his country. At any rate, the volume of poems he was to publish after the war shows that his naval verses were apparently the result of the direct inspiration of events, whereas most of those dealing with military engagements were based upon reports gathered together after the fighting had ceased.

He was at loose ends. His appointment to a consulship, despite Senator Sumner's recommendations to the State Department, did not materialize; and, in the midst of all the excitement that followed the Battle of Bull Run, he had nothing to do. He made his customary visit to Gansevoort in August, where he found his uncle Herman very feeble, but neither he nor Elizabeth was willing to tarry in Albany; and, as cold weather drew on, they could not face the prospect of another winter in the cold farmhouse three miles from town. Elizabeth's share in her father's estate (which was not yet settled but which eventually amounted to $15,114.27) made them more nearly independent than they had been in years and enabled them to spend the winter in the city, where the girls could get the schooling they were now old enough to need.

During the second week of December, accordingly, they closed up the house and the family temporarily separated, Herman and Bessie paying a visit to Gansevoort before joining Elizabeth in Boston on Christmas Eve for the holidays. In January, Herman went on to New York and obtained a house at 150 East Eighteenth Street, where Elizabeth and the children joined him on the eighteenth, found him suffering from rheumatism, and put him to bed before he had a chance to tell his New York friends where he was living. On February 1, however, he was sufficiently recovered to write Evert Duyckinck for some volumes of Elizabethan dramatists and invite him for a housewarming round of whisky punch and a discussion of "the affairs of the universe" on the following evening. Whatever it might have done for Elizabeth and the children, the winter in New York was not very stimulating to Herman, who was too ill on March 18 to make the trip to Gansevoort to attend his uncle Herman's funeral; and he spent most of his time reading the books he had borrowed or purchased and marking the references he found in the latter to literary composition, the high price that had to be paid for pursuing one's intellectual ambitions, and the incongruity between man's desires and his powers of accomplishment. He was obviously meditating something in verse which would reflect the heroism demanded by the times and was just as obviously brooding over his inability to rise to the occasions that were brought to his attention regularly by the newspapers. During this winter he may have expressed his lyrical appreciation of Commodore S. F. Dupont's classic naval maneuver in the "round fight" which took Port Royal on November 7 and composed his lament for the "Stone Fleet" of whalers which were used to block the Charleston harbor on December 20, but the most talked-of victory of the winter—the capture of Fort Donelson in Tennessee on February 16, 1862—went uncelebrated for more than four years. He tried then to recapture the exciting atmosphere of daily bulletins, but his poem "Donelson" could hardly have been written until the various newspaper accounts on which it was based were gathered together in a source he could conveniently use.

The appearance of the Southern ironclad *Merrimac* and the Northern *Monitor* on the naval scene in March inspired him to meditations on the waning splendors of victories gained without glory, and Farragut's capture of New Orleans in April seems to have stirred him to immediate expression; but Melville did not succeed in becoming a spirited war poet. He abandoned New York in April and took Lizzie on a visit to Gansevoort (where his mother and sisters continued to live after the death of his uncle Herman) and returned to Pittsfield before the first of May. There he advertised again for a cook (and by capitalizing his offer of "the HIGHEST wages" apparently got one) and tried to forget that he was a poet. He gave his sister Helen his set of Spenser on May 15, and Frances Priscilla his copies of Shakespeare's poems and those of Collins, Shenstone, and Thomson on May 19. Six days later he wrote Tom that he had disposed of his own "doggeral" at ten cents a pound to a trunkmaker who "took the whole stock" off his hands for lining. He continued to follow military events closely and was pleased to learn that Guert Gansevoort had been placed in command of a fine new sloop of war, but the battles of the spring went uncelebrated. His summer was a quiet one. He was unaffected by the death of his uncle Wessel Gansevoort in Danbury, Vermont, of which Peter informed him on August 8; and his only recorded activities consisted of a two-day excursion into the neighboring Hoosacs with Sam Shaw, who spent the last week of August in Pittsfield, and a trip, in early September, to New York, where he bought a copy of the works of La Bruyère and began to mark passages dealing with the advantages of renouncing the world and taking refuge in a contemplation of the vices of humanity.

He had no intention of renouncing the world, however, by staying on a farm which had gone to grass from neglect and was too far from town for household help or schools for the children in the wintertime. He had again begun advertising Arrowhead for sale on May 22, and, although the advertisement was continued until the middle of August without bringing results, he and Elizabeth decided that they would move into town anyway and rented a square old-fashioned house on South Street. They settled in it during the first freeze of November, and on the morning of Friday, the seventh, Herman hitched up his wagon and in the company of J. E. A. Smith, the editor of the *Berkshire Eagle,* went for his last load of furniture. As they clipped along the frozen road, however, the shocks proved too much for the neglected Melville equipment. A piece of the metalwork broke, the horse bolted, and both driver and passenger were thrown onto the hard ground. Smith fell into the road and, though stunned and bruised, was not seriously injured. Melville hit the angle of the bank and road, broke his left shoulder blade, injured several ribs, and was so badly shaken up that when he was taken to town two doctors were called in to attend him. The accident and the neuralgia which accompanied his gradual recovery had a strange effect upon him. Although his injuries were not dangerous and he was moving around with his left arm in a sling within five weeks, he seems to have spent much of his time in bed meditating death. He also sold his horse and for some time afterward, according to Smith's later recollections, hesitated to enter a carriage. By the middle of the following summer he was sufficiently recovered to rent a carriage in order to drive his mother-in-law over the bad roads to the top of Mount Washington, but he never again lived up to his earlier reputation of being a fearsome but sure driver over mountain roads.

He wanted to move to New York and in early February visited the city in order to discuss his prospects with his brother. Allan's first wife, Sophia, had died on October 3, 1858, and on April 18, 1860, he had married Jane Dempsey of Philadelphia. His house at 104 East Twenty-sixth Street needed repairs and was still mortgaged to his first mother-in-law, and he seems to have been possessed by a restlessness comparable to Herman's. At any rate, the two brothers worked out a deal which would enable Herman to purchase Allan's New York home for $7,750 by assuming the two-thousand-dollar mortgage held by Mrs. Thurston and trading him the unsalable Arrowhead estate at three-quarters of the estimated value of $4,000 currently placed upon it by the tax assessor. The arrangement involved all of the older brother's savings as well as the Pittsfield property, which was in Elizabeth's name. But her brother Sam, who, as one of the executors of Judge Shaw's estate, had become her financial adviser, paid them a visit at the end of February and apparently gave his approval. A legacy of $900 from Herman's aunt Priscilla, who had died on the first of November, would take care of the repairs, and the deal was completed by the latter part of May with the understanding that Herman and Lizzie should occupy their new home in October.

The estate was kept in the family. Allan got a summer home at a bargain and, without knowing it or perhaps ever finding it out, a neighbor who was so "disappointed" in his second marriage that she had determined not to treat him as an old friend but as "only an acquaintance." Herman got a new lease on life. When he had been in New York in February he had taken special pleasure in seeing his cousin Henry Gansevoort, then a lieutenant in the artillery but soon to receive a new commission as lieutenant-colonel of cavalry, and he was corresponding with his old friend "Toby" Greene, who was in service on the Mississippi—and to whom he was to send three copies of *Typee* in August. He was beginning to feel a personal relationship to the war, and when the Southern invasion of Pennsylvania was checked at Gettysburg, in early July, he apparently wrote his first really spirited poem directly inspired by a land battle. Pittsfield had its own military celebration on Saturday, August 22, when its Forty-ninth Regiment returned after nine months of war in Louisiana and staged a parade with Colonel William F. Bartlett at its head. Melville decorated his house on South Street with flags and festoons for the occasion and probably wound up the day at the "brilliantly illuminated" home of J. R. Morewood, where Colonel Bartlett was being entertained and where all the soldiers were honored by a fine display of fireworks. He did not know much about the history of the regiment, but he was greatly impressed by the young "college colonel," who, at the age of twenty-two and with one leg gone and an honorable discharge from the Massachusetts Twentieth, had organized the Berkshire regiment and led it into battle with a crutch at his saddlebow. Now he was bringing his men home with his arm still in splints from a bullet through his wrist at Port Hudson three months before. Melville himself had marched in a parade celebrating the semicentennial anniversary of the Albany Academy on June 26 and, as one of the academy's most distinguished alumni, had sat with his uncle Peter at the speakers' table while his friend Alexander W. Bradford delivered the commemorative oration. With the prospect of removal before him, he allowed himself, in various ways, to be drawn out of his solitude and into the stream of contemporary events.

His move was saddened by the death of Mrs. Morewood, who was still a sprightly neighbor and friend at the age of thirty-nine, on October 7; and he remained involved in the "thousand and one botherations" incidental to moving, redecorating, repairing, and refurnishing until the middle of December. Because of what he called his "vile habit" of destroying most of his correspondence, Herman was not able to respond to the request of an old picnicking friend, Sophie Van Metre, for a supply of autographs to be sold for the benefit of wounded soldiers at the Cincinnati "Sanitary Fair" that December. But he did take an interest in that anticipation of the Red Cross movement and sent his own autograph, attached to a note of commendation, to George McLaughlin of the same city and sent a poetic "Inscription For the Slain at Fredericksburg" to John P. Kennedy of Baltimore for a facsimile volume of *Autograph Leaves of our Country's Authors* which was designed for sale at a similar fair in New York during the following April. He did not have "spirit enough" to review a book for Duyckinck at the end of the year, although he had read it with interest, but in his general escape from his self-centeredness he was becoming more perceptive and humane in his consciousness of other people. His poem "Chattanooga" (which was less artificial in its composition than the apparently later "Look-out Mountain") was focused upon the emotions and the spirit of the soldiers in both armies which clashed on the heights in November, 1863; and "The House-Top" (although certainly not autobiographical, for Melville was not in New York at the time) was an imaginative attempt to interpret the conditions under which the draft riots had occurred in July and the causes of the peculiar Draconian psychology which he probably encountered among the respectable and normally humane residents of the city after he moved there in the autumn.

Whether he ever really settled down in New York that winter is doubtful. Malcolm had been sent to boarding school in Newton Centre, Stanwix was again living with his grandmother and attending school in Gansevoort, and the two girls were going to school in New York, and Elizabeth probably found less strain in the family atmosphere than she had noticed at any time since her marriage. They were together at Christmas, and on New Year's Eve they had a quiet party for Allan and his family and for Mrs. Ellen Brittain of Pittsfield and one or two other friends, who promised to "come early, stay socially, and go early." Herman removed one of the private burdens on his mind by paying the Harpers two hundred dollars on February 9, 1864, thereby clearing up most of the deficit which had annually been an unhappy reminder of his ill success as an author, and shortly afterward made a trip to Gansevoort to see his ailing mother. On his way back he spent the night in Albany and braved a snowstorm in order to see the Arts Exhibition for the Bazaar before having lunch with Peter Gansevoort's family and taking the afternoon train for New York. With the approach of spring he became anxious to see the front and, with Allan, set out for Washington; there they put up at Ebbitt House, while Allan wrote to his former brother-in-law, Richard Lathers in New York, and Herman approached Senator Sumner in an effort to get a pass to visit the Army of the Potomac. Upon Sumner's recommendation of "a loyal citizen and my friend" to the provost marshal, a pass was issued promptly by order of the secretary of war; and when Allan's wife came to Washington on Wednesday, April 13, she learned with surprise and some consternation that the two brothers had departed for the front on the preceding Sunday. If Elizabeth's later recollection that the brothers "called on General Grant" may be trusted, they visited the headquarters of the commanding general at Culpepper, Virginia, on Monday or Tuesday and looked over the Wilderness battle line before making their way to the station of the Thirteenth New York Cavalry at Vienna, where they hoped to find Colonel Henry Gansevoort. But when they discovered that their cousin was away on ordnance business in Washington, Allan hurried back to the city to assure Jane that John Mosby's dread guerrillas had not captured him, leaving Herman (who believed that Lizzie and the girls were still enjoying an unworried visit in Boston) alone in camp.

Herman evidently expected to meet Henry at the divisional headquarters at Fairfax Court House, for he spent an "agreeable evening" there with Brigadier General Robert O. Tyler and made so favorable an impression upon his officers that he was allowed to accompany a scouting party sent out on the morning of the fourteenth under the leadership of the "fighting major," William H. Forbes, of the Massachusetts Second Cavalry. If there were any doubts in his own mind concerning his ability to handle a horse in the wild country through which the Confederate rangers moved at will, he concealed them in a stout heart beneath a flannel shirt borrowed from Captain Brewster and set out, to the "tantara" of the early morning bugles, upon the last active adventure of his life.

As a military action, the adventure did not amount to very much. Major Forbes and his men were back by noon on the following day without having had an engagement, although they did manage to pick up a corporal and five men, one of them with a canteen full of turpentine, who had been sent out by Mosby during the night to harass the Federals by burning bridges. But, as usual with Melville when he had an experience which could be turned into literature, the actual sequence of events which formed the experience were of less importance than the emotional attitude which went with them and which later enabled him to transform "what might have been" into a narrative that seemed more real than the historical occurrences. He could always draw upon other people's experiences for incidents upon which he could work with an imagination quickened by the emotion aroused by a few original perceptions. The scout provided him with an awareness of the contrast between the gaiety of a fresh morning sally and the moodiness of a weary return, of the feelings inspired by the Virginia countryside in the spring, and, more important than anything else, of the almost legendary quality which surrounded the personality of John C. Mosby and filled his enemies with dread.

In the camp at Vienna, to which he returned for a day with his cousin and his recent companions-in-arms, he received other impressions—particularly of the gallant young Charles Russell Lowell, Henry Gansevoort's fellow colonel and commander of the Massachusetts Second, who had recently returned to camp after recovering from a wound. Lowell's bride of six months was still remembered admiringly by the soldiers who had watched her slog through the winter mud, in a waterproof and little gum boots, on daily visits to the hospital tent. The combination of glory in the air and young love in a tent (although Lowell had actually occupied a cottage while his wife was in camp) appealed strongly to a romantic streak in Melville, and sometime after October 21, 1864, when Lowell died of wounds received at the battle of Cedar Creek, he found it irresistible. In "The Scout Toward Aldie," the most ambitious of his Civil War poems, he placed the dashing young colonel in command of the troop and had him leave his bride in camp and be killed in action at the end of an expedition which combined the experiences of Melville's own party with that of another party sent out to surprise some of Mosby's men attending a wedding at Leesburg a week later. Melville probably heard the details of the second foray from his cousin at some later date, and he also incorporated into his poem such later matters as the belief that Mosby had once been captured and allowed to escape unrecognized and the decision, reached during the fall, that the Confederate rangers should be hanged as spies rather than treated as prisoners of war. The quality which made his poem, like his autobiographical prose works, seem like a genuine account of personal experiences, however, was imparted by the awe of Mosby and the feeling for the countryside which he recalled from his own mild adventure.

But the most immediate result of his riding forth to war was a terrific attack of neuralgia which affected his eyes and laid him up during the latter part of April and the early part of May. Elizabeth and the children had returned home in his absence, and he was nursed back into a condition of cheerfulness by May 10, when he wrote his cousin a letter thanking him for his military hospitality and remembering himself to his temporary comrades-in-arms; but he was saddened some days later by the sudden death of his old friend Hawthorne in Plymouth, New Hampshire, on May 19, and may have begun at that time the "Monody" which is often thought to be a memorial poem to the man who had once meant so much to him but whom he had not seen in nearly eight years. Illness and sorrow, however, apparently did not cause the prolonged depression that they had once created when they were piled upon financial worries, and he spent a long and cheerful vacation in Gansevoort with his two boys while Elizabeth and the girls were in Boston. He left them there when he returned to New York on August 8 with Augusta to keep house for him until Lizzie returned and perhaps while she took Bessie and Fanny to visit their grandmother from August 20 to September 9. A legacy of $3,000 to Elizabeth from Dr. Hayward had brightened their spring by enabling them to pay off the mortgage on the house and have a substantial supply of cash ahead, and Herman's good health and spirits seem to have extended through the fall and winter. Tom undoubtedly helped by getting home in time for a family reunion in New York at Thanksgiving.

The war news was also good after Christmas, and, inspired by the reports of Sherman's homeward march from Savannah, Melville composed "The Frenzy in the Wake"; and the fall of Richmond, on April 3, not only moved him to write a triumphant poem on that subject but stimulated him to such an extent that he found the substance of poetry in the events of every week if not of almost every day. Lee's surrender of the Army of Northern Virginia at Appomattox Court House on the afternoon of April 9 and the assassination of Lincoln five days later, of course, provoked the greatest contrasts of feeling which Melville put into verse; but he also found inspiration in a visit to the National Academy Exhibition that month and wrote poems about two of its paintings—"The Coming Storm" by S. R. Gifford, and "Formerly a Slave" by Elihu Vedder. Furthermore, his ambition was stirred for the first time in several years. An invitation from Bayard Taylor to attend a meeting of "The Travellers" club on February 27 undoubtedly brought to mind thoughts of the fame he had once shared with his friends among its members, and the kind of posthumous treatment he received from T. B. Peterson and Brothers in Philadelphia (who had bought the plates of *Israel Potter* from Putnam in the fall of 1857 for $218.66 and published it as *The Refugee,* with Melville's name as the author of several faked titles on the title page, in the spring of 1865) aroused his indignation at being no longer treated with respect. Such feelings operating upon his contemplation of a fairly large and growing collection of manuscripts were enough to make him meditate a book.

He must have proposed something of the sort to the Harpers (with whom he had acquired, in October, a small favorable balance for the first time in a decade) before the end of the year and received the suggestion that a few of the poems be tried on the public through the columns of *Harper's New Monthly Magazine.* For in January, 1866, the February issue of that periodical appeared with "The March to the Sea," and it was followed in March and April by "The Cumberland" and "Philip" (later called "Sheridan at Cedar Creek") and in June and July by "Chattanooga" and "Gettysburg." Although they were all published anonymously, "The March to the Sea" was promptly identified and described as "very inspiring" by Catherine Gansevoort (who had never read any of his verse before but had been told by her aunt Maria that a piece by Herman would be printed in *Harper's*). Tom also thought it was good, and, what was perhaps more important, brought word to Herman that John Hoadley had read it aloud and called it "splendid." Herman's sister Frances passed the word around from New Bedford that it was "thought grand by all." Such widespread and spontaneous approval from his family must have astonished Herman, and it certainly helped him prepare the book for publication and see it through the press without his customary labor pains. The Harpers evidently agreed at some time during the spring to publish it, and its author undertook to expand its size and give a more complete account of the war by writing new verses, mostly descriptive, which were made possible by the appearance of the monumental collection of official documents, newspaper stories, contemporary poems, and miscellaneous anecdotes called *The Rebellion Record*.

Many of these additions were little more than hack work, which may have satisfied either the author's or the publisher's desire for a comprehensive treatment of the war; but, in an encouraging family atmosphere, Melville was at least able to compose them without getting involved in the problems that usually beset him when he began to pad his books. He had not been able or willing to run up to Albany for a party at the Gansevoorts in mid-January, but he did quite a bit of family entertaining at home. After a visit from Tom in January and February his mother came down in early March and became so ill that Augusta was hurriedly called from Gansevoort on the twenty-first to be with her. She improved quickly, however, and was probably well a month before Tom paid his brother another visit about the first of June. On June 29 Jane and Allan Melville returned from a winter in Egypt. Allan was full of his experiences, and the two brothers undoubtedly had to compare notes on the Nile and the Mediterranean. Yet despite these interruptions Herman seems to have been willing, while working on his book, to attend a Sunday night reception at the home of Alice and Phoebe Cary on Twentieth Street and entertain the company with an unusually dramatic and thrilling account of his early life and his later adventures in the Pacific. Such social activity at a time when he was getting a book ready for the press and reading proof was extraordinary with Melville, and, what was even more extraordinary, Lizzie apparently took the children to Boston and left her husband to finish up the book alone. By July 20 it was finished and on the next day, in the company of John Hoadley, he set out on his own vacation for Gansevoort. His cousin Catherine thought he looked "thin and miserable," but he was able to handle a croquet mallet with his accustomed skill and had energy enough for a trip to Saratoga Lake on August 2 with Tom and for visits in Albany and possibly Lansingburgh. He returned on August 6.

Battle-Pieces and Aspects of the War was published eleven days later, with a short Preface explaining that most of the "Pieces" included had been written after the fall of Richmond and with a long Supplement discussing the relationships of the North and South and the problems of Reconstruction. At the time of its appearance, the country was getting ready for congressional elections, new political coalitions were being formed out of the ruins of the "Union party" which had elected Lincoln for a second term in the presidency, and the nation was being divided between the aggressive supporters of the personal and property rights soon to be guaranteed by the Fourteenth Amendment to the Constitution and those who wanted a prompt and peaceful reconciliation of sections and a return to normalcy. Melville clearly aligned himself with the Democrats and the less extreme Republicans who formed the latter group. One of his poems, "The Victor of Antietam," praised John B. McClellan, who had been the Democratic candidate for president in the last election; and another, "Lee in the Capitol," gave a sympathetic guess at what the Confederate commander in chief might have said had he chosen to defend the position of rebel officers before the reconstruction committee of Congress in April, 1866. The speech which Melville wrote for him was one which implied serious doubts concerning the wisdom of the committee's insistence that such men be disqualified for public office at a time when the country needed courageous firmness in meeting its problems.

Even in some of the poems probably written during the war Melville had shown an inclination to see the Southern soldier as a human being, not very different from his Northern brother, rather than an abstract "enemy"; and in the postwar poems, although the conflict itself was invariably represented as being between "Right" and "Wrong," he represented individual Southerners as misguided rather than vicious. His notes to the poems emphasized his attitude, and his Supplement developed it at length and sometimes with eloquence. He pleaded with the North for "common sense and Christian charity" in the work of Reconstruction, and with the South for acknowledgment of error rather than "penitence, in the sense of voluntary humiliation," which he prophesied would certainly "never be displayed." "Patriotism is not baseness," he wrote with reference to the Southern obligation to respect the memory of the many brave men who had died in the misguided cause of secession; and "neither is it inhumanity," he added in a quiet allusion to the advocates of radical reconstruction who had been so vocal in Congress: "The mourners who this summer bear flowers to the mounds of the Virginian and Georgian dead are, in their domestic bereavement and proud affection, as sacred in the eye of Heaven as are those who go with similar offerings of tender grief and love into the cemeteries of our Northern Martyrs." Yet he was careful to avoid an appeal to political passions at a time when passionate controversy seemed to be required to attract attention. His poems and their prose accompaniment underplayed the patriotic emotions which inspired them and the emotions of the political quarrel to which they were related. Melville's voice was so quiet that it was almost unnoticed when he lifted it to "pray that the great historic tragedy of our time may not have been enacted without instructing our whole beloved country through terror and pity."

He may have been disappointed but he could hardly have been surprised at being ignored. For nearly a decade, since returning from his trip to the Holy Land, he had wavered between serious criticism and incidental commentary in dealing with the various literary subjects upon which he touched; and his war poems, as a collection, were characterized by the same uncertainty of purpose which had marked his lecture on Roman statuary. Many of the actual battlepieces showed his awareness of those qualities in human nature which transcended time and political antagonisms, and some of his postwar verses and his Supplement provided a sane and humane basis for criticizing current political policy. But other poems were hack work, inspired only by the desire to make his commentary complete. There was no imaginative force in the book to hold it together and give it an impact, and the author of *Moby Dick* must have felt the absence of this quality even though he had an impelling desire to publish the volume.

Yet there was probably a practical bit of good fortune in the fact that *Battle-Pieces* did not have the imaginative force necessary to make its political implications felt amidst the more gross and violent stimulants to the passions of the times. Melville could not have anticipated making any money from the book, nor could he have expected to live indefinitely upon the capital so providentially supplied by legacies to Elizabeth and occasionally to himself. A part of his wife's inheritance from Judge Shaw was invested in Boston real estate which provided an annual income of five hundred dollars, and she had other income from her inheritance in addition to that from the small trust fund established at the time of her marriage. But Herman, at the age of forty-seven, had nothing except the

New York house, which had been two-fifths paid for by Elizabeth. He needed a job. Henry A. Smythe had just been appointed collector of customs in New York for the purpose of cleaning up a scandalous condition caused by political appointments in the customhouse; and the appointment offered an extraordinary opportunity to a man who had just published a patriotic volume of verse, whose political affiliations had never been strong enough for him to gain federal patronage during twenty years of fairly steady effort, and who, incidentally, had once traveled for a few days in Switzerland with the new collector. The sentiments he had revealed in his volume of poems, had anybody chosen to examine it, were not offensive to either the national administration or the New York politicians; yet they had attracted no attention likely to arouse Congressional opposition to a man whose influential friends would like to see him in a government job regardless of his sentiments. Without so much as a prefatory call on Peter Gansevoort for advice, apparently, Melville applied directly to his old acquaintance for a position in the customhouse, was nominated for it by Smythe on November 28, was approved by the assistant secretary of the treasury on November 30, and was given the oath of office on December 5. At long last, he could draw a monthly salary and take his intellectual ease: he was on the government.

12

The Customhouse

I

A JOB as deputy inspector of customs was not quite up to the dignity of a Melville and a son-in-law of the late chief justice of the Commonwealth of Massachusetts, but by this time the members of the family were convinced that any job would be good if it got Herman out of the house. Among themselves they called him a "District Officer in the Custom House" and watched him carefully for symptoms of melancholia or rheumatism. "Herman's health is much better," his mother wrote Catherine Gansevoort on March 11, 1867, "since he has been compelled to go out daily to attend to his business"; and Catherine passed on the official family translation of the news to her brother Henry: "Cousin Herman has a position in the Custom House and is quite well this winter. His intercourse with his fellow creatures seems to have had a beneficial effect. He is less of a misanthrope." Melville himself probably knew the futility of any man's attempting to combat his family reputation, but he quietly marked three lines in one of the sonnets of Camoëns which he had obtained that spring:

> My senses lost, misjudging men declare,
> And Reason banish'd from her mental throne,
> Because I shun the crowd, and dwell alone.

He was aware of the conspiracy of secret confidences about his "state," and, although he could not do anything about the situation, he could find in his books evidence that his state was not unusual among his own literary kind.

Actually, his job was a good one, less because it kept him from brooding than because it enabled him to brood freely without the pressure of feeling that his meditations should be commercially as well as personally profitable. His wages of four dollars a day were not very large for the father of four children, but they made his income at least equal to that which Elizabeth derived from her Boston property and invested funds, and gave him a greater feeling of independence than he had possessed since leaving Arrowhead. His office on North River, at 207 West Street, was not far from home, his hours were reasonable, and his duties were pressing only when a ship came in to make them fairly interesting. He seems to have kept a good deal of his reserve in dealing with his associates in office, but he was well enough impressed by one of them, Henry L. Potter, to present him with a copy of *Battle-Pieces* soon after he took up his duties; and his relationships, while he was at work, were not disagreeable. His mother's spacious home in Saratoga County had become a summer gathering place for the Melville and Gansevoort clan, and, with room and resources to entertain its members in New York, Herman was in a position to hold his place in the family circle without awkwardness or embarrassment. Certainly his circumstances, both mentally and materially, were eased.

But a normal family life in which his children grew to uneventful maturity was not in store for him. The past hovered over his head. For Melville had in himself something of the parental quality which had made his own father determined that his boys should be kept "off the street," and Malcolm, who had passed his eighteenth birthday in February, apparently possessed a considerable amount of Herman's sensitivity and spirit. A year before he had become a clerk in the office of Richard Lathers, president of the Atlantic and Great Western Insurance Company, at a salary of two hundred dollars a year, and he had all the prospects of advancement that a personable, well-bred, and competent young man might expect. He had never given his family any trouble, and he was a favorite of his Melville grandmother, who had been delighted by his thoughtfulness and attentiveness during her visit to New York in the spring. He had passed his impressionable adolescence, however, in an atmosphere of romantic military glory: his cousins were Civil War heroes, to the family at least, and his father had visited the front and celebrated the war in verse. It was not unnatural, perhaps, that as soon as he became old enough to do so he should have joined a volunteer military company and developed a boyish enthusiasm for its equipment—a handsome uniform with brass buttons, which he bought in the late summer and in which he strutted for the amusement of his younger sisters, and a real pistol with a ball in it which he displayed carelessly to his fellow clerks and kept under his pillow at night. He and his comrades-in-arms also took to staying out late in the evening, and, although he had reached the age at which his uncle Tom was returning from a voyage to China, his father took his house key away from him and probably gave him some definite although unrecorded instructions.

Nevertheless, on the night of September 10 he remained out until three o'clock while his mother, after the house was locked as usual at eleven, stayed up to let him in, remind him of his responsibilities, and kiss him good night. In the morning he answered when one of the girls called him, but when he did not manage to get up his father decided that the most effective punishment would be to let him sleep, be late for work, and face the normal consequences of his actions just as a grown man would have to do. When he did not appear as the day wore on, however, Elizabeth discovered that his door was locked, tried in vain to wake him by calling, and worried through the long afternoon until Herman came home, broke down the door, and found him in his night clothes with his pistol firmly grasped in his right hand and a bullet hole in his temple. The coroner's jury the next day brought in the conventional verdict of suicide while "suffering from a temporary aberration of mind," but the Reverend Dr. Samuel Osgood, who was acting as a substitute for the Melvilles' regular pastor, gave the family the consolation of a "reasonable doubt" and the members of the jury were induced to publish a statement designed "to correct any erroneous impressions drawn from the verdict of 'suicide.'" They believed "that the death was caused by his own hand," they declared, "but not that the act was by premeditation or consciously done." His grandmother and his aunt Augusta were readily convinced that the tragedy was entirely accidental, and the family's respectability was maintained.

Both Herman and Elizabeth bore up stoically under the ordeal of grief and that of putting the best possible face to the world, but Catherine Gansevoort thought them "of such nervous temperaments" that she could "fear for *their peace* of *mind*." A few days after the funeral she wrote a letter to her brother which reveals the quality which eventually drew Herman perhaps closer to her than to any of his relatives. "I sometimes wish we mortals had the power of seeing the heart and feelings of our friends," she said in a charitable qualification of her judgment upon Herman as a "strict parent" and Lizzie as a "thoroughly good but inefficient" one; "I believe there would be greater happiness were such the case. We so often distrust and blame where we should not, because we judge wrongly—and mistake the motives of the actions of others." It is probable that none of the practical things she was able to do to help Melville ever meant as much to him as his gradually acquired perception that this young cousin, who was barely half his age, felt a hidden quality in him and in others which precluded superficial judgments. Such sensitivity was not common among his kindred.

After a brief visit with Allan at Arrowhead during the latter part of September, the family settled down once more into their accustomed routine. They felt Malcolm's loss keenly, but Herman's life was brightened by the prospect of having his brother Tom permanently near home. For Captain Thomas Melville, after the customary scurrying around for letters by members of the family, was elected governor of "Sailors Snug Harbor" on Staten Island—a position providing him with a comfortable home and a salary of $2,000 a year which he expected to have doubled at the next semiannual meeting of the board of trustees on May 18. He planned to bring his mother and sisters down from Gansevoort to keep house for him, and, in the meantime, Herman and Elizabeth urged them to shut up their big home and spend the winter on Twenty-sixth Street. Mrs. Melville, however, had at last reached the age of wanting to stay at home; and, with the coming of cold weather, Herman himself was not very well. The "kink in his back" had returned, and it was serious enough to keep him from work for a while in December and renew his family's worries. Yet he was not despondent about his health. When *Putnam's Monthly* was revived as *Putnam's Magazine* and he was invited to contribute, he wrote with shy stiffness that he felt "much complimented" and might be included "in the list of probable contributors"; and he was doubtless pleased, in spite of the implication that the editors were unconscious of his *Battle-Pieces,* to be called back to the land of the living in the first issue as "a copious and imaginative author" who had "contributed so many brilliant articles to the *Monthly*" but had "let his pen fall just where its use might have been so remunerative to himself, and so satisfactory to the public." Such words were too fulsome to be taken seriously, but some extravagance was necessary to break through the reserve with which a discouraged man normally protects himself.

For *Battle-Pieces* had been an undeniable failure. Despite the fact that nearly one-fourth of the entire edition of 1,260 copies had been sent out to editors for review, only 486 copies had been sold according to the statement supplied by the Harpers on February 13, 1868; and the book was being forgotten so rapidly that only eleven additional copies were to be sold during the next seven years. The New York newspapers that had noticed it had been fairly kind in their reviews, but among the magazines only *Harper's* (which had printed a number of poems from the volume in advance of publication) had shown any enthusiasm for the work, and such elevated journals as the *Atlantic Monthly* and the *Nation* had been frankly contemptuous. Melville had made himself responsible for the expenses of publication and had lost about four hundred dollars on the venture. All of his seven prose works which had been published by the Harpers were still in print, and he was accustomed to having a small royalty account against which he could draw for purchases of other books; but, at the rate they were selling, it would take him six years or more to get out of debt even if he quit buying books entirely. The suggestion by the editors of *Putnam's* that his pen might be "remunerative" was ironic but interesting.

The "probable" contributions to the magazine, however, did not materialize, and almost the only records of Melville's activities during the next year were social. After a half year as the solitary governor of Sailors Snug Harbor, Tom had decided to take a wife instead of his mother and sisters into his establishment, and on June 6 he was married to Catherine Bogart in a ceremony attended by the clan and followed by a party in the home of Richard Lathers in New Rochelle. The party, with refreshments of claret punch and cake and music from an "orchestrian" of twenty-two musical instruments, was an augury of a new spirit in the Melville family. Tom and his wife were to prove hospitable and well able to entertain their friends and relatives comfortably during the winter season. The big house at Gansevoort continued to overflow with guests in the summer vacation period. And 104 East Twenty-sixth Street was a convenient way station between the two which became a pleasant place for visitors to stay in New York. Shortly before Christmas in 1868 Maria Melville changed her mind about being old enough to remain snugly at home while the weather was cold, and started out on a trip which enabled her to see her seven children and six of her seven grandchildren before eating Christmas dinner at Sailors Snug Harbor, where Tom and Catherine entertained nine Melvilles and eight Bogarts. She and Augusta prolonged their visit until early March and then spent six weeks at the home of Herman and Lizzie, where they reported all the family "well."

Herman seems to have genuinely enjoyed the social life and to have begun taking an interest in his old friends, for Evert Duyckinck was invited to attend the annual dinner of the trustees of Sailors Snug Harbor on June 28, 1869, at which Herman was a regular and apparently a cheerful guest. Elizabeth's health, however, was not good during the spring and summer, when she suffered annually from a "rose cold," and her accustomed visit to Boston that year did her little good. Herman was alone all during July and August, except for his customary two-week vacation which he spent with Allan and his family in Pittsfield, and when school opened for the girls in September Augusta had to come down and keep house because Elizabeth was too ill to leave Boston. She came home in early October, but a "persistent neuralgia and weakness" kept her inactive throughout the fall. During her own illness she began worrying about her husband. "If you see Herman," she wrote her aunt Susan, who was visiting in New York, "please do not tell him that I said he was *not well*—but if you think he looks well, I hope you tell him so."

Herman was, in fact, behaving ominously. He was thinking again. During the absence of Elizabeth and the girls in Boston he had, not unnaturally, begun to read more than he had been doing, and one book over which he had meditated was the copy of Matthew Arnold's *Essays in Criticism* he had obtained on July 10. Arnold, Melville discovered, was a man of remarkable understanding. To certain natures, "endued with the passion for perfection," Arnold had observed with reference to Maurice de Guerin, "the necessity to produce, to produce constantly, to produce whether in the vein or out of the vein, to produce something good or bad or middling, as it may happen, but at all events *something*,—is the most intolerable of tortures." This was a torture which Melville had endured for years while feeling obliged to make his living by his pen, and he acknowledged Arnold's acuteness by marking the passage with three emphatic lines in the margin. Other passages he marked dealt with the superiority of "the well-kept secret of one's self and one's thoughts" to the public display of them and of "being to seeming, knowing to showing, *studying* to publishing." And of an observation to the effect that "the literary career seems to me unreal, both in its essence and in the rewards one seeks from it, and therefore fatally marred by a secret absurdity," Melville remarked: "This is the finest verbal statement of a truth which every one who thinks in these days must have felt." He would not do anything so silly as to begin serious writing, but he was beginning to find something attractive in Wordsworth's notion (which Arnold had quoted) "of a mind forever voyaging through strange seas of thought, alone."

The winter was less social than usual, and in January, 1870, the family were upset by the news that Stanwix (who had gone to sea under a friend of Tom's) had jumped ship and apparently disappeared—although, actually, a conscientious letter was en route to them from London. Within a few days, Herman was displaying symptoms which would have been alarming to the family had they not been too preoccupied with Stanwix to notice them. He started buying books. His first purchases, on January 31, both dealt with the scenes he had visited on his Mediterranean trip thirteen years before: W. H. Bartlett's *Forty Days in the Desert, on the Track of the Israelites; or, A Journey from Cairo . . . to Mount Sinai and Petra* and *The Nile Boat* by the same author. His somewhat peculiar present to Fanny on her fifteenth birthday was of the same sort: *The Buried Cities of Campania: or, Pompeii and Herculaneum,* a new book by W. H. Davenport Adams; and a month later, on April 4, he bought Arthur Penrhyn Stanley's richly informative *Sinai and Palestine in Connection with Their History.* By this time Lizzie might have had reason to be worried, but Herman's health and spirits were both good. He had succeeded in avoiding a transfer from his conveniently located office on West Street, and arrangements were being made (by his favorite and sympathetic brother-in-law, John C. Hoadley) to have his portrait painted by Joseph Eaton. A letter to his mother on May 5 was altogether cheerful in its references to his sittings, to the family's health, and even to their failure to have any further word from Stanny. He also gave her a hint of his own private thoughts when he made an anecdote of his efforts to discover how well the hero of Fort Stanwix was remembered around the Gansevoort Hotel and in the neighborhood of Gansevoort Street. Finding that the name was merely supposed to be that of "a very rich family who in the old times owned a great deal of property hereabouts," he retired in indignation "to the philosophic privacy of the District Office" where, he reported in a remark which shows no sign of the bitterness with which he is sometimes supposed to have contemplated such matters, "I then moralized upon the instability of human glory and the evanescence of—many other things."

His uncle Peter, who probably heard the anecdote, sent him a handsomely framed engraving of the hero of Fort Stanwix, and his own portrait proved to be a great success. John Hoadley personally supervised its framing, and Allan's wife was so pleased with the result that she took a carriage and borrowed it for display at a party she was giving on June 14. Stanwix suddenly appeared at his grandmother's home in Boston, looking taller, stouter, and healthy, just a day before Elizabeth and the girls arrived for their annual visit on July 19; and Herman apparently left his work ten days before his vacation time in order to hurry up to see him, afterward taking Lizzie on a visit to North Conway before spending his regular vacation with his mother in Gansevoort. Catherine Gansevoort reported that he was "looking remarkably well" as he stopped off in Albany on his way to New York on the evening of August 13, and "was very cheerful." No one seems to have suspected him of being on the verge of taking up writing again.

Yet he was continuing to buy books and leave in them the record of a mind in ferment. He had bought William Hazlitt's *The Round Table: A Collection of Essays on Literature, Men, and Manners* in May while sitting for his portrait and had marked one significant passage on the "occasions when it is refreshing to escape from the turmoil and final nothingness of the understanding, and repose upon that contentedness of mediocrity, which seems to have attained its end without the trouble of wisdom." He had also scored another comment upon the futility of trying to restore the dead impulse of art to life when the original "inspiration of genius" had fled. There seems to be no doubt but that he was struggling either with or against a literary impulse of his own, pausing over such passages either in discouragement at his inability to get something on paper or because he was searching for an excuse to suppress a growing desire to write. During the summer, he was almost certainly not trying to write, for his recorded book purchases were designed to provide thoughtful recreation for an active mind rather than material which it could exploit: Alexander Gilchrist's *Life of William Blake* and *Passages from the American Notebooks of Nathaniel Hawthorne* in June, and a copy of *The Scarlet Letter* and *The Diary, Reminiscences, and Correspondence of Henry Crabb Robinson* in July. But on September 1 he turned purposeful with the purchase of John MacGregor's *Rob Roy on the Jordan, Nile, Red Sea, and Gennasareth*. His interest in Hawthorne (which he kept up by acquiring the *Twice-Told Tales* on January 6, 1871, *Passages from the French and Italian Notebooks* on March 23, 1872, and *Septimius Felton* as a birthday present from Elizabeth in the same year) was probably largely reminiscent; but if he was buying books on the Holy Land merely in order to refresh his mind on what he had seen on his trip, he was tempting whatever fate there is in a long-established habit. For, normally, book collecting on a single subject by Melville meant either that he was getting his mind worked up to the point of beginning a book of his own or else that he was nearly through one and needed additional material in order to finish it.

He had probably reached the beginning stage by January, 1870, for although his accounts with the Harpers from November of that year to June 17, 1872, suggest that he might have spent as much as a hundred dollars on books from their store alone during that period, the ten or twelve titles he is known to have acquired for his own use are mostly indicative, in their selection and their annotations, of a mind already at work rather than a mind still gathering materials to work with. Only W. H. Bartlett's *Walks about the City and Environs of Jerusalem* (which he gave to Elizabeth for a Christmas present in 1870) and E. H. Palmer's *The Desert of Exodus* (obtained at the time of the latter statement from the Harpers) dealt with the Holy Land. Several of the others, however, contained passages which either reflected Melville's own thoughts or grew into thoughts that he was later to express. In Balzac's *Eugénie Grandet* (which he acquired on December 1) he annotated a sentence with the ironic comment "This describes man in his consummate flower of civilization": "He had received the horrible education of that society, where, in a single evening are committed, in thought and in words, more crimes than the law punishes at the Court of Assizes; where a jest or a sneer annihilates the grandest conceptions; where a man is deemed strong only as he sees clearly; and to see clearly there, is to believe in nothing, neither in feeling, nor in men, nor even in events; for they concoct false events." Emerson (whose *Conduct of Life* he had purchased in November) and Matthew Arnold (whose *New Poems* he bought on February 3, 1871) aroused mixed emotions. The American annoyed him by his contempt for traveling, by his fastidiousness, and by his determined optimism; and the Englishman, by his occasional preciosity. But Emerson impressed him with his command to learn "a wider truth and humanity than that of a fine gentleman" by "humiliations, by defeats, by loss of sympathy, by gulfs of disparity"; and in Arnold he marked a significant passage from *Empedocles on Etna:*

'T is not the time,'t is not the sophists vex him;
There is some root of suffering in himself,
Some secret and unfollowed vein of woe,
Which makes the time look black and sad to him.

The reflections of his secret thoughts in his books were beginning to form a pattern—a pattern which also appeared in his markings and annotations, during this period, of William Habington's *Castara,* Hawthorne's *Twice-Told Tales,* Shakespeare's Sonnets, and Tennyson's *In Memoriam,* and which was to remain fundamentally unchanged through his reading of Sir William D'Avenant in 1872 and Calderón in the fall of 1874.

The pattern was one of distrustful ambition, cynicism toward society, and other dark emotions struggling against control. It was by no means a new one in Melville's life, of course, but its revival after a period of successful repression probably indicates that he had begun once again to suffer the strain of grappling for ideas with written words. The darkness of the pattern was also to be emphasized by the extraordinary series of personal losses, illnesses, and worries he suffered during these three years. Death seemed to be striking at his consciousness from all sides. Malcolm's suicide, as his marking of a defense of self-murder in Crabb Robinson's correspondence indicates, was never far from his mind. In the spring of 1871 the most intimate of his cousins, Colonel Henry Gansevoort, became seriously ill at Nassau; Catherine hurried to bring him home; and Herman saw him in New York, on April 8, only four days before he died on the boat en route to Albany. On February 9 of the following year, his brother Allan, who was suffering from consumption but whose condition was not supposed to be critical, suddenly died "in great agony." His mother, who was visiting Tom in order to have her portrait painted by Eaton, was too ill to attend the funeral and, on February 26, assembled her four daughters and two remaining sons around her bedside to sing "Abide with Me" after she had received Communion. Kate had to interrupt her attendance upon her mother to go to the funeral of her uncle, Captain John De Wolf, and Mrs. Melville died on April 1. Her body was accompanied to Albany for burial by Herman and a solemn party of fifteen others whose feelings were probably expressed by Catherine Gansevoort when she exclaimed in her diary: "How many more of those I love must I see buried?"

The strain was too much for Elizabeth, who, instead of going to Albany, took her two daughters to Boston, where she remained for several weeks of rest and recuperation. Stannie's restlessness, however, brought her home about the end of the month. For, unlike Malcolm, Stanwix was a difficult son. Before sailing for Canton and around the world, on April 4, 1869, he had been Allan's assistant in his law office, but felt handicapped by deafness; and, after his return, he had thought of going to work for his uncle John Hoadley in the mills of Lawrence, Massachusetts, but had gone to Kansas instead, where he drifted around during the greater part of 1871 before returning home sometime before Christmas. His next effort was at dentistry, but after his grandmother's funeral he decided that he wanted to go west again, and both Herman and Lizzie apparently were unwilling to restrain him. They bade him Godspeed at the end of April, and, after a few letters from Kansas, he announced that he was going to New Orleans and disappeared from view on a trip which was to take him through the Indian Nation, Arkansas, Mississippi, and into the Caribbean. His family did not learn until he reached home ten months later that after visiting Havana and various Central American cities he had walked the beach from Limon Bay in Costa Rica to Greytown in Nicaragua, burying one of his two companions in the sand on the way, and then had gone up the San Juan River with a naval surveying expedition for a ship canal through Lake Nicaragua. Nor did they know that afterward he had shipped out of Greytown for Aspinwall and had been wrecked, losing all his clothes and falling ill again of the fever which he had first caught, and from which his companion had died, on the beach. But they worried about him and about the demon of restlessness which made him decide, two months after his return, that he was too nearsighted to be a successful dentist and drove him on April 30, 1873, to take a ship for California and nearly two years of herding sheep.

Every decision and worry involving Stanwix during these years was related, in his parents' minds, to the fate of Malcolm; and after Lizzie returned from Boston in the spring of 1872 to see Stanny off on his second trip to Kansas she started a search for a tinted photograph of her older son which Herman had presented to his military company shortly after his death. Malcolm's regiment of the national guard had been disbanded and its effects sent to Albany, but an investigation traced the picture to the home of a young married couple in New York City; and Herman was able to obtain it in July, presenting the young couple with a framed water color in its stead. The year was a hard one for Elizabeth, and after she spent Herman's vacation with him in Pittsfield (where they celebrated their silver wedding anniversary at Arrowhead) her brother Sam took her off to Quebec in an effort to give her a rest and relieve her hay fever. The trip was a help, and Allan's widow thought that she was "looking very well indeed" after her return; but Sam wrote his mother in distress at seeing "how generally feeble" she was "and prematurely old." In early November the great Boston fire added to her worries, for it destroyed the property she had inherited from her father and forced her, while she was in Boston looking at the ruins, to contemplate the desperate expedient of taking in roomers in order to make ends meet. All the family knew of her situation, however, and Peter Gansevoort sent Herman a check for five hundred dollars—the amount of Elizabeth's annual income from the destroyed property—which Catherine tactfully accompanied with a silver soup ladle in order to represent the gift as a delayed silver anniversary present rather than a gesture of charity. Christmas that year was both quiet and sad.

Herman himself suffered an attack of influenza in early December while Elizabeth was in Boston and Bessie was keeping house for him, and he was to go through a more serious and sudden illness in April. But in other respects he showed no signs of any sort of behavior which would give his friends and relatives cause to worry. Augusta described him, at the time that Stanwix was thinking of going west again, as being "quite like his old natural self," a pleasant companion who seemed to take an interest in everything; and Catherine Gansevoort, while visiting at the house on Twenty-sixth Street in June, 1873, wrote of how much he reminded her of her brother Henry "in manner and in appearance and in little trifling ways" and added that "it does me good to see him." Yet the sensitive and sympathetic Catherine was probably the only member of the family outside Herman's immediate household who suspected that he was engaged in any occupation that would give them worry, for Elizabeth's remark that the "*financial* management" of the family fell on her because her husband's "studious habits and tastes" made him "unfitted for practical matters"—coming, as it did, upon the heels of Bessie's explanation that her father could not thank her for the ladle because of the condition of his eyes—indicated that he was writing again. Such dark suspicions, however, apparently were left unexpressed; and when Herman and Lizzie spent his vacation in Pittsfield, in July and August, 1873, it was only natural that Herman should have been called upon as the practical male to be approached by young Willie Morewood with a request for the hand of Allan's oldest daughter, Maria, in marriage.

Some indication of the feeling toward Melville which was held by those who knew him well may be found in a letter written by John C. Hoadley to George S. Boutwell at a time when the supporters of General Grant's second term were clamoring for the spoils of success and just after Elizabeth had lost her property in the Boston fire. "Proud, shy, sensitively honorable," Hoadley wrote in an effort to preserve his brother-in-law in "the undisturbed enjoyment of his modest, hard-earned salary," "—he had much to overcome, and has much to endure; but he strives earnestly to so perform his duties as to make the slightest censure, reprimand, or even reminder, impossible from any superior. Surrounded by low venality, he puts it all quietly aside,—quietly returning money which has been thrust into his pockets behind his back, avoiding offense alike to the corrupting merchants and their clerks and runners, who think that all men can be bought, and to the corrupt swarms who shamelessly seek their price;—quietly, steadfastly doing his duty, and happy in retaining his own self-respect." There was an extraordinary warmth in the letter which others also felt. His uncle Peter, at the age of eighty-seven, enjoyed calling him "Typee" and apparently thought of him often with a kindness which his aunt Susan shared. Their daughter Catherine's perceptive sympathy had developed into something like devotion, which her fiancé, Abraham Lansing, came to share and which Melville reciprocated in his attitude toward them both. He was always, it seems, a favorite companion of his brother Tom. None of them was quite prepared to become the confidant of his deepest thoughts, but they all bear witness to the fact that he possessed and preserved an attractive human quality which the members of his family appreciated.

He kept his job in the customhouse, and his job kept him too busy to go up to Albany for his cousin Catherine's wedding on November 25. But his life was quiet. Bessie kept house for him after his vacation in 1873, while Elizabeth and Fannie were in Boston, as she did the following summer when she joined him after he returned home from two weeks in the White Mountains. It was probably during these long and lonely summers, from 1871 to 1875, that he did most of his writing. For he was writing—and writing poetry. The secret could no longer be kept. Elizabeth evidently confided it to her family when all of Judge Shaw's descendants with the exception of Stanwix gathered at the family home for Thanksgiving dinner on November 26, 1874. She was sorry afterward and wrote her mother on the following March 9: "Herman is pretty well and very busy—pray do not mention to any one that he is writing poetry—you know how such things spread and he would be very angry if he knew I had spoken of it—and of course I have not, except in confidence to you and the family." But the thing had spread, and when Herman stopped by to see Peter Gansevoort on the first day of his vacation, August 8, 1875, his uncle taxed him with the report and learned that "Typee" had been doing what Peter had once hoped he would do—writing a narrative based upon his trip to the Holy Land. He probably also learned that, since it was in verse, it had little prospect of appearing in print. Whatever Peter thought and what conferences occurred between him and his daughter and son-in-law are not on record. He was approaching the age of ninety; his wife, who had loved her nephew by marriage, had died during the preceding October; and his only surviving child was married to a husband whose disposition was as generous as her own. The only other facts known are that Herman remained in Albany a day longer than he had planned and left on the evening of the ninth deeply affected by his uncle's offer to pay for the publication of his poem even though its estimated cost was $1,200.

Immediately after his return home from his two weeks in Gansevoort and Pittsfield he received a check for that amount, sent through Abraham Lansing, and probably set to work with enthusiasm preparing his poem for its unanticipated appearance in print. He had never seemed better in health and spirits, according to Augusta who had seen him at Gansevoort; and Tom, who saw him just after his return, found him "looking very well." Stanwix was at home, fully recovered from the illness from which he had been suffering at the time of his arrival on June 24; and Fanny, who was acting as housekeeper for her father and brother that summer while Bessie was with Elizabeth, would have had no thought of restraining his labors. His spirits remained high during the fall, when he sent word to his sisters Kate and Fanny that "they both must come down and see us before leaving for the East," and a ten per cent cut in his salary sometime before Christmas probably did not greatly dampen them. The poem was ready for consideration by G. P. Putnam and Sons by the first of the year, and definite arrangements for its publication were completed on January 4. A telegram from Abraham Lansing informed him of Peter Gansevoort's death on the same day.

Elizabeth, however, did not find the prospect of a new book so stimulating. Herman was so determined to get it out immediately that he hurried home from his uncle's funeral in order to spend the following day (which was Sunday) at work, and he probably had kept her hard at work copying, between the sniffles of a lingering hay fever, since her return from Boston in the fall. The poem had proved to be about eighteen thousand lines in length, with an episodic structure and a complicated unity of allusiveness which required careful attention and perhaps some tedious cross-checking; and Herman was undoubtedly both demanding and irritable as he pressed to get the work done while also carrying out his duties at the office. By the time they were half way through the proofreading the strain had become intolerable for both of them, and Elizabeth was obliged to call off a proposed visit from Augusta and another from Catherine Lansing. Her private letter to Catherine, on February 2, 1876, told what she thought of Herman's condition and unconsciously revealed a good deal about her own. "Dear Kate," she wrote:

> I have written you a note that Herman could see, as he wished, but want you to know how painful it is for me to write it, and also to give the real cause.—The fact is, that Herman, poor fellow, is in such a frightfully nervous state, and particularly now with such an added strain on his mind, that I am actually *afraid* to have any one here for fear that he will be upset entirely, and not be able to go on with the printing.—He was not willing to have even his own sisters here, and I had to write Augusta before she left Albany to that effect—that was the reason she changed her plan and went to Tom's. If ever this dreadful *incubus* of a book (I call it so because it has undermined all our happiness) gets off Herman's shoulders I do hope he may be in better mental health—but at present I have reason to feel the gravest concern and anxiety about it—to put it in a mild phrase—please do not speak of it—you know how such things are exaggerated—and I will tell you more when I see you.

Certainly the business of publishing a book was hard on the whole Melville household.

II

The book which was prepared for the press with almost as much distress as went into the preparation of *Moby Dick* was to be called *Clarel: A Poem and Pilgrimage in the Holy Land* and is one of Melville's most mature and revealing works. The secrecy with which he obscured its composition makes it impossible to determine the stages of its development, and his piecemeal method of writing—a method forced upon a man of Melville's temperament by the fact that he never had more than two or three hours of uninterrupted time to spend upon it—forestalls any attempt to trace its progress by a study of literary sources. For the poem was mostly based upon his own observations and meditations, the books from which he most evidently borrowed were obtained near the beginning of the undertaking, and any bits of verse written either at the time of his journey or as late afterthoughts could readily have been inserted into the manuscript at the time he was putting it in order for publication. Yet it was a poem that grew according to a predetermined plan (or, as was usual with Melville, outgrew its plan) which could hardly have been made until after he had settled in the customhouse, escaped from the threat of having to write for a living, and decided that episodic verse would satisfy his need for self-expression without involving him in a work which would have to be driven to completion for economic reasons.

The man who knew the "luckless" feeling of being removed "from action's thrill" and "all that yields our nature room" was one who had become tired of a steady job, not one who was trying desperately to secure regular employment; and the author who sympathized with a character's reluctance, under such circumstances, to take up that "dead feather of ethereal life," the pen, was apologizing for his own need of self-expression rather than writing under the pressure of external circumstances. Furthermore, a bitter reference to

> that parlor-strain
> Which counts each thought that borders pain
> A social treason . . .

was that of a person who was suppressing something more than feelings of disappointed ambition and a longing for philosophical conversation. Such allusions as these could have been inserted into the early part of the poem, where they are found, but they look more like uncalculated reflections of Melville's state of mind at the time he was writing the passages in which they occur; and both internal and external evidence suggest that *Clarel* was not meditated until after Malcolm's death or actually begun in any systematic way until at some time in 1870. He may have thought more than once, after his return from the Mediterranean in 1857, of making literary use of his travels; and he undoubtedly versified more of his impressions than those of Italy, Greece, and Egypt he was later to publish as the "Fruit of Travel Long Ago." But the long poem which grew more or less according to plan was, like Melville's other major works, the result of an emotional and intellectual necessity existing at the time of writing and establishing the design into which the material of his earlier experiences was woven. In it, accordingly, may be found a record of the thoughts and feelings hinted at in the annotations of the books he was reading during these years but carefully kept beneath the surface of his everyday life.

The plan of the poem revealed from the beginning the dual necessity from which it grew. Superficially, its design resembled that of *Mardi* in that it dealt with a young man's quest for happiness, in company with a group of talkative characters representing distinctly different points of view. The happiness in this case, however, was not a vaguely romantic ideal but rather a satisfaction of the conflict between the will to believe and the impulse toward skepticism which for years had existed unresolved in Melville's own mind and which he had now come to see in terms of religious "faith" and "doubt." To that extent, it was a philosophical poem concerned with the problem of knowledge; and if that problem was an intensely personal one to Melville, it had become, by the time he wrote *Clarel,* a commonplace one shared with Tennyson and Matthew Arnold and so many other nineteenth-century writers that it had lost the peculiar emotional and dramatic value it had once possessed for the young author of *Moby Dick.* The mature Melville was able to calculate in advance the philosophical mechanism of *Clarel* and outline its plot. He could arrange the action between the symbolic dates of Epiphany and Ash Wednesday, lay out the route of the pilgrimage or quest, and make his characters represent varying degrees of faith and speculative doubt. More important, perhaps, he could eliminate the problem of transcendental knowledge which had bothered him in his youth: before the poem opened, Clarel had been accosted by a grave stranger on the Jaffa road who had given him the Emersonian advice to escape the superficial narrowness of his shrewd and practical Western mind by discovering the reverent profundities of the East. But in attempting to follow it, after one casual and vain effort at prayer, Clarel showed no traces of the impulse to yield himself to the currents of universal Being and thus acquire an intuitive knowledge which transcended experience. On the contrary, he took to the road and tried to yield himself—as Melville had done on his own pilgrimage—to the traditional associations of holy places. There is no touch of Ahab and very little of Pierre in the young theological student. Melville, for better or for worse, had left his worries about transcendentalism behind him.

Yet with all the mature self-consciousness of his careful planning Melville seems to have found it difficult to focus his attention upon the intellectual design of his poem. The man whose novels had been too philosophical to be fully accepted as novels turned philosophical poet only to find himself more concerned with the psychology of people who used ideas than he was with the ideas themselves. Even with his hero Clarel he was more interested in what he called the "under-formings of the mind" than he was in the conscious intellectual structure which that mind should have erected as a proper conclusion to the poem, and the early characters that he introduced and with whom he lingered were nearly all characters intimately related to his own private emotions rather than to general philosophical problems. The most persistent and pervasive of these emotions was his lonely awareness of the strange attraction one individual could have for another—an "affinity," as Goethe had called it, which sought in vain for satisfaction in words and which was stronger than the recognized demands of sex. The hunchbacked Roman, Celio, in the first part of the poem, was such a character. Set apart from the rest of the world by his deformity, keenly aware from his own loneliness of the unapproachableness of the Deity, and with the passionate temperament of the Latin, he found himself guilty of inadvertent mockery from an excess of earnestness; and he exercised a strange attraction over Clarel without personal contact or verbal communication, involving himself in the student's dreams of Ruth before he died and left behind the journal in which Clarel found his "second self." The attraction was one for which the amateur psychologist might provide a too-easy explanation. The ex-sailor who was not without his share of curious knowledge could only recognize it as a reality and a mystery.

The American recluse, Vine, who was also introduced early in the poem but played little part in its intellectual plan, was another. When they first met, he and Clarel in a single glance "exchanged quick sympathies" which bound them more closely together than any other two characters in the poem, although Vine was to reveal nothing of himself except his deep love for the past and his ability to become alive in appreciation of the luminosity of a perfect symbol. With his suggestion of an "ambiguous elfishness" hiding behind a "virgin soul," he defied analysis. There was no saintliness in his detachment from his fellow man:

> Nay, the ripe flush, Venetian mould
> Evinced no nature saintly fine,
> But blood like swart Vesuvian wine.
> What cooled the current? Under cheer
> Of opulent softness, reigned austere
> Control of self. Flesh, but scarce pride,
> Was curbed: desire was mortified;
> But less indeed by moral sway
> Than doubt if happiness thro' clay
> Be reachable. No sackclothed man;
> Howbeit, in sort Carthusian
> Tho' born a Sybarite. And yet
> Not beauty might he all forget,
> The beauty of the world, and charm:
> He prized it tho' it scarce might warm.

He and Clarel were never intimate, but they were never far apart. Nor was there any suggestion, as there had been in the case of Celio, of a symbolic relationship between the two. Yet throughout the poem Vine was a major character, playing no important part in its intellectual plan but reflecting its author's awareness of his failure to achieve the sort of human companionship for which he longed but which he could not define.

There was probably a good deal of Hawthorne in the character of Vine —although not so much of the Hawthorne with whom Melville had talked freely and shared a common liking for gin and cigars in the Berkshires as of the hidden Hawthorne with whom he had failed to make close contact in Liverpool and who appeared in the hesitancies of *The Marble Faun* and in Mrs. Hawthorne's posthumous edition of the notebooks as the wraith of the man Melville remembered. For, of all Melville's recorded acquaintances, Hawthorne seems to have come nearest satisfying, during a brief period of creative excitement and need, that desire for companionship which was a strong but by no means abnormal quality of his nature. After years of comparative solitude, however, which his intimacy with congenial but uncreative souls could not wholly relieve, his awareness of the desire was stronger than his memory of its satisfaction. The portrait was not true. The relationship between Clarel and Vine was not that of Melville and any man, and the part that his old friend played in the creation of Melville's poem was that of a poorly remembered model for a statue designed to fill an emotional gap which no human being could really close but which his imagination could not leave unoccupied.

But the character most curiously intertwined with Melville's complex internal life was Clarel's first guide, that "flitting tract-dispensing man," Nehemiah, who called himself the lowliest of sinners but who was actually represented as the gentlest of saints. For Nehemiah, though related to the unfortunate Captain Pollard in Obed Macy's history of Nantucket and the Yankee "Deacon" Dickson whom Melville had met near Jaffa, was also conceived as a sort of sanctified ghost of Captain Ahab—the first of Melville's fictitious characters to have any deep emotional significance to his creator and the one who had most steadfastly continued to tease his imagination. Nehemiah had survived one catastrophe at sea with an undaunted spirit and had taken out another vessel only to have it destroyed by the purposeful malignancy of a whale. Surviving to tell the tale, but distrusted by shipowners as a Jonah, he passed through all the stages of Carlyle's transcendental Teufelsdröckh from that of the defiant will through the center of passive indifference and into an "Everlasting Yea" of self-abnegation and acceptance of what he thought to be God's will. He, of all the characters in the poem, was possessed of a knowledge which transcended experience and which had the effect, as Melville represented it, of improving his character and weakening his mind. Clarel found him a man to admire for his goodness but not one from whom he could learn wisdom, and Melville used him not as he had used Ahab as a means of dramatizing his own wild emotions but as a means of quieting them. The old saint, like the boy Malcolm, went to his death in his sleep by his own act, yet left his own memory and his companions blameless. The death of Nehemiah provided a specious consolation to the man who arranged it, perhaps, but it had no point at all except with reference to the emotional outlet which Melville was trying to find through his poem.

The remaining major character to appear in the first part was a young American wanderer named Rolfe who possessed much of Melville's own background and a considerable facility in expressing with enthusiasm all the beliefs that Melville could almost but not quite hold. With a suspicion of historical criticism which caused him to complain sardonically that

> All now 's revised:
> Zion, like Rome, is Niebuhrised,

he was intensely interested in religious problems. Contemptuous of the avowed "rationalist," he revealed that the "under-formings" of his own mind were those of eighteenth-century rationalism when he theorized about the origin of religious beliefs and fears:

> Yes, long as children feel affright
> In darkness, men shall fear a God;
> And long as daisies yield delight

Shall see His footprints in the sod.
Is 't ignorance? This ignorant state
Science doth but elucidate—
Deepen, enlarge. But though 'twere made
Demonstrable that God is not—
What then? it would not change this lot:
The ghost would haunt, nor could be laid.

Yet despite his suggestion that God was only a "ghost" of the mind, created out of human emotions, he was willing to assert that only "fools" would "count on faith's closing knell" for "Time, God, are inexhaustible." Vine found in him "an ocean-waste of earnestness without a buoy"; and he was, in fact, a strange hodgepodge of implicit contradictions. The natural product of an age which he denounced, he was less intellectual than active, more inclined to "heart" than to "head," yet distrustful of his own outspokenness. Melville was as sensitive to what other people thought of his own conversational habits as he was aware of his inner earnestness and uncertainty, and there was probably a considerable amount of ironic self-portraiture in his description of Rolfe as being "more bronzed in face than mind" and in his ascription to Rolfe of the half-apologetic and half-defiant attitude he had adopted toward himself: "as heaven made me, so am I."

These were the characters who—with Clarel's sweetheart, Ruth; her Jewish mother, Agar, homesick for Illinois; and her father, the Puritan skeptic-turned-Jew, Nathan—dominated the first part of the poem. They were all part and parcel of the emotional life of their creator, reflecting his uncertainties, his perturbations, his needs, his defenses, and his apologies; and with them he dallied for more than four thousand lines, exhibiting the interest and curiosity of a novelist who had learned to breathe some of his own life into his fictions and, by so doing, give them an independent life of their own. It was Melville's first extensive and varied achievement of this sort, and if it delayed his calculated quest the delay was probably to his own very considerable satisfaction.

When he set his pilgrimage in motion, in the second of the four parts of the poem, he did so with a certain Chaucerian spirit and the additional characters necessary to his intellectual plan. The "liberal" element in religious thought was represented by an Anglican priest named Derwent and formal dissent by an unnamed Scotch Presbyterian elder who appeared to be a true relic of the days of the Covenant. A wealthy Levantine banker, his mind entirely on his bonds and his gold, represented one of the common ways of the world, while another was set forth through the person of his prospective son-in-law, a Sybaritic youth of Smyrna. A misanthropic Swede, Mortmain, given to wandering the gray places of the world in search of an unknowable power superior to man, completed the party, which (with the four Americans, Clarel, Nehemiah, Vine, and Rolfe, and the representatives of the various Greek and Roman religious orders they expected to encounter) was plainly calculated to reflect almost every shade of professing Christianity. They did not, however, perform their function. Melville's uncalculated interest in people upset the balance of whatever plan he may have had for dealing with their ideas, and the quest, as serious philosophical enterprise, simply did not come off. The pilgrims who did not interest their creator as human problems were dropped from the group. Those who were kept, talked—and talked far more than an exposition of their ideas required.

The first to be abandoned was the Presbyterian elder, who was allowed to leave the party with no other explanation than Rolfe's guess that he could not endure the blank indifference of a desert with which he could not provoke a quarrel. For although Melville's external portrait of the man who criticized St. Paul for lack of zeal was one of the best of his satiric characterizations, he apparently had lost whatever interest he may once have had in the mental processes or psychological problems of anyone who held the Calvinistic doctrines of the church in which he himself had been reared. The Levantine banker and his sprightly companion followed the Scot as soon as Melville had used the young Sybarite for a canto which expressed the amused meditations first inspired during his own trip by the Englishman who had talked enthusiastically about a day's shooting in the Vale of Tempe. Melville may not have wanted to lose entirely either the hardheaded dogmatism or the worldliness of these departed characters, for he replaced them with an apostate Jewish geologist, Magoth, a spokesman for scientific rationalism, who was as aggressive as the Scot and as irreligious as the banker. But Magoth proved to be no more than a caricature, a "Simon Magus run to seed" in the words of Rolfe, who served as a butt for the superior sensitivity of his companions. Melville knew enough geology to have made the conflict between the legendary and the scientific explanations of the phenomena of the Holy Land interesting. Yet he seems to have had little more interest in the purely scientific mind than he had in the mind of the Calvinist or the financier and certainly did not trouble to explore it.

Melville also killed off his two saints during the course of the pilgrimage, bringing the second section of the poem to an end with the death of Nehemiah and the third with the death of Mortmain. For the wild and bitter Swede somehow evolved, during the days and nights he spent alone in the wilderness while separated from his companions, into a type of saintliness—as mad perhaps, as Nehemiah, but with the madness of one whose "naked brain" had been exposed to thoughts which the ties of humanity kept at bay from normal men. He was never quite real to his creator. But he served to fill the same sort of gap in Melville's intellectual life that Vine filled in his emotions: an emblem of something important, but something not to be grasped and understood. To replace him as the embittered critic of contemporary civilization, Melville created one more pilgrim who could be explained in human terms and whose opinions were less absolutely despairing and more simply disillusioned. Ungar, part American Indian, was a mercenary soldier in the service of the Turks, and his attitude was explained, perhaps too protestingly, as the result of his being a scarred and beaten survivor of the defeated side in the Civil War. Yet he was the spokesman for the criticisms of materialism, democracy, and smugness which had appeared in most of Melville's earlier books and were never far removed from his mind. Unlike those of the other travelers, Ungar's thoughts were not generally provoked by the associations of the place in which he found himself. They were apparently gratuitously introduced because Melville could not bring one of his most ambitious books to a close without speaking his mind, even if he had to play the ventriloquist, upon a theme which had been strong in most of his writings from *Typee* to *The Confidence Man*.

Discord, violence, and lust were a part of life which Melville had always accepted, not because they were good but because they were an inescapable part of nature. It was not until these qualities appeared in a context of moral pretensions that they became immoral rather than amoral; and it was the immorality of modern civilization, expressed in the complacent exploitation of one group of human beings by another, in cruelty disguised as competition, and in selfishness idealized, which had always aroused his anger. When he allowed Mortmain to penetrate "Paul's 'mystery of iniquity' " with his insistence that the sins of Sodom did not consist in "carnal harlotry" so much as in serving greed through holy forms or outwitting justice by trading on the coast of crime without landing, he was at last putting into general words a summary of the particulars which had bothered him all his mature life. But the words, he knew, were too general to be effective. Ungar's outburst against the Anglo-Saxon complacency implicit in the proverbial comparison "As cruel as a Turk" bore the same burden but with the shock of a Jeremiad:

> The Anglo-Saxons—lacking grace
> To win the love of any race;
> Hated by myriads dispossessed
> Of rights—the Indians East and West.
> These pirates of the sphere! grave looters—

Grave, canting, Mammonite freebooters,
Who in the name of Christ and Trade
(Oh, bucklered forehead of the brass!)
Deflower the world's last sylvan glade!

The hypocrisies of a civilization which could grow indignant at the story of a Hugh of Lincoln crucified by impious Jews while it was warping the bodies of thousands of Hughs of Lincoln in the child labor of its cotton mills were to Melville more scandalous if not worse than its cruelties.

Yet he could not avoid, in his maturity, facing the fact that this hypocrisy had come to seem almost as natural as the law of tooth and claw. Doubt and skepticism had once been aristocratic qualities of the mind, characteristic of the well-informed few while the mass of men accepted this or that belief in clodlike simplicity. Now, these qualities were commonplace. Almost every clod stirred with doubt, but there was no leaven in the stirring to make him rise. The age was one in which men could accept beliefs without believing, and the real intellectual problem which bothered Melville in *Clarel,* as it turned out, was not the problem of how one could resolve his religious doubts but that of how one could indulge doubt without falling into complacency. It was a human or psychological problem rather than a philosophical one, and it came to dominate his poem, perhaps, both because of the uncalculated diversion of his interest from ideas to people and because his private loneliness and the ineffectiveness of his more thoughtful books made him aware of the veneer of complacency with which the world protected itself from disturbance. During the long years spent in composing *Clarel* Melville became almost as expert as his friends and relatives in disguising the "social treason" of his thoughts by the cheerful countenance with which he faced sickness, death, and disappointment; but in doing so he increased his own isolation, and before the poem was finished social cheerfulness became a preoccupation of his mind greater than solitary doubt. Such a focus of attention preserved his interest in both the mysteriously attractive Vine and the somewhat too obvious Rolfe, and it made the new character Derwent an obsession. For Derwent represented, in human terms, the complacency of the world in its most puzzling aspect. Intelligent, sensitive, kindly, and tolerant, he was in every act and in almost every tone precisely what a Christian and a gentleman presumably should be. As a fictitious character with an independent life, he seemed to fascinate Melville, who let him talk steadily through three-quarters of the poem without revealing a vital chink in the intellectual and spiritual armor which he wore with such grace and facility. But he was armored, and Melville was convinced that a perfect shell was bound to be hollow.

In the canto "In Confidence," Derwent surrounded Clarel with wise answers to more questions than the young student knew how to ask; and Clarel could never think seriously of him later without remembering the occasion and feeling antagonism. He was a Job's comforter who could not say the thing that was right because he was unwilling to face the inexplicable mystery of pain, and his creator's wrath was kindled against him and smoldered throughout the book.

Melville's anger smoldered, however, without bursting into flame. The relative amounts of dramatic sympathy perceptible in his treatment of Ahab and Nehemiah showed, in answer to a question he had once asked, that he would rather be damned with kings than saved with fools; but his pride was at last going before his fall into the obscurity of the customhouse, and, even though he realized with Mortmain that hearts waxed warm oftener through hate than love, he deliberately banked the creative fire which might have made *Clarel* one of the great satiric poems of the nineteenth century. He was writing for himself rather than for the world, and his personal problem was that of adjustment to the sort of civilization that Derwent represented. He did not solve it in *Clarel,* but he moved toward a solution by curbing his anger or by giving it the sort of apologetic psychological justification supplied by the background he attributed to Ungar. Such a move on Melville's part, of course, reflected a decay of the emotional energy he had revealed in *Moby Dick;* but it did not represent any decrease in his intellectual powers. Ever since writing *Pierre* he had wavered between philosophical judgments and human understanding as the proper road to wisdom, and in *Clarel,* despite the temptations of philosophy which caused him to plan the poem, he took the road of understanding. Rolfe was the sort of person who, by temperament, could believe too many incongruent things to accept anything; and Derwent was the kind whose acceptances were easy because of a temperament too shallow for sincere belief. The reserves of Vine appeared to indicate depths of wisdom, but he did not share it, and a suspicion of shallowness eventually settled upon him. Ungar's rejection of everything Derwent accepted could be explained in terms of his past. Nehemiah and Mortmain, with their absolute visions of good and evil, were indefinably mad, bringing the extremes of thought ultimately together in their achievement of a common sainthood. There was no absolute certainty anywhere for a whole man. He could only be what he was made to be, and his dream of becoming anything else through philosophy was a vain deceit. This was the sum of the wisdom Melville acquired while writing *Clarel.*

As for his hero, the seeker after truth, the poem was necessarily inconclusive. Melville's intention had evidently been to allow Clarel to acquire a body of ideas which would have their validity tested by a sense of the finality of death; and he rounded out his narrative according to plan, allowing the travelers to return to Jerusalem on Ash Wednesday and discover that Ruth had died in their absence and was then being buried. But the conclusion had neither the effect of a triumphant resolution of the boy's doubts nor the impact of tragic irony which Melville most probably expected to put into it. Clarel had not acquired an intellectual being which could be put to the test of emotional shock. The conclusion was ironic but arbitrarily rather than tragically so. Melville gave two last glimpses of Clarel. One was on Easter when, by a coincidence of their calendars, all the churches celebrated the arisen Christ while Clarel remembered Ruth and the stone which had not been rolled away from her grave. The second and more effective in its implications was during Whitsuntide. Clarel was lingering on the Via Crucis, still awaiting "a message from beneath the stone." He had no light of the spirit to give him comfort or strength in his afflictions or to defend him against error. He had asked, but nothing had been given to him. He had sought but had not found. He had knocked, but no door had been opened. In the last lines he turns his back on Olivet and "vanishes in the obscurer town."

There was more pessimism in this conclusion, however, than the poem justified, and Melville realized it. He added an "Epilogue" of his own comment, showing that the "under-formings" of his own mind were very much like those he had attributed to Rolfe:

> Yea, ape and angel, strife and old debate—
> The harps of heaven and the dreary gongs of hell;
> Science the feud can only aggravate—
> No umpire she betwixt the chimes and knell:
> The running battle of the star and clod
> Shall run for ever—if there be no God.

The human emotions of faith and despair would find their symbols and, through them, struggle with each other whether or not there was any such thing as absolute truth. The problem of knowledge was not personal, as he had thought while writing *Moby Dick;* nor was it historical, as he had been inclined to believe while meditating his impressions of the Pyramids. It had become, in fact, hardly a "problem" to him at all. As his mind dwelt more upon people than upon philosophy, he began to see inspiration, observation, and introspection as different means for achieving emotional satisfaction rather than as conflicting ways to "truth."

The new clarity of scientific observation was more satisfying than any means the world had known before, but it left many "insignificant thoughts that are in all men" in the chaotic darkness of their "rude elements"; and the modern contrast between clarity and obscurity was frightening to people who had questions which could not be answered by science:

> Degrees we know, unknown in days before;
> The light is greater, hence the shadow more;
> And tantalized and apprehensive Man
> Appealing— Wherefore ripen us to pain?
> Seems there the spokesman of dumb Nature's train.

Yet if the tantalizing light of science could not be shed on all things, the darkness in which they remained was not necessarily the darkness of error:

> But through such strange illusions have they passed
> Who in life's pilgrimage have baffled striven—
> Even death may prove unreal at the last,
> And stoics be astounded into heaven.

Melville was evidently still pretty much of a mind "to be annihilated," but he was finally beginning "to rest in that anticipation." Although prepared to be "astounded," he was unmoved by anticipations of any sort.

For a person who needed the consolations of religion, however, he could recommend an acceptance of the rude elements of belief found in the impulses of the "heart":

> Then keep thy heart, though yet but ill-resigned—
> Clarel, thy heart, the issues there but mind;
> That like the crocus budding through the snow—
> That like a swimmer rising from the deep—
> That like a burning secret which doth go
> Even from the bosom that would hoard and keep;
> Emerge thou mayst from the last whelming sea,
> And prove that death but routs life into victory.

The sort of heartfelt belief he had ascribed to Ahab and Pierre was no longer, to Melville, a tragic illusion but a tolerable and even a necessary one. It was a form of belief which would always exist because some people needed it. The nineteen years that passed between his Mediterranean trip and the publication of his poem brought to Melville no philosophy of myth and monument. His skepticism became, in *Clarel,* the dominant quality of his mind.

But Melville's skepticism did not lead to the pessimism and despair which he seems to have anticipated. Instead of resulting in an unhappy negation of all belief, it simply gave him a detached interest in the human problem of belief which had bothered him for so long. The poem served the "social heresy" of its major purpose by giving expression to all his dark thoughts and painful doubts, but it also served to show that people had become more interesting to him than the ideas which flitted through their minds. In spite of all the distress it caused, for a while, Peter Gansevoort had been right in impelling its completion and publication: *Clarel* resolved the major conflicts in Melville's mind and made him a whole man who could face uncertainty without despair.

III

Although *Clarel* relieved Melville's mind of many of its conflicts and much of its distress, the emotional plot of the poem was unfortunately prophetic. His devoted sister Augusta, who had been directed to Staten Island to visit Tom in order that Herman might not be bothered while he was getting his poem ready for publication, remained there while *Clarel* was going through the press. And there, in early February, 1876, she became seriously ill. Herman was so disturbed about her condition by Thursday, February 17, that he stayed away from work and went over to see her, only to find that she was unable to see anyone and that Dr. Bogart (Tom's father-in-law and the medical director of Sailors Snug Harbor) was calling in a group of New York physicians for consultation the following day. They decided that she was suffering from an "internal hemorrhage" and held out little hope for her recovery. On Saturday, February 26, Herman was back and able to see "Gus" for the first time. "He was deeply moved," according to his sister Frances, and "could hardly control his feelings while with her."

For five and a half long weeks, while he read the proofs of his work, he could hardly have avoided wondering whether matters would not have been different had his sister been visiting him instead of his brother; and when she died, on April 4, he suffered in reality the same sort of emotional shock that he had invented as a test for young Clarel's philosophy. His thoughts while attending the funeral on April 7 and while accompanying her body to Albany for interment in the family cemetery are not on record; but two weeks after his return home, when his book was "at last" in type, Elizabeth wrote Catherine Lansing: "I shall be so thankful when it is all finished and off his mind, and cannot help hoping that his health will improve when he is released from this long continued mental strain." But neither the completion of the odds and ends of work that still remained to be done nor the actual publication of the book brought him the relief which normally accompanied his release from such drudgery. Nearly a year later Elizabeth was still worried about how *"morbidly* sensitive" he was to other people's feeling concerning him and about her lack of success in her constant attempts "to smooth the fancied rough edges to him" whenever she could.

Yet Melville tried conscientiously to enter into the normal life about him. At the *"very strong* representations of the publishers," he agreed to put his name on the title page of *Clarel* and, consequently, dedicated it to Peter Gansevoort with a frank acknowledgment of his uncle's "spontaneous act" of generosity in providing for its publication. He also, on the evening of April 30, took up his old habit of dropping in on Evert Duyckinck. When Catherine Lansing visited New York in the middle of May, she found him apparently "very well" and "very entertaining"; and he insisted that she stay with them for a week and persuade her husband to come down from Albany on Friday to remain through Sunday. The book finally appeared, in two volumes, on June 3; and Tom and his wife helped celebrate the end of the "series of most vexatious delays" which had held it up by coming in from Staten Island to dine on the following day.

Despite his carefully cultivated cynicism concerning literary fame, Melville must have had some hopes for his poem; and secret disappointment undoubtedly contributed something to the sensitiveness Elizabeth observed during the months which followed its publication. A review in the New York *Daily Tribune* for June 16 found it "something of a puzzle, both in design and execution." It seemed to have no plot and no logical course or conclusions to its arguments, and "the reader soon becomes hopelessly bewildered, and fatigues himself vainly in the effort to give personality to speakers who constantly evade it, and connection to scenes which perversely hold themselves separate from each other." Although it contained a vein of earnestness and some good passages of description, it was, on the whole, "hardly a book to be commended, for a work of art it is not in any sense or measure." The *World* was even more critical, and the author's brother Tom was puzzled. But John Hoadley was a loyal admirer and wrote Abraham Lansing that "it will grow on thoughtful reading, and will give Herman Melville a firm footing on a higher plane than anything he has before written." "I wish," he added, "it might make him at once rich, famous and happy! Noble Fellow!" Catherine Lansing, more realistically, worried about the expense of publication. She made Herman admit that although $1,200 had more than covered the cost of printing, it had fallen $100 short of covering the promotion and other added expenses; and for several months she argued with him over the additional amount until, in September, he finally accepted her check and turned it over to the New York Society for the Relief of the Ruptured and Crippled as a gift in her name.

Outwardly, his life moved on an even keel. Elizabeth continued to be forced out of town by her hay fever during the late summer, and Herman spent his August vacation with her and the girls in the White Mountains, returning home at the end of the month by way of Boston, where he paid a brief visit to Helen and George Griggs and their growing daughters. He continued spending occasional evenings with Evert Duyckinck, entertaining friends and relatives in his own home, and regularly urging Catherine and Abraham Lansing to come down often from Albany. An excursion to the Philadelphia Centennial took him away from home for a single day on October 11 to be impressed by the "tremendous Vanity Fair" of the celebration. He read the reviews of *Clarel*—most of which expressed the opinion that it should have been written in prose, although the *Library Table* for August 9 called the verse "flowing and musical"— and discovered an edition of Chaucer that Abe Lansing wanted to add to his collection. Although it is unlikely that he did much writing at this time, the *History of Pittsfield* appeared in 1876 with Melville's memoir of his uncle Thomas in it; and he sometimes browsed through the unpublished manuscripts he had been accumulating. The only results of his browsing, however, were that when he went to inspect the brig *Carolus* (which docked with a cargo of sulphur on March 24, 1877) and discovered that the captain had some fragments of Grecian ruins, he tried to get one to divide with John Hoadley and at the same time sent his brother-in-law a copy of "The Age of Antonines" with the explanation that he "came across it in a lot of old paper" and had no idea of "what the deuce the thing means."

Financially, he was not having an easy time. His book purchases while writing *Clarel* had left him in debt to the Harpers for $84.12, according to their statement of August 31, 1876, and the restoration of the customs inspectors to their four-dollar-a-day wage on October 1 hardly solved his family's difficulties. Stanwix was unhappy and in need in San Francisco and, as the year drew toward a close, secretly writing to Lemuel Shaw, Jr., for financial assistance to go on a prospecting trip to the Black Hills. At the beginning of January, Catherine Lansing tactfully sent Herman another check for a hundred dollars to pay for the deficit on *Clarel,* and this time he kept the money for six months before he returned it. He was able to stand by his earlier decision concerning the extra expense of his poem, perhaps, only because he had received $500 from the estate of his uncle Peter on June 1 and had, as Elizabeth put it, "something to call his own." "Poor fellow," she wrote Catherine, "he has so much mental suffering to undergo (and oh how *all* unnecessary) I am rejoiced when anything comes into his life to give him even a moment's relief." But the legacy could relieve neither his nor her mind. All during June there were dismissals, investigations of dismissals, and fears of dismissals in the customhouse; and it was not until the end of the month that Melville was assured of being retained in his job. In the meantime, however, Elizabeth had been compelled to accept the assistance of her brother Lem in order to go with the girls to the White Mountains for the summer— a trip which her own condition and Bessie's susceptibility to hay fever made imperative although she doubted "being able to leave Herman alone so long, in his state of mental health, with a free conscience."

The extent to which Lizzie's worries about Herman's "mental suffering" and "mental health" were justified at this time cannot be determined. It had long been an established habit of hers to worry about her husband's state of mind whenever she herself was ill and the family was beset by financial difficulties, and Herman seems to have given no evidence to others of suffering anything more than a sensitive man's normal worries about the ordinary affairs of life. Even in August, 1876, when his sister's death was still preying on his mind, he described himself to Catherine Lansing as being "ever hilarious"; and Catherine had found "a warm welcome" in his home in November and had written her husband that "it seems very natural here." During the summer of 1877 he certainly did nothing to justify Elizabeth's worries, taking his normal vacation by spending a day and evening with the Lansings on August 11, strutting through Saratoga Springs in a new linen "duster" en route to Gansevoort, and going on to Jefferson, New Hampshire, to see his womenfolk before returning home on August 27. And Elizabeth—when she got back in the early autumn, free from her fear of hay fever and cheerful enough about finances to set the house "all upside down with painters" and buy new furniture for the bedrooms—could find no excuse for calling him anything but "well."

For the next eight years he lived the normal life of an aging man who was still active enough to follow his daily occupation, who had settled into a routine, and who accepted the responsibilities and the joys and sorrows that came to him in the ordinary rounds of existence while a new generation grew up and an old one died out around him. In the spring of 1878 he suffered the first of his two attacks of erysipelas, which prevented him from using his hands; but he was able to hold a pencil again by the latter part of May, and the worst effects he suffered were the inconveniences of being transferred, apparently during his illness, from his comfortable district near home to an office far, uptown at Seventy-sixth Street and East River. Otherwise, his health was better than that of his family. When Lizzie was not dodging hay fever, she was subject to what she variously called her "run down turns" or "prostrated turns"; and dur-in one of them, in early March, 1879, she wrote Catherine Lansing that she was "hardly able to guide" her pencil and could not "walk across the room without staggering." When she could not find any excuse for worry-ing about Herman, she felt sorry for Bessie—who suffered so from arthritis in the spring of 1879 that she had her fingers straightened by binding and who, in the autumn of 1884, had a serious attack of what the family called "muscular rheumatism" which lasted for several months, required day-and-night attendance by her mother and a trained nurse, and resulted in her head being shaved in January. Stanny's letters from Cali-fornia, too, were full of "pulmonary troubles." Herman's one recorded illness during the early 'eighties, "a kind of rheumatic gout," was hardly worth mentioning.

But his younger daughter Fanny throve, possibly because of the benign influence of a young man from Philadelphia, Henry B. Thomas, who be-gan to make a regular appearance at 104 East Twenty-sixth Street in 1877 and to whom she became engaged in the following April. Her par-ents were pleased with her choice. Herman introduced him to Sailors Snug Harbor on August 1, the family made him "the central figure" in their Thanksgiving Day gathering on November 28, and the marriage was solemnized at All Souls Church on April 5, 1880. They eventually settled in Orange, New Jersey, where Herman's first grandchild, Eleanor, was born on February 24, 1882. His second, Frances, followed on Decem-ber 3, 1883.

Almost every one of these years brought some intimation of mortality to justify Herman's now-habitual observation that "life is short." On October 24, 1877, his aunt Lucy Nourse, with whom Elizabeth had spent her summers as a child, died; and on August 13 of the following year, his friend Evert Duyckinck, with whom he was spending almost as many evenings as he had spent in his company thirty years before, also passed out of his life. In the same month the death of Elizabeth's aunt, Mrs. Martha B. Marett, caused great excitement among the relatives at Ganse-voort who heard the considerably exaggerated rumor that she had left $10,000 to her niece and an equal amount to be divided among the chil-dren. A year later, on August 13, Elizabeth's stepmother died in Boston while Elizabeth and Bessie were spending their summer in the Catskills; and in the spring of 1880, Herman received notice of the sudden death of Abe Lansing's brother John and, in the summer of 1881, of the equally sudden death of his cousin Robert Melville in Davenport, Iowa. Such melancholy reminders of time's winged chariot passed him by during the two years in which his grandchildren were born; but in quick succession in the spring of 1884 his brother Thomas died of a heart attack on March 5 and Elizabeth's brother Lemuel died of apoplexy on May 5. Finally, in July of 1885, his sister Frances Priscilla passed away while staying with Helen in Brookline. These deaths meant not only grief but a narrowing of the Melville orbit: Staten Island became only a pleasant memory after Tom was buried in its Moravian cemetery, Gansevoort was no longer a family gathering place after the death of Frances, and Boston lost most of its attraction even to Elizabeth when neither Mrs. Shaw nor Lem was there.

Yet this pattern of illness and birth and death was woven through a routine of life that remained relatively unchanged. Herman continued to make his daily trip to his district office and inspect cargoes brought from faraway lands. Lizzie continued to gallivant around New England and New York State, fleeing "the enemy" (as she described hay fever) in the summer and visiting "her dear Boston" (as one of Herman's sisters put it) during the holiday seasons in the winter. After spending the summer of 1878 in New Hampshire, she and Bessie decided to try the Catskills, and they apparently spent the next four seasons at the Overlook Mountain House in Woodstock. In 1883, they moved their pollen-season residence to Richfield Spring; and in 1885 they were persuaded to try the more accessible Fire Island in Long Island Sound, but Elizabeth was nervous about the experiment and, after a few days in early July, decided to move to New Hampshire where she and Bessie would be "*sure* to escape." In earlier years her mother's age and her own financial affairs, which were managed entirely by her brother Sam, had provided her with whatever excuse she needed to visit Boston. Among her recorded visits were one for a week or more in July and early August, 1878, and another in the same year which lasted from just before Thanksgiving (when Herman, Bessie, and Fanny held their "little affair" for the "young man" from Philadelphia) until a week before Christmas. She was there again at Thanksgiving time in 1880 and, in early December, Herman was at least expecting her to remain there until the latter part of January. Such visits as these, and shorter ones with Fanny after her marriage, left Herman alone for a great deal of time until Elizabeth—in 1885, and in spite of his vehement objections—found a woman to keep house for him when Bessie was away with her.

Herman himself was losing his inclination to travel. Although he disliked Jefferson, he dutifully spent part of his annual vacation there with Elizabeth; and in the summer of 1878, when his sister Frances was visiting the Hoadleys and the family home at Gansevoort was closed, he probably stopped off in Lawrence with John and Kate. But until 1884 Frances usually kept the house at Gansevoort open, as many of the Melvilles as possible tried to gather there while Herman was free, and one reason, perhaps, why Lizzie turned to the Catskills during the summer was to make it more convenient for him to share his two short weeks with her and with his sisters. Albany was a normal way stop on these trips, and during the summer of 1885, when Elizabeth decided to humor his dislike for Jefferson by going wherever he wished, he paid his last visit to Pittsfield. But he was no longer willing to run up to Albany for a short stay. He was probably being humorous when he wrote Catherine Lansing, after he had spent the week end of August 9, 1878, in Albany, that he would never again visit her and Abraham "if the eventual result is but an augmentation of the blues" he felt at contrasting their hospitality to the loneliness of his own house. Yet he actually found excuses for not accepting all later invitations that required a special trip—staying away on Thanksgiving of the same year because of the affair for Fanny's "young man," refusing an invitation for Christmas in 1879 on the grounds that Elizabeth was not "robust" enough to undertake a journey northward in midwinter, and deciding that he could not come up for a reception by the Fort Orange Club on January 19, 1881, merely because he was an "old fogy."

Staten Island, so long as Tom was alive, and Fire Island, after Elizabeth began to go there regularly, were just about as far abroad as he wanted to go. But he was cordial in urging his female relatives and their husbands (for except for his brother Tom and one Gansevoort cousin with whom he had no contact, he had no close male kin after the death of his uncle Peter in 1876) to visit 104 East Twenty-sixth Street. And, saving one unfortunate occasion when Catherine Lansing apparently expected to spend the night after eating dinner with the family and failed to get an invitation, they all received a warm welcome there. He was not avoiding society but hoarding his energy, and his old friend J. E. A. Smith observed that on his last visit to Pittsfield "he did not evince the slightest aversion to society but appeared to enjoy the hearty welcome that it gave him"; although, he added, "perhaps his manner was a little more quiet than in the old time." During this visit, Smith also observed, he "bore nothing of the appearance of a man disappointed in life, but rather had an air of perfect contentment, and his conversation had much of his jovial, let-the-world-go-as-it-will spirit."

Julian Hawthorne gave contrary reports of him after he had paid Melville a visit in 1883, seeking materials for the biography, *Nathaniel Hawthorne and His Wife*, which he was writing at the time. But Julian made most of his father's old friends almost as "nervous" as he represented Melville as being, and his attitude during the interview was perhaps not only pressing but as supercilious as that which underlay the biography and caused Mary Louise Peebles to suspect that the book's allusions to Melville "would be very trying to a person of his sensitive nature." For Melville had lost none of his pride. Although forgotten by the public at large, the four of his prose works which were still in print—*Omoo, Redburn, White Jacket,* and *Moby Dick*—had been selling about a hundred copies a year between 1876 and 1880 and at about twice that rate during the four years which followed. His readers were few but choice. The popular English writer of sea stories, W. Clark Russell, was reported in the New York *Herald* at the end of 1883 as wondering why someone did not write the life of "that fine writer, Melville," and "let the world know as much as can be gathered of his seafaring experiences and personal story of the greatest genius your country has produced—leagues ahead of Longfellow and Bryant as a poet."

Another Englishman, James Billson, wrote him from Leicester in August of the following year, expressing his admiration for the books he had read—especially *Mardi*—and asking about others. And in the London *Academy* for August 15, 1885, Robert Buchanan paid tribute in verse to *Typee* and *Moby Dick* and added a footnote indicating that while in America he had done practically everything but consult the city directory in his effort to find "this Triton" whom he knew to be living in New York and whom he considered "the one great imaginative writer fit to stand shoulder to shoulder with Whitman on that continent." Melville refused to assist in the founding of the Authors' Club when he was invited to do so in 1882, and, according to the memory of Brander Matthews, he only rarely dropped in for an hour or so among the writers who were still talked about. But he prized his English admirers and entered into correspondence with both Billson and Russell.

His greatest desire seems to have been to live quietly, and, at some time after Elizabeth decided that she was not suffering from "a rose cold" but "the hay fever," he began to grow roses. They appear to have become a modest passion with him, for he started drying the petals and giving a few of them to friends who visited in his home. He grew other flowers in his garden and sent a "superb" box of early blossoms to his sister Frances during her last illness, but his roses provided him with companionship when Elizabeth and Bessie were away during the long months of summer. It was probably at this time, during the years when he realized he had begun "aging at three-score," that he began writing the rose poems he left in manuscript after his death. They were the products of an old man's whimsicality—verse of amused preoccupation in which he punned upon his passion by letting "Amoroso" sing the praises of his "Rosamond" and by stringing "Rosary Beads" of flower worship. He had, as he observed twice in these poems, come unto his roses late; and he smiled at his devotion to them.

But running through the whimsicality of verses was a vein of serious symbolism which reveals the emotional associations his garden had for him. His flowers were closely connected, in his mind, with Elizabeth; and he was doubtless fully conscious that they filled a gap which her long absences left in his life. The rose was love. In a fanciful moment he could play with the conceit that the sons of God had not been tempted to earth by the daughters of Eve but by the more fugitive charms of the rose. But more often the rose was an emblem of eternal love which survived the vagaries of life and continued after death. It was more desirable than any gifts of Mammon. Whether it was a physical or a spiritual love Melville did not know: he had never discovered a satisfactory theology, and he more than once debated the relative claims of the flower and the attar, the body and the essence, with an apparent inclination to put more faith in the former. But with his belief that a man could do nothing better than trust his "heart," love became, in any case, for him a form of religion; and the amused flower worship in his poems was not insincere.

So, under the punning title of "The New Rosicrucians," he expressed the philosophy of his quiet retirement:

> To us, disciples of the Order
>   Whose rose-vine twines the Cross,
> Who have drained the rose's chalice
>   Never heeding gain or loss;
> For all the preacher's din
> There is no mortal sin—
>   No, none to us but Malice!
>
> Exempt from that, in blest recline
>   We let life's billows toss;
> If sorrow come, anew we twine
>   The Rose-Vine round the Cross.

However much he may have been amused by himself and at his fancies, his acceptance of life, his resignation to worldly failure, his contentment with mortality, his genuine love for Elizabeth and his friends, and his lack of malice toward anyone—all of these blossomed, symbolically, in his rose garden.

A major reason why Melville could feel content was that at the age of sixty-five he had outlived the influences of the evil economic star under which he had been born. Mrs. Marett's will was not to be probated until eleven years after her death, and in November, 1878, Elizabeth welcomed a small bequest of $100.00 from Herman's aunt Lucy which she spent on the "back parlor" in order that all the family might share it. But after Mrs. Shaw's death the following summer some provision must have been made for Elizabeth by her stepbrothers who realized that their mother would have remembered her devoted foster daughter had she made a will. Lemuel left each of her children $2,000.00 and made her one of the three residual legatees of his estate, which was formally evaluated at $323,450.70. When the first payments from it were made, in December, 1884, she gave Herman $25.00 a month for the specific purpose of buying books and prints, and the next summer she began doubling the length of time she spent at resorts. The family future, for the first time, was secure. When the specter of dismissals once again hovered over the customhouse that summer and Elizabeth heard about it on a visit to town, she naturally wrote Catherine Lansing to ask Abe to use any influence he might have to keep Herman in his position. But she did not want her husband to know that she had interceded, for "apart from everything else the *occupation* is a great thing for him—and he could not take any other post that required head work, and sitting at a desk." For the first time in Melville's life, although he was not supposed to realize it, work was a luxury.

By this time Melville knew that he would have funds of his own from the estate of his sister Frances, and a small income from the Gansevoort farm, which was then being cultivated by a tenant. When winter came, neither financial necessity nor personal pride required him to make the cold journey uptown to his district office in a wind-swept lumberyard; and Elizabeth evidently decided that he had reached the age at which "head work" was perhaps less dangerous than exposure. In December, 1885, he rounded out nineteen years of "faithful service" in a government office without "a single complaint against him." For some time he had realized that his duties were "too onerous for a man of his years," and there was now no reason why he should continue to fight against the mental and physical exhaustion with which he was sometimes threatened. On the last day of the year he sent in his resignation. Within ten days he was free from the customhouse and had leisure to use as he pleased.

13
Recollection and Renown

MELVILLE HAD a "great deal" of "unfinished work at his desk" to "give him occupation," Elizabeth wrote Catherine Lansing when she announced her husband's resignation from the customhouse. His writing and his reading, she hoped, would prevent time from hanging heavy on his hands while he achieved "a more quiet frame of mind" without having to worry about his ability to perform his duties. For the first time since he had written *Mardi,* she was willing to see him take up his pen. There was no financial pressure to drive him beyond his strength, his motive was primarily one of self-expression, and much of his work would consist of sorting and revising fragments of verse and prose—putting them together in a quiet game of literary solitaire which would provide relaxation to an old man who was tired in body but still alert in mind.

The fragments had been accumulating for years. Some of them dated back to the time he had planned his first volume of poems, for which Elizabeth had failed to find a publisher while he was away on his voyage with Tom. Others were the products of his idle hours in his office. For at some time during the 'seventies Melville had abandoned the legal-size paper on which his novels had been written and had adopted small slips, roughly five and a half by seven inches, which could be slipped into a man's coat pocket and pulled out for use whenever the occasion permitted. Even the fair copies made of his compositions during his later years were on such slips, and he was probably rarely without a small folder of blank paper on which he could scribble or of manuscript which he could meditate or revise without being confined to his study.

The notion of eventually turning out another book or so in a leisurely manner had probably been in his mind since the early winter of 1881 when he began taking the lessons in penmanship from "a High Dutch professor" who taught "all the stylish flourishes imaginable" with such success that his elderly pupil became able to make his own printers' copy without having to depend upon Elizabeth. During the year preceding his retirement he was certainly going through his accumulated manuscripts and thinking seriously of what might be done with them. For on January 22, in a letter to James Billson, he referred to James Thomson's "Sunday up the River" in figurative language directly reflecting his own unpublished poem, "The Cuban Pirate"; on May 17 he published a version of "The Admiral of the White" in the New York *Daily Tribune* and also in the Boston *Herald;* and on October 5 of the same year, in a letter to Mrs. Ellen Gifford, he referred to his verses, "Montaigne and his Kitten," of which she had a copy. But precisely what material he had on hand is impossible to determine. The poems evidently belonging to his Arrowhead period, some of the literary fruits of his Mediterranean trip, and a considerable number of miscellaneous verses were among the papers he carried around with him. Other bits of prose and verse may have existed only in the form of preliminary jottings or crude first drafts.

Within a couple of years these fragments and the new products of his leisure time began to group themselves into three separate literary projects. One was a volume of poems primarily designed for Elizabeth. Another was a mixture of prose and verse something like the "Frescoes of Travel" he had projected thirty years before and something like the Roger de Coverley Papers he had learned to admire and had given to his daughter Bessie as a New Year's present in 1882. A third was a similar collection possibly first inspired by his awareness of the old tars who doddered around Sailors Snug Harbor and by a feeling that, somehow, a part of his own life was doddering along with them. This last project was the one of most immediate interest to Melville during the first retrospective years of his retirement. He was more inclined to look astern then ahead, and he seems often, when he saw an old sailor, to have asked himself what had happened to the friends of his youth or to have let his mind dwell on other mysteries of his seafaring years. Out of these questions grew his volume *John Marr and Other Sailors* which he made ready, with his own improved handwriting, for the printer in the spring of 1888.

Two of the "sailors" in the volume represented the questioner. John Marr himself was introduced by an elaborate prose sketch which described him as having retired to the loneliness of the prairies in southwestern Illinois where he evoked the phantoms of his retrospective musings by trying to recall, in verse, the "merchant-sailors," the "huntsman-whalers," and the "man-of-war's men" whom he had known in the past and for whom he now had that passionate desire for reunion which Melville thought characteristic of "an imaginative heart." The other, in the poem

"Bridegroom Dick," was represented as being "past sixty-five" and quietly sitting with his "old woman" while he let his mind run over his early associates—some of whom were Melville's old officers and friends on the *United States* whereas others included his cousin Guert Gansevoort and the commanders of the *Cumberland* and the *Merrimac* during the battle which had so fascinated him early in the Civil War. It had probably been Melville's intention to include more extensive comments upon various individuals in the form of specific poems or sketches devoted to them, for a partial portrait of Jack Chase appeared among the "sailors" under the title "Jack Roy," and poetic addresses "To the Master of the 'Meteor'" (in the form of a revised version of the lines written and given "To Tom" many years before) and to his old companion Toby Greene (under the name "Ned Bunn") were included among the "Sea-Pieces" which filled out the volume.

But Melville had neither the incentive nor the energy to get out an elaborate volume according to a systematic plan. *John Marr* was a book of scraps. Both the title sketch and "Bridegroom Dick" were introductory to a collection of portraits which were never fully drawn: "Jack Roy" was inadequate if not incomplete, and the only other sailor included, "Tom Deadlight," was portrayed as dying in his hammock while he babbled the "last flutterings of distempered thought" to the measure of a familiar sea-ditty. Yet the prose paragraph and the seven stanzas of verse devoted to Tom Deadlight were probably representative of one of the major interests of Melville's mind at the time he planned the book—the thoughts of sailing men just before they dropped anchor in their last port. Several fragmentary sketches of a morose old man-of-war's man, variously called "Asaph Blood," "A Druid," "Orm," and "Daniel Orme," living apart from his fellows in a sailors' boardinghouse, were probably undertaken for this collection; and so, perhaps, was another which told the story, insomuch as it can be reproduced in its earliest form, of a popular young sailor who was hanged for mutiny and who inspired a deathbed ballad entitled "Billy in the Darbies." Death was very much in Melville's mind as he mused over the phantoms from his past.

He did not strain himself over his books, however, and used only such material as came easily to him. He expanded the published version of "The Admiral of the White" into the longest of his two major "Sea-Pieces" and gave it a new title "The Haglets"; and for the other he used a poem on "The Aeolian Harp" at the Surf Inn on Fire Island. For his "Minor Sea-Pieces" he used some verses, "Crossing the Tropics," from a meditated but apparently unwritten sketch to be called "The Saya-y-Manto," and some others, "The Enviable Isles," from the sketch "Rammon," which hardly belonged to this collection at all. The second of the epigrams or "Pebbles" with which he concluded the volume seems to have been a fragment of some verse intended to accompany the "Daniel Orme" sketch, and the seventh may have been originally connected with the lines on the sea later incorporated in "After the Pleasure Party." Of such fragments of uncompleted work and various short poems—including "The Maldive Shark"—written at various times and revised for publication, he made up the first volume he was able to publish without help and without nervous strain. *John Marr* was done solely for the amusement of its author's leisure.

The first two and a half years of his retirement were not happy but they were not unkind to Melville. Stanwix died alone in a San Francisco hospital, after a long illness, on February 23, 1886; but by this time Herman had become used to death, and his most noticeable reaction to the loss of his wayward son was an increased devotion to Lizzie, who remained grief-stricken and weary for months afterward. For her sixty-fourth birthday, on June 13, he bought for her four books which had been published in the year of their marriage; and it was probably at about this time that he began planning the volume of verse which, according to the date indicated in the original version of the dedication, he evidently hoped to give her soon after their fortieth anniversary. Although he skipped his customary vacation on Fire Island during the summer of 1887, perhaps to work on it in secret while Elizabeth was away, the project did not materialize; but "Bridegroom Dick" (which he completed on December 4), with its affectionate Joan and Darby atmosphere, was a product of the sort of awkward yet real sentiment found in its concluding lines:

> My pipe is smoked out, and the grog runs slack;
> But bowse away, wife, at your blessed Bohea;
> This empty can here must needs solace me—
> Nay, sweetheart, nay; I take that back;
> Dick drinks from your eyes and he finds no lack!

Neither the death of his close friend John C. Hoadley on October 21, 1886, nor that of his other brother-in-law George Griggs on May 8, 1888, made him show signs of bitterness. The years of his preoccupation with his own emotions were over. The writing of *Clarel* had been a genuine turning point in his life.

There were also, during these years, positive consolations for the quiet grief he felt at the loss of his son and friends and at Elizabeth's condition. Although he was "A 'Buried' Author" (according to a headline in the New York *Commercial Advertiser* for January 18, 1886) whose copyrights were expiring and whose publishers were to close out his account with a payment of $50.02 a year later, he was making a few new friends through his books. The newspaper headline was inspired by a poetic tribute paid him by Professor J. W. Henry Canoll before the New York College of Archeology and Aesthetics, and James Billson was continuing to write him from England, sending him copies of the works of James Thomson and a "semi-manuscript" copy of Fitzgerald's translation of the *Rubaiyat*. John W. Barrs also sent him a volume of Thomson "as a small tribute of admiration to Typee and Omoo," and Peter Toft called upon him, at the suggestion of W. Clark Russell, and presented him with water colors of Flamboro' Head (where the *Bonhomme Richard* had met the *Serapis*) and of Redondo Rock in the "Encantadas." Early in 1888 Edmund C. Stedman also wrote to him for a holograph copy of one of his "best known shorter poems" and an engraved portrait to be used in an extra-illustrated copy of his *Poets of America,* and he also asked permission to print extracts from the prose romances and selections from the poems in his *Library of American Literature.*

Melville seems to have been more at ease with his English admirers whom he knew only by correspondence than with the Americans or the English visitors who called on him in person and made him self-conscious by being inquisitive about his South Sea romances. The *Commercial Advertiser,* in a paragraph printed two weeks after his retirement, described him as a man whose "rather heavy, thick-set figure and warm complexion betoken health and vigor"; but he was still as shy as he had been in his young manhood, and his vigor no longer expressed itself in a willingness to talk metaphysics with strangers. Canoll reported that "Though rude Presumption dare not grasp his hand," yet "His palm was friendly," and "his eyes of blue" were "kind"; and Peter Toft later recalled that "though a delightful talker when in the mood, he was abnormal, as most geniuses are, and had to be handled with care." His abnormality, however, seems to have consisted mostly of an unwillingness to talk about his books and in seeming "almost offended" when Toft "inquired so curiously about his falling from the maintopgallant yard of the frigate"—the experience described in *White Jacket* which Toft shrewdly and correctly suspected of being "a tour de force of writing" rather than an actual occurrence.

Yet Melville was cordial to Stedman in sending him an autograph of a selection from *Clarel* which he called a "Ditty of Aristippus" and in giving him permission to print any extracts from his published writings he desired to use. And he was more than cordial in his correspondence with Russell and in his prefatory letter dedicating *John Marr* to him as the man whose recent book, *The Wreck of the Grosvenor,* entitled him to "the naval crown in current literature." There are, in fact, signs of his old loneliness in his relations with Russell—the desire to find a kindred spirit who could speak his own secret language—such as he had shown many years before in his letters to Hawthorne. But the passion approaching desperation which had once marked this desire was no longer present. The author of *John Marr,* unlike the author of *Moby Dick,* was not suffering the self-centering strain of being torn between the need for dollars and the need for philosophy and feeling damned by the one and broiled in hell-fire by the other. "Health and Content," he had decided, were the "most precious things" he knew of "in this world"; and the dollars had come to him, finally, without effort. Elizabeth was well enough off to make his family financially independent, and he himself had inherited $3,019.50 in cash plus a small amount designed for Stanwix from his sister Frances. It was this sum that enabled him to make his last sea voyage—to Bermuda and St. Augustine, Florida, in March, 1888, when he was forced to crawl around on his hands and knees during a rough passage home— and permitted him the luxury of publishing *John Marr* in an edition of only twenty-five copies, only one of which fell into the hands of a reviewer or a critic. He was healthy and had enough money of his own at least to avoid the risk of discontent.

But within the bounds of Melville's quiet old age there was developing a germ of creative excitement. While writing "Bridegroom Dick" he had recalled his cousin "Guert Gan" by name as a hero of Vera Cruz but had been unable to remember him exclusively as a dashing naval officer in a moment of victory. Later on in the poem Guert reappeared as the man of mystery, Tom Tight, who would never tell the story of the young officer who was hung as "an arch-mutineer" in a famed brig-o'-war; and the mutiny on the *Somers* became one of the most teasing phantoms from the past which had appeared in his mind. At the time, however, the most interesting part of the story to Melville seems to have been that of the legendary young sailor, Elisha Small, who was so popular among the crew of the *Somers* and who had fascinated the fleet by exclaiming "God bless the flag!" as he was hanged from the yardarm. He was the original of the "Billy in the Darbies" whose death—rather than the behavior of Guert Gansevoort—was the real mystery to the common sailors who could not believe that he merited hanging. Melville's tentative sketch of Daniel Orme (which he annotated as "omitted of Billy Budd") may have represented his original effort to explain the mystery by using the sort of hypothetical character who could have known the inside truth about the mutiny for which Small was hanged.

Yet it cannot be certain that Melville hoped to get either sketch into *John Marr.* If he did, circumstances changed the focus of his interest before the book was ready for the printer. For the issue of the *American Magazine* for June, 1888, carried an article by Lieutenant H. D. Smith on "The Mutiny on the Somers" which made the whole affair no longer a phantom from Melville's own past but a matter of public interest. The article paid practically no attention to Elisha Small but was concerned primarily with the action of Captain Mackenzie and Lieutenant Gansevoort (as the presiding officer of the court-martial) in hanging Philip Spencer, the son of the secretary of war. Melville was certainly aware of the family's conviction that Guert's action "was *approved* of God," and he had almost as certainly read Thurlow Weed's recently published *Autobiography* in which that old friend of his family recorded his meeting with Midshipman Henry Gansevoort and Henry's report on Guert's only known private statement concerning the case. The inside story and the historical record were at odds in their implications concerning the puzzling actions of Lieutenant Gansevoort and presumably those of Captain Mackenzie, and Melville's interest was diverted from the personality of Elisha Small to the problem of reconciling the conflicting implications. How could a man in a judicial position be held morally free from guilt while condemning to death another human being who was known to be morally innocent of wrongdoing? The problem offered the material for a short novel, rather than for a sketch or a series of sketches, and on November 16, 1888, Melville formally began to write it.

He seems to have fallen easily into the method of composition which he had practiced in his more youthful days—that of telling his story first with the intention of amplifying it, later, with discursive insertions which would give it greater body and significance. At any rate, he made fairly efficient progress, despite the trouble with his eyes which developed in December and the death of his sister Helen on the fourteenth of that month; and on March 2, 1889, he was able to begin the revision. His story was not directly about the *Somers* affair at all. Instead, he gave it the background of an English vessel in time of war, shortly after the outbreak of disaffection in the fleet at Spithead on April 15, 1797, and the mutiny at the Nore on May 20. Neither the still-newsworthy midshipman, Philip Spencer, nor the acting boatswain's mate, Samuel Cromwell, appeared in the narrative; and the lieutenant who presided over the court-martial and allowed his scruples to be overruled by the captain sank insignificantly into the background. But the essential story remained the same. Billy Budd wore the mantle of innocence with which scuttle-butt gossip in the American fleet had clothed the popular figure of Elisha Small; and Captain Vere, although filling the historical role of Mackenzie, had him hanged with the same troubled but conscientious devotion to duty which family tradition attributed to Guert Gansevoort. It was, as Melville called it, "an inside narrative" which bore a close hypothetical relationship to the affair on the *Somers*.

To create his hypothetical "inside narrative" Melville, at first, drew heavily upon his own experiences in the Navy as he had transmuted them into *White Jacket*. He attributed to his hero, Billy, his own horror at the practice of flogging, his own meticulous efforts to avoid so much as a reprimand, and his own imagined desperation at the prospect of unjust punishment. He also gave a prominent place in his story to the two great sources of mental disturbance he found in his period of service: a vicious master-at-arms who had the unassailable power of a privileged informer, and the perpetual threat of the severe articles of war under which the ship was ruled. These, in fact, provided him with his solution to the puzzle he had undertaken to solve. Drawing freely upon his memory of John C. Turner of the *United States* as he had represented him as the character "Bland" in *White Jacket,* he made the master-at-arms a major character in his story—a sort of Iago, villainous by nature and driven to the practice of his particular dark design by envy of the handsome appearance and frank nature of Billy Budd. John Claggart, as he was called in the tale, was represented as falsely accusing Billy of fomenting mutiny; and Billy, feeling the desperation Melville had once imagined he might feel under some such circumstances, struck him dead in his spasmodic inability to answer the accusation. Captain Vere, although fully aware of the situation, was caught between the overt act he had witnessed and the discipline required by the articles of war he was sworn to enforce. He was obliged to compel the court-martial to sentence Billy to death. And Billy, dumbly aware of the good will and even love which existed beneath the surface of the captain's necessity, was hanged with the exclamation "God bless Captain Vere!" on his lips.

Had Melville told such a straight story as this forty years before, at the time he wrote *White Jacket,* he would have placed all the blame for its injustice upon the inhumanity of martial law and would probably have found it difficult if not impossible to defend his cousin and the commander of the *Somers* (who had no overt act to simplify their legal position) for not rising to some higher ideal of justice. But long before 1889 he had accepted the bitter truth of *Pierre* and had reached the understanding of human complexity he had displayed in *Clarel*. A naïve attempt to exercise absolute moral justice might cause more general evil than it would do particular good. Human beings are what they are, and the object of wisdom is not to change but to understand them. His youthful mind could never have appreciated the weight he could now perceive in Captain Mackenzie's argument (as reported by Thurlow Weed) "that there would be no security for the lives of officers or protection to commerce if an example was not made in a case so flagrant as this." As an old man, he could understand Guert Gansevoort's years of tight-lipped suffering as that of a man who had knowingly violated his individual moral impulse in obedience to a moral code required by the general welfare of society. Captain Vere, like Captain Mackenzie, was guided by his perception of the social dangers of listening to the dictates of "the heart"; and, like Lieutenant Gansevoort, he suffered for his wisdom afterward.

When Melville made up a rough folder to contain the "short novel pieces" which were to be inserted into the straight narrative of *Billy Budd,* he probably intended to do little more than add to its length by his customary insertions of factual material, emphasize the pressure placed upon Captain Vere by the low state of morale in the British fleet, and perhaps amplify his characterization of John Claggart. His procedure was his normal one of collecting the books from which he could extract the matter he needed: William James's *The Naval History of Great Britain,* Robert Southey's *Life of Nelson,* Douglas Jerrold's drama on the *Mutiny at the Nore* (which he borrowed from the New York Society Library as late as May 31, 1890), and perhaps others. But, as in the case of *Moby Dick,* something happened which impelled him to do more than piece and splice his short story into a long one. For the June, 1889, issue of the *Cosmopolitan Magazine,* which appeared less than three months after Melville began the revision and expansion of his story, began a new public account of the *Somers* affair aggressively entitled "The Murder of Philip Spencer." Through three monthly installments this new account, by "Gail Hamilton," glorified Spencer and damned Captain Mackenzie while incidentally making Guert Gansevoort's informant, a purser's steward, rather than Guert himself the villain of the drama. How much attention Melville paid to it is uncertain, but it may have called forth the unplanned additions to the novel which helped drag out its revision until April 19, 1891.

The most striking of these additions was the elaboration of Captain Vere's personality until he, rather than Billy Budd, almost became the central figure of the story. In order to make clear that he acted from wisdom rather than prejudice, Melville turned him into a well-read, philosophical individual who was noticeably different from the ordinary naval officer. The villainy of the informer Claggart, too, required greater emphasis; and in his revision Melville descended further into the "dark labyrinth" of Claggart's "natural depravity" than he had been willing to go at first. Other incidental changes—including a good many "dark sayings," as Melville called them, which deepened the speculative tone of the narrative—added "significances" to the book.

In its final form, *Billy Budd* dealt with problems more profound than those involved in telling a hypothetical "inside story" of the *Somers* affair. In "this incomprehensible world of ours," where innocence and infamy naturally exist side by side and where spiritual depravity is not incompatible with fair repute, the philosophy with which Melville consoled himself at the end of *Clarel* would not work. A responsible man could not afford simply to trust his "heart." He had to accept infamy, discount innocence, and conquer his own best and most natural impulses, sometimes, in order to do that which was right. If Melville's long search for a philosophy came to an end in his representation of Captain Vere, it ended with a victory neither for the spontaneous impulses of the "heart" nor for the cold wisdom of the "head." Good will and good sense must modify each other in order to produce good action. When the two seemed incompatible, the resulting compromise might be neither satisfactory nor comfortable—but it was the best thing possible "in this incomprehensible world."

II

If the final version of *Billy Budd* came slowly into being—pinned and pasted together, as it was, in order to save the labor of copying—its slowness was not a reflection of the author's mental processes. Melville had grown old, but his mind remained alert and vigorous, and he had more projects in his head than he had bodily energy to carry out. On June 11, 1888, he had made his will, leaving all his worldly possessions and the eventual disposition of them to Elizabeth; and he was anxious to dispose of his unfinished literary business during the few years that remained to him. "After twenty years nearly, as an outdoor Custom House officer, I have latterly come into the possession of unobstructed leisure," he wrote Archibald MacMechan on December 5, 1889, in apology for not providing him with the "particulars" of his life and literary methods, "but only just as, in the course of nature, my vigor sensibly declines. What little of it is left I husband for certain matters as yet incomplete, and which indeed, may never be completed." *Billy Budd* was only one of such "matters," and Melville was not devoting his time or his thoughts entirely to it.

Another of these was the mixture of prose and verse related to the "Frescoes of Travel" he had projected more than thirty years before. One of the major pieces of verse in it, "Naples in the Time of Bomba," may in fact have been partially composed many years earlier. For it dealt with the things Melville had seen and the impressions he had received while on his own visit to Naples during the reign of King Bomba, from February 19 to 21, 1857, and was written in the octosyllabic verse he used for *Clarel*.

Yet it was revised and given a reminiscent tone later, when he could look back on the time of Garibaldi and after "the flower of flowers," the rose, had come to have a symbolic meaning to him. Some traces of his earlier antagonism toward formalized religion, however, remained in the poem—curiously out of place among his later works, although he did cross out of the version of the manuscript a supercilious line referring to "The god, or host accounted such" in his description of a religious procession.

The framework for this particular project was undoubtedly conceived in the late 'seventies when the death of Charles Sumner, the mistakes of Reconstruction, the political problems of President Grant, and his own resentment of the new Grand Army of the Republic were still fairly fresh in Melville's mind. And it may have been inspired by the renewal of his frequent visits with Evert Duyckinck, shortly before the latter's death, when the two old friends looked back upon the days when "the Knights of the Round Table" gathered in the basement of No. 20 Clinton Place and talked of old books and faraway lands over their punch and cigars. For the scheme evidently called for a series of poetic tales and conversations by a group of gentlemen in "the Burgundy Club"—a "small group of the convivially elect" whose presiding genius and vaporous inspiration was "the Marquis de Grandvin" and whose common interest was in finding relief from "the never-ending daily news." The story of "Naples in the Time of Bomba" was supposedly told by Major Jack Gentian and versified by one of his admirers (who used an "earlier rendering" of the tale and "interspersed ballads and ditties"). Genial Jack, the elderly and well-traveled "Dean of the Burgundians," was one of Melville's favorite characters. Like Ungar in *Clarel,* he was a veteran of the Civil War, affected by the conflict, and the spokesman for his creator's opinions. Yet he had none of Ungar's bitterness. His discourse was "frolic, pathetic, indignant, philosophic" but, throughout, "catholic and humane." Melville could not leave him alone. He sketched him and revised and elaborated his sketches more often than he did those of Captain Vere, John Claggart, and Daniel Orme; and this particular literary project may have become one of those never to be completed primarily because Melville could not forget Jack long enough to characterize the other members of the club.

He did, however, produce a sketch of the marquis and attach it to the introductory poem, "At the Hostelry," in which the marquis evoked the shades of dead artists for "an inconclusive debate as to the exact import" of the current artistic term "picturesque." Evidently written after the original version of "Naples in the Time of Bomba" and in a more flexible variety of the same verse, it nevertheless contains some evidence of having been completed before the death of Garibaldi in 1882. In its introduction and "sequel" it is Melville's passing comment upon what Mark Twain called "the Gilded Age" and Walt Whitman denounced in "Democratic Vistas." But in greater part it represents the lifelong interest in painting which Melville had cultivated in New York and pursued through the galleries of London, Paris, Belgium, Germany, and Italy. No less than twenty-two painters came to life for the discussion—Jan Steen, Fra Lippo Lippi, Spagnoletto, Swanevelt, Claude, Franz Hals, Van Dyck, Tintoretto, Adriaen Brouwer, Carlo Dolce, Teniers, Rembrandt, Van der Velde, Gerard Douw, Paola Veronese, Watteau, Velasquez, Salvator Rosa, Poussin, Dürer, Fra Angelico, Leonardo, and perhaps Caravaggio—and a number of others were alluded to for illustration. Into some five hundred casual lines Melville crowded the literary result of one of his major hobbies, one which had caused him to read books on art, study paintings, and, especially, it would seem, meditate the self-portraits of the artists. Whether such remarkable men could ever be born again into the new age of the commonplace he did not know. Nor did he greatly care. His own mind had already become more at home in the past.

As in the case of *John Marr and Other Sailors,* Melville was able to complete, according to design, only two pieces for the projected volume. A prose sketch including a few lines of verse, called "Under the Rose" and purporting to be "an extract from an old MS. entitled 'Travels in Persia by a servant of My Lord the Ambassador,' " may have been intended to go with the two; and "Rip Van Winkle's Lilac," in form and in one cross allusion, was related to the Jack Gentian sketch and story. They were both probably written during the late 'eighties, and neither quite fitted into the basic plan. The tentative title page which he drew up for the unpublished book (significantly, to be called *Parthenope*) merely called for "An afternoon in Naples In the time of Bomba: with an Introduction merging into A Symposium of Old Masters at Delmonico's." Both this and another title page which identified the Introduction of "Salutatory" as "Touching New Italy and Old Romance" showed that, in his last years, Melville realized that one of his earliest poetic projects was one which would "never be completed."

He was more persistent in his devotion to the volume for Elizabeth which he had planned some years before. On the eve of St. Valentine's day, 1890, he went through his collection of poems, selected some twenty-six of them, and drew up a Table of Contents for a volume to be called *As They Fell.* Half of them were his rose poems. The other thirteen, grouped under the heading "Weeds and Wildings," were the miscellaneous products of various times and occasions. "Lonie," which was later disguised by Elizabeth and called "Shadow at the Feast," apparently referred to a melancholy family guest for Christmas dinner in 1847. "The Cuban

Pirate" and "Madcaps" probably dated from the time his daughters were children at Arrowhead, and "The Old Shipmaster and his Crazy Barn" may have been an even earlier relic of his trip across Cape Cod with Judge Shaw. "Iris" was later dated by Elizabeth as having been composed in 1874. And the "Inscription for Rip Van Winkle" was perhaps a recent composition. On March 23, according to a note on the folder, he also looked over his collection of unused travel poems. A good many of these, perhaps, were not finished to his satisfaction. But before he could do very much with them he suffered his second attack of erysipelas, in April, which, according to his wife's memoir, "weakened him greatly"; and by the time he had more or less recovered in the latter part of May his mind had returned to *Billy Budd*.

For a while during the middle of the summer he was out of town— possibly at Fire Island, where he had gone in July, 1888, or at Jefferson, for Elizabeth had succeeded in getting him both to shore and to the mountains in 1889—but he made his escape and got back to the comforts of home by August 10. There he looked after his roses and cultivated his slowly blossoming literary enterprises. Much of his time must have been spent as his eldest granddaughter remembered him, sitting on the narrow, iron-trimmed porch which ran across the back of the house, smoking his pipe with his cane at hand and looking down into the garden. Little Eleanor also remembered their walks in Central Park and his calls of mock warning, "Look out, or the 'cop' may catch you!" as she abandoned the paths and gaily ran down the hills. In the autumn and early winter of 1890 Melville's daily tramps through the Fort George district of the park became a matter of public notice and a subject of worry for Elizabeth when he persisted in taking them in cold weather despite "a bad cough." Shortly after Christmas "he walked for three-quarters of a mile in bitter cold air," suffered "a turn of dizziness or vertigo in the night," and experienced an immediate loss of strength "which the Doctor feared might eventuate in a serious way." But he gradually recovered, and although by January 8, 1891, he had not gone out or even downstairs, he had every prospect of becoming as well as ever. From that time on, however, he probably spent more time than before at his great mahogany desk or at the wide table in the alcove, warmed by the fire in his own narrow grate.

The preceding year had been generous to the Melvilles in a material sense. The will of Elizabeth's aunt, Martha B. Marett, had at last been probated in October, 1889, and she had received $2,471.45 from her bequest. In the meantime, Mrs. Marett's daughter, Mrs. Ellen Gifford, had died, leaving $15,000.00 to Elizabeth, $8,000.00 to Herman, and $3,000.00 to each of the children, plus a special bequest of $2,000.00 to

Fanny. Stanwix' inheritance was divided equally between his parents, according to an agreement signed March 13, 1890, two weeks after the decree had been passed by the probate court and the executors had signified their intention to begin paying the legacies. A year before, Herman had received $1,123.79 from the sale of the house and farm in Gansevoort, and substantial sums, to the total of $33,516.67, were being paid Elizabeth from her share in the residual bequest of her brother Lem. Her affairs continued to be managed by Samuel Shaw in Boston, and she apparently took care of the family's living expenses out of her income. But Herman could easily afford to pay his share in improving the family lot in the Albany Cemetery and indulge his wish to publish another volume of poems. He had seven government bonds, worth sixteen per cent more than their face value of a thousand dollars each, and nearly five thousand dollars cash in the bank—several thousand more than his total earnings during all his painful years of writing and lecturing. It was the final irony of his life but not the sort that would make him unhappy.

The volume of poems which Melville really did prepare for the press in the spring of 1891 was made ready with the assistance of Elizabeth, who was glad enough to see him occupied at his desk during the cold weather and the raw days which followed. It was called *Timoleon* and consisted of forty-two poems, some new and some old, but all of them representative of their author's old age in the sense that they were all thoughtfully edited and, if necessary, retouched by the color of Melville's autumnal meditations. Just how he ripened the "Fruit of Travel Long Ago," which made up nearly half the volume, cannot be always determined. For his travel pieces were probably considerably rewritten after they were "looked over" in March, 1890, and the six "rejected" poems left in the folder may be the only ones which have survived in something like their original form. If the rejected lines "Suggested by the Ruins of a Mountain-Temple in Arcadia" actually formed the basis for "The Ravaged Villa," they were changed into a poem so entirely different that Melville was justified in not including the published poem among the products of his Mediterranean journey. On the other hand, he had even less justification in putting the "Disinterment of Hermes" in that section, because it could hardly have been written before 1877, when the disinterment took place. Yet there is some sort of coherence in the volume.

How it was achieved may perhaps be suggested by one illustration of what happened to his poem on the appearance of the Parthenon (as he first saw it from the road between Piraeus and Athens on the cold moonlit night of February 8, 1858) which he published under the title "The Apparition." Originally he had compared it with the suspended Cross which converted the emperor Constantine and had written:

With kindred power, appealing down,
Miraculous human Fane!
You strike with awe the cynic heart,
Convert it from disdain.

But, looking back over his life in his old age, he realized that he had not been converted from cynicism or disdain by anything that had happened during his trip, regardless of what he might have thought at the time or soon afterward. Accordingly, he changed the stanza to read:

With other power appealing down,
Trophy of Adam's best!
If cynic minds you scarce convert,
You try them, shake them, or molest.

One of the things he did in this volume of poems was partially to reconstruct his life in the light of his retrospective afterthoughts.

Such a reconstruction, unconsciously pursued, represents a normal process of memory. But Melville, as this deliberate revision shows, was aware of just what he was doing; and the characteristic quality of his last book resulted from a blend of the whimsicality shown in his rose poems and the serious speculations of *Billy Budd*. He let his mind rove backward over his life, recreating it under the influence of literary suggestions or of his settled emotions, and usually attached the poetic outcome to some other personality—partially to disguise the autobiographical implications and partially in acknowledgment of the fact that he was really dealing in fictions. "Shelley's Vision," for example, is somewhat applicable to the author of "Adonais," and the language he used for the poem was gathered out of his recollection of Shelley's. But it was less an interpretation of another writer than it was a reflection of Melville's own desire to believe that he had acquired calm self-reverence by reaction to contempt. "C——'s Lament" seems to have been his effort to find a kindred spirit in the author of the "Ode to Dejection"; and "Lamia's Song," associated with Keats by its title, implied that he had nobly resisted the temptation to gain "more than a wreath" by taking a pleasant "downward way" from the heights of his art. The ambiguity of these and other such poems is rather clearly indicated by the manuscripts, which show the author's fumbling efforts to attach them to an appropriate personality: he thought of Anacreon and Simonides before attributing the "Lament" to Coleridge; he assigned the meditation "In a Garret" to Schiller before finally deciding to print it simply in the first person; and he tentatively made the seemingly confessional "Lone Founts" the "counsels" of Giordano Bruno. Two similar poems, dealing with the flame and the vanity of literary aspiration, which he did not include in the volume, were first linked with Tasso before they were called "Camoëns" and "Camoëns in the Hospital." For years Melville had been reading and marking in the books of other writers thoughts which he was willing to accept as his own. Now, in his last book, he was reversing the process and attributing to other writers the fancies with which he amused his retrospective old age.

This quality of speculative retrospection pervades both of the long poems included in *Timoleon*. The latest of these, the title poem itself, was actually inspired by Balzac's *The Two Brothers* after Melville had acquired the book in an edition of 1887 and checked the passage describing the mother's marked preference for the flashy older son over his unspectacular and often unkempt younger brother. The situation attracted Melville's attention because it was precisely the situation which had existed in his own family for years while he played an unappreciated second fiddle to the brilliant Gansevoort. In recalling it as the subject matter for a poem, however, he transferred it to Plutarch's story of Timoleon and Timophanes, representing the latter as the "pride" and "pet" of a doting and ambitious mother who "made the junior feel his place" and "subserve the senior" but "love him, too." The tragic story of the Corinthian brothers, of course, offered no parallel to Melville's life; but the family relationship did, and so did Timoleon's slow period of self-justification during which he acquired an indifference to the public "fame" (as it was in the original manuscript) or "justice" which came to him after being in such "long arrears." In writing this poem, Melville was licking an old wound and exhibiting its scar, even as he transferred it to another man's soul and insisted that it was entirely healed. The crown of "laurel twined with thorn" which he placed upon his hero was, in his fancy, taken from his own head.

He may have been tending another wound in "After the Pleasure Party," which has no superficial autobiographical significance at all. For the poem deals with such a woman as Maria Mitchell, whom he had met on Nantucket in 1852—a maiden dedicated to Urania but who was imagined as having fallen victim to the god of physical love and was alternately experiencing the pangs of jealousy, resentment against the demands of sex, and inclinations to plunge like Sappho from a cliff, become a cloistered follower of the Christian Virgin Mary, or remain a pagan but more aggressive follower of the "armed Virgin, less benign." Yet Melville, while looking backward over his own life, could hardly have avoided asking himself whether his literary fate would not have been different had he not been forced to meet the responsibilities of a wife and family. Could not his partial failure as a writer be attributed to that "Cosmic jest or Anarch blunder" which made a "human integral" only half whole when it was not linked with a person of the opposite sex? The question could be dramatically asked through the person of a woman but it could not be seriously raised with direct reference to his own life. Melville knew himself. He did not doubt his devotion to Elizabeth and his family (although he sometimes seems to have wondered whether his grandchildren would feel any devotion to him) and he had long ago decided that a person could be only what he was. Neither passionate resistance nor the inspiration of inanimate Art could stand against the assaults of the god of love, whose vindictiveness when wronged was more to be feared than his arrows. Melville may have questioned his life, but he was reasonably content with it.

Yet his wise contentment was not entirely free from illusion. The most consistent theme running through the poems in *Timoleon* was that of devotion to "Art"—often with the implication that the devotion required and received a voluntary sacrifice of worldly success. Melville was not so complacent as to claim, even by implication, that he could have gained and held a great popular reputation had he chosen to do so; but he does seem to have convinced himself that he had pursued "Art" with all the constancy which the "ancient brutal claim" of the material world permitted a husband and a father. Such constant devotion involved a struggle which left its mark upon a man, and Melville may have looked particularly back to the lonely winter of his struggle with *Moby Dick* when, nearly forty years later, he wrote and revised and finished the little poem he called "Art":

> In placid hours well-pleased we dream
> Of many a brave unbodied scheme.
> But form to lend, pulsed life create,
> What unlike things must meet and mate:
> A flame to melt—a wind to freeze;
> Sad patience—joyous energies;
> Humility—yet pride and scorn;
> Instinct and study; love and hate;
> Audacity—reverence. These must mate,
> And fuse with Jacob's mystic heart,
> To wrestle with the angel—Art.

Few of his works were actually the products of such a struggle. But the belief that he had wrestled long and valiantly was a major consolation to a man who professed to find the peace of God in a pipe of tobacco, who anticipated an early entrance into a personal Nirvana, and who yet had a normal longing for some sort of claim to immortality.

The title of *Timoleon* was registered for copyright on May 15, 1891, and in June he affectionately inscribed a copy to Elizabeth, "without whose assistance both manual and literary" the volume "could not have passed through the press." It was dedicated to Elihu Vedder, the artist whose idealized painting of a slave had inspired one of the poems in *Battle-Pieces* twenty-five years before, and was privately published like *John Marr* in an edition of only twenty-five copies. While Elizabeth was preparing the printers' copy, Herman was completing his final draft of *Billy Budd.* He was "tolerably well but not strong" that spring and probably spent a good deal of his time meditating the philosophy of Schopenhauer, whose *Counsels and Maxims* he had discovered in the New York Society Library in February and whose *Studies in Pessimism* and *The Wisdom of Life* he added to his own library later in the year. He was reconciled to leaving the world as foolish and as wicked as he had found it upon his arrival; and, in the hope of belonging to posterity, he was content to be an alien to his contemporaries. Schopenhauer provided as satisfying a substance for meditation as he could have found during the last months of his life.

But he had one more job to do. He had not been alien to Elizabeth, and the volume of poems specifically designed for her had not yet been put together as he wanted it to be. At some time after *Timoleon* had gone to press he once again went through his collection of manuscripts and began a new arrangement of them. On this occasion his mind dwelt more upon the past than it had done when he drew up his tentative Table of Contents the year before: his rose poems were relegated to the end of the collection, a considerable number of poems related to the Arrowhead period were added, and the title became "Weeds and Wildings, with a Rose or Two." Two of the poems he had been thinking of including went back into his collection of manuscripts. Three or four others disappeared entirely and may just possibly have been among those "children" of his "happier prime" which, according to an unpublished poem called "Immolated," he "saved" by burning. The additions brought the total number in the proposed volume up to forty, and most of these, with the exception of the combined prose and verse sketch, "Rip Van Winkle's Lilac," were closely associated with Arrowhead and were given a primary position in the arrangement. Although some of these seem to have been written while Melville still lived in the country, some may have been the products of his retrospective mood, and it is impossible to date most of them with any degree of certainty. It is significant, however, that in the manuscript dedication of the volume he changed his reference to the entire collection from "children of quite another late autumnal aftermath" to "thriftless children of quite another and yet spontaneous after-growth"; and, since most of the earliest could easily have been written within some six years after Herman sold the "brindled heifer" to which he also referred in the dedication, his revised allusion could be applicable to verses composed long before his "autumnal aftermath." But whenever they were written, they were probably, like the travel pieces in *Timoleon,* revised before being copied in their final form and thus were true offerings of the poet's "terminating period."

He had no evident desire to change the spirit of the dedication to Lizzie —or, as he disguised her in anticipation of the public display of his sentiments, "Winnefred" and "Winnie." Once he had thought of wishing her "in this life the after-roses of Paestum, and in the Gardens to come the Eternal ones of St. Elizabeth of Hungary." But this feeling was too genuine to be memorialized in such rhetoric. The common red clover— sweet, abundant, persistent, and useful—was the best symbol of their relationship he had been able to find. Annually he had reminded her of the four-leaf clover he had found in the morning of their wedding day, and the memories he most liked to dwell upon were of their first years among the clover fields of Arrowhead. There he had once rescued a handful of late blossoms from an early fall snow flurry, and Elizabeth had spontaneously called the melting flakes "tears of the happy." The author of *Moby Dick, Pierre, The Confidence Man,* and *Clarel* cherished the phrase, in the privacy of his own mind, for four decades; and when he prepared his last book he did so with the knowledge that Lizzie would find in it evidences of a "melting mood" and with the wish that she would be reminded of her "tears of the happy."

Melville brought the dedication of *Weeds and Wildings* up to date by inserting "four years" into his reference to "a certain bridal month, now four years more than four times ten years ago"; but he was not able to see it through to publication. Elizabeth and Bessie had planned to take him to Fire Island in June, despite his impatience with summer resorts, because he was "not well enough to be left alone." His illness, however, proved more serious than Elizabeth's "rose cold." In July he was placed in the regular charge of a physician, who diagnosed his trouble as an enlargement of the heart, and Elizabeth remained in New York to care for him.

Shortly after midnight, during the first hour of September 28, 1891, the final attack came, and he was dead.

III

At the time of his death, Melville was certainly unknown to the sort of fame which he had called "manufactured to order" in the "almost innumerable journals that enlighten our millions." Arthur Stedman wrote well-informed notices of his death and funeral for the New York *Daily Tribune* and the *World,* and so did J. E. A. Smith for the Pittsfield *Evening Journal.* But when the New York *Times* felt called upon to editorialize his passing, the writer who undertook the duty called him "Henry" Melville; and, although the mistake was recognized and everything except the initial "H" was blurred, the proofreader seems to have been unable to recall his Christian name.

Among the people who read books for enjoyment rather than for conversation, however, he was not forgotten. Some fifty-six new editions and reissues of his various books had appeared in America and England during his lifetime, and four of his prose works were still in print. Only his poems and the two volumes of prose whose plates had been withheld from the sale of Dix and Edwards' effects had failed to achieve at least a second edition. In his later years, when his publishers were losing their vested interest in his copyrights and his position in the public domain was undefined, the printing of his books ceased—to some extent as a courtesy to the author, who refused to overrule Murray's objection to a new English edition of *Typee* and who was helping prepare a new American edition of his romances himself. Arthur Stedman, who had persuaded Melville to help him edit *Typee, Omoo, Moby Dick,* and *White Jacket,* experienced some difficulty getting them published in 1892; but when they did make an appearance, they found a market, and a total of forty-four editions of those four books appeared in America and in England between the time of their author's death at the age of seventy-two and the centennial of his birth in 1919. He lacked renown but not readers.

Some of his readers were of a sort that might make an author famous, and signs of their interest were visible before his death. In the South Seas, John La Farge, Henry Adams, Robert Louis Stevenson, and Charles W. Stoddard were consciously following in Melville's footsteps and mentioning him often in their private correspondence. In England, Billson, Russell, and Barrs were continuing to write to him; and new enthusiasts were appearing in the persons of Henry S. Salt, William Morris, Edward Carpenter, and various others. Russell had dedicated *An Ocean Tragedy* to "the Author of 'Typee,' 'Omoo,' 'Moby-Dick,' 'Redburn,' and other

productions which top the list of sea literature in the English tongue";
and a year later, in 1890, young Havelock Ellis wrote him in connection with an investigation he was making "into the ancestry of distinguished English and American poets and imaginative writers." In
Boston, a columnist for the *Post* in 1889 wanted to see Melville's biography
in the American Men of Letters series and in 1890 described "his best
work" as being "unsurpassed in its way in English literature." Edmund
C. Stedman included one of his stories and three of his poems in the
monumental *Library of American Literature,* and the Harpers began to
train a new generation of readers to appreciate his work by introducing
selections from *Moby Dick* into the new Fifth Reader they published
in September, 1889. Melville did not have the fame, as the columnist
for the *Post* was careful to point out, that he would possess had he been
a Bostonian rather than a New Yorker with the same talents. But a
literary man with a small group of genuine admirers among the younger
writers, an important place in the two major literary anthologies (Duyckinck's and Stedman's) of his century, and a position in the public
school textbooks of an aggressive publisher was in little danger of being
overlooked by posterity.

Yet his achievement remained undefined by either biographer or
critic. Arthur Stedman, who admired him as a composer of South Sea
romances, was anxious to write his biography soon after his death. But
Elizabeth had promised the privilege to J. E. A. Smith, who wanted to
expand his biographical articles into a personal study of a Berkshire
literary character comparable to Oliver Wendell Holmes, whom he had
memorialized in a *Poet of the Hills.* While she protected the right of her
husband's old friend to carry out a project she feared he was too infirm to
complete, Stedman's enthusiasm faded; and the nearest approach to a
biography by anyone who had known Melville in the flesh was a posthumous collection of Smith's articles, which Elizabeth had printed in a small
pamphlet in 1897 "for the family and a few near friends." Five years later,
another potential biographer appeared in the person of Frank Jewett
Mather, Jr. But he, like Stedman, approached the subject as an unhurried
labor of love and did not become active in collecting materials until Elizabeth's death in 1906 made him fear that the necessary documents would
be lost. At his insistence, exercised in part through E. C. Stedman, Bessie
began to gather letters from her father's friends; and a formal "life and
letters" appeared to be under way.

Had Mather succeeded in carrying out his tentative plans, the Herman
Melville who would have been placed on record would have been a different person from the mysterious individual who was to capture the
imagination of a later generation. Probably he would have been the sort

of man James Billson knew through his books and letters—a romancer and a humorist, and the type of good companion who could enjoy paradise with Robert Louis Stevenson and Jean Paul Richter. In later years, Mather was to remember that he had thought of his subject as a great tragic figure; but, at the time, he evidently could give him so few claims to greatness that the Boston publishers who specialized in American authors could not be persuaded that Herman Melville was worth an investment of the seven hundred dollars which a formal biography would require. After the death of Bessie, a year later than her mother, oblivion for Herman seemed inevitable: the collection of biographical documents ceased, and those already in existence began to disappear like sibylline leaves in the several bonfires which still warm the imaginations of seekers after the real man who gradually became lost in a mass of speculation and rumor.

When Melville was finally revived in a number of articles published during the centennial year of his birth, he had become almost as inaccessible, biographically, as a literary figure of the seventeenth century. His books seemed to be the major sources of information about him, and people could read them as they would. Some readers accepted their autobiographical implications with an unquestioning literalness which would have put new life in John Murray's Home and Colonial Library and made Melville a prosperous man had it been characteristic of his earlier readers. To these members of a later generation Melville possessed all the romantic desperation he attributed to the characters in his books, and Fayaway became a more important figure in his life than Elizabeth. It was young Melville as a Byronic hero, the wandering outlaw of his own dark mind, who caught the fancy of the nineteen-twenties; and in his maturity he was supposed to have concealed his bitterness behind his big black beard, through which he muttered his true confessions to a more sophisticated posterity.

Few readers could agree concerning the substance of his confessions, but, during the period between two world wars, practically all his admirers assumed that he was a social rebel. Usually they created in his name an image of what they themselves wanted to be. And *Moby Dick* became their major book of revelations. To the English novelist who longed to lose himself in a Freudian id, the white whale became the symbol of irrational blood consciousness which the ego eternally defied in vain. To the college professor who fancied himself an intellectual radical, Moby Dick represented all property and all privilege which could be defied to admiration but without effect. To the ingenious Swedenborgian, looking for precise parallels between the spiritual world and its material counterpart, the whale was Fate and Captain Ahab was Free Will—and

Ahab was given a whalebone leg as an expression of Melville's belief that the Will was limited by Fate. To list all the symbolic and psychological interpretations of *Moby Dick* would be to call the roll of most of the bugbears haunting the minds of modern intellectuals. The strange Herman Melville who was used to raise these ghosts in print was a medium of revolt against almost everything from fundamentalist religion to society's intolerance of sexual abnormality. The Stoicism in which the man himself took such pride was dissolved in a pool of fantasy in which Narcissus can see himself as in a glass—darkly.

Critics whose impulse has been to worship Art have found in Melville's works a challenge to their ceremonial ingenuity in rationalizing impressions. So satisfactory has been his reflection of their subtleties that typographical errors in cheap editions of his books and mistranscriptions of his difficult handwriting have inspired them to intellectual gyrations of ecstasy. The omission of a comma in modern versions of a sentence addressed to Bulkington in *Moby Dick* has transformed that character from one of Melville's forgotten men into one of his most "significant" heroes. The error which changed a "coiled fish of the sea" into a "soiled fish" in some editions of *White Jacket* has been the basis for a lyrical tribute to the author's unique genius in imagery. The probable misreading of Melville's original spelling of the word "visible" as a reference to "usable truth" in a letter to Hawthorne has provoked discourses on the "usable truth" of both men and inspired a meditation on the "usable past." And an entire book has grown out of a poet's mistranscription of his own correct copy of an annotation in one of Melville's volumes of Shakespearean tragedies. Shakespeare himself has hardly cast his divinity more subtly over all his works in all their manifestations, and only the most rabid of Baconians, in fact, can afford to regard a good Melvillian with anything but awe.

The pool seems to be inexhaustible. As the reflections of one critical group drain off, the waters, without a disturbing ripple, give forth those of another. If Melville appeared to be a type of rebel after the first World War, he smoothly turned into an emblem of the search for security after the second. The young man of the early 'thirties who could write that at the age of seventy Melville's "attitude toward God was still unfavorable" has been replaced by another of the late 'forties who writes that if modern liberalism "has the necessary will to survive, it must come to terms with Herman Melville." The youthful author of *Moby Dick* has become "one of our fathers" who must be sought out as he is supposed to have sought his own father—or, depending upon the personality of the critic, mother —for sanctuary from a hostile world. The author created in their own image by the rebels of one decade has been replaced by an embodiment of the troubles and worries of a new generation. The spirit of Lucifer has been subdued and sent winging its anxious way toward Abraham's bosom.

Melville himself wrote at the end of *Clarel* that the illusions of life were so many and so strange that death itself might prove unreal at the last and Stoics be astounded into heaven. Whether his own Stoicism would have been proof against the illusions through which he has passed in achieving his current renown is uncertain. Careless as he professed to be about literary fame in his later years, he could hardly have continued to strive so diligently with *Billy Budd* and with his poems had he not possessed a natural longing for such immortality as may be found in remembrance. Perhaps, after having been so often baffled in his strife, he would be willing to yield himself to any buoyant theory which would preserve him from oblivion. With his personal drama done, he might even see a certain poetic justice in the fact that the devious-cruising critic, retracing his search through the past for some missing children, could always find in him "another orphan."

Index

Note: This index includes (*a*) separate entries for the names of real persons and of publishing firms, the titles of Melville's separate writings, and the author and title of books and other writings mentioned; (*b*) the names of places in which Melville appeared, the ships on which he sailed, and the periodicals in which his works were reviewed—all indexed under Herman Melville; and (*c*) the names of ships and periodicals mentioned, grouped under the headings "Ships" and "Periodicals."

Abbott, 252
Abdallah, 245, 247
Adams, Henry, 338
Adams, Samuel, 208
Adams, W. H. Davenport, *Buried Cities of Campania: or, Pompeii and Herculaneum*, 289
Addison, 202, 222, 320
Adler, George J., 140, 141, 143, 145, 208
"Admiral of the White, The," 268, 320, 321
"Aeolian Harp, The," 321
"After the Pleasure Party," 322, 334
"Afternoon in Naples In the time of Bomba: with an Introduction merging into A Symposium of Old Masters at Delmonico's, An," 330
"Agatha Story, the." *See* Robertson, Agatha
"Age of Antonines, The," 311
Allen, Ethan, 214–216
    Narrative, 214
Allen, Phineas, Jr., 204
Allen, Senator William, 125
"Always With Us!," 264
Ames, Nathaniel, *A Mariner's Sketches*, 137
"Amoroso," 316
Anacreon, 333
Anderson, Rev. Rufus, 69
Andrews, James, *Floral Tableaux*, 103, 105
Angelico, Fra, 330
Antonio, 251
"Apparition, The," 332
"Apple-Tree Table, or Original Spiritual Manifestations, The," 233
Appleton, 267
Appleton, Thomas Gold, 139
Aristotle, 116, 262

Armstrong, Capt. James, 85, 86
Arnold, Matthew, 270, 298
    Empedocles on Etna, 291
    Essays in Criticism, 288, 289
    New Poems, 291
"Art," 335
As They Fell, 330
Astor, John Jacob, 120
"At the Hostelry," 329
"Authentic Anecdotes of 'Old Zack,' " 106, 110, 164
Autograph Leaves of our Country's Authors, 275
Avery, Lieut. Latham B., 85

Babo, 220
Bacon, Sir Francis, 341
Baker, Rosalie, 151
Balzac, Honoré de
    Eugénie Grandet, 291
    Two Brothers, The, 334
Barrs, John W., 323, 338
"Bartleby, the Scrivener. A Story of Wall-Street," 208, 211, 212, 214, 219
Bartlett, W. H.
    Forty Days in the Desert, on the Track of the Israelites; or, A Journey from Cairo . . . to Mount Sinai and Petra, 289
    Nile Boat, The, 289
    Walks about the City and Environs of Jerusalem, 291
Bartlett, Col. William F., 274
Bates, Joshua, 144
Battle Pieces and Aspects of the War, 271, 280, 281, 284, 286, 287, 336
Bayle, Pierre, *Dictionary*, 131

Beale, Thomas, *Natural History of the Sperm Whale, The*, 162, 167
Beaumont, Gustave de, 138
Beaumont and Fletcher, 165
Belcher, Sir Edward, 161
Bell, Capt., 249
Bell, Robert, 148
"Bell Tower, The," 222, 223
Bells, the, 63
Beneventano, Ferdinando, 110, 209
"Benito Cereno," 29, 218–223, 227, 232
Bennett, Frederick Debell, *Narrative of a Whaling Voyage Around the Globe*, 116, 162
Bentley, Richard, 129, 133, 134, 142, 143, 146–148, 153, 154, 176, 183, 185, 193–195, 198
Bérenger, *Songs*, 267
Bible, 172, 176, 229, 232, 248, 267. See also *Clarel* and Melville, Herman (in Egypt and Palestine)
Billson, James, 316, 320, 323, 338, 340
Billy Budd, 321, 324-328, 331, 333, 336, 343
"Billy in the Darbies," 321
Bishop, H. W., 205
Black, David, 79
Blackburn, Andrew, 55
Bogart, Dr., 309
Bogue, David, 143
Bohn, H. G., 143
Boswell, James, *Life of Johnson*, 149
Bouck, William C., 13
Bougainville, Louis de, *A Voyage around the World*, 115
Boutwell, George S., 294
Bradford, Alexander W., 17, 39, 99, 270, 274
Bradford, Samuel D., 205
Bradfords, the, 40
Brewster, 175
Brewster, Capt., 276
"Bridegroom Dick," 321, 322, 324
Briggs, Charles F., 151, 211, 213
Bright, Henry A., 240, 253
Brittain, Mrs. Ellen, 226, 275
Brodhead, Romeyn, 102, 129
Brouwer, Adriaen, 330
Brown, Capt. Oliver P., 17, 27
Brown, Peter, 27
Brown, Tom, 131
Browne, J. Ross, *Etchings of a Whaling Cruise*, 104, 112, 162, 164
Browne, Sir Thomas, 115, 116, 149, 202
Bruno, Giordano, 333
Bryant, William Cullen, 109, 156
Buchanan, Robert, 316

Bulwer-Lytton, Edward
    Last Days of Pompeii, The, 171
    Pelham, 74
Bunnell, William, 55, 57
Burgoyne, Gen., 33
Burke, Henry, 57
Burke, Joseph, 216
Burney, James, *Chronological History of the Discoveries in the South Sea or Pacific Ocean*, 209
Burton, Robert, *Anatomy of Melancholy*, 105, 115–117, 125, 253
Butler, William Allen, 159
Butler, Mrs. William Allen, 159
"Butterfly Ditty," 264
Byrne, Benbow, 55, 57
Byron, 15, 121, 164, 251, 340
    Don Juan, 74
    Island, The, 114
    Manfred, 164, 172

"C——'s Lament," 323
Calderón, 291
Calhoun, John C., 126
Camoëns, 284
    Lusiad, The, 74
"Camoëns," 334
"Camoëns in the Hospital," 334
Canoll, Prof. J. W. Henry, 323
Capelle, Mme., 145
Caravaggio, 330
Carlyle, 140, 164, 179, 186, 189
    Sartor Resartus, 164, 171, 172, 175, 178, 301
Carpenter, Edward, 338
Cary, Alice, 279
Cary, Phoebe, 279
Cass, Lewis, 123, 125
Cenci, Beatrice, 250, 255
Cereno, Don Benito, 219, 220, 222, 223
Cervantes, *Don Quixote*, 227, 232, 247
Chamberlain, Levi, 69, 70
Chambers, Ephraim, *Cyclopaedia: or, an Universal Dictionary of Arts and Sciences*, 105, 116
Chapman, George, translation of Homer, 263, 267
Chapman and Hall, 143
Chase, John J., 73–75, 85, 138, 141, 321
Chase, Owen, *Narrative*, 45, 166
Chasles, Philarete, 139
"Chattanooga," 275, 279
Chatterton, 212
    "Mynstrelles Songe," 210
Chaucer, 302, 311
Churchill, Thomas, 270

Clarel: A Poem and Pilgrimage in the Holy Land, 37, 246, 248, 295–311, 322, 323, 326, 328, 329, 337, 342
Clark, Thomas, 36
Clarke, Rev. James Freeman, 107
Claude, 330
Cleves, Mr., 148
Clifford, John, 196, 197, 199
Coan, Titus Munson, 262, 263
Coats, Andrew, 27
Cochrane, John, 205
"Cock-a-Doodle-Doo!," 209, 210, 214
Codman, John, *Sailor's Life and Sailor's Yarns*, 104
Coffin, Charles, 64
Coffin, Henry, 64
Colbourn, Henry, 143
Coleman, John B., 47, 63, 64
Coleridge, 114, 140, 165, 171, 172, 333
  Biographia Literaria, 115, 165
Collins, 47
Collins, William, 270, 272
  "Dirge" for *Cymbeline*, 210
Colnet, James, *Voyage to the South Atlantic and Round Cape Horn into the Pacific Ocean, A*, 209
Colt, John C., 208
"Coming Storm, The," 278
"Compensation Office, The" (anonymous story), 227, 228
Confidence Man, The, 36, 37, 227, 230–234, 236–239, 244, 252, 255–257, 304, 337
Conrad, Joseph, *Nigger of the Narcissus, The*, 135
"Continents," 265
Cooke, Philip P., *Froissart Ballads*, 113, 115
Cooke, Robert Francis, 148, 207, 218
Cooper, James Fenimore, 186
  Red Rover, The, 39, 152
Cornwall, Barry, 148
Cowley, Capt., *Voyage round the Globe*, 209
Cowper, William, 81
  Poems, 105
Craddock, James, 81
Cramer, William, 261
Crawford, Thomas, 250
Crisson, Warder, 248
Cromwell, Samuel, 82, 325
"Crossing the Tropics," 321
Croswell, Edwin L., 204
Croswell, Sherman, 204
Cruikshank, George, 101
"Cuban Pirate, The," 264, 320, 330–331
"Cumberland, The," 279
Cunningham, Frederick, 245, 247
Cunningham, Peter, 148

Curiosities of Modern Travel (anonymous), 105
Curtis, Asa G., 85
Curtis, George William, 221, 222, 224, 232, 234
Cushing, Caleb, 204–206
Custises, the, 190

Dallas, Commodore Alexander J., 85, 86
Dana, Edmund, 118
Dana, Richard Henry, Jr., 87, 106, 127, 135, 138, 151, 153, 162, 205, 255, 270
  Two Years Before the Mast, 39, 106, 151
Daniel, Mrs., 146, 147
"Daniel Orme," 321, 322
Dante, *Divine Comedy*, 115, 143, 189
Darley, Felix O. C., 207
Darwin, Charles
  Journal of Researches . . . during the Voyage of HMS Beagle around the World, 105
  Origin of Species, 263
D'Avenant, Sir William, 165, 291
David (hired boy), 195
Davidson, David, 143, 145, 148
"Death Graft, The," 29
Defoe, Daniel, 151
  Robinson Crusoe, 81, 96, 132, 145, 248
  Roxana, 115
Delano, Capt. Amasa, *Narrative of Voyages and Travels*, 218–220
De Quincey, Thomas, *Confessions of an English Opium Eater, The*, 149
De Wolf, John, 5, 8, 16, 49, 93, 292
De Wolf, Mary Melville (aunt), 5, 8, 38
Dickens, Charles, 101, 200
  Barnaby Rudge, 166
  Pickwick Papers, The, 141
Dickson, Deacon, 247, 248, 301
"Disinterment of Hermes," 332
D'Israeli, Isaac, 270
"Ditty of Aristippus," 323
Dix, J. H., 221–224
Dix, Senator John A., 103, 204
Dix and Edwards, 230, 232, 234, 237, 255, 257, 338
Dodge, Mary A., "Murder of Philip Spencer, The," 327
Dolce, Carlo, 330
"Donelson," 272
Dougherty, Conly, 78
Douw, Gerard, 330
Dow, Elizabeth, 207
Drummond, Lady Elizabeth, 144
Duckworth, 241, 303
Dupont, Commodore S. F., 272

Dürer, 330

"Dust-Layers, The," 265

Duyckinck, Evert, 100–103, 105–110, 115, 118, 119, 123, 127, 130, 131, 133, 134, 138, 146, 150–152, 154–162, 165, 173, 174, 177, 181–184, 186, 191, 192, 198–200, 218, 236, 237, 260, 263, 266, 267, 271, 275, 288, 310, 311, 313, 329, 339

Duyckinck, George, 101, 105, 115, 118, 119, 123, 131, 138–140, 151, 158, 181–183, 186, 260, 264, 266

Duyckinck, Margaret, 108

Eaton, Joseph, 289, 292

Ellis, Havelock, 339

Ellis, William, *Polynesian Researches*, 93, 101, 116, 137

Emerson, Ralph Waldo, 130, 179, 232, 298
   Conduct of Life, 291
   Essays, 270
   Poems, 264

Emmons, Richard, 156

"Encantadas or Enchanted Isles, The," 209–213, 215, 323

"Enviable Isles, The," 321

Everett, Edward, 138

"Falstaff's Lament Over Prince Hal Become Henry V," 264, 265

Fanning, Edward, *Voyages Around the World*, 93

Fanning, Nathaniel, *Narrative of the Adventures of an American Naval Officer*, 213, 214

Farragut, Adm. David, 272

Fauntleroy, Lieut., 251

Fayaway, 91

Ferguson, Robert, 270

"Fiddler, The," 215

Field, David Dudley, 155, 156, 159
   History of the County of Berkshire, A, 233

Field, Jenny, 155

Fields, James T., 155, 157

Fields, Mrs. James T., 155

Fitch, "Irish Jimmy," 54

Fitzgerald, Edward, *Rubaiyat*, 323

Flagg, Azariah C., 205

Fletcher, Capt., 148, 149

Fly, Eli James Murdock, 28, 29, 31, 34, 38, 174

Fly, Harriet, 28

"For a Boulder near the spot where the last Hardback was laid low By the new proprietor of the Hill of Arrowhead," 265

Forbes, Joseph, 38–39

Forbes, William H., 276

Ford, Richard, 148

"Formerly a Slave," 278

Forrest, Edwin, 133

Forrestor, Alfred Henry, 148

Foster, John, 146

Fox sisters, the, 156

"Fragments from a Writing Desk," 14, 15, 29, 92

Franklin, Benjamin, 214

Fraser, David, 57

"Frenzy in the Wake, The," 278

"Frescoes of Travel," 320, 328

"Fruit and Flower Painter," 264

"Fruit of Travel Long Ago," 265, 298, 332

Fuller, Margaret, 98

Gansevoort, Catharine (grandmother), 2, 9

Gansevoort, Catherine (cousin), 223, 261, 279, 280, 284, 286, 290, 292–296, 309–313, 315, 318, 319

Gansevoort, Guert, 16, 39, 83, 88, 90, 91, 122, 272, 321, 324–327

Gansevoort, Henry, 255, 261, 262, 274, 276, 277, 284, 286, 292, 294

Gansevoort, Henry (or "Hunn"), 90, 325

Gansevoort, Herman (uncle), 8, 9, 11, 28–30, 105, 107, 183, 185, 234, 236, 271, 272

Gansevoort, Herman (infant cousin), 38

Gansevoort, Mrs. Herman, 9, 11, 227

Gansevoort, "Hunn." *See above*

Gansevoort, Leonard (uncle), 16

Gansevoort, Leonard (cousin), 16

Gansevoort, Mary A., 29

Gansevoort, Peter (grandfather), 33, 289

Gansevoort, Peter (uncle), 1–3, 5–13, 16, 28–30, 38, 90, 100, 103, 200, 203–208, 223, 234, 258, 260, 270, 272, 274, 275, 282, 289, 293–296, 309–311, 315

Gansevoort, Stanwix, 29

Gansevoort, Susan, 90, 288, 294, 295

Gansevoort, Wessel, 272

Gardner, Dr. Augustus Kinsley, 110, 139, 145

Garibaldi, 329

Garritson, John, 55, 57

Gay, John, *Beggar's Opera, The*, 15

" 'Gees, The," 233

George III, 214

German, James, 55–57

"Gettysburg," 274, 279

Gibson, John, 250

Gifford, Mrs. Ellen, 320, 331

Gifford, S. R., 278

Gilchrist, Alexander, *Life of William Blake*, 290

Gill, Henry, 27
Girard, Stephen, 156
Goethe, 179, 194, 299
 Poetry and Truth, 171
Grant, Ulysses S., 276, 294, 329
"Great Pyramid, The," 265
Greeley, Horace, 89
Greene, Richard Tobias, 49, 50, 51, 52, 53, 91, 100, 274, 321
Greenway, F. J., 69
Griggs, George, 190, 207, 212, 269, 311, 322
Griswold, Capt. Robert H., 139–141
Gulick, John Thomas, 262, 263

Habington, William, *Castara,* 291
"Haglets, The," 321
Hall, Judge James, 230
Hall, John, 45
Hals, Franz, 330
"Hamilton, Gail." *See* Dodge, Mary A.
"Happy Failure, The," 215
Harpers, the, 95, 102, 104–107, 110, 113, 127–129, 131, 133, 139, 157, 175, 181, 183, 185, 187, 195, 198, 202, 209, 211, 217, 225, 255, 267, 275, 278, 279, 287, 291, 311, 339
Hart, Joseph C., *Miriam Coffin,* 166
Hartley, Davis, *Observations on Man: His Frame, His Duty, and His Expectations,* 115
Hauser, 245
Hawthorne, Julian, 181, 239, 315
 Nathaniel Hawthorne and His Wife, 315
Hawthorne, Nathaniel, 98, 155, 157, 158, 160, 161, 168, 171, 173–178, 181, 186, 188, 191, 194, 197–199, 201, 203–205, 239–241, 253, 277, 300, 324, 341
 Blithedale Romance, The, 196, 197, 200
 "Earth's Holocaust," 169
 House of the Seven Gables, The, 160, 174, 175, 184
 Marble Faun, The, 267, 300
 Mosses from an Old Manse, 158, 168, 172, 173, 175
 Passages from the American Notebooks of Nathaniel Hawthorne, 290
 Passages from the French and Italian Notebooks, 290
 Scarlet Letter, The, 155, 168, 184, 290
 Septimius Felton, 290
 Twice-Told Tales, 168, 174, 290, 291
 "Young Goodman Brown," 169
Hawthorne, Sophia Peabody, 160, 177, 181, 183, 184, 186, 187, 240, 300
Hawthorne, Una, 174, 181, 239

"Hawthorne and His Mosses," 156, 158–160, 168
Hayward, Dr., 278
Hazlitt, William, *Round Table: A Collection of Essays on Literature, Men, and Manners, The,* 290
Headley, Joel T., 157–159
Heine, Heinrich, 270
Hemans, Felicia, 75
Herbert, George, *Temple, The,* 266
Herrick, Robert, *Hesperides,* 264
Hill, Isabel, 194
Hine, Ephraim Curtiss, 74, 75
 Haunted Barque and Other Poems, The, 75
Historical Account of the Circumnavigation of the Globe (anonymous), 93
History of Pittsfield, 311
Hoadley, John C., 207, 212, 258, 269, 279, 280, 289, 292, 294, 310, 311, 314, 322
Hoffman, Charles Fenno, 98
Holland, Capt., 86
Holme, 12
Holmes, Oliver Wendell, 4, 84, 155–158, 181, 208, 223, 255, 256, 339
 Astraea: The Balance of Illusions, 157
Homer, *Odysseus,* 74. *See also* Chapman, George
Hood, Thomas, 270
"House-Top, The," 275
Hubbard, Henry F., 173

"I and My Chimney," 224, 225, 227, 233
"Immolated," 336
"In a Garret," 333
"In the Hall of Marbles," 264
"In the Old Farm-House," 265
"In the Pauper's Turnip-Field," 264
"Inscription for Rip Van Winkle," 331
"Inscription For the Slain at Fredericksburg," 275
"Iris," 331
Irving, Washington, 96, 133
 Knickerbocker History of New York, 107
Isaiah, 177
Israel Potter, 150, 213–217, 222, 224, 227, 233, 238, 251, 278

"Jack Roy," 321
Jackson, Andrew, 4
Jackson, Joseph, 55
Jackson, Robert, 23, 27, 135
Jacobs, Thomas J., *Scenes, Incidents, and Adventures in the Pacific Ocean,* 105
James, G. P. R., 198
James, William, *Naval History of Great Britain, The,* 327

Jeremiah, 246
Jerrold, Douglas
  Housekeeper, The, 147
  Mutiny at the Nore, 327
"Jimmy Rose," 226, 230, 231, 234
John Marr and Other Sailors, 320–324, 330, 336
Johnson, Dr. Samuel, 222, 266
Johnstone, Dr. Francis, 56, 58–61
Jones, John Paul, 214, 215
Jones, Commodore Thomas ap Catesby, 74, 84, 85
Jonson, Ben, 149, 165
  Volpone, 229
Judd, Dr. Garrit P., 66, 67, 70
Julien, M., 142

Kamehameha III, King, 66, 67, 69
Kant, Immanuel, 116, 140
Kean, Charles, 147
Kearny, Capt. Lawrence, 69
Keats, John, 333
  Endymion, 114, 121
Kemble, Fanny, 130, 165
Kennedy, John P., 275
Kettle, L. A., 27
Kinglake, Alexander William, 148
  Eōthen, 249
Knight, Charles, 148
  Knight's London, 147

La Bruyère, Jean de, 272
La Farge, John, 338
La Motte-Fouqué, Friedrich H. K.
  Sintram and His Companions, 114
  Undine, 113, 114
Lamb, Charles, 144, 165
  Specimens of English Dramatic Poets, 131
  Works, 165
Langford, J. M., 144
Langsdorff, Georg H. von, 49
  Voyages and Travels in Various Parts of the World, 93
Lansing, Abraham, 294–296, 310, 311, 313, 315, 318
Lansing, Catherine G. *See* Gansevoort, Catherine
Lansing, Chancellor G. L., 204
Lansing, John, 313
Lanzi, Luigi, *History of Painting in Italy,* 266
Lathers, Richard, 207, 275, 285, 287
Lawrence, Abbott, 144
Lawrence, Mrs. Abbott, 145
Lee, Gen. Robert E., 278, 280
"Lee in the Capitol," 280
Lefevre, George, 54

Leslie, Charles Robert, 148
"Lightning-Rod Man, The," 216, 217
Lincoln, Abraham, 269, 270, 278
Lind, Jenny, 156
Lippi, Fra Lippo, 330
"Little Good Fellows, The," 264
Lockhart, John G., 144
Lockwood, Henry, 243
Lockwood, Dr. John A., 243, 249, 251
London Carcanet, Containing Select Passages from the Most Distinguished Writers, The (giftbook), 15
"Lone Founts," 333
Long Ghost. *See* Troy, John B.
Longfellow, Henry, 35, 98, 127, 156, 186
Longman, Brown, Green, Longman and Roberts, 238
Longmans, 143, 252
"Lonie," 330
"Look-out Mountain," 275
Lowell, Charles Russell, 277
Lowell, James Russell, 98, 189, 213
Lucia di Lammermoor (opera), 110, 209
Lucrezia Borgia (opera), 118
Lynch, Anne, 118, 140

Macaulay, Thomas B., *History of England,* 131
Macbeth (opera), 249
McClellan, John B., 280
McCurdy, 141
MacGregor, John, *Rob Roy on the Jordan, Nile, Red Sea, and Gennasareth,* 290
Mackenzie, Capt. Alexander S., 90, 214, 325–327
McLane, Louis, 96, 97
McLaughlin, George, 275
MacMechan, Archibald, 328
Macpherson, James, *Fingal, An Ancient Epic Poem,* 115
Macready, Charles, 133
Macy, Obed, *History of Nantucket,* 196, 301
Macy, Thomas, 196
"Madcaps," 264, 268, 331
"Maldive Shark, The," 268, 322
Mangan, James C., 270
Mann, Thomas, 177
Manners, Lord John, 144
Manning, George and Marie, 143
"March to the Sea, The," 279
Marcy, William L., 205
Mardi, 64, 111–129, 131–136, 138, 139, 150, 151, 169, 177, 184, 186, 188, 190, 193, 210, 211, 268, 298, 316, 319
Marett, Mrs. Martha B., 313, 317, 331
Marlowe, Christopher, 165
  "Passionate Shepherd, The," 264

Marryat, Capt. Frederick, 41, 101
Marshall, 249
Mather, Cotton, *Magnalia Christi Americana,* 216, 233
Mather, Frank Jewett, Jr., 339, 340
Mathews, Charles, 142
Mathews, Cornelius, 106, 110, 133, 154–157, 159, 160, 181
Matthews, Brander, 316
Matthews, William, 55, 56
Melvill, Rev. H., 147
Melville, Allan, I (father), 2–8, 10, 15, 17
Melville, Allan, II (brother), 2, 3, 5, 11, 12, 15, 18, 28–31, 39, 89, 96, 104, 108, 110, 111, 118, 121, 123, 128, 129, 133, 139, 145, 146, 149, 153, 154, 158, 159, 180–182, 185, 186, 190, 192, 195, 203–207, 234–237, 267, 269, 273–276, 279, 286, 288, 292
Melville, Augusta, 2, 6, 89, 90, 99, 105, 108, 114, 122, 129, 161, 182, 190, 199, 200, 212, 223, 226, 234, 236, 256, 266, 278, 279, 285, 288, 293, 295, 296, 309
Melville, Catherine Bogart, 287, 288, 310
Melville, Catherine Gansevoort (sister), 2, 90, 207, 212, 236, 292, 296, 314
Melville, Elizabeth (daughter), 205, 208, 209, 236, 265, 270, 271, 278, 293–296, 312–314, 316, 320, 337, 339, 340
Melville, Elizabeth Shaw (wife), 89, 98, 100, 103, 107–110, 114, 118, 122–124, 127, 129–132, 138, 141, 145, 146, 151, 153–155, 158, 161, 174, 180, 182, 186, 190, 193, 195, 199, 201, 202, 205, 208, 209, 212, 217, 218, 224, 226, 234–236, 241, 256, 258, 260–262, 266–274, 276–279, 281–282, 284–286, 288–296, 309–320, 322, 324, 328, 330–332, 335–337, 339, 340
Melville, Frances (daughter), 221, 222, 270, 278, 289, 295, 313–315, 332
Melville, Frances Priscilla (sister), 2, 4, 90, 107, 212, 227, 236, 272, 279, 296, 309, 314, 316, 318, 324
Melville, Gansevoort, 2, 3, 5, 6, 8–12, 14–18, 28–31, 37–39, 46, 89, 92, 94–99, 124, 143, 144, 334
Melville, Helen Maria (sister), 2, 5, 30, 89, 98, 107, 161, 190, 202, 207, 212, 236, 256, 272, 311, 314, 325
Melville, Henry, 91
Melville, Herman
  in Acapulco, 269; Aix-la-Chapelle, 146; Albany, 2–4, 6–12, 31, 100, 227, 234, 256, 258, 269, 270, 275, 280, 290, 292, 295, 309, 312, 315; Auburn, N.Y., 259;

Baltimore, 261; Bermuda, 324; Birmingham, England, 253; Boston, 3, 4, 88, 98, 101, 103–107, 109, 127, 129, 131, 193, 196, 199, 201, 217, 255, 258, 260, 267, 270, 271, 290, 311; Boulogne, 145; Bristol, Mass., 5; Brookline, Mass., 197; Brunswick, Maine, 31; Brussels, 145, 146; Buffalo, 33, 100; Cairo, Ill., 37; Callao, 81–83, 86, 88, 137; Cambridgeport, Mass., 266; Canterbury, 142; Cape Cod, 196; Catskills, 315; Center Harbor, N.H., 107; Charleston, Mass., 259; Chester, 240; Chicago, 35, 261; Chillicothe, Ohio, 259; Cincinnati, 259; Clarksville, Tenn., 259; Cleveland, 34, 259; Concord, Mass., 201; Concord, N.H., 107, 258; Constantinople, 242, 243; Conway, N.H., 107; Danvers, Mass., 266; Deal, 142; Detroit, 34, 259; Dover, 146; Egypt, 243–245; Eimeo, 60–64, 80, 83, 101; Fairhaven, Mass., 40; Fire Island, N.Y., 315, 331; Flushing, N.Y., 265; Galápagos Islands, 47, 209; Galena, Ill., 35, 36, 38, 227, 261; Gansevoort, Saratoga County, N.Y., 227, 234, 236, 237, 258, 260, 261, 269, 271, 272, 275, 278, 280, 290, 295, 312; Germany, 145–146, 252; Greece, 241, 242, 248; Greenbush, N.Y., 28–31; Greylock, Mount, 181, 183, 207; Hadley, Mass., 6; Hancock settlement, Mass., 181; Hawaiian Islands, 64–70, 75, 76, 78, 108; Holland, 252; Italy, 249–251, 328; Ithaca, N.Y., 259; Jefferson, N.H., 312, 314, 331; Lake George region, N.Y., 234; Lansingburgh, N.Y., 12–17, 28, 38, 89–93, 97–99, 106–108, 280; Lawrence, Mass., 258, 314; Lebanon, Mass., 158, 181; Lenox, Mass., 158, 160, 174, 175, 181, 199; Lima, 83, 84; Liverpool, 24–27, 136, 239–241, 253; London, 142–149, 239, 252–253; Lynn, Mass., 262; Mackinac Island, Mich., 34–35; Malden, Mass., 258; Malta, 241; Manzanillo, 269; Marquesas, 48–56, 79–80, 101; Martha's Vineyard, 196; Mazatlán, 85, 86; Milwaukee, 261; Montreal, 107, 258; Mooréa, *see* Eimeo; Mount Washington region, Mass., 107; Nantucket, Mass., 196, 197; Naushon, Mass., 196; New Bedford, Mass., 40, 196, 259; New Haven, 258; New Rochelle, N.Y., 287; New York City, 2–6, 17–18, 37, 93–97, 99–102, 106–139, 150–154, 161, 167, 186, 190, 195, 206, 211, 237, 254, 259–262, 269–272, 275 *et seq.;* Ostend, 146; Oxford, 253; Pales-

Melville, Herman—*Continued*
 tine, 245–248; Panama, 269; Paris, 145;
  Philadelphia, 37, 259; Pittsburgh, 259;
  Pittsfield, Mass., 6, 8–10, 154–236, 256–
  267, 269–274, 286, 288, 293–295, 315;
  Portsmouth, 149; Quebec, 107; Quincy,
  Ill., 261; Ravavai, 64; Rio de Janeiro, 44,
  87–88; Rochester, N.Y., 259; Rockford,
  Ill., 261; Rome, N.Y., 33; Rurutu, 64;
  St. Augustine, 324; San Francisco, 268;
  Sandwich, 142; Sandwich Islands, *see*
  Hawaiian Islands; Santa, Peru, 46; Sara-
  toga Springs, 234, 236, 258, 280, 312;
  Scotland, 238; Southport, England, 239–
  240; Springfield, Mass., 174; Staten Is-
  land, N.Y., 288, 313, 315; Stockbridge,
  Mass., 154, 183, 198; Stratford on Avon,
  253; Switzerland, 251; Sykes District,
  Mass., 11; Tahiti, 56–61, 67, 80; Tumbez, 47; Valparaiso, 81, 82; Vermont,
  108; Virginia, 276, 277; Warwick, 253;
  Washington, D.C., 103, 105, 125, 259;
  270, 275, 276; Wheeling, Va., 37;
  White Mountains, N.H., 295, 311;
  York, 239
 on *Achushnet,* 40–51, 54, 63–65, 69, 72,
  91, 173, 174; *Aquile Imperiale,* 248;
  Arcadia, 243; *Aventine,* 250; *Charles
  and Henry,* 47, 63–67, 72, 80; *City of
  Manchester,* 253; *Cydnus,* 249; *Egyptian,*
  240–243; *Emerald,* 145; *Glasgow,* 237–
  238; *Independence,* 147–150; *Italia,* 248;
  Lucy Ann, 54–60, 65, 101; *Meteor,* 266–
  269; *North Star,* 269; *St. Lawrence,* 17,
  19–24, 27, 135; *Smirne,* 248; *Southampton,* 138–141, 144; *Star,* 67; *United
  States,* 70–88, 109, 243, 271, 321, 326
 reviewed or mentioned in *Academy,* 316;
  Athenaeum, 131, 132, 152; *Atlantic
  Monthly,* 287; *Bentley's Miscellany,* 132,
  142; *Blackwood's Magazine,* 112, 116,
  142, 183; *Commercial Advertiser,* 322,
  323; *Critic,* 132; *Daily Commercial,* 259;
  Daily Journal, 258; *Daily Tribune,* 310,
  338; *Daily Wisconsin,* 261; *Evening
  Journal,* 338; *Evening Post,* 211; *Examiner,* 132; *Graham's Magazine,* 151; *Harper's New Monthly Magazine,* 186, 287;
  Herald, 316; *Holden's Dollar Magazine,*
  151, 191; *Home Journal,* 131, 186; *John
  Bull,* 186; *Leader, The,* 186; *Library
  Table,* 311; *Literary Gazette,* 132; *Literary World,* 131, 186, 197; *Morning
  Courier and New York Enquirer,* 99;
  Nation, 287; *Post,* 131, 132, 339; *Putnam's Monthly Magazine,* 202; *Register,*

  261; *Republican,* 261; *Southern Literary
  Messenger,* 201; *Times,* 338; *United
  States Magazine and Democratic Review,*
  151, 186; *World,* 310, 338
Melville, Jane Dempsey, 273, 276, 279, 289,
  293
Melville, John, 11
Melville, Malcolm (son), 129, 131–133, 138,
  141, 145, 146, 153, 154, 161, 174, 199,
  202, 208, 226, 227, 270, 275, 284–286,
  292, 293, 298, 301
Melville, Maria Gansevoort, I (mother), 1–6,
  8–13, 15, 16, 18, 27–30, 39, 89, 91, 99,
  107–110, 123, 154, 161, 185, 195, 199,
  201, 203–205, 208, 212, 224, 227, 234–
  236, 256, 258, 260, 261, 270, 272, 275,
  278, 279, 283–287, 290, 292
Melville, Maria Gansevoort, II (niece), 133,
  294
Melville, Mary (aunt), 91, 154, 158, 261
Melville, Priscilla, I (aunt), 4, 274
Melville, Priscilla, II (cousin), 91, 108, 212,
  227
Melville, Robert (cousin), 10, 31, 38, 91, 127,
  154, 158, 181, 185, 313
Melville, Sophia Thurston, 104, 108, 153,
  158, 161, 190, 273
Melville, Stanwix (son), 184, 186, 202, 205,
  236, 270, 275, 289, 292–295, 311, 313,
  322, 324, 332
Melville, Thomas, I (grandfather), 3, 4, 6, 8,
  84
Melville, Thomas, II (uncle), 4, 6–11, 31,
  35, 36, 38, 91, 185, 212, 216, 311
Melville, Thomas Wilson, III (cousin), 16,
  38, 39, 49, 88, 91, 93
Melville, Thomas, IV (brother), 2, 12, 89,
  90, 97, 98, 100, 106, 122, 123, 135, 199,
  212, 260, 265–269, 272, 278–280, 285–
  289, 292, 294–296, 309, 310, 313–315,
  319
"Memoir of Thomas Melville," 311
Mendelssohn, Felix, 142
Mercier, James, *Life in a Man-of-War, or
  Scenes in Old Ironsides,* 137
Michelangelo, 255
Miller, Joann, 151, 186
Milnes, Richard Monckton, 138, 144
Milton, John, "L'Allegro," 264
"Minor Sea-Pieces," 321
Minot, Mrs., 247, 248
Mitchell, Maria, 196, 334
Mitchell, William, 196
Moby Dick, 33, 39, 64, 152, 153, 160, 162–
  173, 175–179, 181–183, 185–188, 191–
  196, 219, 220, 223, 228, 229, 231, 237,

240, 244, 259, 281, 297–299, 301, 306–308, 316, 324, 327, 335, 337–341
"Monody," 277
Montaigne, 115, 130
"Montaigne and his Kitten," 320
Montgomery, Isaac, 68–70
Moore, Thomas, 270
Moore, Thomas (sailor), 27
Morewood, J. R., 154, 185, 198, 207, 212, 260, 274
Morewood, Mrs. Sarah, 155, 158, 159, 181–185, 190, 207, 226, 236, 266, 269, 274
Morewood, William, 294
Morrell, Benjamin, *Narrative of Four Voyages,* 105
Morris, G. P., *Poems of General George P. Morris, The,* 269
Morris, William, 338
Mosby, John C., 276, 277
Moxon, Edward, 138, 144, 165
Mudge, Rev. Enoch, 40
Mure, 220
Murillo, 84
Murphy, Father, 59
Murray, John, 95, 96, 99, 100, 102, 110, 113, 117–119, 128, 129, 142–145, 148, 239, 338, 340
Murray, Lindley, *English Reader,* 15

"Naples in the Time of Bomba," 328, 329
"New Rosicrucians, The," 317
Nichols, Thomas L., 95
Niebuhr, Barthold G., 248, 301
Norton, Edward. *See* Russ, Oliver
Nourse, Amos, 151, 270
Nourse, Mrs. Lucy, 107, 202, 313, 317

O'Conor, Charles, 203
"Old Shipmaster and his Crazy Barn, The," 331
Omoo, 56, 57, 62, 67, 97, 100–107, 112, 113, 116–119, 122, 129, 133, 135, 141, 183, 186, 211, 219, 239, 263, 316, 338
Orpheus, Capt., 243
Osgood, Rev. Dr. Samuel, 285

Page, William, 250
Paley, William, 121
Palmer, E. H., *Desert of Exodus, The,* 291
"Paradise of Bachelors and The Tartarus of Maids, The," 218, 224
Parker, Judge Amasa J., 204
Paulet, Lord George, 66,.68–70, 92
Payne, Henry M., 156
Peabody, George, 144
Pease, Capt., 46, 48, 63, 69

"Pebbles," 322
Peebles, Mrs., 1, 14
Peebles, Mary Louise, 315
Periodicals mentioned: *American Magazine,* 324; *Argus,* 9, 204; *Atlantic Monthly,* 255, 256; *Bentley's Miscellany,* 202; *Berkshire County Eagle,* 226, 256, 273; *Commercial Advertiser,* 100; *Cosmopolitan Magazine,* 327; *Culturist and Gazette,* 154; *Daily Tribune,* 127, 320; *Democratic Press and Lansingburgh Advertiser,* 14, 29; *Democratic Review,* 243; *Gazette,* 104, 112; *Harper's Magazine,* 209, 211–213, 215, 217, 218, 222, 226, 233, 278, 279; *Herald,* 320; *Herald,* 120; *Holden's Dollar Magazine,* 174; *Knickerbocker Magazine,* 45; *Literary World, The,* 103, 104, 106, 131, 139, 152, 159, 160–163, 192; *Microscope,* 12; *Morning Courier and New York Enquirer,* 123; *North Western Gazette and Galena Advertiser,* 38; *Putnam's Magazine,* 286, 287; *Putnam's Monthly Magazine,* 208, 209, 211–213, 216, 217, 221–225, 227, 233, 234, 286, 287; *Sun,* 204, 256; *Times,* 123; *Yankee Doodle,* 106, 110. *See also* Melville, Herman
Perry, Commodore Matthew Galbraith, 239
Peters, Mrs., 181
Peterson, T. B., 278
"Philip." *See* "Sheridan at Cedar Creek"
"Piazza, The," 230, 231, 233
Piazza Tales, 234, 255, 257
Picture of Liverpool, The (guidebook), 26
Pierce, Franklin, 201, 203–205
Pierre, 179, 184, 186, 188–195, 197–202, 206, 208, 209, 211, 220, 223, 231, 237, 244, 245, 299, 306, 308, 326, 337
Pistorius, Herman Andrew, 115
Planché, J. R., 142
Plato, 131
Plutarch, 334
Poe, Edgar Allan, 166
Polk, James K., 89, 99
Pollard, Capt., 196, 197, 301
Pomaree, Queen, 63, 80
"Poor Man's Pudding and Rich Man's Crumbs," 213, 215
"Pontoosuc," 264
Porter, Capt. David, *Journal of a Cruise Made to the Pacific Ocean in the U.S. Frigate Essex,* 93, 209
Potter, Henry L., 284
Potter, Israel R., *Life and Remarkable Adventures . . . ,* 139, 148, 150, 213, 214, 218
Poussin, 330

Powell, Thomas, 138
Powers, Hiram, 251
Priestley, 116
Putnam, George Palmer, 96, 213
Putnam, P. S., 233
Putnam's, 162, 200, 224, 278, 296
"Puzzlement," 265

Rabelais, 115, 131
Rachel, 145
"Rail Road Cutting near Alexandria in 1855, A," 265
"Rammon," 321
"Ravaged Villa, The," 265, 332
Rebellious Record, The (compilation), 279
Recreation: A Gift Book for Young Readers, The (giftbook), 105
Redburn, 17, 23, 25, 27, 133–139, 142, 143, 151, 153, 169, 208, 219, 239, 316
Refugee, The. See *Israel Potter*
Rembrandt, 330
Reynolds, Jeremiah N., *Voyage of the U.S. Frigate Potomac,* 106
Reynolds, Stephen, 68, 70
Rice, Alexander, 269
Richter, Jean Paul, 340
Ringbolt, Capt. *See* Codman, John
"Rip Van Winkle's Lilac," 330, 336
Ripley, George, 98
Robertson, Agatha, 197–203, 206, 208, 210, 215
Robinson, Henry Crabb, *Diary, Reminiscences, and Correspondence, The,* 290, 292
Rogers, Samuel, 138, 146, 148
Rosa, Salvator, 330
"Rosary Beads," 316
Rousseau, J. J., *Confessions,* 147, 149
Routledge, 217, 239
Rubens, 146
Ruskin, John, 263
Russ, Oliver, 75, 83, 261
Russell, W. Clark, 316, 323, 338
   Ocean Tragedy, An, 338
   Wreck of the Grosvenor, The, 323
Rutland, Duke of, 144, 146–148

St. Leger, Col. Barry, 33
Salt, Henry S., 338
Sampson, Low, Son, and Co., 198
Saunders, Mr. and Mrs., 247
Savage, Samuel, 180
"Saya-y-Manto," 321
Schiller, 333
   "Diver, The," 268
   Poems and Ballads, 267

Schoolcraft, Henry, 35
Schopenhauer, Arthur
   Counsels and Maxims, 336
   Studies in Pessimism, 336
   Wisdom of Life, The, 336
Scoresby, William
   Arctic Regions, 153, 162
   History and Description of the Northern Whale Fishery, 153, 162, 164
Scott, Sir Walter, 30
   Rob Roy, 74
"Scout Toward Aldie, The," 277
Scribner, 267, 269
"Sea-Pieces," 321
Sedgwick, Catherine, 157
Sedgwick, Harry, 155
Selkirk, Alexander, 81
Seneca, *Morals by Way of Abstract,* 115
Senora, Immanuel, 55
"Shadow at the Feast." *See* "Lonie"
Shakespeare, 115, 130, 165, 168, 169, 171, 194, 231, 232, 253, 272, 341
   As You Like It, 226, 229, 231
   Cymbeline, 231
   Hamlet, 15, 130, 165, 169, 188, 189, 192, 231
   Henry VI, 231
   King Lear, 130, 165, 169, 230, 231
   Macbeth, 74, 130, 165
   Midsummer Night's Dream, A, 231
   Much Ado About Nothing, 131
   Othello, 130, 165
   Richard II, 23
   Sonnets, 291
   Timon of Athens, 165
   Winter's Tale, The, 231
Shaw, Elizabeth. *See* Melville, Elizabeth Shaw
Shaw, Mrs. Hope, 153, 161, 180, 199, 202, 227, 270, 273, 313, 314, 317
Shaw, John Oakes, 201, 205
Shaw, Lemuel, 3, 7, 8, 28, 38, 39, 89, 94, 97, 98, 103, 110, 113, 127, 132, 138, 161, 180, 184, 195–199, 205–207, 212, 227, 235, 250, 255, 256, 258, 260, 262, 264, 266, 269, 270, 273, 281, 283, 295
Shaw, Lemuel, Jr., 118, 122, 199, 207, 255, 256, 260, 311, 312, 314, 318, 332
Shaw, Samuel, 105, 107, 122, 152, 180, 197, 198, 207, 235, 238, 250, 260, 264, 272, 273, 293, 314, 332
Shelley, Percy Bysshe, 250, 270, 333
   Alastor, 114, 121
"Shelley's Vision," 333
Shepherd, Daniel, 234, 237, 264
   Saratoga, a Tale of 1787, 237
"Sheridan at Cedar Creek," 279

Sherman, Gen. William T., 278

Ships mentioned: *Ann Alexander*, 166, 184; *Arabia*, 206; *Atlantic*, 206; *Bonhomme Richard*, 214, 323; *Cambria*, 123; *Carolus*, 311; *Constellation*, 69, 81, 85, 243, 249, 251; *Cumberland*, 321; *Cyane*, 86, 87; *Dublin*, 69; *Essex*, 45, 166, 196; *Grampus*, 90; *Great Western*, 94; *Herald*, 48; *Hermann*, 118; *Highlander*, 136; *John Adams*, 63, 64, 83; *Joseph Maxwell*, 46; *La Reine Blanche*, 54, 58, 80, 101; *Merrimac*, 272, 321; *Monitor*, 272; *Natchez*, 87; *New York*, 136; *Ohio*, 88; *Oregon*, 91; *Perseverance*, 218, 219; *Prince Albert*, 99; *Rousseau*, 49; *St. Louis*, U.S.S., 74; *Savannah*, 85, 86; *Serapis*, 214, 323; *Somers*, U.S.S., 82, 90, 214, 324–327; *Teazer*, 39; *Tryal*, 218, 219; *Tweed*, 44; *Vincennes*, U.S.S., 49; *Vindictive*, 85; *William Penn*, 46; *William Wirt*, 46. *See also* Melville, Herman

Shorty, 61, 62, 64

Simonides, 333

Sixtus V, Pope, 254

Sleeper, S. S., *Tales of the Ocean and Essays for the Forecastle*, 137

Small, Elisha, 82, 324, 325

Smith, Albert, 144

Smith, David, 46

Smith, Lieut. H. D., "Mutiny on the Somers, The," 324–325

Smith, Henry, 54, 56

Smith, J. E. A., 181, 183, 226, 273, 315, 338

 Poet of the Hills, 339

Smith, James S., 55, 56

Smollett, Tobias, 101, 152

 Roderick Random, 137

Smythe, Henry A., 252, 282

"South Seas, The" (lecture), 259, 260

Southey, Robert, *Life of Nelson*, 327

Spagnoletto, 330

Spencer, John C., 82

Spencer, Philip, 82, 88, 90, 325, 327

Spenser, Edmund, 270, 272

 Faerie Queene, 114, 121, 127, 130, 132, 210–212

 "Mother Hubberds Tale," 210

 "Visions of the Worlds Vanitie," 210, 215

Spinoza, 116

Squier, Ephraim George, *Waikna; or, Adventures on the Mosquito Shore*, 225

Staël, Mme. de, *Corinne*, 194

Stanhope, Lady Hester, 248

Stanley, Arthur Penrhyn, *Sinai and Palestine in Connection with Their History*, 289

"Statuary in Rome" (lecture), 257, 281

Stedman, Arthur, 338, 339

Stedman, Edmund C., 323, 339

 Library of American Literature, 323, 339

 Lyrics and Idylls, 269

 Poets of America, 323

Steen, Jan, 330

Sterne, Laurence, *Tristram Shandy*, 164

Stetson, John, 65, 69

Stevens, 144, 148

Stevenson, Robert Louis, 338, 340

Stewart, Charles S., *A Visit to the South Seas, in the United States' Ship Vincennes, During the Years 1829 and 1830*, 93

"Stockings in the Farm-House Chimney," 264

Stoddard, Charles W., 338

"Stone Fleet," 272

Strauss, D. F., 248

Street, Alfred Billings, 200

Stribling, Capt. C. K., 86, 88

"Suggested by the Ruins of a Mountain-Temple in Arcadia," 265, 332

Sullivan, Mrs., 131

Sumner, Senator Charles, 138, 269–271, 276, 329

Swain, Mr., 196

Swanevelt, 330

Swedenborg, Emanuel, 140

Swift, Jonathan, *Gulliver's Travels*, 132

Sylva, Amado, 55, 57

Taghconic; or Letters and Legends about our Summer Home, 198

Talfourd, Thomas N., *Final Memorials*, 165

Tappan, 160

Tasso, 334

Tate, Capt., 240–243

Tawney, 216

Taylor, Capt., 159

Taylor, Bayard, 118, 140, 161, 278

 Views Afoot, 105

Taylor, Father Edward T., 40

Taylor, Dr. Franklin, 140, 141

Taylor, John O., 11

Taylor, Thomas (trans.), *Six Books of Proclus on the Theology of Plato, The*, 119

Taylor, Tom, 144

Taylor, Gen. Zachary, 106

Teniers, 330

Tennyson, 270, 298

 In Memoriam, 291

Thomas, Eleanor, 313, 331

Thomas, Frances, 313

Thomas, Henry B., 313

Thomas, Adm. Richard, 69

Thompson, Waddy, *Recollections of Mexico*, 105

Thomson, James, 270, 272
Thomson, James (19th cent.), 323
  "Sunday up the River," 320
"Thought on Book-Binding, A," 152
Thurston, Mrs., 273
Thurston, Sophia. *See* Melville, Sophia Thurston
Timoleon, 265, 332, 334–337
"Timoleon," 334
Tintoretto, 330
"To David Shepherd," 264
"To the Master of the 'Meteor,' " 265, 321
"To Tom," 265, 321
Toft, Peter, 323
"Tom Deadlight," 321
Tomes, Robert, *Panama in 1855,* 225, 237
Ton, Anton, 27
Tooke, Horne, 214
"Tortoises or Tortoise-Hunting," 209, 211
"Travel Pieces," 265
"Travelling: Its Pleasures, Pains, and Profits" (lecture), 265
"Trophies of Peace," 36, 265
Troy, John B., 55, 56, 60–63, 80, 83, 101, 135, 173
Tupper, Martin F., *Proverbial Philosophy,* 105
Turner, John C., 85, 326
Twain, Mark, 139, 330
"Two Temples, The," 212
Tyler, Brig. Gen. Robert O., 276
Tyler, Wat, 23
Typee, 52, 54, 67, 70, 92–100, 102, 103, 105–107, 112, 113, 117–119, 122, 128, 133, 135, 186, 191, 209, 211, 219, 239, 262, 274, 304, 316, 338

"Under the Rose," 330
Upham, Thomas C., *Outlines of Imperfect and Disordered Mental Action,* 172
Utley, Nicholas, 55, 56

Van Buren, John, 205
Van der Velde, 330
Van Dyck, 330
Van Loon, 12
Van Metre, Sophie, 275
Van Rensselaer, Miss, 99, 122
Vasari, *Lives of the Most Eminent Painters, Sculptors, and Architects,* 266

Vedder, Elihu, 278, 336
Velasquez, 330
Ventom, Henry, 54–58
Veronese, Paola, 330
Vestris, Mme., 142
"Victor of Antietam, The," 280
Vinci, Leonardo da, 330

Watteau, 330
Watts, Charles, 55, 57
Watts, James, 57
"Way-side Weed, A," 264
Webster, Prof., 156
Webster, Daniel, 4
Webster, Noah, *Dictionary,* 105
Weed, Thurlow, 270
  Autobiography, 325
Weeds and Wildings, 337
"Weeds and Wildings," 330
"Weeds and Wildings, with a Rose or Two," 336
Weems, Mason L., 214
West, Edward C., 203, 204
White, Kirke, 270
White Jacket, 37, 134, 135, 137–139, 143, 145, 147, 151, 153, 164, 169, 178, 239, 243, 316, 323, 326, 338, 341
Whiting, Joseph, 65
Whitman, Walt, 98, 316, 330
"Wild-Strawberry Hunters," 268
Wiley, John, 99, 102, 106, 115, 128, 131, 143
Wiley and Putnam, 97, 100, 102, 104, 106, 107, 110, 113, 128
Wilkes, *U.S. Exploring Expedition in the South Pacific, The,* 106
Williams, Mrs., 247, 248
Williams, Griffith, 75
Willie, 62
Willis, George S., 233, 262
Willis, N. P., 98
Wilson, Charles B., 56–58
Wood, George, 248
Wordsworth, William, 238, 289
  Prelude, The, 158
  "Resolution and Independence," 210

Young, Rev. Dr., 107

Zeke, 61, 62, 64